W9-DFT-395

DISCARDED

SHELTON STATE COMMUNITY
COLLEGE
JUNIOR COLLEGE DIVISION
LIBRARY

D
24
.K56   Catastrophe and crisis
1979

Kingston, Jeremy

DATE DUE			
OCT 16 '84			
JAN 17 '85			
MAY 2 8 1986			
FEB 2 4 1987			
NOV 0 2 1989			
MAY 1 4			
DEC 1 0 1997			
MAY 2 4 2000			

DISCARDED

SHELTON STATE COMMUNITY

DISCARDED

17.47
0774
F.OnF.

Catastrophe and Crisis

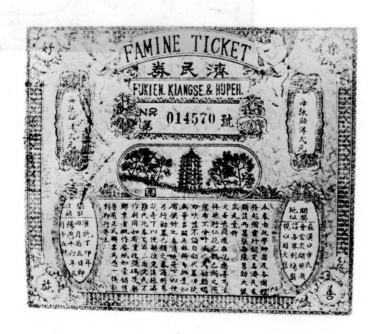

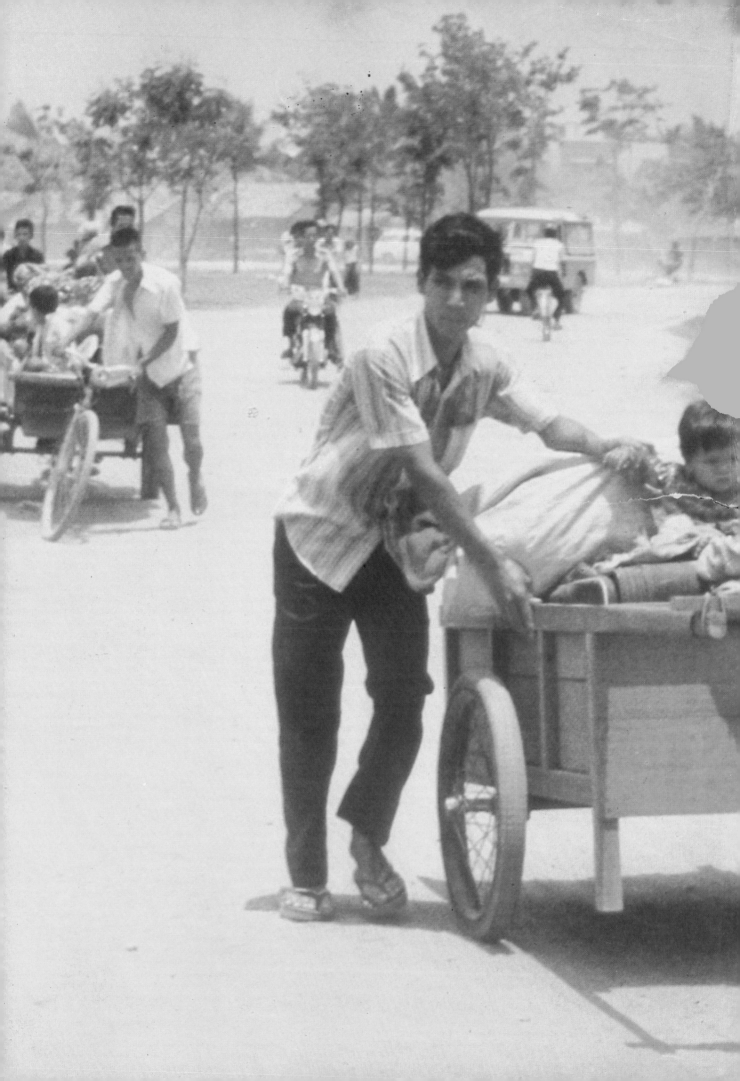

DISCARDED

D
24
.K56
1979

Catastrophe and Crisis

Jeremy Kingston and David Lambert

Facts On File ☑ **New York**

Editorial Coordinator: John Mason
Art Editor: Grahame Dudley
Design: Adrian Williams
Editorial: Damian Grint
Research: Marian Pullen; Sarah Waters

ISBN 0-87196-409-0
© 1979 Aldus Books Limited, London
First published in the United States
by Facts on File, Inc.,
119 West 57 Street
New York, N.Y. 10019
Printed and bound in Hong Kong
by Leefung-Asco.

Introduction

History is full of dramatic and often devastating events that have left their scars on the earth's surface or in the minds of men. Earthquakes, fires, floods and volcanic eruptions; plague and pestilence; assassinations, and crimes against humanity; economic and scientific disasters, and tragic accidents that aroused worldwide concern – this book looks at all these events. Each category is defined and described, and, in the case of assassinations and other violent crimes, their causes and effects upon subsequent events. Natural disasters such as earthquakes and epidemics, famines and volcanoes, are tackled scientifically, and practical means of predicting and coping with them are also described. The result provides a worldwide historical survey of the crises and catastrophes that have dogged mankind from the beginning of recorded history up to such recent events as the assassination of President Kennedy in 1963, the Chinese earthquake of 1976, and the Indian cyclones of 1977.

Contents

Chapter 1

Man and Disaster

Primitive man saw his gods as arbitrary and even vindictive influences upon his daily life on this earth. When we look at the appalling catalog of natural disasters that still dog us in our own sophisticated, scientific 20th century – earthquakes, storms, volcanic eruptions, famine, fire, flood – we can perhaps appreciate his point of view. It is man's own nature, however, that frequently makes him his own worst enemy. Greedy, aggressive, and cruel toward his fellow men, he compounds his perilous existence by his own actions. The first chapter of this book looks at the background to man's struggle against catastrophe and crisis – his environment and his own nature. It forms the prologue to the subject of the book: man and disaster.

Opposite: an avalanche of coal-slag that engulfed a school and part of the town of Aberfan in Wales in 1964, killing 144 people, mostly children. In this case, thoughtless dumping of coalmining waste softened by rainwater combined to bring about the disaster. Despite this terrible event, similar waste-heaps – that spoil the visual environment, sterilize the land, and overshadow nearby dwellings – continue to exist.

9

Our Perilous Planet

Man lives on a perilous earth. The dangers that beset him take many forms, some natural, some man-made. They range from the periodic to the persistent, from the microscopic to the cosmic. At one end of the scale is the tiny microorganism *Pasteurella Pestis*, the plague bacillus that in the pandemic known as The Black Death killed an estimated 43,000,000 people in Europe and Asia between 1345 and 1350 when it petered out in the extremities of Europe – Ireland, Scotland, and Scandinavia.

At the other end of the scale is the sun, whose ceaseless stream of radiation brought life into being on this planet, and in the form of heat and visible light, is now the basic fuel of all life forms. But the radiation that living organisms make use of occupies only a narrow band in the spectrum. Beyond the ultraviolet rays lie wide bands of X rays and the deadly gamma rays that destroy the bonds holding organic molecules together. If these lethal rays were not largely absorbed by the layer of ozone in the earth's stratosphere, all but the most primitive forms of life on earth would be killed.

In many ways man has made his environment much more hospitable over the past few centuries, yet with all the armory of modern science at his command he is still in danger from the same age-old enemies that have pursued him down the ages: earthquakes, fires, floods, volcanic eruptions, plague and pestilence, and assassination and crimes against humanity. Modern medicine has been able to control the deadly outbreaks of diseases such as plague, cholera, and yellow fever. But these same controls can sometimes cause bacteria to develop new and more virulent strains. Similarly, modern science now probably possesses the means to punch holes in the ozone layer surrounding the earth, our outer and most essential defense against solar death.

Many of the achievements of science and technology that are beneficial to man are really attempts to bring nature under his control. Dikes are built to keep out the sea, embankments raised to limit the course of a river, marshes are drained to make good farmland. Nature merely bides its time. Sooner or later, it seems, the waters sweep away the work of centuries like so many flimsy barriers, and wreak their own retribution on those who put their trust in the work of their hands.

Because today the human population of the world is the largest in man's history, people continue to use the potentially dangerous places such as fertile mountain slopes and the low-lying land around rivers and sea coasts. There is a desperate need to feed the many hungry mouths around the world. The im-

Above: all the memories of the Black Death are captured by the 16th-century Dutch artist Pieter Bruegel in his *Triumph of Death*.

proved strains of food grain that have been developed have been found to draw more nutrients from the soil than before, exposing the land to erosion and turning it into wilderness. The consequent replenishment of the soil with artificial fertilizer then alters the character of the soil. Medicine, hygiene, industrialization, city life are all departures from nature.

These departures and interferences have made man

what he is today. His struggle to overcome nature is, in a full sense, the history of man on earth. The early cultures that grew up beside the great rivers knew only too well the horrors of flood – and in the case of Egypt, the calamity that would occur in the *absence* of the floodwaters that deposited the rich, fertile silt on the surrounding land. Deluge, earthquake, famine, and the other calamities of nature came to be under-

stood as marks of disapproval or punishment meted out by their gods. Man being man, it was never difficult to select, after a destructive flood or earthquake, some offense or shortcoming that must have roused a particular god to anger. When an earthquake opened a wide crack in the forum of ancient Rome the priests declared that the gods would not close it until Rome's most costly possession had been thrown into

11

it. A youth named Marcus Curtius stepped forward and said that Rome's true wealth was her brave men. Mounting his horse he jumped into the crack, which instantly closed. Even today, during eruptions of Mount Etna and Vesuvius, priests carry the relics of local saints in procession toward the volcano in the belief that this will bring the eruption to an end.

Eruptions, earthquakes, even cyclones are local events compared to the wholesale horrors of war and epidemics – phenomena that frequently go hand in hand. Plague, typhus, syphilis, dysentery raged through medieval and Renaissance Europe as state warred against state and armies marched and counter-marched to feed men's ambitions or greed. In the summer of 1528, during the long struggle for supremacy between the French and the Holy Roman Empire, a French army came close to defeating Emperor Charles V's Spanish troops near Naples when typhus struck. Within a month only 4000 of the 25,000 French remained alive. This remnant was cut to pieces and the Hapsburgs and Spain dominated Europe for another century. When the fate of nations was decided by the bite of a louse it is no wonder that man's attitude to the world about him was one of nervous uncertainty and fear.

The campaign that ended in disaster outside Naples was just one of the world's seemingly endless succession of wars. Whatever the reasons for the many wars of history: territorial expansion, trade rivalry, the imposition of a religion, or self-aggrandizement, their aims are never achieved without suffering, atrocity and death. But over and above the senseless violence of war there is the cruelty that man inflicts on man, sometimes so monstrous that it leaves the mind numb with horror. Nor is man's inhumanity to man something that stopped with the persecution of the Christians by the Roman emperors, or with the ending of the Black slave trade. Our own century has provided fresh evidence of man's capacity for appalling cruelty to his fellow creatures – the hardly credible systematic slaughter of Jews, Slavs, Gypsies, and other "undesirables" by the Nazis. And in the post-war years the long catalog continues – most horribly in areas of Africa and Southeast Asia – it is a list that grows longer each decade.

There are those who seek to achieve their political aims or ambitions by murdering their opponents. Indeed, assassination of one's opponent has long been an accepted weapon of political warfare. From the stabbing to death of Julius Caesar in 44 BC to the shooting down of Martin Luther King in 1968, the murder of one man has often seemed, but rarely been, the simple answer to a complex political problem. In the event, most have provoked the very crisis that the murder was meant to prevent. Not a few have proved a turning point in the course of world history.

Until man has conquered the beast within himself there seems little he can do at present to prevent the systematic cruelty of individuals or even states. He can, however, do much more to alleviate the suffering

Above: the Fire of London and (below) chlorine gas victims of World War I. Fire and war are two worldwide scourges of mankind.

of those caught up in the wake of natural disasters. The immediate reaction is to respond quickly with relief supplies. The long-term prediction methods of such disasters and potential disasters as earthquakes, volcanic activity, and cyclones are being improved all the time. Medical science has made great strides in the battle against the diseases that bring so much misery and death to so many people throughout the world. Pesticides and fertilizers increase crop yields to feed an ever-growing world population. But here, too, the very tools that science provides man with to improve the quality of his life can also be used as weapons against him. The use of broad-spectrum pesticides by which many different kinds of insect are killed is already causing grave concern among environmentalists. Not only the pests, but the pests' predators are killed. Because the predator belongs to

Above: an oil-pollution victim and (below) a tornado. Pollution and natural disaster claim many victims every year.

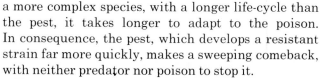

Above: famine is a constantly recurring problem in the Third World.

a more complex species, with a longer life-cycle than the pest, it takes longer to adapt to the poison. In consequence, the pest, which develops a resistant strain far more quickly, makes a sweeping comeback, with neither predator nor poison to stop it.

Exactly the same thing can, and does, happen with antibiotics as diseases build up resistant strains. Another worry is the pollution from chemical factories, either through carelessness or accident. In the mid-1960s, for instance, 68 people died, 330 were permanently disabled and some 10,000 others were affected with mercury poisoning as a result of eating fish and other seafood caught in Minamata Bay in Japan. It was discovered that a chemical plant in Minamata City was discharging mercury-bearing waste into the Bay.

In 1498, the year Savonarola was burned at the

stake for trying to bring about a spiritual and moral revival in Florence and in which the ill-famed Machiavelli was made a secretary to the war committee of the same city, the German artist Albrecht Dürer drew one of his most celebrated engravings, the Four Horsemen of the Apocalypse. Those same dreaded riders – Pestilence, War, Famine, and Death – still ride through the lives of men as they have done since long before Saint John recorded his vision, which survives as the last book of the New Testament. Man will never conquer Death and may never fully conquer the other three. The misery they bring can nevertheless be significantly reduced. To do this, however, requires an understanding of these catastrophes and what causes them, both those that are called natural and others that originate within man, who is after all himself part of nature.

Chapter 2

Our Restless Earth

Most people take for granted the stability of the earth under their feet. They plan their lives and build their cities and roads on that assumption. Many languages have such phrases as "solid as a rock" or "on safe ground." The fact is, however, that we stand on a restless earth – not *terra firma* at all. It is because the ground itself cannot be trusted that the experience of an earthquake is uniquely terrifying.

On average the world has a million earthquakes a year – about two a minute. The majority can be detected only by instruments; about 300,000 are strong enough to be felt; 20 are sufficiently violent to wreck a town but do not because they occur in thinly populated areas of the globe; about five cause destruction and death. Since 1900 some 850,000 people have been killed as a result of earthquakes. If a way exists to reduce this fearful toll, it must come through a fuller understanding of the still mysterious forces involved when our earth quakes.

Opposite: the devastation caused by the earthquake in Alaska in 1964. Severe earthquakes, often arriving without warning, are an awe-inspiring phenomenon that have intrigued man since earliest times. By understanding something of what causes earthquakes, and the apalling damage they can do to property and life, we can at least meet the dangers half-way.

What Causes Earthquakes?

Most earthquakes begin with a low loud rumbling coming from below ground. Then, in open country, there appears a ripple in the earth – the ground swells into a low ridge that travels over the land like a wave on the sea. These features make it understandable that early peoples imagined earthquakes to be the work of some subterranean monster. In Japan it was thought to be a giant spider, in India a gigantic mole.

The ancient Greeks tried to find a natural explanation. Aristotle suggested that underground gases caused earthquakes when they escaped from subterranean cavities, and his view prevailed for nearly 2000 years. New ideas also had to struggle against the religious belief that an earthquake was a sign of wrath from God.

The first instrument to record the direction of an earthquake was a pendulum inside a jar, designed by the Chinese astronomer Chang Heng in about 130 AD. A device based on spillage of water came in 17th-century Italy and one involving a cup of mercury in 18th-century Europe. These instruments are termed seismoscopes (from *seismos*, a Greek word meaning to shake or quake).

During the 19th century the seismograph was invented to register distant earthquakes, and a network of seismic stations was established around the world. The seismograph is designed to indicate not simply the direction of an earthquake but also its time of occurrence. It also records the shock waves that radiate from the tremor. Most seismographs measure earth movements in only one direction, so receiving stations use three instruments – one for vertical movement and two others for north-south and east-west movements. It was then found that earthquakes were caused by sudden earth movements, mostly along *fault lines*, that is, where the crust of the earth is weakest. What triggered this activity has not yet been fully solved.

The point on the earth's surface immediately above the origin of the shock is called the *epicenter*, and the surface vibrations at this point are likely to be most intense. The point of origin within the earth is called the *focus*. Shallow earthquakes originate 60 miles or less below the surface, deeper earthquakes 400 to 500 miles below. By analyzing the time it takes for the different types of shock waves to reach three or more receiving stations, seismologists can pinpoint the position and depth of the earthquake.

The impact of an earthquake used to be expressed as the degree of intensity on a scale that ranged from I (hardly felt) to XII (damage total). But intensity is not

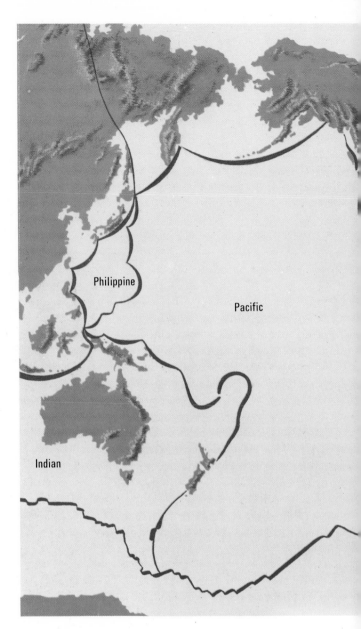

Philippine

Pacific

Indian

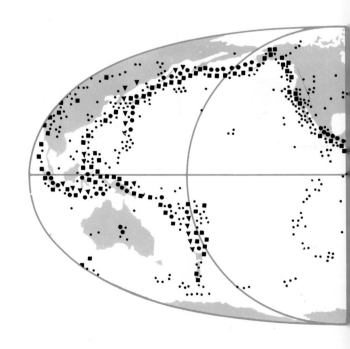

16

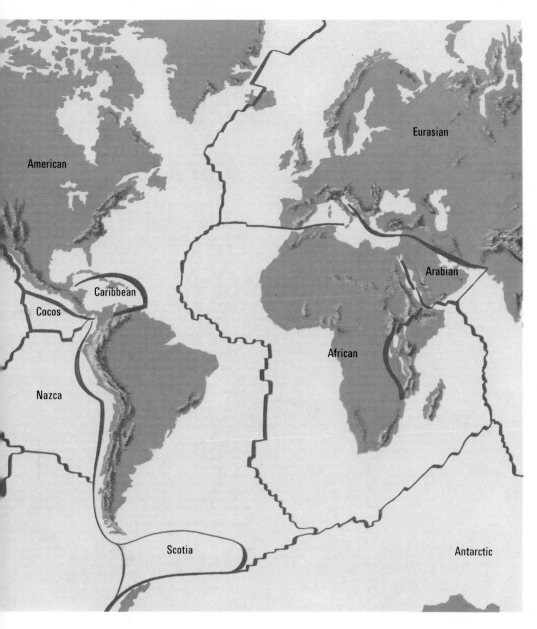

American

Eurasian

Arabian

Caribbean

Cocos

African

Nazca

Scotia

Antarctic

Left: a world map with lines representing the edges of the largest of the 19 plates that make up the earth's crust. **Below left:** a map of the world showing where earthquakes occur. As can be seen most are concentrated around the Pacific, central Asia, the Mediterranean, and the mid-ocean ridges. Severity of earthquakes range from the small dot symbol for normal earthquakes to the large symbols for major earthquakes – divided into surface (square symbol), intermediate (large dot), and deep (triangle). **Below:** this diagram of a cross section of the earth illustrates how new crust is formed. New material wells up from the mantle at the oceanic trenches, spreads over the ocean floor, and descends again into the mantle at the oceanic trenches.

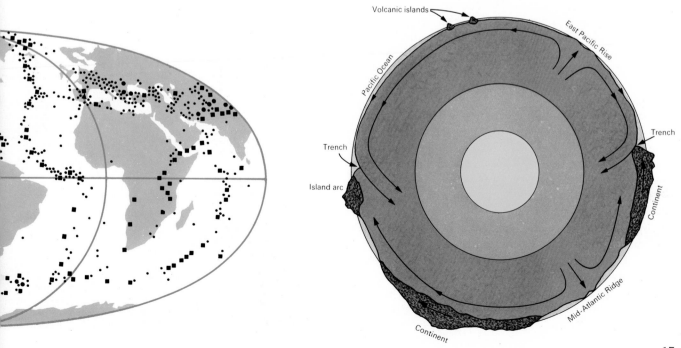

Volcanic islands

East Pacific Rise

Pacific Ocean

Trench

Trench

Island arc

Continent

Continent

Mid-Atlantic Ridge

17

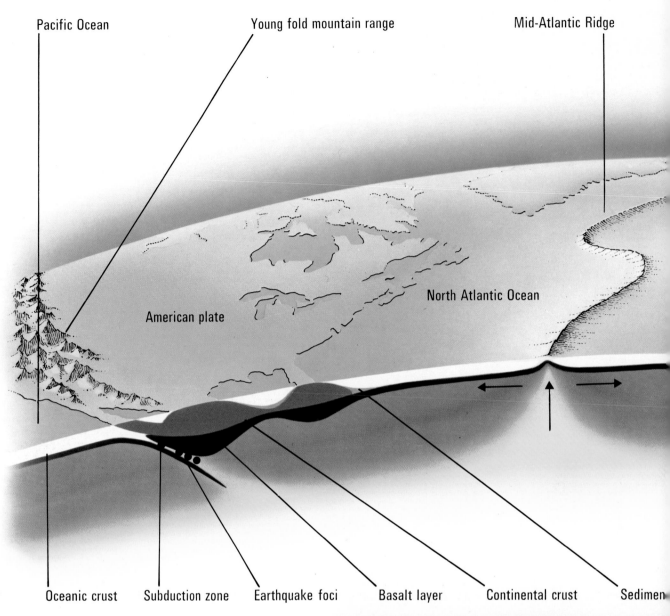

Pacific Ocean · Young fold mountain range · Mid-Atlantic Ridge

North Atlantic Ocean

American plate

Oceanic crust · Subduction zone · Earthquake foci · Basalt layer · Continental crust · Sedimen

a reliable indicator because it varies from place to place and is affected by the nature of the ground, the solidity of the buildings, and not least, the subjective response of the observers. Nor can it usefully be applied to earthquakes that occur under the sea. Today, earthquakes are generally measured in terms of their *magnitude*, which is the amount of energy released at their source.

A convenient magnitude scale was devised in 1935 by Charles F. Richter, who became a professor of seismology at the California Institute of Technology. He based it on the maximum deflection shown on a seismograph, taking into account the distance of the instrument from the epicenter. The Richter Scale is logarithmic – that is, magnitude 6 is 10 times greater than magnitude 5 and 100 times greater than magnitude 4. It is 1000 degrees less than magnitude 9. The largest earthquake of the 20th century was the Colombia-Ecuador shock of January 31, 1906 which recorded a magnitude 8.9. The energy released was equivalent to that of a 100-megaton nuclear bomb.

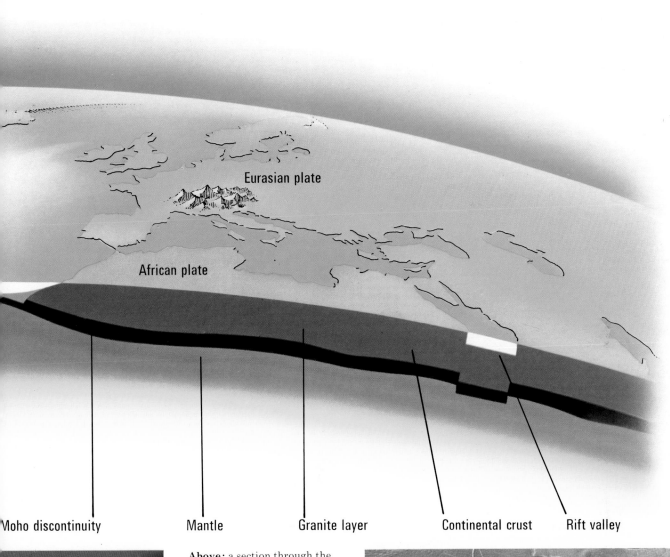

Eurasian plate

African plate

Moho discontinuity   Mantle   Granite layer   Continental crust   Rift valley

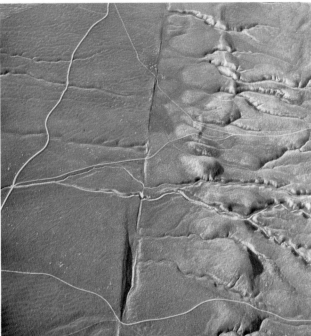

Above: a section through the earth's crust showing the forces that shift continents, build mountains, and trigger earthquakes. The Mid-Atlantic Ridge is formed where material wells up from the mantle and pushes continents apart. Iceland, which straddles the Ridge, is the scene of considerable volcanic activity (**left:** lava crater on Surtsey). The American Plate overrides the Pacific Ocean Plate forcing up mountains at the edge of the plate and creating earthquake zones.

Right: an aerial view of the San Andreas Fault on the American Plate. It is caused by friction between the American and Pacific Plates.

A large number of earthquakes were found to occur under the sea in certain well-defined areas. In the Atlantic the earthquake belt is within a central band extending the length of the ocean from Iceland almost to Antarctica. In the 1950s oceanographic expeditions using depth recorders discovered that this band consisted of the longest mountain range in the world, rising two miles from the ocean floor, and

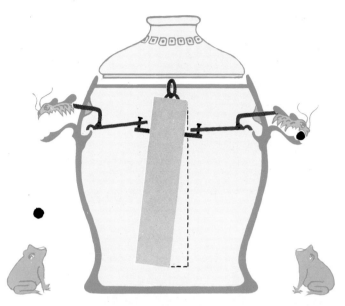

Above: a Chinese seismoscope designed about 130 AD. A pendulum suspended within the jar is linked with the moveable upper jaws of eight dragons' heads arranged around the outer surface of the vessel. Shocks cause the pendulum to swing, releasing a ball from one of the dragon's jaws into the mouth of a hollow frog.

extending hundreds of miles wide and many thousands of miles long. This previously unsuspected feature of the Earth goes around the south of Africa, up through the Indian Ocean, and into the Gulf of Aden. It divides in the southern Indian Ocean, and the branch goes between Australia and Antarctica to connect with

another ridge in the East Pacific. Sizeable sections of this oceanic mountain are offset from each other by transverse fractures, and nearly always the middle of it is marked by a deep rift valley.

Discoveries such as these, and others in allied subjects such as magnetic variation in rocks, led to the first comprehensive and convincing explanation of the earth's structure.

The outer 45 miles of the earth – the crust and the upper layer of the *mantle* (the thick layer of rock below the crust) – is made up of six large plates and a number of smaller ones. These plates bear the continents and oceans on their backs and, along the mid-ocean ridges that mark the boundaries between two plates, molten or basaltic material rises from below the surface and pushes the plates apart at the rate of a few inches per year. Such movement in the long distant past created our separate continents of today. Around 100 million years ago, for example, South America was joined to Africa, and North Africa and Europe were alongside Greenland, Canada, and the United States.

Since the earth is not getting any bigger, the rise of material to the surface means that elsewhere material is being returned to the mantle. This exchange takes place in the deep oceanic trenches – zones, like the mid-oceanic ridges, of high earthquake and volcanic activity. When the edge of an oceanic plate collides with the edge of a continental plate, the ocean edge has to dip into deeper, hotter areas of the mantle, and is eventually consumed. The dip forms the trench.

When two continental margins converge, neither of them sinks. Any trench between them is filled up, and the two land masses slowly fuse together. Further convergence builds mountains. Several million years ago the Indian plate bumped into Asia, pushing up the Himalayas. The same process is occurring today as the Africa plate moves north; it is squeezing out the

Above: a seismograph used for detecting earthquakes. A traveling pen traces a line across a revolving arm. Tremors cause waves in the line, which then reveals both strength and duration of the earthquake shocks. **Left:** a trace from a seismograph which records an earthquake shock that occurred in Iceland in March 1963.

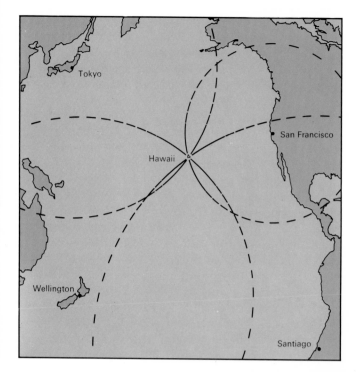

Mediterranean and raising the Alps still higher.

Molten rock can also rise to the surface in continental areas of the plates, splitting them and causing rift valleys. The largest of these stretches from East Africa through the Red Sea to the Dead Sea and Jordan River, and is thought to be the start of a new ocean. If the process continues, the Jordan River will have widened to the size of the Atlantic in another 100 million years.

When two plates grind sideways against each other but neither dips under, a fault, or vertical crack, develops in the earth's crust. The jerky movement of the plates along such a fault can be anything from mild to severe. The San Andreas Fault in California and others in New Zealand, Turkey, and the Philippines are constantly in motion.

The surface of our earth is a restless jigsaw of plates slowly jostling each other in a variety of ways that can cause them to be compressed, driven apart, consumed, or sheared. All these processes cause earthquakes.

Above: by plotting the distance of an epicenter from at least three widely scattered recording stations, scientists can determine the site of the earthquake. The map above shows arcs plotted from stations in Japan, New Zealand, the USA and Chile. As the arcs intersect at Hawaii, this is where the epicenter of the earthquake is located.

Right: a cartoon of 1906 following the earthquake in San Francisco in 1906. The caption to the picture read *The earth: " I hope I shall never have one of those splitting headaches again."* The artist must certainly have been voicing the opinion of the survivors of the earthquake, which devastated the city. Some observers, however, believe that they can see a pattern of severe shocks emerging – the next should be around the year 2000.

Destruction of a City
Lisbon: 1755

Lisbon in 1755 was renowned for three things: piety, trade, and wealth. A city of some 275,000, it was the nerve center of the Portuguese empire consisting of possessions in Brazil, Africa, and the Far East. The ships that sailed up the Tagus River to its bustling quays brought goods from every major port in the world. Lisbon, prosperous and happy, was famous the world over.

On the morning of All Saints Day, Saturday November 1, most of the people were attending Mass in the innumerable churches whose towers and spires rose like a forest above the housetops. About 9:30 am the first of three shocks struck the unsuspecting city. First came a loud rumbling noise like thunder underground. After a brief pause, this was followed by two minutes of frightful shaking that brought down houses and shops, churches and palaces in a deafening roar. A third tremor completed the destruction, and day turned into night as a dark cloud of dust smothered the ruined city. When the dust had settled and

survivors began to emerge, a disastrous fire broke out among the ruins. Within the hour came a further horror. Three 20-foot-high ocean waves (known by their Japanese name, *tsunami*) struck the waterfront with appalling force and caused utter destruction there.

Observers on higher ground around Lisbon reported that the buildings seemed to sway like corn in the wind before they fell. Of the 20,000 houses in the city, 17,000 were destroyed, and what the quake spared the fire consumed. The royal palace and the magnificent new opera house, which had been only lightly damaged by the quake, were both gutted by the flames. The same fate was suffered by innumerable other palaces, public and religious buildings, warehouses packed with goods, and entire streets of houses in the fire that turned the major part of the city into a charred desert. Many of the unfortunate citizens were trapped in the ruins and burned alive. Others who had taken refuge from the fire on the quays were swept away by the tsunami and drowned. The blocked streets and squares were filled with the cries of people pleading to be confessed before they died. Estimates of the number of deaths run as high as 60,000.

More than one third of Europe felt the shocks. In churches 1000 miles away chandeliers were observed to swing, acting as primitive seismographs in recording the passage of the earthquake waves. The level of water in the Swiss lakes and as far away as Loch Lomond in Scotland began to fluctuate, and continued to rise and fall for an hour, the rise ranging up to three feet. In canals and rivers in the Netherlands, the oscillations were so great that large vessels snapped their cables. Sea waves caused by the quake crossed the Atlantic and sent a wave 22 feet high crashing against the islands of the Lesser Antilles. Even the major shocks were not restricted to the area around Lisbon. Severe tremors struck North Africa, causing great destruction in Fez. Smaller shocks continued in Lisbon for at least a year. In July 1756 the British ambassador to Madrid wrote to a colleague in Lisbon, "Will your earth never be quiet?" By then there had been upward of 500 aftershocks that kept the people in a state of hysterical fright.

When the distraught King José I asked what was to be done, his minister Pombal replied succinctly, "Bury the dead and feed the living." The fire had consumed many of the bodies. Some of the remainder were buried, but others were collected in barges, towed out to sea, weighted, and sunk. Tents and huts were quickly erected for shelter, and the arduous work of recovery began. Recovery, however, was hampered by the religious mania of many priests. When many people wondered why Lisbon had been singled out for destruction, these stern priests warned that God was angry with its sinful people and would punish them again if they did not repent. The hundreds of sermons on this theme, delivered daily, induced a mood of dejected apathy in the people and seriously

Above: the Marquez de Pombal, a Portuguese government minister, sent a questionnaire to every parish in Portugal after the Lisbon earthquake, to discover the time and the length of the shock. It was one of the earliest attempts to assess the intensity of earthquake shocks in terms of surface damage.

Above: an engraving of the 1755 Lisbon earthquake. After the tremors had shaken down most of the buildings fires broke out and gutted those that had been only lightly damaged. Survivors that fled to the waterfront area were swept away by three 20-foot high ocean waves that struck in the aftermath of the earthquake.

Right: the remains of Lisbon Cathedral after the 1755 earthquake. Many Portuguese were attending Mass for the Feast of All Saints when the tremors occurred and perished as the massive stone structure collapsed on top of them.

hindered efforts to restore the city's normal life. Eventually the more frenzied priests had to be imprisoned.

The religious conflict gives the Lisbon earthquake a particular significance. Knowing how many children and other innocents had perished on that dreadful day, people began to question God's mercy and compassion. The ingenuity of the priests was put to the test in having to explain why God allowed the destruction of so many churches, yet spared a street full of brothels. The battle of opinion was carried out through numerous pamphlets and writings. Among these were some by scientists who maintained that the earthquake was caused not by the sins of Lisbon but by movements under the earth. It was a turning point in human attitudes toward natural disasters.

"Roaring in the Streets"
San Francisco: 1906

Above: this view of California Street in San Francisco gives some idea of what the city looked like before the earthquake and fire all but obliterated the city (below). San Francisco lies across the San Andreas Fault, where two of the earth's plates scrape laterally against each other. The movement is slowly ripping a slice of land stretching from San Francisco to Baja California in Mexico, away from the continent and up toward Alaska.

Even when San Francisco, the 11th largest city in the United States, was little more than a village of wooden huts, the Californian coastline on which it was situated was known as "earthquake country." Today, geologists realize this is because it lies at the boundary between two plates moving past one another at a rate of some 2.5 inches a year. In some places the plates slide past harmlessly, elsewhere they stick for a few years or a few decades. The strain builds up until finally the rocks are forced to yield and the plates jerk past each other. The movement is sudden, violent, and the result is an earthquake.

After an earthquake in Southern California in 1857 the channels made by many of the streams that flowed across the boundary area (known as the San Andreas Fault) of the two plates were found to be displaced by as much as 30 feet. This is believed to be the largest horizontal movement caused by an arthquake in modern times. There was another earthquake in 1857 but the details are scarce because the area was then thinly populated. Information is even scarcer for the earthquake that occurred in the San Francisco area of Central California in 1800. It is in these two areas of California that the crustal plates stick and that are therefore exposed to major earthquake risk. They seem to take it in turn: San Francisco in 1800, Los Angeles in 1857. If there was to be one in the early 1900s, it would be San Francisco's turn.

At 5.15 on the morning of April 17, 1906 the people

Above: a house in San Francisco that survived the 1906 earthquake and fire. It slid upon its foundations a distance of four feet. **Right:** a print of 1906 showing the execution of looters following the earthquake. Such was the havoc caused first by the tremors then by widespread fires that the city was put under martial law in an effort to bring some organization into relief and rescue work.

of San Francisco awoke to "the groaning of timbers, a grinding and creaking sound, and then a roaring in the street." To the north, at Tomales Bay, directly over the San Andreas Fault, a two-story hotel sprang from its foundations and landed in the sea. The fault also ran under the Skinner dairy ranch at Olema where a line of cypresses and a rose garden that had stood beside the house slid along to a new position in front of the barn. The cows stampeded and one fell into a rift caused by the moving Fault.

The outer suburbs of San Francisco stood a mere five miles from the Fault. The quake came thundering in across the Bay from the north and the buildings began to dance. Cornices broke off, façades of houses slid away, streetcar tracks twisted. Electric cables snapped and every light in the city went dead. Some water pipes broke but the most serious damage of all occurred a few miles south of the city where the earthquake split the great pipes that brought in the city's water supply. This meant that if fire broke out there would be no water to extinguish it.

The earthquake damage was particularly severe to buildings in the downtown area where the tenements had been constructed on old marshland covered with sand and which the quake shook like jelly. On the harder ground buildings tended to survive – though one that did not was the City Hall. Recently completed

at a cost of $6,000,000, it had taken 20 years to put up. It collapsed in less than a minute.

Yet relatively few of San Francisco's buildings were destroyed directly by the quake. The very low figure of 390 people killed was point one percent of the city's population – and that included those shot as looters while the city was under martial law. It was the uncontrollable fires that destroyed San Francisco – "the most combustible city in the world." They devastated the business area, burned down nearly all the public buildings, the millionaires' palaces commanding the city from the heights of Nob Hill, and 28,188 houses. With no water available to put them out, the fires raged through the city for three days. The desperate firemen hosed the blazing buildings with anything could find, even sewage, but nothing halted the inferno until the wind changed. A few men helplessly trapped by debris were shot as an act of mercy when the flames were about to burn them alive.

If the earthquakes follow the pattern so far established – 1800 . . . 1906, then San Francisco may be safe until the end of the century. But what about Los Angeles? Along the San Andreas Fault in Southern California the accumulated strain is sufficient to produce a jerk of over 20 feet. Eventually the rocks must yield. Meanwhile the population of Greater Los Angeles has reached 7,000,000.

Disaster in Japan
Tokyo: 1923

Earthquakes shake Japan an average of 1500 times a year. Because of this, the Japanese traditionally built their houses of light strips of wood with sliding panels of paper for the internal walls – materials that cause the least possible damage if they fall during an earthquake. On October 28, 1891 a severe shock struck the provinces of Mino and Owari in central Japan. Ground on the north side of a 70-mile fault moved up to 13 feet sideways. In the villages, whole streets of houses collapsed like houses of cards. Some 197,000 homes were destroyed, but happily the number of deaths, 7300, was relatively low.

Very different were the effects of the quake of Magnitude 8.3 that rocked Tokyo and the surrounding Kanto region at two minutes before noon on September 1, 1923. In the densely populated cities of Tokyo and its great port Yokohama, and in the villages and small towns along Sagami Bay, a total of 140,000 perished. The earthquake's epicenter was in the middle of Sagami Bay. Some areas of the bay floor rose by 800 feet, others were depressed by 1500 feet – a difference in relative level of nearly half a mile. City authorities in Yokohama had been considering a plan to deepen the harbor so that more big liners could moor there. The earthquake deepened the harbor for them.

In Japan the first day of September is called Nihyaku-toka, meaning Two Hundred and Tenth Day, and it is traditionally said to be a day for something unpleasant to happen. The unpleasantness began happening two minutes before noon, as the charcoal braziers were being lit for the midday meal in more than half a million homes. The preliminary tremors were as violent as the main shock of an ordinary quake. The main shock knocked all the seismograph needles in the locality off their drums.

As severe as the quake was, it is thought that only 5000 of Tokyo's half a million buildings collapsed. The story that only the Imperial Hotel survived because of its revolutionary design by the American architect Frank Lloyd Wright is a popular legend, but untrue. Numerous buildings in traditional style remained standing, as did many others built with reinforced brick walls a yard thick.

In Yokohama, which was 17 miles nearer the epicenter, the shock brought down 12 per cent of the 100,000 buildings. In one odd occurrence, an occupied bathtub that had been on the second floor of the Grand Hotel descended gradually, supported by the piping, until it came to rest in the street with a woman still in it – and most of the bathwater as well.

In tragic contrast, 200 school children on an excursion train were buried alive in Yokosuka when a high embankment collapsed on top of them. Further west, a landslide of mud poured down onto the village of Nebukawa, pushing its houses into the bay and burying them completely. A crowded train waiting at the village station was knocked down a 150-foot precipice into the sea, and all but one of the passengers drowned.

In Tokyo the shocks were greatest on reclaimed swampy land such as the Asakusa amusement district. The Twelve Storey Tower, which resembled the Tower of Pisa without the tilt, and which was Tokyo's highest structure, stood in that area. For a few moments after the quake, the tower leaned like its famous counterpart, then it split into two pieces at the eighth floor.

The worst damage by far was caused by the outbreak of fire. The quake could not have happened at a worse moment than mealtime. Hundreds of thousands of cooking braziers overturned and set the wood and paper buildings alight. There was no hope for them because all firefighting equipment had been destroyed. In Yokohama, oil from burst storage tanks poured down through the canals, catching fire on the way. Thousands were trapped inside circles of flames. Some tried to force their way into the supposedly fireproof Yokohama Specie Bank, but they were burned to death on the steps. The hundreds who did shelter in the cellar of the bank died of heat and suffocation. Flames advancing along the select residential district called the Bluff cornered the residents against the edge of a 100-foot cliff at the end. Forced to jump, they

Above and below: scenes of some of the destruction that followed the Tokyo earthquake of 1923. Apart from the widespread collapse of buildings some eight square miles of the city were demolished by fire and 140,000 people died. **Right:** some of the bodies of victims burned to death in a city bank vault where they were sheltering from the appalling fire tornadoes that criss-crossed the city.

landed on those who had jumped before and were lying too injured to crawl away. The screams of the dying continued through the night.

Thousands in Tokyo fled to the bridges across the Sumida River. Sparks that fell onto their bundles of belongings ignited the bridges, and all but one were burned with everyone upon them. The exception was the Shin-Ohashi. There one courageous policeman allowed no one carrying anything to step onto the bridge. His good sense saved the lives of 12,000.

Forty thousand people took refuge on the 25 empty acres by the waterfront known as the Army Clothing Depot. During the afternoon the multitude of small fires produced fire tornadoes that criss-crossed over the burning city, either roasting people alive or poisoning them with carbon monoxide. At four o'clock the most violent of the fire tornadoes roared into the depot, and, said a survivor, "hundreds of people were taken into the air like beans." Pillars of fiery smoke ranged through the ranks of huddled refugees. Of the 40,000 a "few hundred" who had been on the outskirts or protected under a pile of bodies survived.

Three fifths of Tokyo was destroyed, four fifths of Yokohama. The Kanto earthquake of 1923 remains Japan's greatest single catastrophe.

Avalanche in the Andes
Peru:1970

between it and the Huascarán protected it from avalanche danger. It was there that Dr Morales had eaten lunch on the day of the earthquake, greeted two visiting geophysicists and then, overcome by a strange nervousness, had decided to drive out of the valley. On the way to Huarás the earthquake struck and an estimated 10,000 cubic yards of rock fell off the

Left: startled and terrified spectators at the Monterrico Hippodrome, Lima, on May 31, 1970. They are running out on to the race course just as the first tremors are felt of the earthquake that wrecked the town of Huarmey about 150 miles farther up the coast.

Huascarán is Peru's highest mountain, soaring 22,204 feet up in the Cordillera Blanca range of the Andes. Its last 2500 feet is a vertical granite cliff topped with thick layers of ice and snow. In July 1962, part of this icecap broke away and set off a rock and ice avalanche that hurtled down to the valley, overwhelming eight villages and half the small town of Ranrahirca, killing 3500 people. The avalanche weakened and fractured the west face of Huascarán, which now overhung the valley. Peru's leading glaciologist Dr Morales remembers, "immense rock slabs nearly separated from the bedrock and counterpoised." All that was needed was a trigger to set the rocks loose.

The earthquake of 1970 served as that trigger. The epicenter was about nine miles off the coast and the coastal towns of Casma and Huarmey were totally wrecked. Yet fewer than a dozen people died there because the streets are wide and when everyone ran into them the buildings collapsed harmlessly behind them. It was a different matter in the thickly populated Rio Santa valley at the foot of the Cordillera Blanca. Here, because cultivable land is at a premium, the towns are crowded into as little space as possible and streets are narrow. People who ran from their houses in Huarás, chief town of the Santa valley, were buried as the sun-dried brick adobe buildings burst into the narrow streets on top of them. Around 10,000 died, nearly half the population.

Fifty miles along the Santa valley stood the rebuilt town of Ranrahirca and beyond it Yungay, a pleasant town confident that the 650-foot-high spur of rock

cliff of Huascarán. With it came its thick covering of ice, some of which melted in the frictional heat to form a rapidly moving torrent of mud, bearing great chunks of ice and slabs of rock, some bigger than houses. This irresistible avalanche ricocheted down the narrow gorge at 180 miles an hour totally burying Ranrahirca beneath a blackish, semiliquid mass. A major lobe of the avalanche soared over Yungay's protective hill and descended on the town like a cataract, smothering it but for the tops of four palm trees in its central square. Most of its inhabitants lay dead beneath it. Among the few survivors were Dr Morales' two geophysicists. In an article published in the *American Alpine Journal,* Morales wrote, "The two ran as if possessed for the cemetery, the highest point in town. As the muck swept about their feet, they gained the steps that led upward. For three nights and two days, with around 200 other people who were saved, they cowered there among the open graves waiting for the encircling mud to harden."

Dr Morales' duties include planning measures to lessen the danger from natural disasters. Peru will always suffer from earthquakes, but ordinary risks can be reduced by reconstructing towns like Huarás in stronger materials and with wider streets. Little or nothing can be done to prevent rock avalanches from Huascarán and Dr Morales advised that Yungay, Ranrahirca, and the other villages be rebuilt some miles from their former sites. Whether these sites can be left unbuilt on, in a land-starved, relatively poor valley remains to be seen.

Above: the town of Yungay nestling below the Huascarán mountain in Peru. An earthquake on May 31, 1970 dislodged a huge mass of rock and ice, causing a 200-mile-an-hour avalanche which buried the town under some 15 feet of mud.

Below: Yungay after the avalanche. Some 20,000 people perished under the watery debris. Among those who were saved were two visiting geophysicists who with about 200 townspeople sheltered in the highest point in the town – the cemetery.

A Community Destroyed
Italy: 1976

The mountainous region of Friuli in northeast Italy lies in a known seismic area but for hundreds of years no major earthquake had disturbed the picturesque red-roofed houses and medieval churches of its old towns. Surrounded by the foothills of the Alps, the towns are small and the villages remote. The life of the peasants is hard but the struggle to make a living is common to all and bound the communities close. The long ordeal that began on May 6, 1976, destroyed more than the towns and villages – the old tight-knit community spirit of Friuli has gone, perhaps for ever.

Above: the ruins of the 12th-century church of Gemona del Friuli.

The first shock occurred at 8 pm and many people who were at home eating dinner ran into the streets. This preliminary shock and its mildness saved the lives of thousands when the main shock (6.0 on the Richter Scale) occurred and shook the buildings down. The epicenter was near Udine, the provincial capital, but the towns worst hit were farther north. In the village of Maiano some 50 families were trapped when two housing blocks collapsed. Sixty people were buried under the rubble of a restaurant where they were having a banquet. Outside Gemona posters invited tourists to visit this attractive hill town and see its medieval castle. But 80 percent of Gemona had become a wasteland of rubble and all that was left of the castle were a few shattered walls.

The tremors were felt from Yugoslavia to Belgium where they caused hundreds of occupants of high-rise buildings to rush into the streets. In Venice, 60 miles from Udine, the city was plunged into darkness and people ran from the houses and out of cinemas in panic. Saint Mark's Square was empty as people sought safety in other open spaces, fearing the collapse of the 322-foot-high bell tower.

In the Friuli area itself 939 people were dead and 50,000 homeless, nearly a third of the total population of the region. Tents were hastily sent to shelter them; the luckier families moved into empty railroad coaches. Help from outside was clearly necessary but the Friulani were unimpressed by government promises of massive aid in equipment and money. As it turned out their mistrust of government offers proved justified. The supply and construction of prefabricated houses was continually delayed as a result of Italy's cumbersome administrative system. Eventu-

ally some reconstruction work was done but September brought many demonstrations against the government by people, many of them elderly, who saw no likelihood of their being housed before the winter.

The earthquake was probably caused by the release of accumulated pressure built up by the rocks beneath the Adriatic Sea pushing northward against the Alps. Unfortunately, the pressure released in May and in the 188 aftershocks of the following four months had not succeeded in settling the earth. On September 12 two severe shocks destroyed four months of reconstruction in a matter of seconds. Buildings already weakened now collapsed entirely. Road and rail links were blocked again and villages were cut off by landslides hurtling down the mountains.

As if this were not enough, an early autumn brought freezing temperatures and torrential rain. Many of the 119 tent sites were flooded and deep in mud; the building of huts for the homeless (now 60,000) was far behind schedule. By September 13 the mood of the Friulani had turned from resentment to despair. Plans for evacuating the area in the summer had been abandoned because people did not want to move from their home areas. Now cars, buses, and army trucks took them away in thousands to empty holiday apartments and single-story chalets on the Adriatic coast. Within a week four fifths of the population of Gemona had left, two thirds from Maiano. Silence fell over many villages. The following April when nearly all the prefabricated houses had been built many people came back – but not all. They had gone to seek relatives in France, Venezuela, the United States – anywhere were the earth kept still. The old life of Friuli had indeed been broken for ever.

Above: some of the workers attempting to salvage belongings after the destruction caused by the earthquake that struck the Friuli district of northeast Italy. **Left and right:** one of the worst hit places in the district was the medieval hill town of Gemona where some 80 percent of the town was reduced to rubble.

Annihilation of a City
China:1976

"One of the worst natural calamities in human history," is how a Chinese government official described the appalling earthquake that killed an undisclosed number of people – perhaps 750,000 – in the city of T'ang-shan on July 28, 1976.

T'ang-shan no longer exists. When it did it stood in the heart of China's most thickly populated region, 85 miles southeast of Peking. Although the Chinese have had some success in forecasting earthquakes, this one – in a part of China not considered to be a danger area – came without any warning. At 3.45 am a major 2 minute-long shock of magnitude 8.2 convulsed this coal-mining city with a population of 1.6 million. The devastation seems to have been total – a rare, possibly uniquely terrible catastrophe. After even the worst of the world's previous earthquakes parts of some buildings have remained standing. An especially horrifying detail concerns the fate of the thousands of miners on night shift who were caught underground and on whom the walls of rock closed for ever. A hospital and a train were virtually swallowed into the ground after a huge subsidence took place into the mining shafts that ran beneath the city.

Mr Gough Whitlam, the former Australian Prime Minister, happened to be in Tientsin, China's third largest city, 40 miles south of T'ang-shan. In the 7th-floor room of his hotel furniture was overthrown and a heavy dressing table crashed onto the bed. "A Chinese official with us found a torch," he recalled, "and guided us down the stairs. We had to jump over a foot-wide gap which had split the hotel from top to bottom."

Sixteen hours after the main shock the area was hit by an aftershock (magnitude 7.9) of exceptional severity. In Peking police warned people to move out of doors because of the danger of further tremors and that night, in torrential rain, 6 million people camped in the streets under tents and makeshift shelters. For the next 16 days the capital resembled a vast refugee camp. Every available tree, bush, telegraph pole, or railing was utilized to form an anchor for the walls of temporary shelters.

Aftershocks continued and over the next few days the epicenters moved ominously toward Peking. People in the capital were forbidden to enter buildings. Foreign diplomats camped on the lawns and tennis courts of their embassies. Peking's railroad station was sealed off and travelers were allowed to enter only minutes before the trains were due to leave. They had to run to their platforms through the long passages beneath the station, fearful that they might be trapped in the tunnels by new tremors.

All this time the Chinese had released no firm information about the situation in T'ang-shan. The official announcement stated merely that the area had sustained "damage in varying degrees" although foreigners returning from Manchuria reported seeing military aircraft arriving filled with wounded. The number of injured was later estimated to be 800,000.

After a week, however, the Chinese practice of turning everything to political account was illustrated by the story published in the *People's Daily* of a certain Che Cheng-min, described as a member of the T'ang-shan party committee's permanent committee. After he had managed to drag himself from the ruins of his wrecked home his two children cried, "Quick, daddy, come and save us." As he was about to go to their aid, he heard another call from the nearby house of Chiu Kuang-yu, secretary of the local neighborhood party committee. At once Che told his wife, "I am going to rescue old Chiu first." When he had done so, Chiu asked him, "What about your children?" "Let us not bother about them," Che replied. "You are secretary of the local neighborhood party committee and you have no time to lose. Go and organize the rescue work immediately." When he returned to his home he found his children dead but he felt neither remorse nor grief. He had not hesitated to sacrifice his own children, the report concluded, in the interest of the people of the neighborhood.

Above: members of the Chinese army marching to assist peasants clean up the devastated industrial city of T'ang-shan after one of the world's worst earthquakes struck the area on July 28, 1976. The natural phenomenon was made worse by the honeycomb of coalmines below the city that collapsed as a result of the tremors.

The railway system (below) was particularly badly hit by the combined earthquake and subsidence in which more than 655,000 people are thought to have died. **Right:** Peking inhabitants camping out of doors because of the dangers of secondary tremors.

Unofficial Chinese sources gave the number of dead as 655,000 though later information increased this figure by a further 100,000. Not until 11 months had passed were foreign journalists allowed to pass through the ravaged area. Peter Griffiths of *The Times* of London wrote: "Approaching the city, one can see scores of rebuilt villages and bridges, row upon row of fresh, peasant-style burial mounds and occasional piles of rubble dotting the fields. It does little to prepare the traveller for the horror of T'ang-shan, reminiscent of Hiroshima after the bomb. The transition from rural near-normality to scenes of vast urban destruction is swift and shocking. One minute the train is speeding by waving fields of wheat, the next it is crawling through a desert of rubble stretching as far as the eye can see, across what used to be a city [of a million people]."

Prediction and Prevention

The destruction and misery created by major earthquakes is so great that an accurate means of predicting them would be of incalculable benefit to mankind. There have been successful forecasts in the past: The earthquake of 1042 in Tabriz, Northern Persia, for instance, was correctly predicted by the astrologer Abu Tahir Shirazi. He was unable to persuade the people to leave the city, however, so that when the earthquake came, 40,000 perished. In 1549 another Persian earthquake killed 3000 at Qayin. This one had been forecast by the local leader who was equally unsuccessful in persuading his people to sleep in the open that night. He stayed out alone but, as the night was cold, he returned to his home after a time, and later perished with the others.

The prediction methods used by these seers is unknown. It may be that some people share with certain animals a heightened sensitivity to minute physical changes occurring in the earth or the atmosphere in the period immediately preceding a quake. Not all the signs require heightened sensitivity to be noticed, however. On the afternoon before the Agadir earthquake pictures on hotel walls were seen to have shifted and were hanging at a tilt. It is said that a small boy in the Casbah was scolded when the contents of a bucket slopped over, though he swore he had not touched it. That evening dogs howled, cats prowled uneasily, and the mules kicked against their shed walls. In Tokyo and Yokohama flocks of birds left the area some hours before the earthquake of 1923. On the eve of the 1935 Quetta earthquake an unusual degree of electricity was noticed in the air.

Such phenomena may be significant pointers, but they suffer the fatal drawbacks of lacking both precision and the power to persuade. The mysterious slopping of a bucket of water could never have roused the Casbah to interrupt its business and flee, as Abu Tahir Shirazi and many like him have discovered.

Only a few years ago the scientific prediction of earthquakes was looked on as an impossible hope. Since then matters have changed so far that seismologists in the United States, Japan, and the USSR believe that given sufficient funds, earthquake prediction could be a practicable proposition some time in the 1980s.

Soviet investigations began in 1949 when a disastrous earthquake in Tadzhikistan, which borders on eastern China, set off landslides that killed 10,000. After 20 years of study the Russian scientists established that certain measurable changes take place in the earth before an earthquake. Variations in electrical resistance and in the speed of seismic waves passing through the rocks occur at particular depths in the earth. The concentration of the radioactive gas radon in the water of wells increases dramatically, and the land above a threatening quake is slightly uplifted. A slight doming of the land preceded the 1923 Kanto earthquake, although Japanese scientists did not at that time know what interpretation to put on the phenomenon. Doming is occurring now over a vast area of Southern California which has uplifted 10 inches since 1960.

California, in fact, is the scene of some of the most intense efforts to understand the physical changes that precede earthquakes. The Southern California doming, known as the "bubble," is centered over the San Andreas Fault. This notorious feature is the boundary between the Pacific plate moving northwestward against the plate on which the rest of America rides. If the San Andreas Fault were straight, the two plates would creep past each other relatively easily with fairly frequent short jerks giving rise to small tremors. But the east-west range of the San Bernardino Mountains obstructs and bends the Fault and prevents an easy release of the never-ceasing strain. In three areas where the Fault subdivides into many smaller branches minor earthquake activity is frequent and harmless. These are known as areas of "creep." They separate two areas where the Fault is

Above: the Saada Hotel in Agadir on the west coast of Morocco. **Below:** the Saada Hotel after the earthquake of February 29, 1960, when the hotel collapsed "like a house of cards."

Above: devastation in the town of Port Richardson, Alaska, following the earthquake on March 27, 1964. **Below:** the Transamerica building, San Francisco. All new buildings in this potentially dangerous earthquake zone are built to withstand earth tremors.

seen as a single continuous line. One of these, extending northward from San Francisco, was the scene of the 1906 quake. The other runs southward past Los Angeles to San Bernardino: this was the scene of the 1857 quake in the course of which land west of the Fault jerked northward by up to 27 feet. In each of these two areas the Fault changes direction in the middle and this bend may be what locks the two plates together until the accumulated strain abruptly and violently gives way. Because both these areas are regions of high density population, and in both (but particularly in Los Angeles) the rock-strain is approaching breaking-point, scientists see a method of prediction and, if possible, prevention, as a matter of urgency.

Remarkable progress in prediction has taken place in China. In addition to the range of scientific observation conducted by seismologists, thousands of people in other walks of life throughout China have received instructions on supplying data of unusual phenomena. These include muddying of wells, streams that dry up or alter color, and many kinds of observations concerning animals – rats abandoning buildings, snakes in large numbers emerging from their holes, odd behavior in dogs, or birds reluctant to roost. Some of these observations may turn out to have nothing to do with earthquakes. Nevertheless, the Chinese attitude is that diagnosing the earth is like diagnosing the human body: "one must look in many directions for symptoms and take every hint that is presented."

35

In 1970 seismologists identified the town of Hai-cheng in Southern Manchuria as a future danger area. By 1974 reports from local observers were becoming increasingly ominous. A crisis point seemed to be reached and scientists issued an immediate warning. The inhabitants spent two nights out of doors in sub-zero temperatures. This warning was a false alarm but early February 1975 seismologists announced that a major quake would occur within two days. "Without delay," a Chinese report states, "the broad masses of people were notified to build temporary living huts . . . to move the old and the weak." In some communes, open-air movies were shown to encourage the people to leave their threatened homes. On February 4, five hours after the warning was issued, an earthquake of Magnitude 7.3 destroyed Hai-cheng.

Many of the long-term signs had been observed before the terrible T'ang-shan earthquake of July 28, 1976, but unfortunately there were no strong signs immediately before the fatal date. In consequence no warnings could be issued to save the 755,000 people who died in the greatest killer earthquake ever recorded.

In California evidence published in 1978 established that before an earthquake, concentrations of a rare heavy gas, radon, in the water of wells increases sometimes as much as fourfold. The radon enters the wells from traces of uranium minerals and occurs, so

Above: seismological reading room in the Earthquake Research Center Menlo Park, California. Throughout the world there are over 1000 seismograph stations particularly in known earthquake areas such as China, where this seismologist (left) is checking readings on a seismograph. Some instruments can record an earthquake of magnitude 4 or greater occurring anywhere in the world.

Left: an earthquake in the Philippines during August 1976 wrecked this building on Mindanao Island. Earthquake prediction and building techniques are vital to the economies of developing countries.

Above: neatly planted rows of trees in an orange grove over the San Andreas Fault, the crack in the earth's surface that runs nearly half the length of California. It is under this area that two of the crustal plates meet and pass each other. The enormous strain that builds up when the plates stick is released in earthquakes – some violent, some minor tremors. In 1906 horizontal movements in the earth's crust along the 600-mile fault caused the great San Francisco earthquake.

scientists believe, because shortly before an earthquake the rocks deep underground suddenly become porous, crack, and expand. This releases the radon into the soil to be concentrated near the surface of the earth. Seismologists have already dug 20 boreholes along the San Andreas Fault at roughly two mile intervals and an extension of these, examined weekly, appear to give the most reliable predictions yet found.

In 1962 the US Army dug a well two miles deep at their Rocky Mountain Arsenal in Colorado to dispose of water contaminated during the manufacture of nerve gas and insecticides. Six weeks after the first water was pumped into the well Denver, the state capital of Colorado, had its first earthquake for 80 years. An old fault below the city had been lubricated by the water and reactivated. Earthquakes continued almost daily until the US Army stopped using the well in 1966. They reached a peak the following year and have since subsided.

The discovery that earthquakes could be triggered off by man gave seismologists the idea that the strain on the San Andreas Fault might be relieved by inducing a series of controlled, minor quakes along its course. The critical factor here is, naturally, the control since it would be no good setting off by accident the major earthquake everybody wants to avoid. In essence, the plan is to bore a series of holes in sets of three, each hole reaching about 2.5 miles into the earth. The outer holes, about 1000 yards distant from

each other, would be pumped dry, to lock the fault at those points; water would then be pumped into the middle hole and any earthquake set off by this would not, scientists hope, extend beyond the locked outer holes.

Not every earthquake region of the world could be made safer by such methods. Although they might be applied in Turkey and Persia, scientists believe it will neither be possible nor desirable to interfere with the earthquakes that originate below the deep oceanic trenches. For Japan and Chile, therefore, hope lies in accurate prediction and sensible building. Even in California, the disastrous consequences of a mishap must make any interference a highly dangerous game. With the San Andreas Fault approaching a critical point it may be unwise to attempt preventive measures until after the next major earthquake but then to use them regularly to prevent the strain from ever dangerously building up again. Many buildings have actually been built over the Fault itself. When the earthquake comes these will be torn apart but many others will also be demolished. The ruined cities can then be rebuilt using materials capable of resisting earthquakes and leaving the immediate vicinity of the Fault clear. Any future earthquakes in the area it is to be hoped, will be of a minor kind, engineered by man. San Francisco, "The City that Waits to Die," may change its nickname to "The City that Only Died Twice."

Chapter 3

Storm and Flood

All living forms and all living processes require the presence of water if they are to survive. Yet this necessity and sustainer of life also possesses a terrible power to destroy. It is a power that is recognized in the myths of many of the world's religions, which tell how a wicked or neglectful mankind was punished by a deity who sent a great deluge that overwhelmed the earth. Whether or not these myths recall an actual widescale flood in man's early history, they do at least show the extent to which our ancestors stood in awe of the might of the sea and the fury of tempests.

Some storms, though initially destructive, bring long-term benefits. For centuries, Egypt survived on the annual flooding of the Nile. But these are unexpected cases. Ruin and desolation are the usual results of what an American newspaper once aptly summed up as "Hell and High Water."

Left: the violent whirling action of the winds is the main characteristic of the windstorms known as hurricanes and tornadoes. The hurricane covers larger areas and is the most destructive windstorm known to man, the tornado the most violent, though its destructive path is generally short and narrow. For anything in the path of either, the result is usually the same – utter destruction.

The Destructive Power of Wind and Water

Above: the USAF Base in Oklahoma after a 98-mile-an-hour tornado had hit it in March 1948. Some wind gusts reached 250-miles an hour at times. The tornado destroyed the base and 50 aircraft, doing damage estimated at around $15,000,000 in aircraft alone.

When the Hwang-ho (Yellow River) burst through its 70-foot embankments in 1887 the resulting flood drowned 900,000 people. In the Kansas-Missouri floods of 1951 only 28 people died but the damage caused by this most costly of American floods was $935,224,000. These bare statistics indicate the scale of destruction that can be brought about when water breaks out of the channels nature or man have provided for it.

Water is heavy. A cubic foot weights approximately 62 pounds and a large bathful (a cubic yard) weighs 1680 pounds. This weight is one explanation for the great damage done by floodwaters; a second is its rapid mobility, and a third is the added force it can derive from surmounting the obstacles – dikes, dams, levees (flood embankments) – that man has placed in its path.

Broadly speaking, there are two kinds of flood: inland flooding, such as a river overflow or dam-burst, and coastal flooding, where the sea breaks over the land. Each of these can be caused in several different ways and the two types can overlap. The most violent sea flooding occurs as a side-effect of a submarine earthquake or the eruption of a coastal volcano. During the 1883 Krakatoa eruption 36,000 people were drowned when giant waves swept over the low-lying settlements on Java and Sumatra. The epicenter of the terrible Messina earthquake of 1908, in which 82,000 were killed, lay in the Strait between Sicily and Italy. Three large waves raced outward, reaching a maximum height of 43 feet. The second wave was the most powerful and at the Calabrian port of Reggio it moved a concrete block weighing 15 tons, a distance of 22 yards. These waves are called by their Japanese name, *tsunami*, to distinguish them from ordinary tidal waves (brought about by the action of the moon and sun), storm waves, and surge waves.

Surge waves are a regular threat to Holland and the eastern counties of England. Violent north winds combine with low atmospheric pressure – similar to that found within the *eye*, or calm center, of a hurricane – to raise the level of the sea. If the water cannot escape south through the Strait of Dover it floods the coast. The most famous instance of this occurred in 1953 but there are records of similar disasters going back 1000 years. In 1287 a dreadful storm laid the whole country on both sides of the Zuider Zee under water and 50,000 people were drowned. In 1421 southwest Holland was overwhelmed with a loss of life totaling nearly 100,000.

Over the years the coastal defenses have been improved but unfortunately this has been largely canceled out through the tendency for tides to become higher. One cause of this is the continuing melting of the glaciers. Enough water is locked in the form of ice in Greenland and the Antarctic to raise the sea level throughout the world by several hundred feet. Other processes within the earth can cause parts of the landmass to sink. Eastern England is sinking relatively quickly and barriers that were heightened along the tidal river Thames in London in 1972 have already had to be raised a second time. In January 1978 strong east winds blowing up the Thames coincided with the monthly period of extra high tides (confusingly known as Spring tides) and the water level rose to within a few inches of the Red Alert danger level. Luckily for London, the previous days had been free of rain and the headwaters of the river were not swollen. London cannot rely on being so lucky another time.

Inevitably, some endangered cities will one day have to be abandoned. Venice seems to be one of the unfortunate ones unless some way is found to reverse the processes causing it to sink into the Adriatic. Even so, it is unlikely that anything man can devise will do little more than postpone the inevitable. The world's many legends of drowned cities have their basis in fact.

People have sometimes expressed surprise that so many millions of peasants should choose to live close to such dangerous rivers as the Hwang-ho, the Ganges, and the other rivers of Southeast Asia liable to devastation by flood. But the choice is between that and starvation. Land is scarce and the earth watered by these rivers is enormously fertile.

The devastating floods of Southeast Asia are generally the result of tropical cyclones, which are vast masses of rapidly circling air that form over all tropical oceans except the South Atlantic. In Asia they are also known as typhoons, in the Philippines they are known as baguios, in Australia willy-willies, and in the Caribbean and North Atlantic they are hurricanes.

Why tropical cyclones develop is still uncertain, despite intense meteorological research. The way

Top: a mansion in Pass Christian on the Mississippi coast before Hurricane Camille struck in August 1969. At the height of the hurricane's fury gusts of 200 miles an hour were reported.

Above: the same Pass Christian Mansion reduced to rubble after Hurricane Camille had swept over it. Devastation during the storm was increased by a storm tide 25 feet above normal.

tion, and then, after the brief interval of the central eye, from the opposite direction. Much destruction is caused by the wind and the rain but more than three fourths of the deaths in cyclones are caused by the violent storm waves. As these waves approach the coast the geography of the seabed affects the height of the wave, so that the shallower the seabed the greater the height of the waves. The area around a bay or channel in the path of a hurricane is always in great danger, which is why Bangladesh, at the head of the Bay of Bengal, suffers so terribly from inundation.

The best-known of all floods is of course the biblical flood – "Noah's Deluge" – when "the waters prevailed exceedingly upon the earth, and all the highest hills, that were under the whole heaven, were covered." References to a great flood abound in the literature of ancient Mesopotamia and in 1930 the British archaeologist Sir Leonard Woolley, excavating in the royal city of Ur – Abraham's birthplace – uncovered physical evidence of a flood so devastating that it had left a

Above: a stained-glass window from Ulm Cathedral showing Noah in the ark – one of the best known flood stories.

they are formed is well understood but not what makes a cyclone begin at a certain place one day and not elsewhere. An area of moist air, heated by the equatorial sun, begins to rise. Cooler air moves in to take its place and also rises. Because of the rotation of the earth the winds do not blow directly into the center but obliquely – counterclockwise in the Northern Hemisphere and clockwise in the Southern. Soon an immense mass of air is circling around a central eye, rather like a gigantic phonograph record. Within the eye, where air pressure is very low and temperature relatively high, winds are light. But the eye is surrounded by a steep bank of clouds rising layer upon layer up to 35,000 feet above sea level. It is these clouds that produce the torrential rains associated with hurricanes.

Just as a top, while spinning rapidly, moves forward only slowly, so a hurricane advances at about 15 to 20 miles an hour while its circling winds commonly whirl around at speeds of over 100 miles an hour with guests of over 200 miles an hour. As the hurricane passes, the winds are first felt raging from one direc-

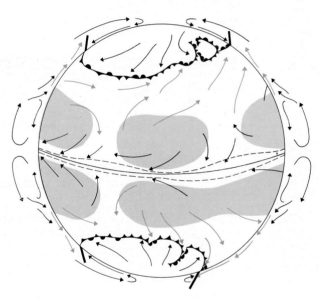

Above: a simplified diagram of the pattern of world pressure and winds. Winds blow outward from tropics and poles, which are high pressure areas to the low pressure areas of temperate and equatorial latitudes. Changes in weather generally occur when two different air masses meet. **Below:** the formation of a cyclone. The black arrows show the movement of air as it flows in at the bottom of the cyclone, or hurricane, and out at the top. The low pressure area pulls down warmer air from the stratosphere, forming a typical warm "eye" of the hurricane.

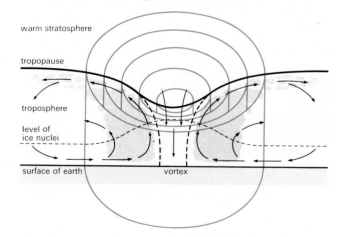

warm stratosphere

tropopause

troposphere

level of
ice nuclei

surface of earth   vortex

Above: Venetians crossing St Mark's Square on a gangway during the winter high tide flood. Unlike other northern Italian cities, Venice is not built on solid ground but on a series of small mud islands that are slowly sinking into the Adriatic Sea.

layer of sediment eight feet thick. Below this layer, Woolley found all the signs of a Stone Age culture that did not appear in the levels above it. The catastrophe that deposited the sediment had wiped out a culture.

"Eight feet of sediment," Woolley wrote, "imply a very great depth of water, and the flood which deposited it must have been of a magnitude unparalleled in local history." Shafts dug elsewhere in Mesopotamia indicated that the flooded area was perhaps 400 miles long by 100 miles across and dated from about 4000 years BC. "It was not a universal deluge," Woolley concluded. "It was a vast flood in the valley of the Tigris and the Euphrates which drowned the whole of the habitable land between the mountains and desert; for the people who lived there that was all

the world. The great bulk of those people must have perished, and it was but a scanty and dispirited remnant that from the city walls watched the waters recede at last. No wonder that they saw in this disaster the gods' punishment of a sinful generation and described it as such in a religious poem; and if some household had managed to escape by boat from the drowned lowlands the head of it would naturally be chosen as the hero of the saga."

The exact nature of the disaster will probably never be known, but a tropical cyclone or a tsunami caused by an earthquake seem very probable explanations. Sweeping from the Arabian Sea into the narrow Persian Gulf the waves would crash up the flat Mesopotamian valley as a vast wall of water ". . . all the foundations of the great deep [were] broken up."

43

"Long Island Express"
New England:1938

Hurricanes are born in the Caribbean and in the tropical waters of the Atlantic. They move westward and frequently turn northward, striking the southern coasts of the United States. Destruction is caused by the appalling winds, the unbelievably heavy rain and the great waves that generally accompany the hurricane. In the days before it was possible to issue advance warnings, the death toll was very high. After a hurricane had ravaged the coasts of Georgia and South Carolina in August 1893 it was reported that, "hundreds of corpses were strewn among the farms, unknown except to the vultures that flocked above them." In September 1900, 6000 people died at Galveston when a violent hurricane accompanied by high waves struck the Texas coast. An estimated 2000 million tons of rain fell during the life of this hurricane. One of its grisly achievements was to wash hundreds of coffins from the Galveston cemetery into the Gulf of Mexico.

Even advance warnings have sometimes proved unavailing. The hurricane that tore into Florida on September 2, 1935 was one of the most violent ever recorded. Known as the "Labor Day hurricane," it was of small diameter but tremendous force. Peak winds were estimated to have reached 200 miles an hour and the barometer reading of 26.35 at Long Key was the lowest ever recorded for the Western Hemisphere. About 700 war veterans were in a relief camp at the point where the hurricane crossed the keys. The train sent to rescue them was swept off the track. 286 veterans and civilians were killed and a further 90 never found. Some of the victims were literally sandblasted – stripped of all clothes except belt and shoes, and the skin rasped from their bodies.

For over a century hurricanes had spared New England. But on September 20, 1938, a hurricane moving westward toward Florida unexpectedly turned due north. At the same time it increased in speed. Most north-moving hurricanes are deflected harmlessly out to the Atlantic by the prevailing westerly winds but on this occasion a high pressure area unusually close to the American coast closed this escape-route. When another high-pressure area advanced from the west it left the hurricane a narrow lane of low-pressure air leading straight for Long Island. The vast mass of circling air rushed along it at 60 miles an hour, a phenomenal rate that earned it the name of the "Long Island Express." The wind speeds within the hurricanes were of course much greater. At Blue Hills Observatory Massachusetts, the wind speed for a five minute period was timed at 121 miles per hour, with one gust of 183 miles per hour. On September 21 these hurricane winds smashed into densely populated Long Island and New England and

Left: the steeple of the Community Church at Dublin, New Hampshire was blown off and upended by a freakish twist of the hurricane that struck New England on September 20, 1938. The steeple smashed through the roof and its point pierced the pew normally occupied by the minister's wife. **Right:** one of the houses wrecked on Long Beach, Long Island by the September 1938 hurricane.

Right: bodies of World War I veterans killed during a hurricane that struck Florida in September 1935. They are being transported from the wreckage of their camp at Matecumbe Key on crude sledges attached to cars. **Below:** a couple sit around the ruins of what was once their home after the hurricane of September 1938 smashed into Rhode Island.

began the orgy of destruction that would isolate 7,000,000 people.

After making an aerial reconnaissance, journalist Rudy Arnold described the scene of devastation, "Acres of trees were scattered about like matchsticks. Automobiles were lying on their sides, half buried in mud. Houses were flattened out as though they had been crushed under steam rollers. At one spot, nearly 15 houses were whirled together as though they had been in the grip of a giant egg-beater."

Some 275,000,000 trees were destroyed or damaged, electric power lines and telephone wires brought down throughout the area; torn-up roots smashed gas and water pipes. The elms in the main street of East Hampton, Long Island, planted to replace elms blown down in the 1815 hurricane, now met the same fate. In Dublin, New Hampshire, the steeple of the Community Church was blown off and plunged upside down through the church roof. The wind scratched paint off cars and stripped painted houses down to the bare wood.

As much as 11 inches of rain fell throughout an area of 10,000 square miles. Floods poured down the hillsides, the sea surged in across the shore. In flooded Providence, Rhode Island, the water short-circuited the horns of cars which added their blare to the roar of the hurricane. Thousands of coastal houses were washed away and in many places the shoreline changed shape. A man who had just paid $1000 for an ocean-front lot found his purchase had been washed out to sea.

Six hundred lives were lost and $350,000,000 worth of damage done, greater than in any previous storm in human history. Since 1938 New England has been savaged by other hurricanes but the "Long Island Express" probably remains the most memorable. It served as a warning that no place along the Atlantic seaboard of North America is 100 percent safe from these mighty destructive forces.

Tsunami Terror

The warning signs for the seaquake are well known down the long earthquake-shattered coast of Chile. On the afternoon of May 22, 1960 the inhabitants of the 200-mile coastal stretch from Valdivia to Chiloe Island saw the sea steadily rise some way above the high-tide mark. This phenomenon is known as "the smooth wave." The water then abruptly retreated, very fast, as though being sucked through a straw or vanishing down a drain, far beyond the lowest low-water mark. Old wrecks came into view, fish were seen struggling on the seabed, but few of the onlookers waited to study this strange occurrence. The experience of centuries had told them what was shortly to happen. The cry went up "the sea has retreated"

these terrible and destructive waves. They are generally the result of an underwater earthquake or the eruption of a coastal volcano, but underwater landslides on sloping parts of the continental shelf have sometimes caused them, while the greatest wave ever recorded in human history occurred after a massive rockslip into Lituya Bay, a fjordlike, almost land-locked bay in Alaska. On July 9, 1958, 90 million tons of rock fell 3000 feet into the head of the bay. A wave raced across the bay and surged over the opposite side to the incredible height of 1740 feet, twice as high as the Eiffel Tower. Four square miles of forest were wiped clean to the bare rock.

Earthquakes, however, are the single greatest cause of these powerful waves, and though known in the Mediterranean and Middle East they are most common in the Pacific Ocean where earthquakes occur all around the perimeter. Like ripples caused by a mighty stone, the waves travel thousands of miles across the vast ocean. The Japanese call them *tsunami* and scientists have adopted this name.

Where the ocean is deep the *tsunami* travel at

Left: an engraving of the Royal Mail steamship *La Plata* being struck by a tsunami off the Virgin Islands in the West Indies, 1867. Caused either by quakes or undersea volcanoes, tsunami race across the oceans at speeds of 500 miles or more per hour and approach coastal areas as huge walls of water – 50, 100, or even 200 feet high.

and everyone fled to the hills. It was the *Maremoto,* the seaquake. The French vulcanologist Haroun Tazieff has described what followed at the small port of Corral, 10 miles from Valdivia.

"The wave came 20 minutes later, 26 feet high traveling at the shocking speed of 100 to 125 miles an hour. The screaming of the women mingled with its dreadful roar.... The wave, like an enormous hand crumpling a long sheet of paper, crushed all the houses, one after another, with a prodigious crackling of shattered planks. In 20 seconds it had heaped up 800 houses, smashed to matchwood, at the foot of the hill."

No dam, no breakwater, no protective barrier built by man can successfully stand in the path of one of

fantastically high speeds, 300 to 500 miles an hour, but are only a few feet high. This is why they are seldom noticed by observers in the open sea. In 1896 a severe earthquake occurred in the sea east of Japan and a succession of giant waves scoured the Sanriku coast. Yet fishermen 20 miles offshore noticed nothing and were totally unprepared for the devastation that greeted them on their return to what had been their home ports. Thousands of boats in the harbors had been crushed to fragments and 28,000 people were dead. Only when the tsunami approaches the coast does it rear up to become a wall of water. It loses speed but is still traveling at about 60 miles an hour when it smashes against the shore.

Because of its central position in the Pacific, Hawaii is exposed to *tsunami* from all quarters. The city of Hilo was devastated in 1946 by a huge wave that originated in the Aleutian Islands. The Chilean earthquakes of May 1960 were so severe that, according to one scientist, "the whole body of the earth, down to its center, rang like a bell." The *tsunami* generated by them were appropriately impressive but this time Hawaii was prepared. When the wave stuck Hilo again, only 61 people who had disregarded the warning and remained in the city were drowned.

The *tsunami* swept on past Hawaii across the Pacific. The Japanese meteorological station received a warning but the two young meteorologists in charge misunderstood the warnings to refer to the South Pacific only and no action was taken. Nine hours later a succession of 22-foot-high waves suddenly pounded the coastal towns of north Honshu and Hokkaido, leaving behind the familiar wreckage of splintered boats, 50,000 ruined houses and in this case an unnecessary toll of death.

Left: it was a tsunamilike seawave, triggered by a massive rockslip into the bay that caused this promontory at Lituga Bay, Alaska to be cleared of trees down to the bare rock to a height of almost 1800 feet. **Below:** the devastation left after a tsunami struck Kodiak Island, Alaska, 1964. It was the aftermath of one of the severest earthquakes ever to hit North America and affected some 100,000 square miles.

The North Sea Overflows
February 1953

North winds had blown at gale to hurricane force for 24 hours. In the Orkney Islands gusts of 120 miles an hour were reported. Two ships sank off the Scottish coast. In Scotland and England an estimated 4,000,000 trees, mostly mature plantation conifers, were blown down by the violent and repeated gusts. But this destruction, though very serious, was as nothing to what was to follow. On the night of January 31–February 1, 1953, the North Sea overflowed.

The persistent north gales were the worst ever recorded in the British Isles and drove thousands of millions of tons of water to the south, sufficient to add six to eight feet to the predicted height of the tides. Along the Essex coast the afternoon tide scarcely went down at all. On the other side of the North Sea the strong winds, blowing onshore, totally prevented the tide from ebbing from the southern estuaries of the Netherlands. The high-water level stayed constant for a few hours, then started to rise still higher. The unusually low barometric pressure had further raised the level of the sea and the furious winds had whipped up the surface into waves in some places reported to be 16 feet high.

The most serious flooding in England occurred in Essex. At the port of Harwich waves were washing over the quay three hours before high tide. Shortly afterward the water broke into the town, racing down the narrow lanes and trapping people in their basements. All down the coast the waves flung water over the sea walls where it began the deadly work of undermining the walls from the landward side. In one place after another this led to collapse and water poured through the gaps. In the single-story houses and lightly built chalets people were overwhelmed and drowned, on one occasion while the householder was on the telephone urgently calling for rescue.

On Canvey Island, first reclaimed by Dutch engineers in the 17th century, the whole land lay below high-water mark. Some 11,500 people lived there, mostly in single-story houses, protected by the high sea walls and connected to the mainland by a single bridge. Shortly before midnight the sea poured over an exposed section of wall like a waterfall and a stretch of the wall collapsed. Other breaches followed in swift succession and the torrent poured in onto the now defenseless community. Most people had no warning of the disaster but awoke as the icy water swept into their homes. Many who clambered onto their furniture found it swept away from under them. Others clung to the tops of doors, their heads in the air space between water and ceiling.

In England a total of 307 people were drowned but in the Netherlands the loss of life and destruction was even more terrible. Not since the notorious flood of November 1421 had so great a disaster struck this nation where 40 percent of the land would be submerged each high tide were it not protected by its 700 miles of dikes and dunes.

Above: police making a house-to-house search on Canvey Island, England, for survivors of the 1953 North Sea flood. Like Holland, British east coast towns suffered severely during the terrible gales and lashing floodwaters of the night of January 31–February 1, 1953.

Left: a Dutchman walks along a wrecked railway track through the inundated and ravaged countryside in Holland after the night of January 31–February 1, 1953. Near hurricane-force winds and high tides combined to raise the level of the North Sea until it overtopped the dikes of Holland and broke down the sea defenses on the east coast of Britain. **Above:** flooded houses at Lieriksee, Holland. **Below:** the bridge of a British trawler smashed by one wave during the North Sea gales.

High tide was due shortly after midnight on the night of January 31–February 1 but well before this the gale-driven sea was level with the top of the dikes. Quantities of water were flung over onto the inner slopes and began the process of erosion so that when a sudden surge of the sea occurred just before high tide the dikes were already severely weakened. Warnings of a higher tide than usual had been issued but a surge had not been expected and most people were asleep when the catastrophe struck. More than 50 dikes burst at about the same time and 400,000 acres of *polder* (reclaimed land) were overwhelmed by the raging sea. In the provinces of Zeeland, South Holland and North Brabant, situated around the estuaries of the Rhine, Maas, and Scheldt rivers, the work of centuries was destroyed in minutes.

Church bells were rung but went largely unheard in the howling gale. In Stavenisse on Tholen island a wall of water 12 feet high demolished the farmhouses in the shelter of the dike and swept the heavy roof and wall beams into the village where they became battering-rams that shattered the walls of the houses. Over 200 people were drowned – and the village was left "looking as if hit by a land mine." In another village on Tholen a 10-year-old girl saw her father, mother, and eight brothers and sisters drowned in front of her. At Spijkenisse, five miles south of Rotterdam, a husband and wife clung to the roof of their house, she holding onto the chimney with one arm and with the other holding on to the man. "For over 24 hours the swirling tides and currents dashed the man's foot against a metal gutter, so that when they were finally rescued his whole foot was gone except for a few smashed pieces of bone."

Altogether, 1800 people died and nearly 100,000 had to be evacuated from the floods that rolled over farther inland until 625 square miles were inundated. The history of the Dutch people is one of ceaseless struggle against the sea. The ordeal of the night of January 31–February 1, 1953, shows there can never be any relaxation against this sleepless adversary.

The Florence Flood
November 1966

Above: the streets of Florence, thick with mud after the waters of the Arno river had cleared. An estimated 500,000 tons of mud were deposited in the "city of the lilies," and greatest art center in the world by the floodwaters on November 4, 1966.

October 1966 was a wet month throughout Italy. The first two days of November were sunny but torrential rain fell on November 3 – one third of a year's normal rainfall in 24 hours. Serious flooding occurred in many places but nowhere with such catastrophic results as in the Arne valley. By early morning on November 4 the citizens of Florence saw that the normally placid green river Arno had become a brown roaring torrent, its surface snarling with whirlpools and matted with debris. Logs, oil drums, uprooted trees, and the corpses of drowned cows were bucking and plunging in the violent waters.

Although dams had been built on the upper reaches of the river, the sluices did not cope with the enormous volume of rainwater on that night. A massive surge of water was allowed into the river and the level in Florence rapidly reached the top of the river walls and flowed over them in an uncontrollable deluge of filthy, oily water. It raced through the streets at speeds of up to 40 miles an hour, tossing cars over and over as though they were toys and pouring through the thousands of small shops and artisans' workshops that line the streets of the city, sweeping their contents away. The water brought with it an estimated 500,000 tons of mud deposited inches and sometimes feet thick in the streets and basements. But worse than the water and the mud was the oil that coated every place the water reached with a foul-smelling, blackish-brown slime.

For 18 hours the river continued to rise, then it began to fall. By the morning of November 5 the water in the river had dropped by 18 feet – and Florence, Europe's greatest cultural treasurehouse, began to take stock of the damage.

The galleries of the Uffizi and the Palazzo Pitti were on upper floors and the numberless masterpieces they contained had not been threatened. But the damage done in other galleries, churches, and museums was grievous. The water that raged through the Piazza del Duomo had torn out five of the 10 panels on the magnificent bronze doors created by the 15th-century sculptor Ghiberti, a creation so superb that Michelangelo declared them fit to be the doors of Paradise. The missing panels were recovered but damaged. The marble statues erected throughout the city wore hideous drapes of black oil. The Church of Santa Croce in the ancient part of the city contained, among other treasures, priceless frescoes by the city's 14th-century artist Giotto and the *Crucifixion* by the 13th-century artist Cimabue, and considered a landmark in the development of European painting. All the frescoes were imperiled because even though water lapped just below them, damp seeped up through the wall and pressed salts out to the surface where they pushed off the paint. The *Crucifixion* was found face down in the mud, large areas of the paint washed away.

Irreplaceable treasures suffered throughout the city; some were totally ruined. Not only paintings but old maps, documents, rare musical instruments (now all in splinters) at the Bardini Museum, illuminated manuscripts, tapestries, and books. At the National Library 300 students formed a living chain extending from the far depths of the basement galleries – where the air was so poisonous they had to wear gas masks – to the higher levels passing from hand to hand, hour after hour, the mud-saturated rare books and manuscripts. Many items would have been entirely destroyed had it not been for the students and the Florentines called them "angeli del fango" – angels of the mud. New techniques of restoration have had to be devised because never before has so wide a range of objects been damaged by both water and oil.

Elsewhere in Florence 6000 of the 10,000 shops were destroyed. The flood swept through the famous row of goldsmiths' shops on the Ponte Vecchio. Some of the goldsmiths had come down on the night of November 3 and made their way onto the shuddering bridge to save their stock before the water burst through. Those less fortunate lost everything. Poorer artisans and shopkeepers who lived in their shops escaped with their lives but nothing else. That winter there was great poverty in Florence.

Children in Italy receive gifts not on Christmas Day but on Twelfth Night when the kindly old witch *La Befana* brings candies and toys to good children and a sock stuffed with coal for the bad. On Twelfth Night 1967 there appeared in the middle of the Ponte Vecchio, hanging down above the water, a sock as tall as a man, packed with coal and labeled "To the River Arno." It was *La Befana's* present to the river.

Above: what was once a library of rare books has been turned into a mush of pulp-paper after the River Arno flooded. Basement galleries were particularly vulnerable to the muddy waters and to the even more destructive thick oil they brought with them.

Below: some of the rescued fine leather book bindings drying on lines festooned across a room in Florence after the disastrous flood of 1966. Hours of patient cleaning were followed by further hours of leather dressing and application of fungicide.

The Bay of Bengal
A Disaster-prone Region

Throughout history the lands bordering the Bay of Bengal have been cruelly exposed to the horrors of flood. The state of Bengal – later called East Pakistan and now Bangladesh – lies at the head of a funnel-shaped bay, a flat, lowland region crisscrossed by the deltas of two great rivers, the Ganges and the Brahmaputra. It has the deserved reputation of being a luckless country. Flood disasters strike it both from land and from sea. Every year in April and May when the Himalaya snow melts there is always the risk of flooding from the rivers. But the period of greatest danger is July and August, the time of the monsoon. Torrents of rain fall in the steep hills of northeast India, which has the world's heaviest rainfall, and as this mass of water descends onto the Bengal plain there is flooding almost annually, particularly along the Brahmaputra.

Unprecedented heavy rain even for that area was the cause of the disastrous floods of 1974. The monsoon began earlier than usual, in late June, and fell almost without ceasing for 50 days. Five inches in a day is not unusual in this part of the world. But five inches in a day four days in the week for over seven weeks defeated all the emergency measures that existed in the newly independent state of Bangladesh, still recovering from the disorder of recent civil war. Cattle and thatched homesteads were swept away and people perched in trees or on the roofs of those huts that were still standing. In a village near Fulchari Ghat, about 100 miles northwest of the capital, Dacca, the houses stood on a mud embankment above the level of the floods. This did not save them, however. Slowly the mud embankment dissolved into paste. Attempts to patch it up only delayed the inevitable. One day the houses simply fell down and the inhabitants knotted their few possessions into a cloth and waded to the high ground of a railway.

By mid-July half the country was under water, an area of 15,000 square miles – about the size of Switzerland. The rain-swollen Brahmaputra poured in uncontrollable torrents across the plain. In the process 800,000 houses were washed away.

But flooding from the rivers is not as terrible as the tropical cyclones that rage against the coast with appalling frequency. The worst one to hit the area within living memory was the cyclone that roared over the delta on November 12, 1970. Thousands of people were swept away by an irresistible wall of water 20 feet high, their bodies later to be found scattered in paddyfields or tangled in the branches of trees. Blood from the battered corpses of cattle stained the fields where their carcases had been flung. The offshore island of Bhola took the full impact of this savage cyclone. Ali Hussain, a 25-year-old soldier, was one of the only two people in his family of 15 to survive. "We were all sleeping when it hit at mid-

Above: a woman survivor of one of the numerous floods that ravage Bangladesh. **Above right:** villagers gather around relief supplies, desperate for food. Many of the villagers live on the poverty line often growing only enough food to pay rents for their lands and meagerly feed their families. In times of disaster they are very quickly reduced to starvation. **Right:** villagers queue for blankets flown in by amphibian aircraft after severe flooding has wiped out their villages. **Left:** livestock suffers heavily in time of flood. The loss is a serious blow to the peasants.

night," he recalled. "I caught hold of a palm tree and climbed it and hung on until the waters went down at dawn." Death toll was greatest among the children who were not strong enough to hold on to the trees. Luckier than the vast majority were six children aged between three and twelve who were pushed into a wooden chest by their grandfather. Three days later the chest was washed ashore with the children in it still alive. 150,000 people died from this cyclone and the cholera epidemic that followed it.

The coastal regions of India farther south along the Bay of Bengal suffer less from cyclones but are by no means immune. As recently as 1977 two cyclones struck different parts of the coast on successive weekends. The first state to suffer was Tamil Nadu (formerly Mysore) where several hundred people were killed by a cyclone that afterward crossed the southern tip of India and then turned around, bringing heavy rain and gale-force winds to the western coast.

Meteorologists said this phenomenon had never been known before. More serious damage was caused by the cyclone of November 19, which hurled its fury against the coast of Andhra Pradesh (formerly Hyderabad) 400 miles to the north. Entire villages disappeared and hundreds of thousands of farmers lost all their standing crops. The death toll was believed to be around 20,000 people.

In Bangladesh the endless repetition of calamity seems to have bred a fatalistic attitude in the population, an apathy that has often irritated relief workers. In southern India, however, there was an immediate and active determination to repair the cyclone damage. Within a few days work had begun to remove the debris, rebuild the houses and clear the irrigation channels so that water could flush the salt out of the fields. But in this disaster-prone region of the world everyone knows that the next catastrophe can never be very many years ahead.

Warning and Defense

Since earliest times the suffering caused by storm and flood, both in terms of human misery and economic loss, have stimulated people to find the means to protect themselves. Against no other natural threat have so many defensive schemes been devised, and as engineering techniques have improved so defenses have grown surer. There can unfortunately be no protection against the devastation of a tsunami, but against flooding from seas and rivers man has built dikes, levees, or embankments. Natural channels have been straightened and deepened to improve their flow and discharge capacity; emergency channels and reservoirs have been constructed to direct and store surplus water. Measures such as these help in the task of keeping water off the land and have been employed in one form or another for hundreds of years. But only recently has it become possible to start providing the most fundamental of all defenses: adequate warning.

Hurricane forecasts began in 1898 when the head of the US Weather Bureau, Willis L. Moore, persuaded President McKinley to establish forecasting centers in the West Indies at the time of the Spanish-American War. With the invention of wireless telegraphy ships hundreds of miles from land could provide reports of tropical cyclones (as hurricanes are properly termed) from the earliest stages of their development in the tropical Atlantic. In 1960 the first weather satellites were launched and for the first time man was able to see weather systems as a whole. Polar orbiting satellites provide a detailed look at the weather situation from an altitude of several hundred miles. From altitudes of 22,000 miles satellites orbiting above the equator at a speed matching the rotation of the earth are able to see half our planet at a time.

Up till now hurricanes have been given girls' names – something girls are entitled to consider unchivalrous. Maybe it has something to do with a wish to soften the hurricanes' savagery. From 1978 boys names also will be used in the Pacific area, and later, in the Atlantic as well; 26 names are chosen and the first hurricane of the year is given a name beginning with A, the second with B and so on boys' and girls' names alternating. If a name has been used for an unusually destructive hurricane, it will not be used again for 10 years. This was the case with Diane 1955 which caused $750,000,000 worth of damage as it hurtled from North Carolina to Massachusetts, flooding ground already saturated with rainwater.

The most accurate forecast in the world is unable to

Above: an avalanche of water hurtles down through a street in the city of Putnam, Connecticut, during the Eastern States floods in 1955. Connecticut was the hardest hit of the six states affected by the disaster.

Above: the narrow, highly fertile strip on either side of the Nile river is evidence of one of the more useful effects of flooding. In this case, rich, black silt brought down from the African interior by the Nile is flooded onto the river banks annually. **Right:** cloudbursts and flat terrain are often the cause of "flash floods," one of which has engulfed this township near Brisbane, Australia. In an arid zone like this, shallow stream beds peter out into flat country and cannot cope with sudden floods. Luckily they tend to be brief and are often valuable in recharging essential ground water.

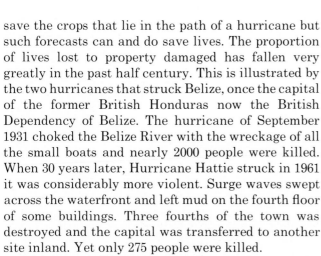

save the crops that lie in the path of a hurricane but such forecasts can and do save lives. The proportion of lives lost to property damaged has fallen very greatly in the past half century. This is illustrated by the two hurricanes that struck Belize, once the capital of the former British Honduras now the British Dependency of Belize. The hurricane of September 1931 choked the Belize River with the wreckage of all the small boats and nearly 2000 people were killed. When 30 years later, Hurricane Hattie struck in 1961 it was considerably more violent. Surge waves swept across the waterfront and left mud on the fourth floor of some buildings. Three fourths of the town was destroyed and the capital was transferred to another site inland. Yet only 275 people were killed.

Various suggestions have been put forward for taming hurricanes. Attempts have been made to seed them with dry ice but with no outstanding success and at least one attempt that ended in disaster: the hurricane of October 1947 had passed over Florida and was moving out into the mid-Atlantic. Some dispute exists as to what happened next but it seems that after the hurricane was seeded it made a hairpin turn back to the United States coast and did $3,000,000 damage in Georgia.

Another suggestion for coping with hurricanes is to prevent them forming at all. They need warmth to begin. If cold water was raised to the surface of the sea beneath the early stages of a hurricane this might stop it developing.

But even if some method is found to abolish hurricanes or destroy them safely out at sea, is it sensible? The British author Frank Lane in *The Elements Rage*, published in 1966, discusses this point: "Maybe a worse evil would result. Hurricanes appear to be important agents in the general circulation of the atmosphere, and the maintenance of heat balance. If hurricanes were prevented altogether, who knows what consequences would follow? It can be highly dangerous to frustrate Nature's forces."

Being caught in a hurricane is unpleasant, to say the least, and while being lashed by winds of 100 miles an hour and soaked in torrential downpours it is understandably easy to forget that the rain is actually doing a great deal of good – even though unseen – by recharging essential ground water. To minimize the suffering caused by such floods efficient rescue services must be provided. During the floods in Northern Australia in December 1974 planes, boats, and helicopters all played significant parts in removing

55

stranded people and livestock to places of safety.

The floods on the Nile have been turned to economic advantage. Without the annual inundation of the narrow strip of land either side of the river, Egypt would never have come into being. But in the valleys of the world's other great rivers flooding is not life-bringing but death-dealing. The Hwang-ho, the Indus, the Ganges have each spilled their waters again and again over the surrounding, densely cultivated land. In the United States the vast river system of the Mississippi has twice in the present century spread a vast yellow sheet of water over tens of thousands of square miles. Its waters are drawn from 31 states of the USA and 2 provinces of Canada. In March 1927 heavy rainfall of 12 to 24 inches in the states bordering the Lower Mississippi brought immediate flooding on a scale exceeding all previous records. Highways and bridges were unusable for weeks. Over wide areas of the valley all crops were destroyed and people left destitute. Some 18,000 square miles were inundated and over 300 lives lost in floodwater so deep that relief boats were moving among treetops 15 feet off the ground. Once the water had topped or broken the levees it moved so fast that, for example, "the streets of Arkansas City were dry at noon, and by two o'clock mules were drowning in them before they could be unhitched from their wagons." The levees were cut some miles north of New Orleans to divert the flood water from the city.

The catastrophe of 1927 led to a complete overhaul of the system of flood defense. The job was taken largely out of the hands of the local states and made a federal responsibility. But nature has a habit of varying the mean tricks it plays. In May and June 1951 unusually heavy rain fell in the normally dry state of Kansas. Some flooding occurred but on a small scale only. The ground, however, was still thoroughly sodden when 16 inches of rain fell in three days of July. A bucket will only hold so much water. All along the Kansas River the water-soaked levees collapsed and people fled with nothing but the clothes they were wearing. So high was the floodwater that it overtopped the levees farther down, but this time from behind, pouring back into the river. Damage was estimated at a phenomenal $870,000,000 but would have been a further 250 million had it not been for work carried out since 1927 by the federal flood control bodies.

Naturally, the carrying out of defense schemes at a federal or national level does not do away with individual responsibility. The tradition of individual duty is vividly expressed in the story of the Dutch boy who kept his finger in the dike. In the 1951 floods someone omitted to secure a 6000 gallon oil tank and it later floated into a high-tension wire that started fires that gutted several oil refineries with a total loss of $10,000,000. Both individuals and governments have a duty to perform when the adversary is water. Nor does the battle get easier. The Water Resources Policy Commission reporting to President Truman in 1950 said, "However big floods get, there will always be bigger ones coming." The events of a year later proved them right. Unhappily, at some future date they will be proved right yet again.

Above: an engineer in London's Flood Room – an emergency flood warning service. Behind him is a large-scale map of the Thames river, showing danger points as shaded areas. In many countries throughout the world man is at last tackling ways of predicting and preventing floods.

Right: a machine used by the United States Weather Bureau for rapid plotting of data based on computer-processed readings.

Below: a weather-satellite picture of a cyclonic storm in the making about 1200 miles north of Hawaii.

Below left: the town of Marysville, California completely protected by levees from rising flood waters.

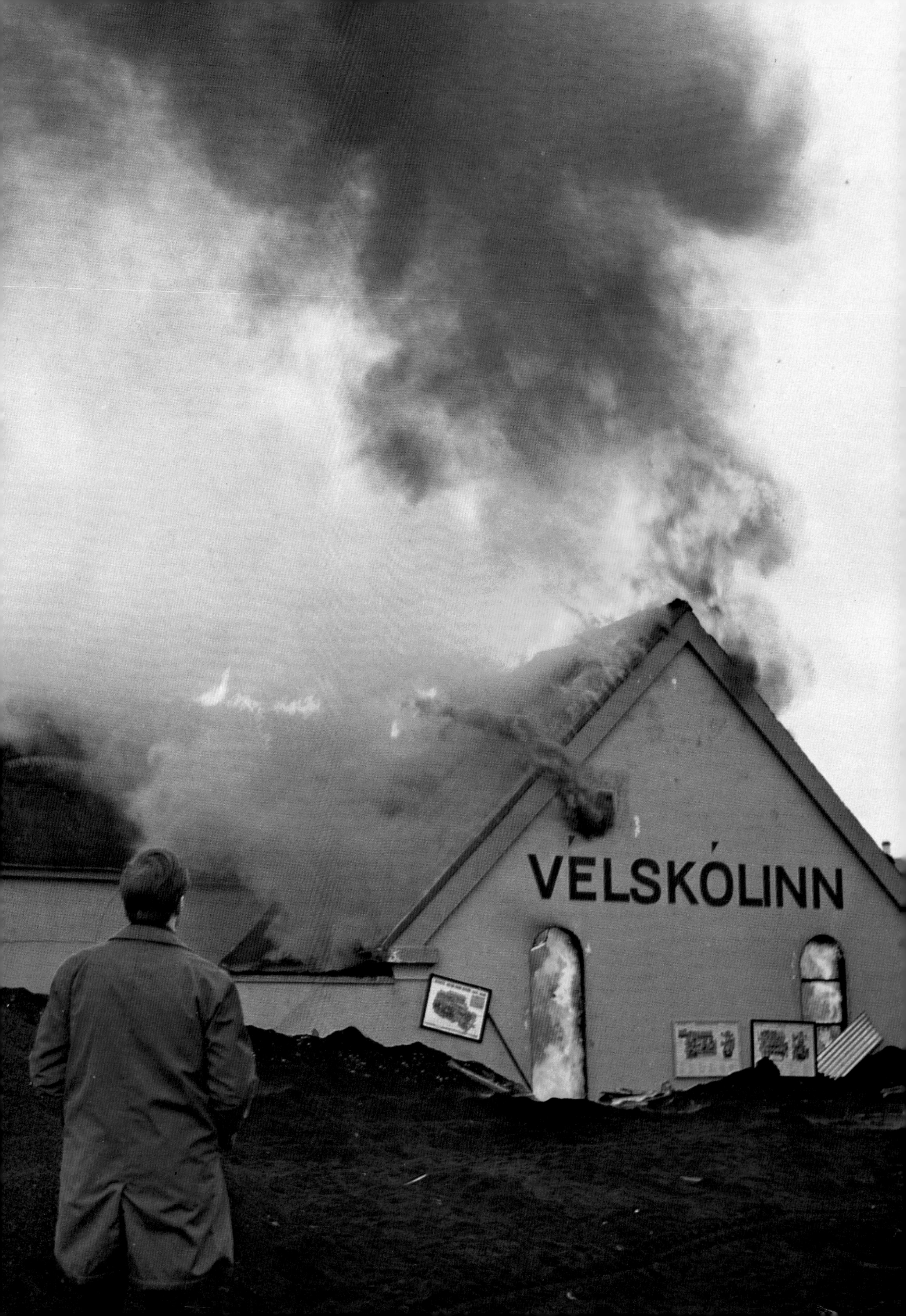
VELSKÓLINN

Chapter 4

When Volcanoes Erupt

A volcano in full eruption is the most awe-inspiring and amazing spectacle nature has to offer. The earth shakes. Dense clouds of ash and hot gases soar into the air, sometimes accompanied by flashes of lightning and the crack of thunder. Within the crater incandescent lava explodes in fountains of brilliant fireworks. Pieces of rock hurtle through the air, and down the sides of the mountain flow rivers of glowing, liquid rock, overwhelming all in their path.

Volcanoes are looked on mainly as agents of destruction and it is true they have destroyed hundreds of thousands of humans as well as animals, plants, and other organisms. Yet they also bring inestimable benefits. Volcanic ash and lava are rich in minerals, and throughout the world crops flourish in the fertile soil that comes from eroded volcanic rock. Equally significant, deposits of gold, copper, silver, and many other valuable ores are associated with volcanoes, both active and extinct. The story of volcanoes is intimately bound up with the story of man.

Opposite: Heimay Island's school of Engineering engulfed and set on fire by red-hot lava during a recent eruption in Iceland.

What is a Volcano?

In ancient times volcanoes were worshiped as dwelling places of gods. The Romans believed that Vulcan, the god of fire, lived beneath a volcanic island off the coast of Sicily. The island was named for him and the word *volcano* came to be used generally for any vent in the earth that produced molten rock, steam, and ashes. Later, it was thought that eruptions were caused by winds trapped underground – a belief that persisted until scientists discovered that the earth becomes hotter the deeper you descend into it. At a certain depth the interior must be entirely molten, they argued. Following on from that, volcanoes came to be seen as essential safety valves allowing the escape of excess heat.

At the center of the earth is a very dense core, believed to be composed of a mixture of iron and nickel. The inner part of this core is solid, the outer part liquid – and movements within the latter are thought to produce a dynamo that generates the earth's magnetic field. Overlying the core and making up the bulk of the earth's mass is the mantle, rich in silicon, iron, and magnesium. In the upper part of the mantle the rock has the consistency of a very thick, extremely viscous liquid. Convection currents carry hotter (and so lighter) material up toward the surface. There it cools, becomes heavier and cracks into sections or plates, and later (millions of years later) sinks back again into the lower regions of the mantle. These same convection currents cause the drifting of the crustal plates and in certain areas of the world particularly under the oceans molten material from the mantle, known as *magma*, breaks through the thin ocean crust as underwater volcanic eruptions. The mid-ocean ridges are the result.

As this magma cools it turns into one of a variety of black, fine-grained, heavy rocks known as *basalts*.

Left: a cross-section showing the earth's interior and the formation of volcanoes as visualized in the light of 17th-century knowledge.

A great deal has been learned about the earth's interior since then, however. We know, for instance, that the interior of the earth is not entirely molten. The earth is made up of a number of concentric layers, of different chemical nature and density. Seismologists have measured the density of these layers by tracing the way shock waves from large earthquakes and controlled atomic explosions travel through them.

They compose the whole of the ocean floor. Oceanic volcanoes that surface above the water, like those in Hawaii, Iceland, or Tristan da Cunha, also produce basaltic magma.

In certain parts of the world the spreading oceanic plates collide with lighter, continental plates and are forced to dive beneath them. The deep oceanic trenches mark the site of these descents. The collision generates enormous quantities of frictional heat that

Right: Mount Kilimanjaro, Tanzania, part of the East African Rift System – a long narrow valley with straight sides formed by geological faults. The African volcanoes along this rift system occurred 20,000,000 years ago not as a result of crustal plates either colliding or overriding, but as a consequence of the splitting apart of the land into the Rift valley and the formation of the Red Sea. **Below:** view taken at 8000 feet on the African Rift Valley wall, looking north toward Lake Rudolf.

tinental side of the oceanic trench. The presence of sediments and continental material gives this lava a different composition from the basaltic lavas. It is called *andesite* lava, after the Andes Mountains where thousands of such volcanoes (no longer all active) are to be found.

The majority of the world's volcanoes occur at the edges of the continental plates where new plate material is rising up or old plate material is sinking down. The Pacific Ocean, almost encircled by deep trenches, is likewise encircled by long ranges of volcanoes – the so-called "ring of fire." The European volcanoes were formed by the movement of plates whose edges meet beneath the Mediterranean.

Most volcanoes are located within a few miles of the sea because this is where the plates tend to meet. The apparent exceptions to this rule occur in East Africa where a number of volcanoes – Kilimanjaro and Mount Kenya are among the best known – are to be found 500 miles or more from the coast. These, however, are all located along the East African Rift System, a geological feature that extends for 3000 miles north through Ethiopia and along the Red Sea. This long rift valley is the first stage in the formation of a new ocean that will one day split the African plate in two. Oceanic crust is already being generated on the floor of the Red Sea and elsewhere along the rift valley the underlying magma is close enough to the surface to have produced volcanoes along its flanks.

melts some of the rock of the oceanic plate, some of the deep sea sediments it has collected, and a portion of the lower part of the continental plate. All this molten material then moves upward. A lot of the material solidifies a few miles below the surface of the thick continental crust into enormous masses of *igneous* (from Latin for "fire") rock, generally granite. The rest reaches the surface, erupts as lava and ash and builds up a line of volcanoes along the con-

61

In Europe the river Rhine flows along a rift valley between Bingen in the south and Bonn in the north, marking a possible attempt to give birth to a new ocean between France and Germany. The movement appears to have come to a stop for the time being but has left a number of volcanoes in the Eiffel region that' only ceased to be active in geologically recent times.

An erupting volcano produces gas, lava (molten rock), and an assortment of solid material collectively known as *tephra*. Material in a shower of tephra can range in size from large blocks (or "bombs") through pebble-sized material called *lapilli* to fine ash – which despite its name is pulverized lava, not the product of burning. Some lavas are very fluid and when they emerge from below ground – white-hot and at a temperature of 2012° F – they flow very rapidly, faster than a man can run. As the lava cools the color changes to yellow and then to red and eventually a dark crust forms on the outside. This can be relatively smooth but as the lava cools further the surface wrinkles until it has a plowed-land appearance. This sort of lava is common in the Hawaiian volcanoes and is known by the Hawaiian name *pahoehoe*. In other lava flows the lava develops an irregular, rubbly surface, very unpleasant to walk across when cool. This type of lava is called by another Hawaiian word, *aa,* and its appearance when in motion has been compared to a shuffling slag heap.

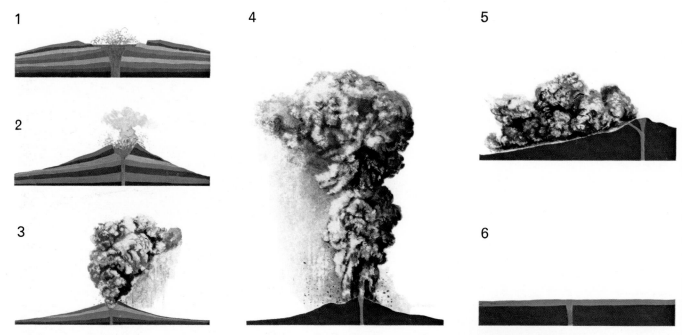

1 4 5

2

3 6

Above: the six different types of volcano. 1 Hawaiian, 2 Strombolian, 3 Vulcanian and Vesuvian, 4 Plinian, 5 Pelean, 6 Icelandic. **Below:** Mauna Ulu pit crater – an example of a Hawaiian eruption. Here the liquid lava is beginning to overflow, revealing the red-hot undersurface of the thin congealed crust. **Below right:** diagram showing the earth's crust, some 25 miles thick, below which is the 1800-mile-deep zone of plastic rock that makes up the mantle, then the 1300 mile zone of liquid outer core, and finally an inner core with a radius of 850 miles.

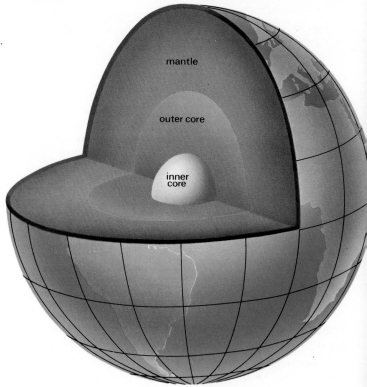

mantle

outer core

inner core

When the molten magma is under pressure within the earth the volcanic gases it contains remain in solution. But as the magma rises toward the surface at the start of an eruption the pressure drops and the gas bubbles out. It is the way in which the gases escape that to a large extent decides the form the eruption takes. If the magma is very fluid the gas escapes easily and the eruption is likely to be fairly quiet. But when the magma is of a more viscous, granitic composition or is forced very rapidly to the surface, the gases are released explosively and the lava turns into a kind of froth. The resulting eruption makes a great amount of noise and may be exceedingly violent.

The scientists who study volcanoes recognize several distinct types of eruption. The main ones are:

Icelandic These are sometimes called fissure eruptions because instead of issuing from a central cone the lava erupts from long cracks in the ground. Enormous quantities of exceedingly mobile lava pour from the cracks, quickly filling up all valleys and hollows in their path and forming vast level plateaus. It is named for a type of eruption found in Iceland.

Hawaiian The lava in these eruptions is also highly mobile but gently sloping mountains are formed, sometimes called shield volcanoes. Eruptions are frequent and mild. Often a lake of lava forms in the crater and high fire fountains are thrown up in the center. Some of the drops from these fountains solidify in the air into black, glassy teardrop shapes and are known as Pele's tears, after the Hawaiian goddess of fire. Similarly, long glass threads of solidified lava are known as Pele's hair.

Strombolian These more explosive eruptions are named for the small volcanic island off the toe of Italy. The lava in this type is not quite so fluid and gas escapes spasmodically, with short intervals ranging from a few moments to an hour or two. Blocks of semisolid lava are flung out but do not travel very far. The eruption cloud above the crater is white, indicating that it contains little ash. Stromboli itself has been in continuous moderate eruption for over 2000 years and is known as the "Lighthouse of the Mediterranean."

Vulcanian and Vesuvian Only 40 miles south of Stromboli is Vulcano but its eruptions are very different, long intervals separating periods of strong activity. The lava is viscous and pasty, and large volcanic bombs are ejected, accompanied by dense ash clouds that often assume a "cauliflower" shape as they rise. Violent electrical storms range within the cloud. Lava flows do not occur on Vulcano itself (which has not erupted since 1890) and scientists now sometimes refer to a *Vesuvian* type, which is a Vulcanian eruption with lava.

Plinian The more violent Vesuvian eruptions conclude with an enormous explosion that sends a cloud of gas and dust 30 miles or more into the air, ejects vast amounts of ash and pumice and frequently blasts away a part of the crater. This type was first described by Pliny the Younger after the catastrophic eruption of Vesuvius in 79 AD.

Pelean In this type, first observed in the devastating eruption of Mont Pelée in 1902, the lava is so viscous that it blocks the vent leading to the crater. Pressure from below gradually raises the block into a dome. When finally this splits, a cloud of gas and intensely hot incandescent solid fragments is blasted out sideways under great pressure.

Although grouped into one or other of these headings for scientific classification, there are many factors that combine to give each volcano its individual character. Some are calm, almost companionable presences – but there are others that are definitely not to be trusted.

Above: a typical cauliflower-shaped eruption of ash towers miles above Vesuvius in March 1944. This is an example of a Vulcanian and Vesuvian-type eruption.

A Civilization Destroyed
Thera: c1470 BC

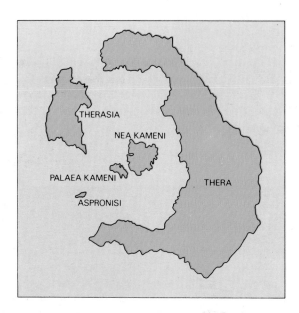

Above: the volcanic caldera of Thera, with the volcanic cones of Nea Kameni and Palaea Kameni in its center. Comparison with Krakatoa indicates that the destruction caused by the Thera eruption and its effects must have been immense.

Europe's best known volcanoes are the four in the south of Italy and Sicily. There, is, however, a fifth active volcano farther east – and it was a cataclysmic eruption of this volcano around the year 1470 BC that had a more profound effect on the history of civilization than any other in man's history.

The volcano is Thera (sometimes called Santorin) and it is now a group of small, odd-shaped islands in the Cyclades archipelago midway between southern Greece and Turkey. These islands are the surviving fragments of what used to be a volcano of very considerable size, 10 miles across and perhaps as much as 4500 feet high. During its last great eruption such massive quantities of pumice, ash, and other solid material were ejected that the cone of the volcano collapsed into the exhausted magma chamber below it. The sea rushed in to occupy the great saucerlike space, and formed what is known as a *caldera*.

The terrible events of that day, nearly 3500 years ago, have had to be pieced together from evidence drawn from geology, archaeology, and incidents in the legends of Greek mythology. No account of the eruption written at the time it happened survives. Perhaps none was ever written. The Greeks on the mainland had not yet evolved as a nation and the people directly involved – those few who survived – were too shattered by the experience to do much else than flee from their ruined homeland.

These people were the Minoans of Crete, a highly civilized, spirited, and by all the evidence, a happy race, who ruled over many islands of the Aegean Sea – including Thera. The Minoan civilization was overwhelmed in its prime by a catastrophe so complete that all knowledge of Minoan achievements soon passed from men's minds. All that survived were legends of a Golden Age and of King Minos and his bull-man monster, the Minotaur. Europe knew no more of this accomplished Late Bronze Age race until in 1900 the English archaeologist Sir Arthur Evans dug up the vast palace of King Minos at Knossos on Crete and uncovered objects that astounded the world.

Evans discovered that other palaces and settlements along the north coast of Crete had all been destroyed at the same time. He blamed barbarian invaders, but a different explanation was suggested by the Greek Professor Spyridon Marinatos after he had dug along the coast north of Knossos. He found quantities of pumice among the ruins and noticed that building stones had been tilted as though by the powerful suction of water. Could the catastrophe have been caused by a volcanic eruption of unimaginable violence?

In 1967 Marinatos began excavating on Thera, 75 miles north of Crete, and from the first day astonishing

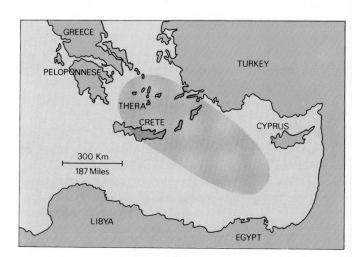

Above: the eastern Mediterranean showing the extent of the ash fall-out produced by the Thera eruption. The map is based on geological evidence of sediment cores from the seabed.

Right: a fresco from the West House on Thera. It depicts a coastal city with ships offshore, a forested land and plentiful deer. It was painted by an unknown Theran at the height of Minoan civilization.

64

Right: the ring-shaped submerged caldera of Thera with its central active volcanic islands, photographed during series of eruptions from 1938–41.

discoveries were made of Minoan vases knocked from their stands by volcanic stones and superb frescoes preserved beneath the ash. Few bodies were found, suggesting that the inhabitants of Thera had had time to evacuate their homes before the first eruption. The reconstructed sequence of events seems to have gone like this:

After 20,000 years of inactivity, Thera's volcano came to life again around 1500 BC and ejected coarse pumice, probably covering the whole island, to a depth of 13 feet. Intermittent minor activity continued for about 30 years, ending in an explosion, or series of explosions, that certainly rival and may well exceed the celebrated Krakatoa eruption of 1883. The violent outburst was probably heard from end to end of the Mediterranean. Thera was covered with ash 220 feet deep. A dense cloud of darkness spread out above the entire area bearing ash southeastward in the prevailing winds. Cores of sediment brought up in drills from the sea bed show that 600 miles away the fall-out was two inches. Closer to Crete a core of ash 30 inches thick was brought up. The effect on land of such thick falls can be imagined when a mere four inches on Iceland was sufficient to kill trees and wreck the country's agriculture for several seasons. The final calamity, it seemed, came from the tsunami, the great waves that swept out from Thera at incredible speed and found the exposed north Cretan settlements an open target. So many cities were washed away, so many people drowned or left starving, that the brilliant Minoan civilization never recovered.

It was dimly remembered as a Golden Age and may have given rise to the legend of Atlantis. Nearly 1000 years after the eruption Egyptian priests told a Greek traveler, Solon, of a disaster that had overwhelmed a people "far to the west." To the Egyptians, Crete was the westward limit to their world but by the time Plato came to weave Solon's story into his saga of Atlantis, the Greek world was larger and the far west was the Atlantic Ocean. The end of Plato's Atlantis, where the bull was worshiped (as in Crete), came with "violent earthquakes and floods; in a single day and night of misfortune . . . the island of Atlantis disappeared in the depths of the sea."

When Vesuvius Erupted
Pompeii: 79 AD

The eruption of Mount Vesuvius in 79 AD, when Pompeii, Herculaneum, and several other thriving Roman towns were overwhelmed, is perhaps the most famous eruption in history. The Romans believed Vesuvius to be extinct – there had been no activity for probably 3000 years – and its slopes were cultivated with olives and vines to the very summit. In 62 AD a severe earthquake shook the area but nobody supposed this had anything to do with the pleasant green mountain that rose above what is now the Bay of Naples. Minor earthquake activity continued for 17 years until on August 24 in the year 79 the volcano burst into terrible life.

The sequence of events can be traced in two letters written by Pliny the Younger describing the death during the eruption of his uncle, the naturalist, writer, and lawyer Pliny the Elder. The Plinys were staying in their villa across the Bay. The first signs that something unusual had occurred was the appearance of a huge cloud over Vesuvius: "like an immense tree-trunk it was projected into the air, and opened out with branches. . . . sometimes white, sometimes dark and mottled."

The elder Pliny, who was in the command of a fleet, set off in one of the galleys to see what was happening but the hot ashes and pieces of pumice had fallen so thickly along the shore that landing was impossible and Pliny directed the ship some miles to the south. Here they were able to land and make their way to a friend's villa. Toward what should have been dawn

the falling pumice, ash, and frequent earth tremors drove the party back to the shore, only to find the waves too rough for any escape by sea. Choking in the clouds of sulfurous fumes, Pliny fell down dead, either suffocated or from a heart attack.

Meanwhile, across the bay, the earth tremors were becoming so violent that Pliny's 17-year-old nephew

Left: a 19th-century lantern-slide picture of Vesuvius during an eruption.

Right: Pliny the younger's description of the terrible eruption of Vesuvius in 79 AD, is the obvious inspiration behind this painting from around 1820 by the British artist John Martin, which he titled *The Destruction of Pompeii and Herculaneum*. **Below right:** casts of three of the citizens of Pompeii who died under the smothering ash and sulfur fumes when Vesuvius erupted.

and his mother left their villa and joined a panic-stricken crowd struggling to get out of town. Above the volcano there now "loomed a horrible black cloud ripped by sudden bursts of fire, writhing snakelike and revealing sudden flashes larger than lightning." This terrifying situation lasted for some time, with ash falling so thickly that they had to shake themselves clear occasionally for fear of being buried in it. When eventually the darkness lightened and the sun shone dimly through they saw that the whole top of Vesuvius had been blown off, and where once there had been fields, farms, and rich vineyards, a silent gray carpet of ash now lay over all.

The city of Pompeii was buried beneath 15 to 25 feet of ash and pumice. Plaster casts taken of some of the 2000 bodies found so far show that many of the inhabitants died with hands or cloth to their mouths trying to keep out the poisonous fumes of the ash cloud.

The smaller city of Herculaneum met a different end. Though nearer to Vesuvius it lay up-wind of the volcano and escaped the worst of the ash-fall. But after the main eruption was over, torrential rain turned the ash on the upper slopes into a mass of mud that avalanched down onto Herculaneum and engulfed it completely. Like its more famous neighbor

Pompeii Herculaneum remained buried for 1600 years.

Ash and pumice continued to be ejected periodically after 79 AD and in 1036 the first lava flow appeared. A quiet period followed, but then more serious eruptions involving loss of life and property occurred in 1631, 1779, 1872, and 1906. The last eruption of Vesuvius took place in March 1944. The next eruption could be any time in the near future. Far more people live around the Bay of Naples now than in 79 AD, and though an eruption is unlikely without warning, an unexpected one could cause death and chaos.

67

Europe's Volcanic Island
Iceland: 1783

Above: a house being engulfed in a sea of basaltic ash during the 1973 eruption on Heimaey. The people of Iceland live under constant threat of volcanic action as their country sits over a crack in the earth's crust where new material is being forced up from the mantle.

Iceland – land of fire and ice – was created by its volcanoes. An island of 40,000 square miles, about the size of Ireland, it sits astride the northern end of the mid-Atlantic ridge. Volcanoes reach the surface at other points along this huge, mostly submerged mountain on the ocean's floor, but only in Iceland does the ridge itself rise above sea level. The rift valley in the center of the ridge is a striking feature of the harsh Icelandic landscape. Over 50 million years, basaltic lavas have welled up from the earth's interior to form vast lava fields on either side of the ridge. In the course of eons, as North America and Europe have drifted apart, western Iceland moved west and eastern Iceland east, widening the center at an average rate of nearly an inch a year.

Volcanic eruptions in Iceland typically occur not from a central crater but from long fissures or cracks in the ground. Such eruptions produce enormous quantities of lava that spread in layers over the surrounding countryside. Almost the whole of Iceland was formed in this way, as were the Deccan Plateau of India and the Columbia and Snake Rivers regions of the northwestern United States, among others. The only fissure eruptions of recorded history have occurred in Iceland, and the greatest of these was in 1783. It was the most remarkable eruption mankind has ever witnessed as far as production of lava goes. It was also the worst catastrophe Iceland has ever experienced.

Toward the end of May 1783 farmers in the sparsely populated settlements of southeast Iceland noticed a peculiar bluish haze hanging thickly over the desolate headwaters of the Skafta River in the vicinity of Mount Skaptar. On June 1 came the first of a succession of violent earthquakes that continued for eight days. The alarmed inhabitants of the area deserted their houses and pitched tents in the open fields.

The morning of June 8 began with several tremendous explosions and darkness caused by the emission of a vast cloud of dense smoke that blotted out the sun and rained down ash over a wide area. Winds carried the ash eastward in sufficient quantities to damage crops in Scotland and Norway.

The eruption proper commenced two days later when jets of lava burst from a row of small craters along the 10-mile-long Laki Fissure and flowed southwest. The liquid lava quickly reached the steep-sided valley of the Skafta and proceeded to fill the river to the brim, although in places the valley was 600 feet deep and 200 feet wide. It then inundated the neighboring fields, laying waste the pastureland, farm buildings, and churches of the various settlements in its path. The main stream continued all the way to the sea, a distance of 15 miles. In the lowland areas the

Above: the summit crater on Hekla volcano emits an ash-cloud similar to the catastrophic eruption of 1783 when more than 10,000 people, 190,000 sheep, 18,000 horses, and 11,500 cattle died as a result of heavy falls of ash blotting out crops and grasslands.

flow spread to a maximum width of 10 miles, with an average depth of 100 feet.

The eruption had melted great quantities of glacier ice, and volcanic steam had condensed into water that fell in heavy rains. With the channel of the Skafta dammed by lava, the waters poured over the land. Many homes and churches that had escaped the lava were then carried away by the flood.

Periodically for the next two months the whole area was enveloped in almost pitch blackness. At noon on midsummer day it was impossible to see a sheet of white paper held up against a window.

A further eruption on August 3 produced more vast outpourings of lava. Unable to escape toward the Skafta, the molten mass flowed southeast to the Hverfisfljot River. It soon filled this stream to overflowing and flooded the plains with devastating rapidity. When the eruptions came to an end in August, lava had covered the enormous area of 220 square miles. The total volume of the flow is estimated to have been 2.6 cubic miles.

Nobody was directly killed by this massive deluge of lava and the blue haze that came with it, but the ill effects were felt for a generation. The falls of ash drove the fish from the coasts. The blue haze, which was observed throughout much of the Northern Hemisphere and which even dimmed the sun over Italy, sickened both animals and humans. The lack of sunlight during the summer had stunted all the grass growing in Iceland that year. As a result, half the cattle and three quarters of the sheep and horses starved to death. So did many people. In the ensuing famine, known as the Haze Famine, a quarter of Iceland's population of 49,000 perished. People were reduced to chewing raw hides and pieces of rope. Sheep devoured each other's wool. Horses ate each other. Finally a plan was drawn up to abandon the island and transport the remaining population to West Jutland in Denmark, but it came to nothing. For the survivors of the Laki volcanic eruption, the years following 1783 were the grimmest period of Iceland's long history.

Right: part of the Mid-Atlantic Ridge on land is the 15-mile-long Laki fault or fissure in Iceland. New material wells up from the Laki fault pushing the two halves of Iceland away from each other at the rate of nearly an inch a year.

The Most Terrible Eruption
Krakatoa:1883

The most catastrophic eruption of a volcano ever recorded in human history issued on August 27, 1883 from a little-known and scarcely visited scrap of land between Java and Sumatra – the island of Krakatoa. Unlike the higher and more celebrated volcanic peaks of Indonesia, known to be active, the small cones of Krakatoa were considered harmless. The highest, Rakatam, was only 2700 feet high.

In May 1883 Krakatoa came abruptly to life with a succession of violent explosions audible in the then Dutch colonial city of Batavia (now Jakarta) 100 miles away. A great cloud of vapor and ash rose above the island, spreading ash over a wide area. The deck of the Dutch mailboat *Zeeland* making its way through the Sunda Strait between Java and Sumatra was strewn with pieces of pumice as large as hen's eggs. This initial activity did not last long but for the rest of the summer sporadic eruptions continued. These reached their climax in the appalling events of August 26 and 27.

The few witnesses in the coastal towns and villages who survived were so stunned by the terrible experience they had lived through that a coherent picture of events took some time to establish. The opening

Right: a 19th-century engraving of the eruption of Krakatoa in 1883. The island between Java and Sumatra, was the scene of the most appalling volcanic explosion in recorded history and could be heard in Australia – 2250 miles away.

salvo came at 1 pm on Sunday, August 26 with a series of shattering explosions, at first occurring at intervals of 10 minutes but soon blasting off every two minutes. At 2 pm a dense black cloud was spewed out of Krakatoa's new crater and soared to an estimated height of 17 miles. Vast quantities of ash and pumice began falling over the sea and coastal areas and by 3 pm all visibility in the area was blotted out. Within a radius of 50 miles of the volcano the darkness of this unnatural night was to last for 57 hours.

Several ships were caught making their way past Krakatoa at the time of the eruption. The captain of the British vessel *Charles Bal* recorded in his log – "The blinding fall of sand and stones, the intense blackness above and around us, broken only by the incessant glare of varied kinds of lightning and the continued explosive roars of Krakatoa, make our situation a truly awful one."

Unpleasant though conditions were at sea, they were preferable to those on land where heavy waves were pounding the shores, smashing boats and houses. Nobody within 100 miles of Krakatoa slept that night – the noise from the volcano was almost continuous. Survivors described the sky as "one second intense blackness, the next a blaze of fire."

But all this was merely the preliminary to Krakatoa's culminating outbursts on the Monday evening – a succession of explosions vaster than anything man has heard before or since. The greatest occurred at 10.02 when 11 square miles of Krakatoa Island collapsed into the exhausted magma chamber. The sea rushed into the gaping hole and the explosion that followed – Krakatoa's death cry – was heard over a large part of the earth's surface. In central Australia 2250 miles away, it was loud enough to be mistaken for rock-blasting. The farthest report came from tiny Rodriguez Island, 2968 miles to the west near Mauritius in the Indian Ocean, where an alert coastguard heard it and took the sound to be gunfire. The intensity of the explosion can be appreciated by supposing the eruption to have happened in New York, in which case it would have been heard in Western Europe.

In Batavia the force of the blast cracked walls and blew a gasometer out of its well. In southern Sumatra hundreds were killed by a heavy rain of hot pumice and burning ash. Survivors were tormented by thirst yet unable to find any drinkable water. But the greatest destruction was caused by the terrible tsunamis that raced out again and again from what was left of Krakatoa. These were responsible for most of the 36,417 known deaths. Towns and villages ceased to exist as the great wall of water swept everything before it. In the inky blackness people never saw the water coming and could not help themselves when it struck. The few survivors were those who happened to be washed into the tops of trees.

A total of 295 towns and villages were wholly or partly destroyed. In the Javanese port of Merak the wave was high enough to destroy the stone houses on top of a hill 130 feet high where most of the 2700 in-

habitants had taken refuge. Only two survived. In Sumatra at the port of Telok Betong the Dutch gunboat *Berouw* was carried well over a mile inland and left stranded 30 feet above sea level behind a hill. It is still there, a permanent reminder of the fearful power of Krakatoa. Telok Betong itself was totally destroyed and for a long time remained a desolate swamp.

Within a few years the surviving islands of Krakatoa were cloaked once more in thick vegetation. In 1927 a new volcano began to grow from the caldera floor. Named Anak Krakatoa – "Child of Krakatoa" – it broke surface in 1952 and its cone is now over 300 feet high. The world has not heard the last from this deceptively insignificant scrap of land.

Above: a steamer carried inland by the giant tsunamis that followed the eruption of Krakatoa in 1883. The gigantic waves wiped out towns and villages and claimed more than 36,000 victims. **Below:** Anak Krakatoa "child of Krakatoa" that grew from the remains of the old volcano, erupting in 1969.

71

A Caribbean Explosion
Mont Pelée:1902

Above: six months after the disastrous eruption of Mont Pelée, Martinique, that obliterated the city of Saint Pierre, this lava plug topped 800 feet, before collapsing into the volcano's throat.

"This date should be written in blood," wrote the Vicar-General of the Caribbean island of Martinique to his bishop on May 8, 1902. "Saint Pierre, in the morning throbbing with life, thronged with people, is no more. Its ruins stretch before us, wrapped in their shroud of smoke and ashes, gloomy and silent, a city of the dead."

The thriving and elegant port-city of Saint Pierre, and until that morning the leading city of Martinique, lay between a wide bay and the slumbering volcano of Mont Pelée. A minor eruption 50 years earlier had sprinkled gray ash on the slopes of the mountain but nothing had occurred since to give cause for alarm. The first signs of renewed activity were observed in April. Ominous rumblings were heard, clouds of steam rose over the summit and light falls of ash lay like snow over Saint Pierre. As the days passed the falls became thicker. Mrs Prentiss, wife of the US Consul, wrote home, "The smell of sulfur is so strong that horses in the street stop and snort, and some of them drop in their harness and die of suffocation. Many of the people are obliged to wear wet handkerchiefs to protect themselves from the strong fumes of sulfur." On May 5 a torrent of boiling mud swept down a valley two miles from the city, destroying a sugar mill near the sea and burying alive the 30 workers.

Despite these warning signs, the editor of the local newspaper *Les Colonies* assured his readers there was nothing to worry about. "Where could one be better than at Saint Pierre?" he asked in the very last issue of his paper.

At about 7.50 am on May 8 the volcano exploded with four deafening reports. A great black cloud pierced with lightning flashes emerged from just below the crater and like an avalanche swept effortlessly, remorselessly down the slope. A few moments later 30,000 people were dead or dying, scorched by the fearful blast of superheated gas and dust. The force of this blast uprooted mature trees and smashed stone walls three feet thick. Within minutes the entire city was ablaze. All but two of the 18 ships in the harbor were capsized and sank as the fiery blast swept over them. On one of the remaining ships, the American SS *Roraima,* the masts and smokestack were struck off as though a knife had cut them. Everyone on deck was instantly killed but below decks a few people managed to survive. A Barbados nursemaid gave a moving account of her ordeal:

"I was assisting with the dressing of the children when the steward rushed past and shouted "Close the cabin door – the volcano is coming!" We closed the door and at the same moment came a terrible explosion which nearly burst the eardrums. . . . We were all thrown off our feet by the shock and huddled crouching in the corner of the cabin. My mistress had the baby girl in her arms, the older girl leaned on my left arm, while I held little Eric in my right.

"The explosion seemed to have blown in the sky-

Right: the town of Saint Pierre at the foot of Mont Pelée today. The eruption of 1902 was the final phase of volcanic activity in this particular type of volcano before years of rest or even extinction.

Below: enormous clouds of superheated steam and molten rock were forced through a vent in the side of Mont Pelée because the mouth of the volcano was blocked. Like a monstrous blowtorch it razed the town and harbor killing over 30,000 people and incinerating 10 square miles of country.

light over our heads, and before we could raise ourselves, hot moist ashes began to pour in on us; they came in boiling splattering splashes like hot mud. In vain we tried to shield ourselves. . . . When we could see each other's faces, they were all covered with black lava. The baby was dying; Rita, the older girl, was in great agony and every part of my body was paining me. A heap of hot mud had collected near us and as Rita put her hand down to raise herself up it was plunged up to the elbow in the scalding stuff. . . .

"The first engineer came now, and hearing our moans carried us to the forward deck and there we remained on the burning ship from 8.30 am until 3.00 pm. . . . My mistress lay on the deck in a collapsed state; the little boy was already dead, and the baby dying. The lady was collected and resigned, handed me some money, told me to take Rita to her aunt, and sucked a piece of ice before she died."

In the city itself two men survived the holocaust, a shoemaker on the outskirts and a young murderer locked in the dungeon of the jail.

The destruction of Saint Pierre was caused by a swiftly expanding cloud of hot gases, ashes, and highly viscous lava. After the eruption an enormous spine of the stiff lava was pushed up above the crater, finally reaching a height of 1020 feet, and for a year remained as a sort of natural monument to the 30,000 who had died at its feet.

Is Prediction Possible?

A volcano in eruption may be "the greatest show on earth" but the show is not free. A price has to be paid in loss of buildings, ruined crops and vegetation, fields put out of cultivation by layers of ash, sunlight dimmed by dustclouds and affecting weather, and, not least, destruction of life.

It is probably impossible to prevent a volcanic eruption altogether – and in the unlikely event of it becoming technologically feasible, the risks are high and a beneficial outcome doubtful. The bombing of volcanoes has been considered, sometimes to stop and sometimes to start an eruption. The Guatamalan volcano Santa Maria began a mild eruption in 1946 that was soon doing greater damage than many briefer but more violent eruptions. The volcano emitted no solid materials, only sulfurous vapors – but these killed many acres of formerly excellent coffee plantations. The gases continued to pour out for seven years. Among suggestions for ending this threat to Guatamala's staple crop was a scheme to bomb the crater

and so block, if only temporarily, the vent through which the gases came. Before any decision could be reached Santa Maria solved the problem by ceasing to emit fumes.

In World War II the possibility was considered of bombing Vesuvius and certain Japanese volcanoes. If an eruption could be started it was hoped this would distract the Italians and Japanese from their war effort. Vulcanologists were skeptical about the military value of such an enterprise and again the operations were never carried out. Vesuvius did erupt when Allied troops were in the area. The runways of Naples airport were covered with ash, hindering take-offs, but otherwise the eruption caused hardly any inconvenience.

But if prevention is impossible or unwise, incalculable benefit comes from reliable prediction of when an eruption is going to occur. Careful study of his barometer saved the life of Fernand Clerc, one of the leading planters on Martinique at the time of the Mont Pelée eruption. He woke early on May 8, saw that the needle of his barometer was constantly jerking and acted immediately. British author Frank Lane described Clerc's reactions in his book *The Elements Rage*, "He ordered his carriage at once, piled his family into it and soon after 7 am drove out of the city. His friends laughed at his fears and waved as his carriage sped away. He made for Mont Parnasse, a

mile from Saint Pierre. On arriving there he and his family got out of the carriage and looked back. It was 7.50 am on May 8 – zero hour for one of the world's greatest tragedies."

Measurements of the events that precede an eruption have made considerable progress since 1902. Seismometers can record the increase in local small earthquakes, known as microearthquakes, that indicate movements of magma within a volcano. The rise of magma up a volcano alters the local gravitational and magnetic fields and these changes announce the approach of an eruption. Observatories have been set up at some volcanoes (not very many, unfortunately) to monitor their behavior. An instrument that has led to considerable success in prediction, particularly in Hawaii and Japan, is the *tiltmeter*. In some cases, before an eruption magma enters the chambers and fissures of a volcano, causing it to swell to a small but measurable degree. The essential structure of a tiltmeter consists of two containers of liquid, usually mercury, connected by a tube. A swelling of the ground will alter the height of one of the containers relative to the other and the liquid will flow downhill from the upper one to the lower. Two instruments are generally placed at right angles so that the direction of the tilt can be determined.

Not only do tiltmeters give warning that an eruption is due – they can also indicate that a lull in activity is only temporary. An example of this occurred at Kilauea, the youngest of Hawaii's volcanoes and famous for the lava lake named Halemaumau, "Home of Everlasting Fire" a remarkable volcanic feature that is no longer as everlasting as it used to be but comes and goes over the years. In 1957 the tiltmeters on Kilauea indicated that the entire surface of the mountain was swelling. Swelling steadily continued over the next two years until a rapid increase in the rate, occurring in November 1959, showed that an eruption was near. It happened on November 14, from a crater near the summit, but not much lava emerged and the action ceased in December. The mountain was still very swollen, however, so it was evident the eruption was not yet over. Seismic records suggested the lava was moving underground and on January 13, 1960, cracks appeared in the center of the town of Kapaho, nearly 30 miles from the summit crater. A half-mile crack opened outside the town and vast quantities of lava poured down toward the sea. Embankments were flung up to protect Kapaho and a lighthouse but all were overwhelmed by the flow that had totaled 150 million cubic yards when the eruption was over four weeks later. By this time the tiltmeters indicated that much subsidence had taken place, and a few months later Kilauea had returned to its pre-1957 level.

The first known attempt to divert the course of a

Above: Mount Etna in an eruption in May, 1971. The eruption caused serious damage to the villages at its feet and also engulfed the Mount Etna volcanological observatory (left).

Right: a scientist places a probe stick containing a tiny tiltmeter five feet into the South California earthquake fault area. The inset shows a close-up of the sensitive one-inch tiltmeter device. The use of tiltmeters greatly improves prediction of volcanic activity, particularly where ground swelling occurs over a period before an eruption. Two separate liquid reservoirs widely spaced and connected by a tube are the simple principle behind the tiltmeter. When the ground beneath one reservoir rises, the liquid runs down from the higher to the lower reservoir and the level of the rise can be measured.

lava flow occurred in Sicily during a serious eruption of Etna in 1669. A man from Catania named Pappalardo dressed himself and 50 of his fellow citizens in wet cowhides as a protection against the heat and with crowbars and iron hooks they dug an opening in the solidifying crust at the side of the flow. Lava poured through the gap they created and considerably lessened the force and speed of the flow moving upon Catania. Unfortunately, the new flow threatened the small town of Paterno and 500 of its citizens took up arms and drove the men of Catania from their work. The gap in the wall soon crusted over again and the main flow continued once more toward Catania. It piled up against the city walls, which were 60 feet high, then poured over them in a fiery cascade that overwhelmed part of the city.

In modern Sicily so many villages cluster around the fertile flanks of Etna that it is now illegal to attempt to divert the flow of the lava. No such restriction stood in the way of the determined endeavors of the Icelanders on the Nestmann Islands (a group that includes the new volcano of Surtsey) when a fissure opened up on Helgafell, a hillside only half a mile from Heimaey, Iceland's biggest fishing port. The eruption began in January 1973 and within a few hours many roofs of the town had collapsed under the weight of ash. The population was evacuated but the lava looked likely to block the harbor and overwhelm

the hoses had played the temperature was 1300°F. When the eruption ceased in June the town was in ruins but by narrowing the mouth of the harbor the lava flow had actually improved it, making it more sheltered than before.

An eruption in 1935 from Mauna Loa, Hawaii's largest volcano, threatened the port of Hilo. Dr Thomas A. Jaggar, then Director of the Hawaiian Volcano Observatory, suggested bombing the swift-moving lava flow at strategic points to start small diversionary flows. Two targets were selected and blasted with 600-pound bombs. By the following day the lava flow had slowed from 800 feet per hour to only 44 feet per hour and later on the same day all movement had stopped. The shock of the bombing appeared to have "frozen" the lava right back to the source, which spent its energy in lava fountains. The operation cost $25,000. Had the flow reached Hilo, the damage would have run into millions.

The most difficult volcanic outburst to control is the sort that destroyed Saint Pierre. This is because of the fiery cloud's intense heat and speed. But it has been suggested that, where communities are threatened, a notch could be made in another part of the crater wall so that the deadly gas clouds escape down another path.

Ambitious engineering works were required to make Kelut in Java safer for the Indonesian villagers

the town. To cool the lava, sea water was pumped onto the advancing front in the hope that this would solidify it. With special high-capacity pumps flown in from the US, the operation was more successful than was expected. Boreholes drilled into parts of the lava that had not been hosed with water showed that 15 yards inside the temperature was 1830°F. Where

Above: the fishing port and main town of Heimaey, Iceland. During the 1973 eruption the islanders cooled the lava with water in an attempt to divert the flow.

Above: an engineer at the exit of a drainage tunnel built from the crater lake of Mount Kelut, Java. Tunnels were built to minimize mud flow during an eruption. Below: a scientist wearing protective clothing tests the temperature of a volcano at the crater's edge. Temperature variations are an important clue to imminent activity.

at its feet. The problem was that the summit of the volcano contained a deep crater lake. Kelut's eruptions tend to be violent but brief, yet they can be disastrous because the lake is ejected from the crater, mixes with ash, and turns into mud that sweeps down the slopes destroying everything. In 1919 some 5000 people were killed and the Dutch authorities decided to bore a system of tunnels that would drain most of the lake. Over 30 years passed before the next eruption, in 1951, tested the tunnels. This time no mud flows formed and only seven men died – two of them vulcanologists who happened to be in one of the drainage tunnels when the volcano erupted. The eruption blocked the tunnels, however, and a new deep crater allowed a large lake to form in it. New drainage tunnels were not constructed and in 1966 an eruption formed mudflows and killed many hundreds of people. Since then, drainage tunnels have been re-introduced.

Volcanoes thought to be extinct and scarcely visited in the remoter parts of the world sometimes erupt and cause great damage. It is impossible to monitor every volcano in the world but in Japan, Hawaii, and parts of Indonesia and the Phillipines – densely populated regions regularly threatened by volcanoes – surveillance is considered important and it is nowadays unlikely that an eruption will take the neighborhood by surprise. Given good warning, the inhabitants can all be evacuated in time. Volcanoes are as different as individuals and the only general rule applies to those on islands, besides lakes, or otherwise associated with large tracts of water: If you want to enjoy the spectacle of an eruption, don't watch from the shore. Remember Krakatoa and make for the top of a hill, the higher the better.

Chapter 5

Drought and Famine

Unlike other natural catastrophes famine is not a sudden disaster but a long-drawn-out process passing through several stages. The rains fail, vegetation withers for lack of water, food gradually dwindles. Shortage becomes scarcity and eventually complete dearth. It may take many months before this final, dreaded stage is reached. Drought is still the main traditional cause of famine. Some famines have followed upon calamitous floods. There have been cases – fortunately rare – when a new disease attacks the main food crop of a people, as in the terrible potato famine of Ireland. Armies have inevitably brought famine in their wake, killing the men who should be working the land or by deliberately laying waste the land itself.

In this century a new danger looms – one that threatens not a single unfortunate region but the entire world – overpopulation. The world's population at present is 4000 million of which, it is estimated, 2400 million are undernourished or malnourished. Population figures are expected to reach 7000 million by the end of the century. Will there ever be enough to feed them all?

Opposite: a scene in the Australian desert. Desert and semidesert lands make up to 20 to 25 percent of the world's total land surface. These are the regions where there is scant rainfall and populations in or near them eke out a precarious living while existing within the constant shadow of prolonged drought and the inevitable famine that follows.

Why Do People Starve?

certainty. Except for the unfailingly wet rainforests of the tropics, all regions of the earth can experience a disturbance in their normal climate. Rain at the wrong time and insufficient sun affect harvesting but the greatest damage is done not through too much rain but too little.

Indian agriculture depends on the monsoon rain that sweeps in from the southwest in June and July and continues until September. The main crops are reaped in December. The last weeks before the monsoon arrives is a period of great anxiety. Even a week's delay will affect the quality of the crops. The monsoon has never totally failed over all India – and meteorologists believe this to be impossible – but it has failed over areas where as many as 50 million or more people live. The great mass of the population do not have the means to store grain from the occasional bumper year. When the monsoon fails, they starve.

The poor communications that exist in most of the countries exposed to famine danger make the situation there that much worse. In the 1870s a three-year drought afflicted north China. Famine resulted and in five provinces law and order disintegrated. Grain

Above: part of a carving from the temple of King Unis at Sakkara, showing an emaciated Egyptian of around 2350 BC. The problem of famine has a history as old as man himself.

Deserts are as natural to the earth as rainforests or gassland. Climate is determined by interactions between the atmosphere (in particular the humidity and direction of the wind), the physical features of the land, and the rotation of the earth. Large areas in the western regions of Australia, South Africa, and South America in the Southern Hemisphere, and in central Asia, North Africa, and the southwestern United States and in the Northern Hemisphere receive little or no rainfall. There are places in the Atacama Desert in northern Chile where no rain has been recorded for centuries. These conditions are likely to continue into the foreseeable future, perhaps until another Ice Age changes the global pattern of the winds.

Some peoples have adapted to life on the edges of these deserts but the great majority of the world's population, whether hunters, farmers, or city-dwellers, have chosen kinder habitats, lands where animals have access to sources of food and water, and where crops have a near-certainty of reaching maturity. Unfortunately, a near-certainty is not an absolute

piled up in the coastal ports but the transport available to take it inland was woefully inadequate. Between 9 and 13 million people starved to death, perished from disease, or died in food riots.

The British nutritionist and famine relief expert Dr W. R. Aykroyd says in his book *The Conquest of Famine,* "Famine can be recorded in terms of area, duration, the size of the population affected, the scarcity and cost of food, the death rate and other features. But essentially it means a lot of miserable people suffering from starvation, and physically and mentally damaged as the result. . . . People without food do not simply lie down quietly and die. The way to death is nasty and brutish and often not short."

In the first stage of famine food is in short supply but still available. People in good health can lose 10 percent of normal weight without this adversely affecting their fitness. In this state they are still able to search intelligently and actively for food. Hunger very quickly occupies their thoughts to the exclusion of everything else. With continued weight-loss physical changes occur in the body cells, which has the effect of reducing the energy required to keep the vital

processes going. The victim sinks into a state of apathy after 20 percent of the body weight is lost. Men on hunger strike can survive an astonishing number of days because they drink any amount of liquid, do nothing but rest and have the consolation of knowing they can end their self-imposed fast whenever they wish. Men dying of starvation have no consolation. Despair sometimes rouses them to utter appalling moans but then they subside into a semicomatose state of depression. After more than 30 percent of the body weight has been lost death is almost inevitable.

As the point of death is approached the victim becomes indifferent to his surroundings and, even more distressing, indifferent to the sufferings of others. A doctor in Ireland during the potato famine wrote, "I have seen mothers snatch food from the hands of their starving children; known a father to engage in a fatal struggle with a son for a potato; and have seen parents look on the putrid bodies of their offspring, without evincing a symptom of sorrow." It is hardly surprising that those who undergo the agonies of famine and survive suffer mental damage that long outlasts the physical symptoms.

Left: a Kenyan tribeswoman collects water from a well.

Right: Mali farmers plow the baked earth. **Below right:** an Indian plants rice after the monsoon. All these peoples adapted to a desert way of life are especially vulnerable to even minor changes in rainfall.

Below: map of the dry belt (red) which runs eastward from northern Africa, through the Levant and Central Asia to the Far East. Areas reduced to complete desert are in brown.

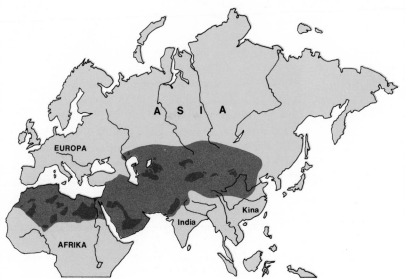

81

The Great Potato Famine
Ireland:1840s

Above: a cartoon from a British magazine of 1847, when the Irish potato famine was at its height. John Bull, representing the larger British Isle, is depicted giving alms to the starving, workless Irish. In fact it was largely through government neglect that the Irish suffered so appallingly.

In 1844 a blight that had never appeared before attacked the potato crop in North America. Little attention was given to this fact at the time in Europe. In 1845 the blight appeared in the potato fields of Ireland, where virtually the whole population had come to depend on the potato as the sole source of food. The spores spread with terrifying swiftness destroying a great part of the crop. The following year the entire crop rotted in the fields. In 1847 there was no blight but famine had so disorganized the country that only an eighth of the normal quantity of seed had been sown. In 1848 the famine was again total. By the end of 1849 when a good potato crop was at last harvested 1,500,000 Irish people had starved to death, died of famine fevers, or perished from exposure after their landlords had evicted them from their huts. Ireland, then an unwilling partner in the United Kingdom, has never forgotten that English stubbornness, mismanagement, and greed paved the way for the famine and then did less than enough to combat it.

Ireland had no industries. About half its people lived on small farms and grew potatoes for food. Others worked as tenant farmers on English-owned estates. They grew grain and raised cattle but these were sold to pay rents to their absentee landlords. They, like everyone else, grew potatoes for food. They were easy to cultivate and an acre produced food for four people for a year. To feed their families on grain would have required three or four times the acreage and there was fierce competition for land among the swarming population. A diet of potatoes with buttermilk produced a nourishing fare. Even so, there were dangers in the widespread cultivation of a single crop species. Potatoes did not keep, and in very wet or very dry years the crop often failed. As there was no alternative source of food, the people went hungry. The blight of 1845 was a new and incomprehensible enemy but the Irish had suffered famine before and though many people went hungry that year, by the spring and summer of 1846 the new crop promised well. In May and in June the plants flourished – then disaster struck. Overnight, fields of luxuriant plants withered and turned black. The air was filled with the stench of rotting potatoes. Women sat at the edge of their stricken potato patches weeping and wringing their hands. The Irish potato crop was annihilated.

The English government, unwilling to accept the scale of the disaster, refused to alter what was called "the normal course of trade" by dispensing large sums of money to feed the Irish. It was arranged that the Irish should work (building roads, digging canals) for payment; this money would then, by "the normal course of trade," attract food imports from foreign merchants. Free enterprise was to be encouraged. This policy failed totally. In the event the workmen were paid too little and as harvests had failed throughout Europe, the price of corn rocketed and hardly any reached Irish ports. Gaunt, famished men began to trudge the roads in search of foods; women and children chewed weeds. Meanwhile, and incredibly, exports of grain *from* Ireland continued – to pay the rents.

The winter of 1846–47 was the coldest in living memory. Snow covered the ground for months. Nicholas Cummins, a magistrate of County Cork, described in a letter to *The Times* of London a visit to the village of Skibbereen. He found the place apparently deserted but inside one mud cabin he saw, "six famished and ghastly skeletons, to all appearances dead, were huddled in a corner on some filthy straw, their sole covering what seemed a ragged horsecloth, their wretched legs hanging about, naked above the knees. I approached with horror, and found by a low moaning they were alive – they were in fever, four children, a woman, and what had once been a man. In a few minutes I was surrounded by at least 200 such phantoms, such frightful spectres as no words can describe, either from famine or from fever."

Many landlords took advantage of the situation to evict the tenants for non-payment of rent. Destitute and starving families were dragged weeping from their huts and the roofs and walls knocked down. Whole villages were depopulated so that wheat could be grown instead of the potato. The wretched peasants tried to shelter in ditches but were driven from there too. Clearing the land meant clearing it of people.

The English introduced soup kitchens – but insisted that those must be paid for by rates found locally. There was now virtually no money in all Ireland but the government in London was unmoved. "Arrest, remand, do anything you can," was the solution suggested by the Chancellor of the Exchequer, Charles Wood (later to become Viscount Halifax), "send horse, foot and dragoons, all the world will applaud you, and I should not be at all squeamish as to what I did, to the verge of the law, and a little beyond."

In 1848 the failure of the potato was as bad as in 1846. Typhus killed tens of thousands. Cholera spread. In the ominously named town of Skull the dead bodies were so thin that when they lay on their backs the stomach fell in and the vertebrae on the spine could be counted. Those who could afford the passage crossed the Atlantic, emigrating to Canada and the United States. Many died on the way. Those who survived retained a hatred of England that has only recently and only partially begun to subside.

Right: clothing being distributed at Kilrush in Ireland during the potato famine. There were many individual acts of charity throughout the famine, but the combination of rapacious absentee landlords and a totally uncomprehending government made the plight of the Irish unbearable. People died in their tens of thousands from famine, disease, and exposure and an estimated 1,250,000 found refuge overseas, especially in the U.S.A. and Canada – some in England. **Below:** an engraving depicting Irish families leaving Ireland for North America.

India's Starving Millions

The teeming millions of India fight a desperate battle against starvation. Early historical records and legends tell of terrible famines that laid waste the land. In Kashmir in 917 AD the ground was covered with the bones and skulls of the unburied dead while the king and his ministers, so it is reported, amassed huge fortunes by selling rice at an exorbitant price.

Indian agriculture has always been dependent on the monsoon rain and periodically these fail over large areas. Even in normal times the diet of the people is barely adequate. It is deficient in protein and vitamins, and does not allow the accumulation of body fat that could be drawn on in times of scarcity. Only a small shortfall of grain is required to turn scarcity to famine. In the past, poor communications between regions made it hard or impossible to move grain from one part of the country to another, and before the British imposed a kind of unity, India was a patchwork of innumerable warring states.

The behavior of the last Mogul emperor Aurangzeb during a famine in 1660 contrasts with the usual pattern of kings feasting while their people starve. The emperor bought grain in other parts of his wide domain and sold it in the famine area at a low price. The following year some corn was distributed free and peasants in areas affected by famine were not taxed. Aurangzeb's policy saved hundreds of thousands of lives.

British influence in India grew during the 18th century but the idea that governments should be responsible for relieving famine was slow to develop, despite the example of Aurangzeb. What has been described as "one of the most terrible of famines"

Above: a late 19th-century print showing starving Indians begging for food from Europeans. Government policy of unrestricted trade hindered relief for the victims of famine in India during the first half of the 19th-century, but in 1873 Warren Hastings had this granary (below) built at Patna for the "perpetual prevention of famines."

occurred in 1769–70 after an almost total failure of the rains in Bihar and parts of Bengal. Some 10,000,000 people, about one third of the population, are thought to have died. The stench from dead and rotting bodies filled the air, and millions of starving and diseased peasants flocked from the countryside into Calcutta and the other cities. By the time the next season's monsoon rain fell many villages had been entirely depopulated. After another famine in 1783 the governor-general, Warren Hastings, ordered the construction of an enormous granary at Patna in Bihar. It bore the inscription, "For the perpetual prevention of famines in these provinces." Unfortunately, the granary was never filled.

British economic policy in the first half of the 19th century was dominated by the theory that unassisted trade would solve all problems. Rigidly adhering to this doctrine, through famine after famine, British governments refused to control prices or stop exports of grain from famine areas or import grain from elsewhere. During the 1866–67 famine in Orissa a grain ship ran aground on the coast. British officials would not let the grain be taken to relieve the famine because the ship was bound for Calcutta. The grain rotted in the holds of the ship while officials debated on how to transport it there.

The workings of "unassisted trade" failed to solve the Orissa famine and there again the death toll is believed to have reached 10,000,000. British governments finally learned their lesson. In the 1870s when drought brought the threat of famine once more to Bihar, grain and money were swiftly despatched there. A Famine Code was devised to recognize danger in its earliest stages and the construction of railways ended the problem of poor communications. For 60 years India was spared the horror of severe famine and the efficient prevention system only broke down at a critical period in World War II.

In 1942 the Japanese army occupied Burma and refugees fled over the mountains into Bengal. In preparation against a Japanese invasion of India, the British removed from Bengal excess stocks of rice. At the end of October a severe cyclone caused great destruction to the crops shortly before harvest and this misfortune, combined with the invasion scare, set off a sharp rise in prices. In January 1943 rice was three times its normal price. In May it was eight times the normal price and far beyond the reach of poor peasants. Speculators exploited the situation and some organizations, both Hindu and Moslem, made colossal fortunes. Preoccupied by the war, British officials did not realize the extent of the catastrophe until streams of starving refugees began converging on Calcutta. Living skeletons shuffled through the streets and died in the gutters. Even then the provincial government of Bengal was slow to establish efficient relief measures, and not until the army took over the organization of relief in October 1943 did the situation begin to improve. Food was taken to the countryside in convoys and distribution centers set up; the famine retreated but the weakened population continued to succumb to cholera, malaria, and smallpox. The British nutritionist W. R. Aykroyd, who served on the Inquiry Commission, believes 3,000,000 people perished. Outside China and Soviet Russia it is the worst famine of the 20th century.

Right: a starving Indian family photographed during the Orissa famine of 1866–67. Such sights were a typical, and all-too-frequent, occurrence in the cities, where the arrival of starving families from the countryside was usually the first indication to the administration that crops had failed and famine was widespread.

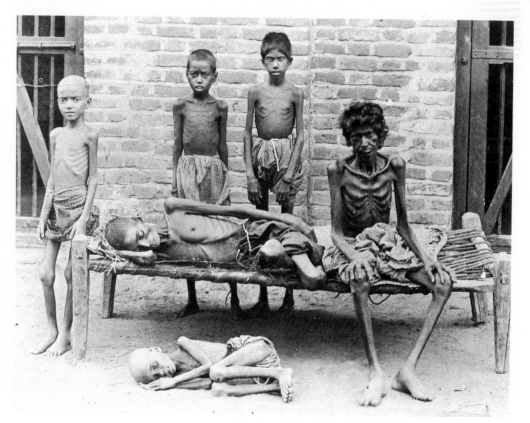

An Imposed Starvation
The Netherlands: 1944-45

last months of World War II when some 10,000 people died and hundreds of thousands were brought to within two or three weeks of death by starvation.

The liberation of the Netherlands was long delayed. Paris was liberated on August 23, 1944, Brussels 10 days later, and on September 5 jubilant crowds filled the streets of Rotterdam, Amsterdam, The Hague, and Haarlem, to celebrate what was believed to be the imminent arrival of Allied armies. But after the excitement of *Dolle Dinsdag* ("Mad Tuesday") the Dutch had to wait eight months for their freedom. They were to be months of agony.

During September 1944 the Allies launched the airborne attack on Arnhem, destined to end in failure. The exiled Dutch government in London instructed the Dutch railwaymen to strike, so as to hinder the German armies, and the railwaymen obeyed. Artur von Seyss-Inquart, the German high commissioner of the Netherlands, retaliated by stopping all movement of food into the western provinces of the country, a densely populated region that has always been dependent for food on the predominantly agricultural regions of the north and east.

Food soon became scarce. By mid-November the inhabitants of the larger towns were spending two or more days a week scouring the countryside on bicycles or with prams or handcarts in search of food.

In modern times famine in Europe is uncommon. Agricultural expertize and the generally benign climate mean that good use can be made of the land without exploiting it. But famine is only uncommon, not unknown. Efficient husbandry is no match for policies of starvation deliberately imposed in time of war. This was the experience of the Netherlands in the

Above: a small girl photographed as she searches trash cans for anything edible during the famine-winter of 1944–45 in the Netherlands. **Right:** an Allied attack on the strategic bridge at Arnhem on the north bank of the Lower Rhine. It was to assist this attack by glider-borne troops that the Dutch railway men went on strike. In retaliation, the Nazis carried out a policy of deliberate and cold-blooded starvation of the major cities in the western Netherlands.

Some potatoes and sugar beet could still be found but there were 4,500,000 people confined west of the river Ijssel and the situation steadily deteriorated. In the first week of December the week's rations were given as: 21 ounces of bread; $2\frac{1}{2}$ lbs of potatoes for children up to 14 years, none for older people; no butter, no fats, no sugar, no beans. Foodships arriving at the liberated Belgian capital of Antwerp unloaded flour, corned beef, canned soup, and other provisions but there was no way of transporting them to the Netherlands. In obedience to Seyss-Inquart's orders, potatoes were allowed to rot in the northeastern provinces rather than let them be taken west to relieve the sufferings of people starving in Rotterdam, Amsterdam, Utrecht, Dortdrecht, Delft, Haarlem, Gouda, and The Hague.

Five years of wartime shortages due largely to the fact that 60 percent of agricultural output was confiscated by the Germans had affected the general health of the people and the continuing rail strike led to depletion of fuel stocks. This together with the lack of food made it increasingly difficult to keep warm. In October the daily rations had amounted to 780 calories. By January 1945 they had dropped to 460 calories and by March to 320 calories – just over one tenth of the amount considered necessary for the needs of normal life. In January many people began

Above: one of the many starving young children during the famine. The young were particularly badly hit by the lack of protein essential to their diet up to the age of 14. Altogether, 10,000 people died.

ARNHEM BRIDGE, 5pm, THE SECOND DAY — David Shepherd —

to develop the symptoms of *famine oedema,* the "bloating" characteristic in famine victims when water accumulates in the spaces left between shrunken cell tissues. Fuel supplies were exhausted. Most areas were without a proper water supply and had no means of heating water or cooking what food they had. The majority of the deaths occurred among children below the age of 14, who require a high-protein diet for survival, and people over the age of 40. Many elderly people, particularly those who lived alone, starved to death in their beds. In Amsterdam the bodies of those who had died in the streets were taken into the churches and laid there by exhausted people without the strength to bury them.

Not until the beginning of May, one week before the end of the war, did Seyss-Inquart attend a meeting between Allied and German officers to work out means of relieving the famine. Food supplies were to be dropped by air; foodships entering Rotterdam – largely destroyed by Nazi sabotage – were to be conducted by the Germans to a safe harborage. With the end of the war Allied forces entered the Netherlands, accompanied and in some cases preceded by relief workers and supplies of food. Those who had survived the famine made good recoveries but in the words of the official report, the famine had come close to being a "very terrible catastrophe. Had the German occupying forces held out another two or three weeks against the Allied attack, nothing could have saved hundreds of thousands in the towns of the western Netherlands from death by starvation."

African Emergencies 1960-1969

enemies early in the fighting. An area that normally only just supported about 2,000,000 people now had to cope with the arrival of a further 300,000 exhausted and hungry refugees. Starvation was inevitable.

True famine did not occur. Instead, tens of thousands of children developed the distressing protein-deficiency disease, *kwashiorkor*. Given this name by

"Languid and misshapen, their feet and faces swollen, their stomachs distended with fluid and air, their arms wasted to the bone, their hair changed to the color of tobacco ash." This was the description of the hundreds of children, sleeping five to a bed or lying in the dust of the hospital grounds at Miawi, near Bakwanga, in the Congo.

When the Belgians withdrew from their former colony (now Zaire) in 1960 fighting broke out between the Luluas and the Baluba tribesmen in the Kasai province. The Baluba were beaten and fearing, with every justification, reprisals at the hands of their triumphant opponents, began streaming back from the north and west of Kasai to their homeland in the south. A clever and sophisticated people, the Baluba make competent administrators and shrewd traders but the poor soil and rolling grassland of south Kasai produces little surplus food. What meager stocks there were had been looted or destroyed by their

the Ga tribe of Ghana, it means literally "first-second" because symptoms tended to develop in a first child after a second had been born with the resulting deterioration in the quality of the elder child's diet. Growing children need protein as much as they need vitamins and a lack of protein will kill them. They lose weight, develop the bloated symptoms of oedema, the color of their hair becomes ashen or reddish, and they sink into a state of apathy – very distressing to witness – in which they no longer respond to external stimuli. A few weeks feeding with a protein-rich diet (generally skim milk) restores them to physical health, but the setback of kwashiorkor at a critical stage of childhood permanently affects their growth and mental development.

In south Kasai the only food the Baluba refugees could find was cassava, the tapioca root, which is almost pure starch and contains no protein. In November 1960 the first reports were coming in of starving men and women and of children dying at the rate of 200 a day. The United Nations Organization which had intervened in the civil war swiftly introduced relief operations. Vehicles and special foods were flown in. Skim milk and a gruel made of cassava were given to the children and by the end of January the estimated daily death rate had been reduced to

Above: bags of powdered milk being despatched to the starving region of eastern Nigeria which had seceded from the Nigerian Federation as "The Republic of Biafra." **Left:** a group of Biafran children rescued from the fighting. They are suffering from irreversible protein deficiency disease and are doomed to die. Throughout the eastern region some 2,000,000 people, mostly children, died. **Right:** a mother-and-child health clinic in Zaire operated by the Save the Children Fund. Its object is to improve child care and health and to eradicate such diseases as *kwashiorkor* the deadly protein-deficiency disease.

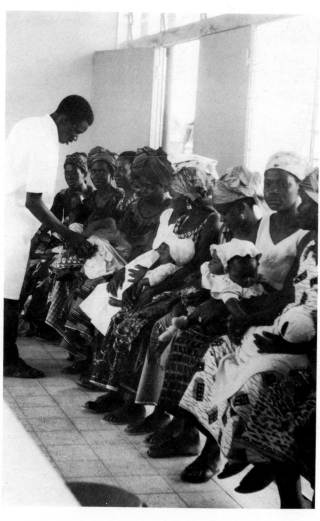

world only through a small air-strip at Uli. The Ibo people, who numbered 14 million at the start of the war, were crammed into a continually diminishing area. Cassava kept adults alive but the deaths of children from kwashiorkor were extremely heavy. Charitable organizations throughout the world were stirred by the plight of the Biafrans and organized

about 40. The dead and dying no longer lay unattended by the roadside. The new crop was being sown that would, in June, provide food to help make the region self-sufficient again.

Seven years later another civil war 1000 miles to the northeast of Kasai brought about severe famine to Nigeria, until then a famine-free area of Africa. Shortly after independence a struggle for power developed between the mainly Christian Ibo people in eastern Nigeria and the Moslem tribes of the north. Two bloody coups d'etat were followed by the defeat of the Ibos and, as in the Congo, their flight back to their homeland. In 1967 they declared their independence as the Republic of Biafra and a desperate war began that was to last 30 months.

After some initial successes the tide of the war turned and the Biafran frontiers were steadily eroded. Biafra became a steadily shrinking enclave, soon land-locked and eventually linked to the outside

"mercy flights" to the beleaguered people. At great personal risk pilots flew over Federalist Nigerian positions to reach Uli and unload hundreds of tons of stockfish, corn meal, dried milk, and other high-protein food. Perhaps because of this assistance the war dragged on until January 1970 and some people have blamed the relief system which although mounted to save lives actually prolonged the sufferings in which an estimated 2,000,000 people, mostly children, died.

The cost of such relief is enormous. The "mercy flights" each cost between £1250 and £1450, depending on the size of aircraft, and 2500 flights had been run by July 1969. The Red Cross alone was by then sending each month £800,000 to Nigeria and £500,000 to Biafra. The amount of aid received by the two sides would, as one Geneva worker put it, "keep a reasonably sized peaceful country in luxury for about five years."

Crisis in the Sahel 1968-1974

"sea." In normal years a small amount of rain between 4 and 20 inches falls in the summer. Wells are replenished and lakes form in old watercourses. In the southern Sahel fast-growing crops such as millet and sorghum are cultivated. Further north grasses spring up, reach maturity, and spread seeds.

For untold generations the Sahel had supported

During 1973 reports began to filter out from the interior of West Africa that a major disaster was looming for the nomadic herdsmen living on the southern fringes of the Sahara Desert. A prolonged drought had caused wells to dry. Men were starving and animals dying for want of pasturage. Television cameramen were quick to make their way to the area and the outside world became aware for the first time of the fascinating but sorely threatened belt of land that extends eastward across Africa for some 2000 miles – the Sahel.

Sahel comes from an Arabic word meaning "shore" and describes the area bordering the arid Saharan

settled farmers in the south and nomadic stock-breeders in the north. The most famous of the nomads are the Tuareg, a northern, Berber-speaking people, and their herds were traditionally limited by the quantity of dry-season pasturage within reach of their base well. At the end of the dry season the grass begins to grow throughout the region and the cattle move away from the grassy area around the well, giving it chance to recover before their return later on. A very subtle trading relationship developed between the nomads and the farmers who allowed the cattle to graze on the stubble in their fields after cropping. The soil would then be organically fertilized with their droppings. Famines had occurred in the past but the way of life was designed to withstand drought and minimize its effects.

A sequence of abnormally dry years began in 1969 but the warning signs passed largely unnoticed. The Sahel stretches from the port of Dakar, in Senegal on the west African coast, across what used to be French

Above: the despair in the faces of the women from Upper Volta, in the Sahel region is echoed in millions of other people who live in this area of prolonged drought. Luckier ones, like these women from Niger (**left**) can draw water from deep wells, but without rain to replenish the ground water they, too, will dry up – as many already have. **Right:** Europeans sinking new wells in Chad, another drought-struck country. New wells are not the whole solution; peoples of the area need to live in equilibrium with their harsh environment if new disasters are not to occur.

West Africa but is now six very poor nations – Senegal, Mauritania, Mali, Upper Volta, Niger, and Chad. All but the first two are landlocked and communications with the interior are rudimentary. Unconsidered development degraded the land both before and after independence from France in 1962. The sinking of deep wells dried up the older wells. Vaccination of animals led to the formation of herds greater than the land could feed. Overgrazing stripped the soil. In all the Sahelian states, attempts at industrialization and the introduction of a money economy disrupted a traditional system that had worked well enough. An emphasis on increased productivity led to

desertification of the land – the familiar "dustbowl" effect. Drought was all that was needed to bring about catastrophe in the area. Even so, drought was the trigger, not the prime cause of what was going wrong in the Sahel.

The first signs of crisis were noticed when the Tuareg appeared in towns much farther south than they usually visited, trying to sell off their animals. The men were famished, the cattle just skin and bones. Deaths among humans from famine as such were few, but starvation had weakened them and an estimated 100,000 died from famine-linked diseases, tuberculosis and typhus. Cattle losses were enormous. In the last two years of the drought Mauritania lost 1,600,000 cattle from a total of 2,100,000. When the drought was over Mali had to start the herds again from scratch. Crop losses ranged between 50 and 70 percent.

The Sahel region has been extended to include the former British colony of the Gambia, where the rice crop failed, and the Cape Verde Islands where no substantial rain has fallen for nine years. For these now desolate and wind-eroded islands – stripped of their timber by the Portuguese colonists – funds from international organizations have been provided to help conserve the soil and at the same time conserve the self-respect of the people.

This last factor has to be borne in mind in all relief programs. As soon as the Tuareg can gather together a small herd of around 2 camels, 3 cows, and 10 sheep, say, for a group of six or seven persons, they will leave the relief camps and return to the life they know best. They have now been taught to grow tomatoes and onions near the wells but essentially they are nomadic herdsmen still. To destroy their way of life is to destroy them. There will always be periodic droughts in the Sahel. Plans for development must ensure that man does not make them worse.

A Famine Averted
Bihar:1967

The fickle weather that plagues the long-suffering people of northeast India was at its most fickle in the mid 1960s. In 1964 a good monsoon brought a bumper crop, but throughout 1965 there was extensive drought and the surplus grain was used up. The 1966 season opened badly in all parts of India. Cyclones flattened the crop in Assam but nearly everywhere else the monsoon was late or failed almost entirely. In Bombay trading in the stock exchange was interrupted while stockbrokers prayed for rain. Many villagers fell back on ancient but unforgotten rites and sent maidens out to plow the fields at night, naked or dressed in men's clothing in the belief that it would bring rain and fertility back to the land.

Bengal neighbors its people have always been cruelly exposed to the vicissitudes of the weather. In the summer of 1966 the monsoon rains came for a few days and then stopped. The extensive rice crops that had begun to grow withered with the return of the hot dry weather. No further rain fell.

By October it was realized that the crops usually harvested at that time were an almost complete loss. Further, the ground had been baked so hard that farmers were unable to break it with their wooden plows and even where it could be broken it was too hard for seeds to be planted. Only in a few more fortunate areas could some be sown for the small spring harvest. For the majority of the 47 million people of Bihar there would be no food for the best part of a year except what was brought to them.

Bihar soon became a depressing spectacle of barren land, dry canals, and emaciated peasants. In those few areas where the crops could still be saved farmers worked night and day to draw what underground supplies of water were available. Bihar state government was sharply criticized for not having under-

Right: emaciated cattle in Bihar during the emergency of 1966–67 when the rains failed for the second year running. There is a large cattle population in Bihar but not enough good grazing land. In consequence, any drop in the rainfall means there is not enough grass to support the cattle. Drought is disastrous.

Bihar is one of the largest states in India. Here in the 6th century BC, at Gaya, near the state capital Patna, the young prince Siddhartha attained enlightenment and became Gautama Buddha. On the rich northern plains rice, corn, oilseeds, barley and wheat, sugar cane (Bihar is the original home of the sugar cane), jute, and tobacco are grown. But like its

taken the relatively minor irrigation schemes that could have lessened the approaching disaster. Less than seven percent of the agricultural land was protected by irrigation although in large areas of the state considerable sources of water exist underground, even during the worst droughts.

Wheat from the United States saved the Biharis.

Some 600 shiploads, arriving in India at the rate of three a day, brought 9,000,000 tons – one fifth of the United States annual crop – to Bihar and the other drought-stricken areas. In Bihar itself there was little confidence in the competence of the state government to distribute the food fairly. Many officials were inefficient, some corrupt. Fortunately an election in February 1967 resulted in the defeat of the ruling politicians and a new government tackled the problem with intelligence and energy. Assisted by an international force of relief workers, including several hundred members of the American Peace Corps, new wells were sunk, old wells improved, and pumps installed.

blow struck Bihar. Totally unexpected spring rains caught the harvested crops and did great damage to the state's profitable mango groves.

The great influx of foreign grain kept famine at bay. Food was short – and for a time water supplies became very short – but no one died of starvation. Cholera, smallpox, scourges that in the past invariably accompanied famine, never developed and the Biharis themselves proved capable of distributing the grain that came to them. Inevitably, there were cases of corruption and injustice, but when the summer monsoon brought the Bihar Emergency of 1967 to a close it was seen to have been one of the happier episodes in man's age-old campaign against famine.

Right: Biharis engaged in their centuries-old system of irrigation. There has never been enough water storage to meet the not-infrequent periods of drought.

Right: one of the many projects carried out by relief workers after the 1967 emergency was the installation of water tanks to hold reserves of water.

The new government opened "fair price shops" throughout the state, one in every fourth village, where the people could buy rations at controlled prices. To enable the people to pay for food work of various kinds, including irrigation schemes and stone-breaking, was started. In March the smaller than usual spring crop was harvested but then another

The War Against Drought

The chief responsibility for causing famine has shifted in the past half century from nature to man. Nature can still produce calamitous droughts when the monsoon fails or when changes occur in the pattern of rainfall distribution. But man can make the harmful effects of a drought very much worse.

Mankind has always had the ability to alter his environment for the worse. When the Roman Empire ruled the Mediterranean world North Africa was the "granary of Europe." Camels were unknown. Early Arab writers said that it would be possible to walk from one end of North Africa to the other without leaving the shade of trees. But the goats of those same Arabs destroyed the trees, and over-cultivation may have impoverished the soil. The sands of the desert now blow between the broken columns of once-flourishing Roman cities.

The current threat – some say the most serious danger man has ever had to face – is not one of too much destruction but too much creation. The world's present population of 4000 million is expected to rise by the end of the century to between 6000 and 7000 million. It has been pointed out that we already live in a starving world, where 2000 million people go hungry every day, where another 1500 million barely manage, and where the remaining fortunate 500 million need only worry about over-feeding. If nothing is done to alter the direction of present trends, conditions must become unimaginably worse by the year 2000. Then even the fortunate few millions will be affected.

The population of the earth increased only very slowly until the start of the 19th century. The reasons for this are simple. Infant mortality was high – only 2 out of 10 babies could expect to reach maturity – and in the prevailing state of medical ignorance, fewer people reached the age of 60, most died much younger.

Medical discoveries and improved standards of hygiene altered all that. In Europe and North America more infants survived, and by the 20th century many of the diseases that had been killers in previous ages (scarlet fever, diphtheria, smallpox) were brought under control. In the course of the Industrial Revolution in the 19th century the population of England quadrupled. If this trend had continued serious over-population could have resulted, but the danger was averted in the industrialized nations by the widespread desire to limit the size of families. Whereas families of 15 or 20 were by no means exceptional in the mid-19th century, so large a family today would be considered antisocial. In most of Europe and North America today population growth has stopped or is climbing only slowly.

It was only to be expected that doctors and missionaries should carry these discoveries of how to save lives to the rest of the world. It is a merciful mission

Above: an example of soil erosion brought about by deforestation for agriculture. With the loss of the covering canopy of trees, rains progressively wash away layer after layer of topsoil, scoring the hillside into deep gullies and exposing bare rock. Eventually the site is abandoned by the farmers.

that has proved to be a two-edged sword, however. In Asia, Africa, and South America the diseases native to those countries were controlled, infant mortality hurtled down – and the population rocketed up. The ordinary people had no special reason to limit the size of their families. The ambition to acquire material possessions played a large part in persuading Western couples to practice birth control. Where there are few material possessions, no such motive exists.

Doctors are understandably irritated when it is suggested they are responsible for the overpopulation threat that hangs over the world. They see the saving of life as their duty. The morality of restricting the application of life-saving remedies (death-control) only to those countries that practice birth-control is a very dubious one. Yet this has been seriously suggested as one of the solutions to the problem. Most people prefer the alternatives: more food and more birth control.

In many parts of the world attempts have been made to reclaim the desert, to make it, if not exactly the granary of the Middle East – at least produce useful food crops. After all, not only North Africa but much of the Middle East – Israel, Jordan, Iraq – was once fertile country covered with trees, which is how it got the name "the Fertile Crescent" in the first place. In Israel modern technology has been brought in to help with the problems of conserving water. The result is that in the semi-arid Negev peppers and tomatoes are now being grown under protective polythene cloches. Similar reclamation schemes are in progress elsewhere but the work is slow and costly.

Above: picking tomatoes on a kibbutz in the Negev. Piping water and establishing communes can turn a potentially fertile soil such as the semidesert Negev into an important economic factor in a country's life. Another area where this has happened in the Libyan Kufra Desert (below) where grasses and crops are now made to grow.

Irrigation is being extended in India but such work has to be carefully planned so as not to damage the existing water supply pattern. Indiscriminate sinking of boreholes can remove much of the underground water reserves and dry up the wells on which other communities depend. As in the Sahel region of West Africa, too many wells can lead to overgrazing and the disappearance of essential woodland. The increasingly higher prices of domestic fuels – kerosene for example – has led to widespread felling of trees and shrubs for firewood among poor communities. At Ouagadougou, the capital of Upper Volta, the fire-

and seepage through the porous sandstone banks of the lake. The spread of irrigation canals has brought with it the snail-borne disease of bilharzia where formerly the majority of the snails were swept away by the annual flood out to sea. To cap this tale of disasters, in a few decades the dam will have silted up so that it will no longer even do the job for which it was constructed.

Another approach to the solution of worldwide famine is the development of better-yield crops. Work in the Mexican International Maize and Wheat Improvement Center under its director Nobel-prize-

Right: dwarf hybrids, shown here on right of picture stand up to wind and rain much better than the long-stemmed variety (on left of picture), which have bent or snapped because their stalks are too slender – a fault that causes enormous losses in annual cereal yields.

wood reserves have been exhausted within a radius of 40 miles from the city, so that many people have to spend up to one quarter of their income buying expensive firewood from farther away. The use of dried dung as a cheap fuel prevents its prime use as a natural fertilizer. Cattle manure is traditionally used for fuel in India, an act of waste that would deeply shock a Chinese farmer where drought, floods, and war have brought famine in the past but where great ingenuity has been applied to minimize the harm caused by them. River irrigation brings water and fertile soil with it but the fertility of the fields is chiefly maintained with a manure of treated human excreta.

A sad example of a bold enterprise that was not thought through for possible drawbacks is the Aswan High Dam in Egypt. This was designed to extend irrigation by storing the floodwaters of the Nile for gradual release during the dry season. But the dam, built without sluices, retained the all-important silt and organic matter that had made the Nile Valley the richest farmland on earth. It held back, too, the plankton that had fattened the sardines and crustacea of the Eastern Mediterranean. Along the Nile there is a gain in water but a loss of fertility that has to be made good by artificial fertilizer – using much of the electricity generated at the dam. Not as much water as was expected has accumulated in Lake Nasser above the dam because of the loss through evaporation

winning Dr Norman E. Borlaug, has led to the evolution of "dwarf" varieties of wheat that give yields three to four times larger than previous varieties grown in the same locality. The principle behind the discovery is that plants with shorter, stiffer stems can use larger quantities of fertilizer to grow bigger ears without becoming topheavy and snapping off. This "Green Revolution" increased production of wheat in Mexico from 1,190,000,000 tons in 1960 to 2,100,000,000 tons in 1970. For the first time Mexico became self-sufficient in grain. Since the dwarf varieties were used in India, wheat production has nearly doubled. Other countries where they are now widely grown include Turkey, Lebanon, and Morocco. Similarly improved strains of rice have been developed. Japan is now self-supporting in rice and will soon become a rice-exporter. The Philippines already export 1,000,000 tons of rice a year.

But the Green Revolution is another mixed blessing. The new varieties of grain need heavy dosages of nitrogen fertilizer that not all countries have in sufficient quantity and which are expensive to obtain. Borlaug has stressed the need for chemical pesticides and even DDT, which has been shown to have highly destructive repercussions on animal life. But if the Green Revolution has been only a qualified success it has achieved one of Borlaug's aims, to give the world a breathing space of perhaps 20 years during which the dangers of overpopulation can be attacked.

Most governments now recognize the dangers and promote family planning schemes. Only natural forms of contraception are sanctioned by the Catholic Church but many of the laity seem to disregard this injunction. In Catholic Latin America some governments support family planning but not all, and in the states of Central America the population is doubling every 21 years. The work of persuading rural communities in developing nations of the urgent need to limit the size of families comes up against centuries of tradition in which exactly the opposite practice was encouraged. But in India, Thailand, China, Turkey, and many other developing nations Family Planning posters can be seen contrasting two happy parents and their two happy children with two miserable parents and their all-too-numerous, glum-faced, and hungry children.

Unless large-scale nuclear war or worldwide chemical poisoning drastically reduces the population of the world, birth control must be made to work. It is both the painless and the most certain way to avoid the horrors of such natural checks on human populations as widescale disease and the misery of untold millions of starving, dying humans.

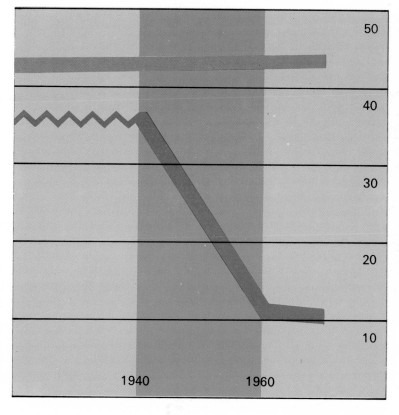

Above: a plague hospital in the 15th century. Plague and disease had a controlling effect on population growth before the advent of modern medicine

Above: a chart of birth-rates (top) and death-rates (bottom) of eight countries shows that birth-rate between 1940 and 1960 rose only a little, while death-rates fell staggeringly. It is death control, not any slight rise in birth-rate, that has caused the population avalanche.

Right: India is one of the countries where a vigorous propaganda campaign is being carried out to encourage people to limit the size of their families. This poster stresses the material benefits of a smaller family.

Chapter 6

Fire as Enemy

The roar of the flames, the searing heat, the wild uncontrollable terror of a forest on fire, were probably man's first introduction to an element that can change in minutes from a gentle flame to a monstrous killer. As the centuries passed man learned to harness fire to warm his caves and to keep away wild animals at night. Later he used it to cook food, shape weapons, change clay into pots.

But though fire is a good friend, it remains a bad enemy. As man congregated first into settlements, then towns, then great cities, accidental fires destroyed what he had so painstakingly built up. Most of the world's cities have had at least one major conflagration in their past, and many have had a regular history of smaller ones.

In modern times, war and earthquakes are the most likely cause of large-scale fires – but accidental fire in single buildings can still produce tragically high death tolls. And forest fires, the oldest fire danger of them all, continue to be a seasonal danger in large areas of the world.

Opposite: a bush fire in Australia. Forest and bush fires are an ever-present hazard in countries with extensive woodlands and low density population, such as Australia, America, Canada, and the USSR. Every year millions of acres of forest are consumed by fires – which can be started by lightning or, more frequently, lighted matches, cigarettes, or neglected campfires.

Fire Hazards

On February 1, 1974, a fire broke out on the 11th floor of the 25-story Joelma Building in Sao Paulo, Brazil, trapping hundreds of office workers on the upper floors. The building had been designed with virtually no fire escapes. Highly flammable plastics and paint were used on windows and flooring, and to make matters worse, although Sao Paulo had a population of 6,000,000, it possessed only 13 fire stations – with totally insufficient equipment to cope with such a blaze. The ladders were far too short and as the fire roared through the upper floors desperate people,

their hair in flames, flung themselves off the upper ledges. Helicopters could not approach the building for two hours but then rescued about 100 people who had managed to reach the roof. After the fire 227 bodies, with heads, arms, or legs burned away were recovered. Others just disappeared in the 700°C inferno.

In the depths of the forest near St Laurent du Pont, 20 miles from Grenoble in Southern France stood a hangarlike building known as the Club Cinq-Sept. The inside walls and columns were covered with shaped plastic to give the building a grotto effect – the plastic was highly inflammable, however, and should never have been used in any building work. On November 1, 1970, the Club was packed with young people and shortly before 2 a.m. a youth dropped a match onto a cushion. After he and his friends had failed to beat it out themselves they called "fire," and those who heard them were able to make their way safely out of the building. Suddenly a giant flame streaked down the length of the dance floor and within seconds the interior of the Club was an inferno of smoke and flame. The plastic arches melted onto the dancers, many of whom died where they stood, in each other's arms. The main exit, worked by a turnstile, jammed; the other two had been locked; the two fire exits were not illuminated and one was obscured behind stacks of chairs. Countless safety regulations had been ignored in building and approving the Club Cinq-Sept – neglect and incompetence that cost the lives of 146 young people.

There is perhaps something especially terrifying about even the thought of being trapped in a blazing building. Even so, how much more horrifying to

Above left: people escaping by ladder from the blazing Joelma Building in São Paulo, Brazil, on February 1, 1974. **Left:** some of the extensive damage to the Joelma Building can be seen in this gutted office.

escape the building only to find that every building is on fire, every street. Such is the situation for those caught within a burning city. Clouds of stifling smoke confuse fugitives as to which direction safety lies. Glowing cinders fall on all sides. There is the added shock of having to abandon home and contents to certain destruction, the agony of searching for children or other relatives, lost, or perhaps lying trapped or injured, calling for help. The eventual loss of life, surprisingly, depends on how the fire is started and how it progresses.

Fires that spread from building to building and eventually burn large areas, sometimes whole towns, are generally called *conflagrations*. They burn quickly but most of the population manages to escape. For example, only eight people died in the 1666 Great Fire of London. In World War II several cities heavily attacked by incendiary bombs developed huge fires that were caused by enormous numbers of separate fires all burning together. What are called *Firestorm* conditions developed and the population was trapped. In the Hamburg raids of July 1943 over 100,000 people perished.

Not all fires are caused by man's negligence or aggression. Forces of nature such as earthquakes can produce straightforward conflagrations, as in San Francisco in 1906. Then, a few fires gradually spread across the city because no water was available to put them out. In the case of the Tokyo earthquake and fire of 1923, which occurred at lunchtime, it was not lack of water, but tens of thousands of charcoal braziers, lit only a few moments before, that overturned and started tens of thousands of fires. Terrifying fire tornadoes raged across the city, one of which

swept into a park where 40,000 had taken refuge and roasted alive all but a few hundred on the outskirts.

Fire has always been employed as an instrument of war. In the Ancient World cities were sacked, set alight, and razed to the ground so that the site would never again be occupied. This was the fate of Troy, whose whereabouts disappeared from the knowledge of men for 3000 years. Cities have also been set ablaze as acts of persecution and revenge. Hideous scenes marked the massacre of the Greek and Armenian Christians of Smyrna (now Izmir) in 1922 when the Turkish soldiers fired the city and utterly destroyed some three fifths of it. The loss of life was impossible to calculate.

Cities have been fired to prevent them giving shelter to an enemy. Moscow in 1812 is the most celebrated example, but during the Thirty Years' War Magdeburg was burned by its Lutheran defenders on the day it fell to the Catholics. In the strong wind the largely wooden city was a furnace within minutes. Lutherans and Catholics, about 25,000 in all, perished in the inferno and for 14 days afterward a train of wagons carried the charred bodies to the river.

Modern improvements in building and in firefighting technique mean that, except when caused by earthquake or war, large conflagrations are now rare. Unfortunately, faults in construction still expose individual buildings to risk and the destructive fire of today is usually of this sort. Because people inside the building usually find themselves trapped the deathtoll tends to be tragically high.

Typical fires of today are different from those of the Ancient World but the horror of death by fire has not diminished.

Above: a fire chief tests some of the highly inflammable plastic material use on the walls of the Club Cinq-Sept. **Left:** the interior of the club Cinq-Sept dance hall at St Laurent du Pont, France, after the fire of November 1, 1970.

When Rome Burned
64 AD

In 64 AD the greatest fire of the ancient world all but destroyed its greatest city – Rome. The contemporary Roman historians agree that the fire was started on the orders of Nero, the vain, capricious, and bored emperor of the time, but disagree as to his motives. Some say he was offended by all the drab old buildings of Rome and wanted to expand his palace – which already covered two of the seven hills on which Rome stood. He may have wished merely for a new sensation – not the mock disasters of the theater and gladiator show, but the real thing.

Shortly before the fire one of his favorites, probably his chief adviser and evil genius Ofonius Tigellinus,

of stores by the Circus Maximus at the foot of the Palatine Hill. Fanned by the wind, it quickly swept the whole length of the Circus where there were no walled mansions or temples or any other obstruction to arrest it. From the Circus it spread into the surrounding districts, its swift progress aided by the narrow winding streets.

The historian Tacitus was an eyewitness and vividly describes the scene: "Terrified, shrieking women, helpless old and young, people intent on their own safety, people unselfishly supporting invalids or waiting for them, fugitives and lingerers alike – all heightened the confusion. When people looked back, menacing flames sprang up before them or outflanked them. When they escaped to a neighboring quarter, the fire followed – even districts believed remote proved to be involved. Finally, with no idea where or what to flee, they crowded on to the country roads, or lay in the fields. Some who had lost everything – even their food for the day – could have escaped but preferred to die. So did others, who had failed to rescue

Left: the Emperor Nero, who, rumor had it, started the fire of Rome in 64 AD and, to the accompaniment of his lyre, sang of the destruction of Troy, comparing the misfortunes of the time with calamities of the past. **Right:** the fire of Rome. It started at the Circus Maximus and fanned by the wind, destroyed a large part of old Rome.

happened to quote a line from a Greek play, "When I am dead, may fire consume the earth," but Nero replied that the first part of the line should read, "While I yet live." What was decided between the two is unknown but on July 17 the emperor departed for the coastal town of Actium and two days later Rome was a sea of surging flame. The fire began in a street

their loved ones. Nobody dared fight the flames. Attempts to do so were prevented by menacing gangs. Torches, too, were openly thrown in, by men crying that they acted under orders."

The fire burned for six days and seven nights. Among the countless buildings destroyed were mansions, shrines, and temples dating back to Rome's earliest days. Oldest was the temple dedicated to Jupiter by Romulus, the founder of the city 800 years before. Nero returned to Rome in time to see his palace on the Palatine Hill overwhelmed by the flames. He watched the burning city from a tower in his gardens, enraptured by what he called "the beauty of the flames"; then he put on the costume of a tragedian and sang verses from *The Fall of Troy* in his husky voice, accompanying himself on the lyre.

The fire was only brought to an end when buildings in its path were demolished. Three of the city's 14 districts were totally consumed, another seven were reduced to a few scorched and mangled ruins. Nero refused to let anyone search the rubble even of his own mansion, wanting, Tacitus says, "to collect as much loot as possible for himself." He rebuilt his palace on a colossal scale with a statue of himself 120 feet high in the entrance hall and a pillared arcade a mile long. The gardens contained lakes and entire woods. "Good," he declared when he moved into it, "now I can at last begin to live like a human being."

At least he had Rome rebuilt sensibly. A certain proportion of every building had to be of fireproof stone. Heights were restricted and porches projected from the front so that fire-fighters would have easier access in the event of future fires.

To suppress the rumor that he had started the fire he searched for scapegoats and picked on the considerable numbers of Christians living in Rome. Arrests were made and torture produced the names of a great many others – among them, it is believed, Saint Peter. Some were crucified, others met their death in the Circus where they were dressed in the skins of wild animals and torn to pieces by dogs. The gruesome spectacle continued after nightfall in Nero's gardens where more Christians were used as living torches. Tacitus, though no lover of Christians, adds that these victims of Nero's cruelty were pitied, no one believing them to be responsible for the fire. Their horrible fate in the first of the Persecutions, and the image of the emperor "fiddling while Rome burned," kept the memory of the fire alive down the centuries.

The Great Fire
London: 1666

into the city center, the fire had taken on the shape of a "great bow of flame." The fire spread from the slums to the better-class districts and a desperate scramble began for boats and carts to carry furniture away. The boatmen, their own homes already destroyed, were able to charge tremendous prices for their services. Above the roar and crackling of the flames

Left: people scrambling into boats as fire consumes London in 1666. **Right:** part of a panoramic map of crowded, congested London. Old Saint Paul's Church can be seen in the right of the center of the map.

Below: a Dutch painting of the Fire of London. London Bridge is seen on the left, the Tower of London on the right.

When the weary, disheveled Lord Mayor of London, Sir Thomas Bludworth, surveyed his city on September 6, 1666, five sixths of the largely medieval city lay in smoking charred ruins. Some 85 churches, and over 13,000 houses had been burned to the ground in this most famous of all fires.

The fire began on Sunday September 2, 1666 in a baker's shop in Pudding Lane, a mean little street sloping down to the river between London Bridge and the Tower. The smell of smoke awoke the baker's servant at 2 a.m. and he aroused his master who escaped with his family by climbing out of the garret window onto the roof of the house next door. His maid-servant was too frightened to follow and became the Fire's first fatality.

At that time London, with its narrow, congested streets of oak-framed houses, its back-to-back poorer dwellings, covered with weatherboarding coated with pitch, their projecting upper stories nearly touching those across the street, was one enormous fire hazard. Soon the flames had spread to the Star Inn across the lane. The inn yard was a storeplace for straw and fodder and houses on all sides were soon alight. By 3 a.m. the Lord Mayor had been roused and brought to the scene. Sir Thomas was unimpressed and went back to bed. But Pudding Lane was crossed by Thames Street where the wharves were stacked with hemp, pitch, oil, and spirits. Once this inflammable area was ablaze the fire grew fiercer. By 8 a.m. the houses on the north end of the bridge had burned and collapsed, destroying the pumps that worked most of the city's water supply. The first church was burning and its high roof was sending embers floating onto the surrounding houses.

Moving rapidly along the riverside but more slowly

the church bells could be heard ringing reverse peals. This was the traditional warning of fire although few Londoners can have heeded the warning.

The following day, Monday, the fire reached the quarters of the wealthy merchants but worse was to follow on the Tuesday. "It made me weep to see it," wrote the diarist Samuel Pepys. St. Paul's was ablaze

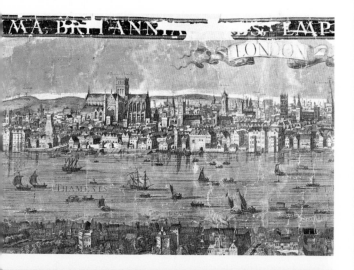

Above: many of the refugees from the fire automatically made their way toward the river Thames where they escaped by boat – while boatmen made handsome profits for their services.

and its six acres of leaden roofs poured down into the churchyard "like snow before the sun." The fire consumed 34 churches that day together with nearly all the richly decorated medieval halls of the city companies. The king, Charles II, joined the fire-fighters and was to be seen "smoke-grimed and ash-covered, handling spade and bucket, his laced coat wet and filthy." Eventually gunpowder was brought in from the dockyards and house by house entire streets were demolished. A barrel of powder would be placed in a house and ignited by a long fuse; when the explosion had destroyed the building seamen with ropes and chains dragged the debris away into the side streets. This way the fire was at last halted on the Thursday. Miraculously, only eight people died as a direct result of the fire, but more than 100,000 people were homeless and thousands ruined beyond hope of recovery. Many once-prosperous merchants ended their lives in the misery of the debtors' prison.

Although the architect Sir Christopher Wren's plans for rebuilding London would have made it the finest 17th-century city in the world, the citizens resisted his splendid conception and the houses went up again on the same old sites. Admittedly, building regulations specified the materials (brick or stone) and limited the height, but the opportunity to create a spacious and gracious city was lost.

Flames of Defiance!
Moscow: 1812

Above: the old city of Moscow ablaze after the French army occupied it in 1812. Nearly the whole city was destroyed.

Moscow in the 19th century, like most cities in the Russian Empire, was almost wholly built of timber, with the result that accidental fires were always breaking out – small ones, usually, but sometimes severe. In Moscow's most famous fire, the Fire of 1812, the great city that was to be Napoleon's prize was deliberately set alight and Napoleon found himself surrounded by ruins. It was one of the biggest disappointments of his life.

The French emperor's *Grande Armeé* marched into Russia on June 24. The Russian army withdrew before the French and by August 18 Napoleon entered Smolensk. On September 7 the armies met at Borodino where 50,000 men were killed. The battle was indecisive but the Russians retreated again and on September 12 the *Grande Armeé* had advanced to the top of the range of hills south of Moscow and saw the green, and blue, and golden domes of the city's 2000 churches glittering in the distance. Napoleon hastened forward to the view and gazed down at the city that would mark his greatest triumph. He was observed to smile.

The hours passed and the expected deputation of Muscovites did not emerge from the gates. A party of French officers managed to get through the walls and sent back word that the city was deserted. Napoleon could hardly believe it, "Moscow deserted!" he said, "A most unlikely event! We must enter it and ascertain the fact."

Enter it they did and found the streets and houses silent with no sight or sound of a Muscovite anywhere. Napoleon himself entered the city that evening and lodged in the suburbs. That night the fires began. At first it was thought French soldiers must have started them while looting because the flames were coming from the merchant's palaces in the wealthier quarter of the city. But the next morning Napoleon was shown "houses covered with iron roofs; closely shut up and without any marks of violence or an attempt to break into them: yet a black smoke was already issuing from them." Napoleon entered the ancient citadel of the Kremlin, thoughtful and uneasy, but daylight made the task of controlling the fires simpler. Order was re-established and the French went to their beds with easier minds. At midnight the city was ablaze again. Palaces were enveloped in huge flames; flakes of burning material were being borne in the wind toward the Kremlin's roofs. This time there was no doubt who was responsible. Before their departure the Russians had released prisoners from the jails and given them access to huge quantities of combustible materials and fuses. Preparations were laid with the greatest secrecy. Evidently the Russian authorities did not trust the citizens to destroy their own city. On the other hand, the secrecy would have allowed them to blame the French for the fire if this failed in its objective of driving Napoleon out.

Napoleon gave orders for incendiaries to be shot although he found it hard to accept that the Russians could wish to destroy so great a city. He kept hurrying to the Kremlin windows – where the glass was too hot for him to touch – to study the progress of the fire. The fire gained ground every moment, the bridges were alight as well as the neighboring houses so that he was almost a prisoner within the Kremlin walls. At last came the cry, "The Kremlin is on fire!" A tower was blazing and French grenadiers were bayoneting the man who had set it alight. Napoleon was now convinced the Russians proposed to destroy everything and he prepared to leave.

The flames, dust, and thick smoke made it almost impossible to find a way across the city. The Emperor selected a narrow street "crooked and in every part on fire . . . amidst the perils of dividing roofs and falling beams, and domes covered with melting iron, all scattering tremendous ruins around him. They were walking on a soil of fire, under a sky of fire, and between walls of fire."

Napoleon managed to make his way out of the inferno. Next day the fires were still burning. To the French camped in the fields around the city, Moscow looked like an ocean of flame. It continued to do so until the first rains came on September 18 and the French moved back into a rain-soaked ruined city. Nine tenths of it had been destroyed. After waiting a month the first snow began to fall and Napoleon led his army out of Russia. The Great Retreat with all its attendant horrors had begun. The burning of Moscow had turned Napoleon's hollow victory into a catastrophic defeat.

Above: Napoleon makes his way out of the burning city that was to turn his victorious prize to ashes.

Right: the Muscovites themselves burned their city of 2000 churches and innumerable palaces and mansions to deprive Napoleon of his goal.

The Blazing Church
Santiago, Chile: 1863

"Never was there anything more hideous than the catastrophe at Santiago." So began the leading article of the London *Times* when news at last reached Europe, after an eight week journey from Chile by mailboat, of the fire that on December 8, 1863, burned to death some 2500 women and children in the Jesuit church of La Compania. Over a century later this figure for deaths caused by fire in a single building had still not been surpassed.

December 8 was the Feast of the Immaculate Conception. For a month beforehand the Jesuits had been celebrating a splendid festival in their great 17th-

century church. The interior was festooned with drapes of muslin, pasteboard, and paper, and illuminated by 20,000 colored lamps hung in festoons, in niches, on ledges, and wherever it was possible to place them. The lamps were fed with camphene, an oil distilled from turpentine, and it took so long to light them all that the church servants had to begin in the middle of the afternoon. Every night the church was packed with worshipers, mainly women, kneeling or sitting on the small hand-carpets they brought with them. There were no chairs and the congregation, perhaps 3000 in all, were packed closely together. Fewer men attended the ceremonies and those that did so stood near the back, segregated from the women by an iron grating.

On the fatal evening, climax of the month's celebrations, more lamps than ever before had been lit. A certain Father Ugarte had ordered this after hearing that the visiting Apostolic Nuncio (a papal representative) had said the illuminations at Santiago could not be compared with those he had seen in Rome. Father Ugarto retorted, "I will give him . . . such an illumination as this world has never seen!" No one can deny that he kept his word.

The church was packed, the lamps had almost all been lit and were gleaming along the nave, high up in the wooden roof, and in the lofty dome. In the middle of the high altar stood a statue of the Virgin Mary, her feet upon a crescent moon in imitation of the painting by Murillo in the Louvre. At 7 p.m. the last lamps inside this canvas and wood half-moon were lit – and set fire to one end of it. The flame spread instantly to the paper garlands on the altar and swept from there up the vast muslin drapes to the roof. There was a scream of horror and a surge to escape. The men behind the grating left without difficulty by the side door. Father Ugarto and the other priests hastened to the sacristy door which they then *shut*, apparently so as not to be inconvenienced while they removed the church silver to a place of safety. For the women in the body of the church the only exit was the main door opening onto the Plazuela de la Compania.

A few hundred managed to escape but in the panic some women tripped and fell, others fell over them and

Left: the ruins of the Church of La Compania, Santiago, Chile, after the horrific fire on December 8, 1863. Right: the blazing Church at Santiago reconstructed in this picture from eyewitness reports. A gaucho can be seen trying to pull people out of the inferno with a lasso. In the foreground are women with their dresses on fire.

the door was soon blocked by a living barricade of screaming women in layers on top of each other. As the flames raced along the roof the festoons of lamps exploded and a rain of burning oil poured down onto the women below, setting fire to their fine clothes, their fans, their mantillas, their hair. Would-be rescuers outside were unable to enter the church because of the blocked doorway. A passing gaucho threw his lasso into the church "and a thousand hands tried to catch hold of it. Some did seize it, and were dragged out by the man and the strength of the horse; but the second time the same attempt was made the lasso gave way."

What followed next was described in a Santiago newspaper as "the most harrowing sight that ever seared human eyeballs."

"To see mothers, sisters . . . dying that dreadful death . . . within one yard of salvation – within one yard of men who would have given their lives over and over again for them! It was maddening; the screaming and wringing of hands for help as the remorseless flames came on – and then their horrible agony – some in prayer – some tearing their hair and battering their faces."

Within 15 minutes the horror was over. "Women seized in the embrace of the flames were seen to undergo a transformation as though by an optical illusion, first dazzlingly bright, then horribly lean and shrunk up, then black statues rigidly fixed in a writhing attitude."

The following day 200 cartloads of human remains were removed from the ruined church. Two thirds of the dead were servants; the remainder were "the flower of Society." Most of the victims were between the ages of 15 and 20. The priests were held responsible for the catastrophe and feeling against them ran very high. Those priests who returned to the blackened ruin to say mass for the dead were driven off by sentinels with the butt end of their muskets. The church was never rebuilt.

Chicago in Flames 1871

In the space of 39 years Chicago grew from a settlement of a few hundred people to an important grain, stock market, railroad and farm machinery center. In 1871 block after block of offices and marble-fronted stores lined the streets in its business section and the city boasted a population of 334,000 people. Yet in only 27 hours, fire burned the heart out of this prosperous, populous city, destroying all the great hotels, all the banks, all the theaters, the Opera House, the City Hall, and 18,000 other buildings – including, in the sixth hour of the fire, the Water Works.

The fire began at 9.30 in the evening of October 8, 1871, in Patrick O'Leary's barn. Some say Mrs. O'Leary went out to milk one of her cows and the cow kicked a lighted kerosene lamp into a pile of shavings. Mrs. O'Leary claimed she was in bed at the time. Obscure though the cause of the fire remains to this day, the O'Leary barn was soon ablaze and set fire to two others. The barns burned briskly and before the firemen had reached the scene the flames had burned diagonally through the block, crossed the street and were swiftly burning into the next block, driven on by the strong southwest winds. The O'Leary barn stood in the southwest area of Chicago, separated by the river from the more valuable areas of the city. Two miles distant (but due northeast) stood the towers and battlements of the Water Works – but no one supposed the fire would reach the river, still less cross it.

These fond hopes were soon shattered. In the busi-

Above: Mrs O'Leary and her cow. According to tradition, the cow knocked over a lighted kerosene lamp setting fire to the barn and eventually burning down most of Chicago in 1871.

ness area of the city the newer and higher buildings were of marble, stone, and brick; elsewhere the city was largely constructed of wood: wooden walls, wooden roofs, wooden sidewalks. There had been no rain for six weeks. As if this were not sufficient to start an inferno, in the path of the fire lay numerous stables, lumber depots, distilleries, grain stores, and coal yards. The wind-driven fire had soon reached the river and at 20 minutes past midnight a huge blazing board was blown across to land on the roof of a three-story tenement, dry as a tinderbox. The roof was instantly in a blaze and within seconds flames were racing at an incredible speed through the joining wooden houses and littered alleys. The flames spread as fast as a man could walk. So intense was the heat that six-story buildings took fire and disappeared within five minutes. Marble burned like wood. The First National Bank was supposed to be fireproof. Its walls did not burn but so great was the heat coming from outside that the iron girders expanded upward, "breaking the iron ceilings, crashing the exterior walls, and leaving the building a wreck and a ruin."

Two journalists from the *Chicago Daily Tribune* wrote an eyewitness account of the fire: "Flames would enter at the rears of buildings, and appear simultaneously at the fronts. For an instant the windows would redden, then great billows of fire would belch out, and meeting each other, shoot up into the air a vivid, quivering column of flame, and

poising itself in awful majesty, hurl itself bodily several hundred feet and kindle new buildings.... The whole air was filled with glowing cinders, looking like an illuminated snowstorm. Interspersed among these cinders were larger brands, covered with flame, which the wind dashed through windows and upon awnings and roofs, kindling new fires. Strange fantastic fires of blue, red, and green, played along the cornices of the buildings. On the banks of the river, red hot walls fell hissing into the water, sending up great columns of spray and exposing the fierce white furnaces of heat which they had enclosed."

The leading fires swept northeastward across the city until they reached the lake. Subsidiary blazes spread sideways and then they too swept northeastward. People who piled their valuables into a trunk and dragged it to some other house or open space soon had to flee for their lives, abandoning what they had saved, as the flames raced to yet another part of the city thought to be safe. Falling sparks kept igniting the clothes of the fugitives, 76,000 in all, as they hurried through the streets, in the stifling smoke, buildings ablaze in every direction, the horrible roar of the fire behind. Groups of panicking horses plunged through the pressing crowds. The desperate howling of chained dogs, abruptly stilled, gave another dimension of horror to the terrible scene.

In all, 96,000 people were made homeless. An area of three and one third square miles was entirely de-

Above: citizens of Chicago camping out in the ruins of their city after the fire. **Left:** the fire at its height. There had been no rain for six weeks when the fire started and the still largely wooden city was soon a mass of flame.

stroyed except for the mansion of Mahlon D. Ogden. All the carpets and blankets in the house were hung over the fronts and roofs, and kept soaked first with water and then with barrels of cider until the flames had passed by on either side. The buildings and properties destroyed were valued at $196,000,000. Patrick O'Leary's house was undamaged.

Forest Fires

Above: a new method of fighting a forest fire – by helicopter. Chemicals are being sprayed on the fire to deprive it of oxygen.

"It came in great sheeted flames from heaven," said one survivor. "The atmosphere was all afire," said another. This awesome description could fit almost any of the world's great forest fires. In fact the two speakers were from the town of Peshtigo, Wisconsin, They had lived through the fierce horror of America's worst forest fire, a tornado of flame that swept along the northwestern shores of Lake Michigan destroying 1,280,000 acres of forest on October 8, 1871.

Fires were considered a seasonal hazard in the states of Wisconsin and Michigan. Normally they gave little cause for alarm. The summer of 1871, however, had been excessively dry, with small fires continually breaking out in the sparsely populated Green Bay region. The local people had taken the usual precautions, what changed the situation from normality to disaster was the wind of gale force that sprang up on the evening of October 8. By a sinister coincidence the same wind that same evening fanned the Great Chicago Fire 200 miles to the south. It was shortly after 9 pm when the townspeople of Peshtigo first became aware of a terrible roar approaching. The sky glowed red with clouds of flame. Survivors emphasized that the fire did not advance upon them gradually, burning from tree to tree, but came as a

whirlwind of flame high above the tops of the trees, towering flames that fell upon the earth beneath and enveloped everything. Men who breathed the intensely hot air died at once. In some cases their bodies were found scarcely burned; more often they were reduced to heaps of charred bones.

From the head of Green Bay a belt of fire 15 miles wide swept north for 40 miles and nothing could stop it. Farms, sawmills, small factories, all were reduced to cinders, and 1152 people died. In one settlement the entire population had tried to save themselves by climbing into a well. After the disaster 32 bodies were brought out, all drowned or crushed to death.

Only certain areas of the world are exposed to such risks – and the loss of life has seldom approached the high death toll of Wisconsin in 1871. Fires rarely occur in the tropical rain forests and only in unusual circumstances do they cause extensive damage to the broad-leaved deciduous forests of temperate zones. But coniferous forests are always at risk after a dry hot spell, the resinous needles, alive or dead, forming an ideal fuel. The great fire of Maine and New Brunswick in 1852 destroyed 3,000,000 square miles of forest. The leaves of evergreen broad-leaved trees (holly, evergreen oak, eucalyptus), covered with a natural

112

inflammable wax also make an ideal fuel. In Australia, where the open forest land is known as *bush*, eucalyptus grows over extensive areas and assists the spread of bush fires in the hot dry season of December to February.

Nothing today compares in horror with the notorious Black Thursday of February 6, 1851, when the temperature in Melbourne reached 117°F in the shade at 11 a.m. The whole of Western Victoria was like one vast hayfield, bleached by weeks of scorching sun and inflammable as tinder. By the afternoon the entire state seemed to be ablaze. Flames surged across the grassland faster than a horse could gallop and when they reached the bush flew along the treetops while through the tangled undergrowth there roared a sea of fire. Even today, with increased population, better warning systems, and more effective firefighting equipment, wide tracts of grassland and forest are destroyed most years, with more devastating outbreaks occurring about once in a generation. The summer of 1951–52 brought appalling fires to New South Wales, burning more than 6,000,000 acres of bush. So great is the heat generated by these bush fires that steel girders and machinery are twisted as though they were made of fine wire.

In Europe the forests most often endangered are the great pine forests of southern France, particularly those of the Landes. In this region, between the river Garonne and the Bay of Biscay, some fires occur every year and the poorer people locally benefit, collecting charred trunks and branches for winter fuel. Occasionally these fires get out of hand, as happened spectacularly in August 1949. Drought had been more or less continuous since the previous October and had become intense since June. The fires started near the village of Saucats, 15 miles south of Bordeaux, and swept north and west, encircling villages and hamlets. Pine trees are the basis of the economy in the region, producing turpentine and timber for pit props, but 500 square miles were destroyed before the fire could be brought under control. The Mayor of Saucats lost his life fighting the fire and 83 others died – the majority on August 20 when a sudden shift and rise in the wind revived a dormant fire and suddenly changed its direction, fatally trapping 60 civilian and soldier firefighters. A day of National Mourning was announced. Throughout France flags flew at half mast. In the words of one commentator, "A peaceful corner has suddenly been turned by fiery disaster into a charred district of mourning."

Above: a firefighter moves in to deal with a bush fire in Australia. Bush fires are some of the most difficult fires to deal with because of the rapidity with which they move. **Left:** a forest fire in the hills around San Bernadino, California.

Fire Services and Fire Prevention

On Christmas Day 1971 a gas stove exploded in a coffee shop on the second floor of the Daiyunkuk Hotel in Seoul, capital of South Korea. The fire that raged through the 222-room hotel – opened only two years before – killed at least 165 people, possibly more. Some of the heaps of charred bones could be identified only by the rings or wristwatches found among them. Mattresses were put down to break the fall of the 38 people who jumped from the upper floors – but in vain, all were killed. Inquiries later revealed that although the original designs for the hotel had been officially approved, changes were subsequently introduced that contravened safety regulations.

seven-story building were used as a hotel and nightclub. A bed in a hotel room caught fire from a cigarette and flames roared through the top two floors. Of the 88 people who died, 64 of them were young couples trapped in the nightclub because the doors were locked – apparently to make sure no one left without paying the bill.

Fires in high-rise buildings present one of today's greatest problems to fire-protection services. In Europe the aerial ladder can be extended to 150 feet, in the United States to 100 feet. Yet the world's highest building, the Sears Building in Chicago, is 1450 feet high, and buildings of more than 20 stories are commonplace in all the world's major cities. Helicopters have been used to rescue people trapped in high buildings but this cannot always be attempted until the fire has passed its peak. When the Joelma Building in São Paulo caught fire, smoke and flames prevented helicopters getting near until two hours after the blaze took hold. The heat peeled paint off the helicopter doors. In this "towering inferno" some fire-

Left: the death-toll at the Cocoanut Grove Club in Boston in 1942 reached 474 because of a reckless disregard of safety measures. Many guests were crushed and smothered in the stampede to get through the tiny vestibule and jammed swing doors at the club's entrance.

The difficulties of enforcing adequate fire protection are well illustrated by the disturbing fact that three years later two other serious fires occurred in hotels in Seoul. In the fire that gutted the nine-story Namsan Hotel in October, 1974, 19 people died. These deaths were attributed to insufficient fire-fighting equipment in the hotel and to the thick smoke and gas that came from the burning carpets and wallpaper. The following month casualties in the Daowang Corner Building fire were four times greater. The top two floors of this

men heroically rescued people trapped on window ledges by swinging over to them on ropes from adjacent buildings. Sergeant José Rufina saved 18 in this manner – although he nearly met his death when hit by a man falling from the 16th floor.

For fire safety in high buildings the answer is adequate provision for fire *prevention* and *detection*. Modern building codes require exit stairs to be separated from the floors by heavy self-closing doors of metal. Fire-retarding paints have been developed

Right: firemen at a fire in London in 1971. Every year Central London receives over 100,000 fire alerts. Regulations specify that there has to be a minimum of three firetrucks to every call. One of the biggest problems in large cities is the increasing number of tall buildings that present special fire hazards and require new techniques of firefighting.

Below: an idea for saving lives in burning skyscrapers is this Japanese invention. It consists of a long slide made of nylon and linen with supporting cables and spiral springs sewn inside. Inside, people can regulate their speed of descent by stretching out their arms.

that delay the spread of flame, and fabrics can be treated chemically for the same purpose. Automatic detection devices are now of several kinds. The heat-sensitive detector works on the principle of a broken electrical circuit that is completed (thus setting off an alarm) when heat reaches a certain level. Smoke detectors take advantage of atmospheric alteration caused by the presence of smoke particles. The simplest of these, a photoelectric device, is triggered when smoke density obscures the transmission of a beam of light.

While methods of detecting fires at an initial stage are of prime importance, the safest guarantee is to be found in safe building and the observance of safety precautions. Lighted cigarettes are notorious for starting fires. In the inquiries following the destruction of the Belgian and the British Pavilions at the Brussels Exhibition in August 1910 it was alleged that not only had the firewatchmen been smoking but the men detailed to make sure the firewatchmen did not smoke were also smoking.

Early man's ability to control fire set him firmly on the road to civilization and the technological achievements of the modern world. Even so, we must always be on guard to prevent this "good friend" becoming the "bad enemy." In this struggle, as against other enemies, some men prove to be traitors to their own side. It is sobering to recall a British report published in the summer of 1977 that two fifths of all fires causing £20,000 damage or over are due to arson.

SENIS ME PINXIT ANNO DNI · ☉ · CCCC · XXXI

Chapter 7

Plague and Pestilence

Most people today expect a long life span. Relatively few expect to die young, and then usually only through some kind of accident. Before modern medicine evolved, however, life for everyone was much more chancy. At any time an outbreak of disease could ravage town and countryside, striking down families to untimely graves.

For thousands of years diseases have unpredictably cut swathes in the world's population, bereaving millions, impoverishing millions more. Often the almost continual warfare that swept back and forward through the known world provided all the conditions for the diseases that followed in its wake. As pestilence struck trader, soldier, ruler, it helped dictate the rise and fall of nations and empires.

Medicine has largely freed the world from such catastrophes. But lethal crowd diseases live on in certain poorer nations. Most agents of disease are just subdued, not vanquished. Man's old enemies deserve continuing respect, for some remain potentially as great a threat to life as global war.

Opposite: a hospital in Renaissance Italy. Generally in the West it became the duty of monasteries to care for the sick, but although simple herbal remedies were available, all forms of medical help, religious or secular, were powerless against the death-dealing plagues and pestilences that ravaged mankind from time to time.

117

The Causes of Disease

To ancient peoples epidemics seemed to kill like blows from some invisible enemy. Indeed, the word *plague* comes from a Greek word meaning "a blow or stroke." The idea that epidemics could have some sort of natural origin dates from the Greek philosopher Empedocles, who lived about 400 BC. But for many centuries people blamed epidemics on unseasonal weather, which they believed corrupted the atmosphere. Fumes from earthquakes and volcanoes were given as other likely causes of disease. Sun, moon, stars, and planets were thought to stir up disease, too. In 1580 Italians condemned the influence of heavenly bodies for the disease they therefore christened "influenza." Many doctors thought that some diseases rose and spread like a bad smell from corpses, swamps, and cesspits. The notion that disease could hop from man to man or from animal to man was old but held only by a minority. Apart from some herbal remedies developed in the monasteries there were few really useful remedies produced in the Middle Ages to ward off or cure epidemic diseases – or any other disease for that matter.

A true grasp of how diseases start and spread awaited the discovery of germs. In 1658 – when men were still developing the microscope – a German priest-scholar, Anthanasius Kircher, daringly suggested that invisible microbes caused plague. But it was not until the 1860s that France's Louis Pasteur put the germ theory of disease on a scientific footing by experiment. At the same time the British surgeon Joseph Lister put forward the theory that epidemics might be spread by a fine airborne dust, like pollen.

Soon, people learned that epidemic illnesses were caused by microscopic organisms that invade the body and multiply inside it. But decades passed before researchers had identified the four groups of organisms that between them are responsible for most epidemic outbreaks. The four are protozoans (minute creatures causing malaria and other ills); bacteria (plantlike microbes responsible for plague, cholera,

Above: the discovery in 1796 that a virus from cows could prevent smallpox was at first greeted with ridicule. This cartoon shows people who have been vaccinated growing cowlike deformities.

Left: the medieval concept of the cause of disease is shown in this 12th-century illustration to the Book of the Revelations of Saint Hildegarde. It depicts the breath of demons as the cause of disease.

and many more diseases); the still smaller rickettsias responsible for typhus; and the submicroscopic viruses, which cause such diseases as influenza, smallpox, and yellow fever.

We now know that different germs spread in various ways. The influenza virus, for instance, migrates through the coughs and sneezes of its hosts and gets into the body of a new host by way of nose, mouth, and lungs. Cholera and typhoid bacteria enter the human body through food or water contaminated by infected feces. Yellow fever, malaria, typhus, and the bubonic form of plague invade the bloodstream through punctures in the skin made by insects bearing microbes of one of the diseases.

In certain areas of the world a disease such as cholera or typhoid may be ever present, and a few cases break out from time to time, the disease is said to be *endemic* there. When social life breaks down through war or famine, the germs may find a broader footing in the population, and an *epidemic* starts. Rarely, an epidemic becomes a worldwide outbreak or *pandemic*.

Millions of people may die in certain germ explosions. But certain organs in the survivors' body,

munity is provided against a battery of old-time killers. It was mass vaccination that was responsible for bringing the deadly smallpox disease to the brink of extinction by the late 1970s.

Health authorities check the spread of sickness by placing immigrants suspected of incubating a danger-

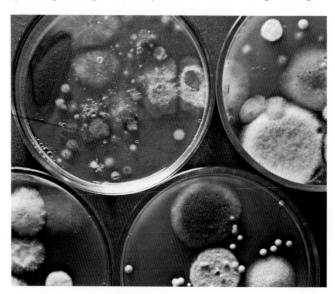

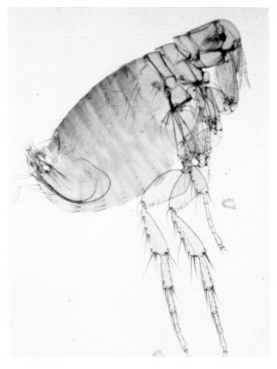

Above: molds from earth samples used in research into antibiotics. **Left:** a photomicrograph of the plague flea from a rat. Several kinds of flea carry plague bacteria (bubonic plague bacillus, below), which multiply in the flea's stomach to be regurgitated into the next host bitten.

spleen, liver, thymus gland, and others, manufacture a substance known as antibody, which is released into the bloodstream and combats the disease. In many cases an antibody will protect its owner from any subsequent invasion by the kind of germ that stimulated the antibody in the first place. These individuals have become immune to that disease. Nowadays, by vaccinating people with germs that have been killed or rendered harmless, the manufacture of antibodies is stimulated without the fear of contracting a deadly disease and an artificial im-

ous infectious disease in isolation, or *quarantine*, because some days usually elapse between acquiring an infection and developing the signs and symptoms. True, antibiotics can now treat bacterial diseases, but the best defense against most epidemics remains prevention, which is why the World Health Organization has set up a worldwide early warning system. It is worthwhile looking at some of the harrowing accounts from the past to remind ourselves what happened in epidemics and pandemics where no cure or method of prevention was available.

119

Enemy Within the Walls
Athens: 430 BC

The city-state of Athens, which included most of Attica, lay already deep in trouble in 430 BC when it was struck by a grave disease. The Peloponnesian War between Athens and its rival, Sparta, was already in its second year. A powerful Spartan army was ravaging Attica. Unable to repel the enemy, the Athenian leader Pericles herded his people protectively inside the city walls. Some refugees camped on open spaces.

detail by the Greek historian Thucydides, who was living in the city at the time. According to him, the epidemic raged from 430 to 428 BC, tailed off until 427 BC, then raged for one more year. "There is no record of so great a pestilence occurring anywhere or of such a destruction of human life," Thucydides wrote.

The first signs of the disease were burning headaches followed by inflammation of the tongue and throat. Breathing became difficult, the breath fetid. Sneezing and hoarseness followed and in a short time the disorder, accompanied by a violent and painful cough, reached the chest. The disease then affected the stomach with aching, retching, and vomiting. The body became red broke out in "pustules and ulcers." Sufferers felt so feverish that they could not bear the

Others huddled in or around the temples, or crammed themselves in nooks and towers of the city walls, or else in cabins, sheds, and even huts adjoining them.

Athens grew desperately overcrowded. Conditions must have been unspeakable in a city where many homes were mud-walled huts, most streets were alleys, and people defecated in the open. The heaps of dung and garbage lay and stank around the city's rim. The overflow of refugees made all this worse and helped produce a situation ripe for disease.

What eventually happened was described in painful

finest linen garmet, but lay naked, long to plunge into cold water, and grew desperately thirsty. Many died after a week – others later, exhausted by severe diarrhea.

Those who did survive found themselves immune to subsequent attacks and believed themselves immortal. But some lost eyesight, memory, fingers, toes, or genitals.

The disease spread with appalling speed from man to man. Those who nursed the sick died like flies so that many of the victims had to be abandoned, and some "hardly alive, wallowed in the streets and crawled about every fountain craving for water." Most dismaying of all was the loss of will to live. Anyone contracting the disease believed that death was inevitable.

Those worst affected were the peasant refugees. Without proper homes, many suffered from the intense summer heat while lying in their stifling makeshift huts. The death rate among them reached enormous proportions. Thucydides writes: "They perished in wild disorder. The dead lay as they had died, one upon another." Temples became tombs filled with the corpses of those who had sought sanctuary there. Strangely, according to Thucydides, carrion-eating birds and dogs ignored the piles of dead or "died if they touched them."

tagion by overcrowding Athens.

This anger faded, however, probably when Pericles' own sister and only legitimate sons died in the epidemic, leaving Pericles a broken, heirless figure, soon himself to perish from disease.

Another possible cause of the plague was that the gods had been neglected or angered in some way, and the pestilence was their retaliation. Apollo was one of the deities controlling pestilence. In the second outbreak of the plague, the citizens dug up and shipped out all the bodies buried on the isle of Delos, once sacred to Apollo. They hoped that by purifying the island they could avert his anger.

At last the plague abated. Historians still disagree about its cause. Bubonic and pneumonic plague, smallpox, and typhus have all been put forward as

Left: Spartan ships attack the Athenian harbor of Piraeus. It was in Piraeus that the mysterious "plague of Athens" started. Athenians at first thought the Spartans had poisoned the drinking wells.

Right: when the plague reached its peak the citizens of crowded, besieged Athens died in their thousands. Hardest hit were the refugees and the poorer classes but eventually all classes suffered.

Some families clung to the old tradition and burned their dead. But fuel grew scarce and gatecrashers would often toss their own corpses in the flames or light pyres before the rightful owners were prepared.

The Athenians vainly sought a cause and cure for the disease. At first they blamed the enemy. The Spartans, they believed, had poisoned the wells of Piraeus, the port of Athens where the outbreak started. According to the Greek biographer Plutarch, the desperate Athenians then rounded on their leader Pericles, blaming him for spreading the con-

candidates. Scarlet fever comes nearest to Thucydides' description of the signs and symptoms of the Athens plague, but neither it nor any of the other diseases in their modern form fits this description exactly.

Whatever it was, the plague severely sapped the city's power. Possibly one third of the people died. Lawlessness erupted. The armed forces lost so many men that they were no longer able to harry the invaders. In these ways the epidemic probably prolonged the war that eventually smashed the Athenian Empire and closed a chapter in world history.

The Black Death

No pandemic ever killed more people than the Black Death, the outbreak of true plague that occurred in the middle of the 14th century. Headstones from Christian burials near Lake Issyk-kul (now in the Soviet state of Kirghis) show that plague was already active in Central Asia by 1338. Within 13 years the pestilence had struck all Old World lands in trading contact. In places 9 out of every 10 infected individuals perished. It is estimated that some 75,000,000 people died.

The first hints of this almost global tragedy reached European ports in 1346. Rumors told of mass deaths in Asia. Some said that India had been depopulated, and that dead bodies littered much of southwest Asia. Eventually plague reached the Crimea on the eastern edge of Europe. From this Black Sea region plague leaped into Western Europe. According to a con-

Below: the prophet Solomon Eagle from Daniel Defoe's *A Journal of the Plague Year*, a vivid, though fictitious, 18th-century account of the plague of London in 1665.

temporary Italian chronicler, plague attacked a Tartar army besieging the Genoese trading port of Caffa (now Feodosiya) in southwestern Crimea. Using huge catapults, the Tartars lobbed plague-ridden corpses over Caffa's defensive walls, infecting the base's inhabitants. Plague-bearing refugees then leaped aboard their galleys. With crewmen actually dying of disease as they rowed, the vessels – and the pestilence – made their way to the Mediterranean.

The Black Death reached Sicily late in 1347. From there ships bore the disease to Corsica, Sardinia, North Africa, and southern Italy. Meanwhile, infected vessels reached north Italian ports including Genoa and Venice, from where the plague spread north and west in an arc embracing France, the Low Countries, Germany, and Scandinavia. By the summer of 1348 a ship had set plague ashore in southern England.

Writers in various countries painted ugly word pictures of the course taken by the disease. In Italy, the writer and poet Giovanni Boccaccio described the "tumors" (buboes) in the groin or the armpits, some as big as an apple, others egg size, some smaller. "Black or livid spots also cropped up on the body," he wrote. In France, Guy de Chauliac the papal physician noticed that the plague took two forms: one with fever, blood spitting, and death in three days: the other with buboes and death in five days.

We know now that true plague may take on the bubonic swelling form, the septicemic or blood-poisoning form, or the pneumonic or lung-infecting form. Each is produced by the bacterium *Pasteurella pestis*. In bubonic plague, man contracts the disease from fleas – especially those living on the black rat, an agile climber haunting homes and warehouses. Even today the bubonic form can be found in Asia among wild rodents especially the squirrel-like tarbagan or Manchurian marmot. In the second, septicemic, form of true plague, blood poisoning kills before buboes have a chance to appear. The pneumonic form spreads directly from man to man as people inhale bacteria sneezed or coughed out by others. The Black Death began with the rat-flea-man chain of infection. But this bubonic form gave rise to the pneumonic version as coughs and sneezes spread plague far and quickly.

Doctors were powerless. Quacks advised useless remedies like drinking vinegar or downright dangerous practices like letting blood. At Venice the physicians hid indoors while laborers tended the sick. The city authorities there issued orders for containing the plague; the locking up of infected houses, cleaning filth from the streets, setting up plague hospitals, and burying dead at night.

Chroniclers related frightful stories. In Italy, no city suffered more harshly than Florence, whose fate Boccaccio described to introduce his *Decameron*. Boccaccio tells how people dropped dead in the street or died unnoticed in their homes, from where the stench of rotting bodies later told the neighbors what had happened next door.

There were mass funerals but few mourners. Hired corpse-carriers bore whole families on a single bier to the nearest church. There, the priest would hastily consign the dead to the first vacant tomb he could find. As graves overflowed, men dug a huge trench where they heaped corpses "hundreds at a time, piling them up as merchandise is stowed in the hold of a ship. . . ."

More than half of all Florentines probably perished in six plague-stricken months. Plague cut similar swathes in Siena, where it halted work on the new cathedral. At Parma, the poet Petrarch bemoaned the loss of a friend, whose sons "and all his family" died within three days of each other.

Horrors like this were soon commonplace all over Europe. In France, 56,000 reportedly perished at Marseilles. Only one in eight of Perpignan's physicians survived. At Avignon 7000 houses lay empty, and the pope consecrated the Rhone so that people could cast bodies into the river. In Paris one church gained 419 bequests in nine months – 40 times the rate before plague struck the French capital. Plague even forced a truce between France and England, then embroiled in the Hundred Years' War.

Of Flanders and the Low Countries one writer claimed the death rate almost impossible to believe. Travelers described cattle wandering untended through towns; wine cellars standing open; fields uncultivated. In Tournai in 1349 the bishop was among the first to die, and soon the funeral bells rang "morning, evening, and night."

Plague deeply infiltrated Germany and Austria by

Above: a European doctor during the plague. He is wearing a spice-filled mask and using a stick instead of his hands to touch patients.

Left: a scene common throughout Europe and the world during the Plague Years – a mass-burial pit, the only way to cope with the multitudes of dead. This one is at Aldgate, London.

late 1348. Each city counted corpses in their thousands and Vienna lost 960 victims in a single day. One in three of the German higher clergy perished and many monasteries and parish churches closed.

In 1349 death struck England from the biggest city to the smallest and remotest hamlet. So devastated was the population of one Buckinghamshire manor that its surviving income after the disaster was the rent from one small cottage. At another manor rents ceased altogether when plague killed all the tenants. At Winchester Cathedral plague halted an ambitious rebuilding program, forcing the hasty erection of a new west front intended to be only temporary. It still stands, over six centuries later. At Rochester in Kent the bishop lost "four priests, five gentlemen, ten serving men, seven young clerks, and six pages, so that not a soul remained who might serve him in any office." In London at least two successive archbishops of Canterbury perished, and perhaps more than half of all the citizens. New cemeteries were consecrated to take the teeming dead. As in other cities, moral standards sagged and crime boomed.

Records speak similarly for other parts of Europe. We learn that the Byzantine Emperor lost a son. At Split, in what is now Yugoslavia, wolves set upon

themselves by whipping. It was a form of penance that had begun even before the Black Death broke out and was particularly popular in Germany. Hundreds of Flagellants, trudging two abreast, made their way across the countryside. They would halt in market squares, the men would strip to the waist and form a circle lashing their bare torsos with leather thongs studded with metal. One account describes how blood ran from their bodies, already swollen and blue with beating. By 1349, however, the German Flagellants had formed themselves into an heretical sect and were condemned by the Church. Hundreds were thrown into gaol, tortured, or killed.

Meanwhile scapegoats were sought among social or racial minorities in European cities and blamed for spreading plague among the main community. Cripples, lepers, pilgrims, the Arabs in Christian Spain – all suffered at least verbal condemnation. But the Jews endured the heaviest of all attacks. Rumors claimed that Jews had spread the plague by poisoning the Christians' drinking wells. In May 1348 the Jews of Provence were massacred. In Basel the town's Jewish citizens were shut up in wooden buildings and burned alive. By November German towns were busily engaged in the slaughter of their Jews. At

Left: the mental anguish that accompanied such a widespread disaster as plague gave rise to fanatical groups such as these flagellants who proclaimed the wrath of God against corruption and invited penitents to atone for their sins by self-imposed flagellation. This miniature of 1349 shows a group of flagellants, each one carrying a small whip.

surviving citizens. Plague reportedly reached Norway aboard a drifting ship whose crew had perished of the sickness. In Spain King Alfonso of Castile caught plague and died – though Europe's other ruling monarchs were luckier.

Christians saw plague as God's punishment for sin and prayed for forgiveness. At Rome barefoot penitents with ash-strewn heads and ropes around their necks climbed the marble steps up to the Church of Ara Coeli, where they begged the Blessed Virgin for deliverance.

Groups of penitents called Flagellants punished

Speyer men piled Jewish corpses in wine casks and rolled them into the Rhine. Thousands of Jews perished at Strasbourg before plague had actually arrived. Flanders, too, saw massacres, and anti-Jewish riots flared in Spain.

By 1351 persecution and plague abated. Europe had lost perhaps one third of its inhabitants. For three centuries recurring outbreaks made plague a major cause of death in Europe, disrupting urban life and inspiring artists with grisly dance-of-death motifs and commemorative paintings. Not until the early 1800s was Europe freed from this terrible disease.

The Fearefull Summer:

OR,

Londons Calamitie, The Countries Difcourtefie, And both their Miferie.

Printed by Authoritie in *Oxford*, in the laft great Infection of the Plague, 1625. And now reprinted with fome Editions, concerning this prefent yeere, 1636.

With fome mention of the grievous and afflicted eftate of the famous Towne of New-Caftle upon Tine, with fome other vifited Townes of this Kingdome.

By IOHN TAYLOR.

Above: a German woodcut of 1492. It shows Jews being burned as scapegoats for the plague. **Left:** the cover of a publication about plague in England in the year 1625. The woodcut on the front shows Death triumphant in the countryside. Soldiers at right try to keep refugees out of the city. **Below:** a commemorative diorama of the Black Death in Florence, Italy.

125

The Yellow Fever War!
St. Domingue: 1794-1804

In 1789 the French colony of St Domingue on the Caribbean island of Hispaniola ranked among the richest colonial possessions anywhere. Thirteen years later the land lay ravaged, its population decimated. From the shattered colony emerged the world's first fully independent Negro republic – a nation born of war and yellow fever.

For more than 200 years, yellow fever ranked among the worst epidemic killers in the Caribbean area. It is a tropical disease, found among the forest monkeys of West Africa, yet curiously absent from East Africa and alien to Asia. How and when it first reached the Americas is uncertain, though old Mayan chronicles from Mexico suggest that yellow fever could have broken out from time to time before Columbus landed.

reported after chance contact with various forest-based mosquitoes. But yellow fever epidemics among humans are usually due to one "domesticated" species of mosquito: *Aedes aegypti*. It breeds in any puddles and pools however small.

Although the female *Aedes* can survive by sipping nectar, it needs the nourishment obtained from blood to manufacture fertile eggs. *Aedes* seems to prefer the blood of humans, which is why many are found in or near houses. Yellow fever epidemics, then, occur where *Aedes*, yellow fever virus, stagnant water, and a concentrated population without immunity to the disease all come together.

By the 16th century, settlements of Europeans in the West Indies may have been providing all these conditions abundantly. The Spaniards were the islands' first colonists. Because Spain lay outside the major yellow fever belt, few of its people had ever had the illness and so had not formed any immunity to later attacks of the disease. Also, the cause of yellow fever was unknown for centuries, so no one knew they could help prevent an outbreak just by draining ponds and puddles.

Left: slaves working on a Spanish sugar plantation on the island of Hispaniola. Soon after their colonization of the Caribbean in the early 16th-century, Spanish settlers began to be hit by outbreaks of Yellow Fever. Their slaves, imported from Africa, were only lightly affected by the deadly disease.

Opposite: the storming of the Bastille in 1789. It was the spark that led to the French Revolution – which in turn spurred the revolt of the black slaves in the French half of Hispaniola, St Domingue.

The organism causing yellow fever is a virus. In humans it attacks and damages the liver. Because the liver is no longer able to function properly yellow bile pigments collect in the victim's skin, turning it yellow and giving the disease its name. In its natural state the virus breeds in mammals such as monkeys and is transmitted from animal to animal by mosquitoes. Cases of yellow fever among human beings have been

It was not long after the Spanish had settled around the Caribbean that the first epidemics were recorded – for Puerto Rico in 1508, and Cuba 12 years later. Some medical authorities, however, believe that true yellow fever arrived in the West Indies only in the 17th century, when many outbreaks hit the islands. This coincided with another inflow of non-immune European colonists – the British, Dutch, and French. In

1635 yellow fever savaged Guadeloupe. Within the next 20 years St Kitts (sometimes known as St Christopher), Martinique, Barbados, Jamaica, and St Lucia fell victim to the malady.

One incident above all others shows how fiercely yellow fever preyed on people fresh from Europe. The British warship *Tiger*, based in Barbados had to replace the equivalent of its entire crew of 200 men three times during its two-year stay. As naval personnel died, Captain Sherman kidnaped sailors from newly arrived merchant ships. When yellow fever struck these down as well, he just collected more.

The West Indies held another big and growing group who suffered relatively lightly from yellow fever. These were the black slaves shipped in from Africa to work the European's tropical plantations. It may have been that yellow fever first slipped in with them. Scientists specializing in the disease think that long exposure to yellow fever back in West Africa had produced a kind of immunity among the native population. Certainly attacks of the disease that decimated European settlers in the West Indies touched the black slaves there relatively lightly. Then,

Without yellow fever, black independence might have been delayed until the middle of this century. As it was, this frightful killer provided black revolutionaries with a biological weapon that helped expel their masters by the early 1800s.

The overthrow of France's monarchy was the spark that lit the fuse of revolt on St Domingue. In 1791 black slaves on one plantation killed the local Europeans and burned their buildings. Soon, murder, pillage, and arson swept across St Domingue's fertile North Plain. A French government official named Sonthonax then secured power for himself. France sent out a governor-general, but Sonthonax drove him out, encouraging the revels to loot and smash the town. Then he declared all slaves free – a decree at first approved by France's revolutionary rulers. Economic chaos followed, and in 1793 the European colonists appealed for help to Britain, then at war with France.

The British governor of Jamaica responded by landing 7500 troops in southwest St Domingue. The British quickly crushed black troops and seized most of southern St Domingue. By May 1794 they held

too, natural increases and imports of fresh shiploads meant that by the late 18th century the blacks in the West Indies heavily outnumbered their European masters. It was slave labor in the sugar cane and coffee plantations that enriched the French colony of St Domingue on the western third of Hispaniola, the second largest island in the Caribbean. Then revolution – and yellow fever – struck the colony.

Port-au-Prince, the capital, and seemed about to overrun the island.

Then the British met a new and formidable adversary in the black leader Toussaint L'Ouverture, invading with a force from Santo Domingo, the eastern, Spanish part of Hispaniola. Toussaint – ex-slave, ex-coachman – went to the aid of official French forces pinned down in northern St Domingue. The British troops were soon halted by a combination of mountain-based guerilla warfare by Toussaint and summer heat that helped sap their vitality. But their troubles were only beginning, for soon yellow fever struck.

British troops suddenly began to suffer headaches, backaches and a high temperature. They felt sick and vomited dark blood. As the virus attacked their livers, skins and eyeballs turned yellow. Many bled from bowels and stomach. Diarrhea and inability to urinate were further and strongly sinister signs – few men with these complications recovered. All victims felt wretchedly exhausted.

Reinforced by fresh troops from Jamaica, the expeditionary army clung on for years. But the toll of life was cruel. By May 1797, the number of British soldiers that had died had reached 7530 (more than the initial force dispatched to St Domingue). Some, of course, had died in combat, but far more had been killed by enemies too small for them to see.

Largely immune to yellow fever virus, the blacks suffered no such slaughter. In October 1798 Toussaint accepted the British surrender on behalf of France and let the remnants of the British army sail back to Jamaica. By 1801 the black leader had crushed all rivals on Hispaniola, and ruled it in the name of France. Prosperity began reviving.

But Napoleon Bonaparte now decided to smash black rule and reestablish slavery in the virtually independent island. In February 1802 his brother-in-law Charles Leclerc landed at Cap Francais at the head of a French force 23,000 strong. The French soon captured Toussaint and drove the rebels back into the mountains.

The rebels were still holding out when only two months later in April French troops started going down with yellow fever. By June disease and heat had halted their campaign in St Domingue. The catastrophe that followed dwarfed even the British disaster of a few years earlier. By late November, disease and battle had killed off nearly half the French army, including its commander. By next spring France held only a handful of ports – "literally hospitals as the French troops die by hundreds in a day," declared a report in *The Gentleman's Magazine* of London. The entire inland area, the writer claimed, lay in Negro hands.

Although 10,000 reinforcements had managed to arrive in autumn 1802, in 1803 a British naval blockade began to make the French position untenable. By November 1803 Cap Francais alone remained in French control. War and yellow fever had killed 24,000 of the total French force of 33,000, and 7000 more were dying, mainly from the virus. General Rochambeau surrendered to a British admiral, and

Left: the rebellious black slaves surrender to the British troops called in by European settlers on St Domingue. The British were soon to meet a more formidable enemy than the ill-armed rebels – Yellow Fever. Below: General Charles Leclerc, sent by Napoleon Bonaparte to crush the slave revolt.

British ships bore off the pathetic rump of an army that had once appeared invincible.

On January 1, 1804, St Domingue formally became the independent black nation of Haiti. A microscopic germ and mountain-based guerilla fighting had broken a contingent from an army that no power in Europe could withstand.

Above left: Toussaint L'Ouverture, the black rebel leader who ruled St Domingue in the name of France until Napoleon decided to reintroduce slavery and smash black rule in the island.

Above: part of the 23,000-strong French force that nearly succeeded in ending rebel rule in St Domingue. **Below:** the town of Cap Francais set ablaze by black rebels. Exhausted, decimated by disease, the French troops finally left St Domingue, which became Haiti in 1804.

The Cholera Pandemic

Above: a costume suggested to the citizens of Vienna during a cholera epidemic in the 19th-century. Pockets around skirts hold herbs, basket has medicines, thick overshoes and many other "preventions" point to a frantic guesswork on the part of doctors in the face of cholera epidemics.

Rain fell heavily on much of India in 1817. Fields flooded in the crowded Ganges Valley. In May came the first of a new crop of cases of cholera. This disease, which attacks the intestines, causing diarrhea and vomiting, severe dehydration and death, was not new: Hindu physicians had first described it about 400 BC. By 1800, cholera outbreaks had slain thousands of troops manning British East India Company garrisons in India. The Netherlands East Indies also suffered outbreaks. But on the whole cholera remained an ever-present scourge within India alone until 1817.

That year, cholera spilled over India's borders and began penetrating the countries around it. This slow march of the disease from its borders was soon overtaken by another outflow that would scour the world. Cholera infected the trade routes sailing first from India aboard ship to Arabia. From Arabia it seeped into Persia, Turkey, and then into southern Russia. At the same time another wave of cholera spread east to Malacca and Japan. The disease moved slowly. It took until 1831 to reach Moscow and Berlin but less than a year later it was in France, the British Isles and North America.

The area around the North Sea port of Sunderland in northern England provided the first British victims. On August 5, 1831, a "painter of earthenware"

suffered what one report described as "vomiting and purging of a watery whitish fluid, like oatmeal and water. His hands and feet were cold, his skin covered with clammy sweat, his face livid, and the expression anxious, his eyes sunken, his lips blue, thirst excessive, his breath cold, his voice weak and husky, and his pulse almost imperceptible." The man grew feverish, but recovered. Three days later, a nearby farm laborer suffered similarly and died.

More deaths followed. But British doctors familiar with bowel infections explained most as severe cases of what they vaguely termed "summer diarrhea." Britain's first official death from Asiatic cholera was that of a 60-year-old Sunderland keelman named Sproat. After two weeks' diarrhea, the old boatman suffered a severe attack of vomiting and diarrhea. Then he rallied, taking "toasted cheese for supper," and next day, "a mutton chop for dinner." Hours later, Sproat collapsed with telltale muscle cramps and "rice-water" diarrhea. He died three days later.

Between October 23 and December 31, 1831, there were 202 deaths in the Sunderland epidemic. By early January cholera had appeared in other parts of northeast England. In February 1832 London's dockland area was invaded, and in summer the capital was badly hit. Altogether, in 1832, London had 11,000 cases, and nearly half the patients died – about one quarter of the year's mortality from cholera in the whole of England and Wales.

·Britain escaped this first pandemic lightly compared with other countries. Then a second, worse, pandemic struck Europe and North America in 1848–49, and outbreaks flared up for a decade. In Russia, some 18,000 British, French, and Piedmontese troops succumbed to cholera in the Crimean War. In France 140,000 people perished; in Britain more than 50,000.

This outbreak, which had every likelihood of establishing cholera as a recurring disease throughout the world proved also to be a turning point, when men discovered how cholera spreads and how its spread might be prevented. The hero of this story was John Snow, a British doctor. Snow doubted the popular theories that bad air or touching cholera patients spread the disease. Observation convinced him that people contracted cholera by either drinking water or eating food that had been contaminated with material from the body of someone already suffering the disease.

Snow's chance to test this theory arose in 1849. In just 10 days, 500 people perished in a local outbreak involving London's Soho district where Snow then practiced medicine. On a map he marked the houses where the deaths occurred. He also marked the stand pumps above the wells from which the district's residents had drawn their water. Most deaths appeared clustered around one manual pump in Broad (now Broadwick) Street. Snow had the handle of the pump removed, and deaths dramatically ceased.

Above: the British founder of modern nursing, Florence Nightingale nursing troops during the Crimean War of 1853–6. She did much to alleviate the sufferings of cholera victims.

Although it was another 34 years before the German bacteriologist Robert Koch identified the rod-shaped bacterium that causes cholera, Snow was able to show that simply keeping drinking water free from sewage can help to halt the spread of cholera and other waterborne diseases. Years, and more pandemics had to pass before all cities possessed the pure, piped drinking water that has saved the Western World from further outbreaks.

The Indian subcontinent – that ancient home of cholera – remains less fortunate. By the 1970s a staggering 200,000 people still died there annually from this preventable disease.

Above: the British Doctor John Snow who discovered how cholera was passed on to victims. Before Snow's research people adopted a fatalistic approach to the disease. The triumph of death theme (left) was a frequently seen device in art before medical breakthroughs in the world's major diseases. **Right:** in Granada, Spain, fires were used to disinfect the streets during the cholera epidemic of the 1830s.

Worldwide Influenza 1918-1920

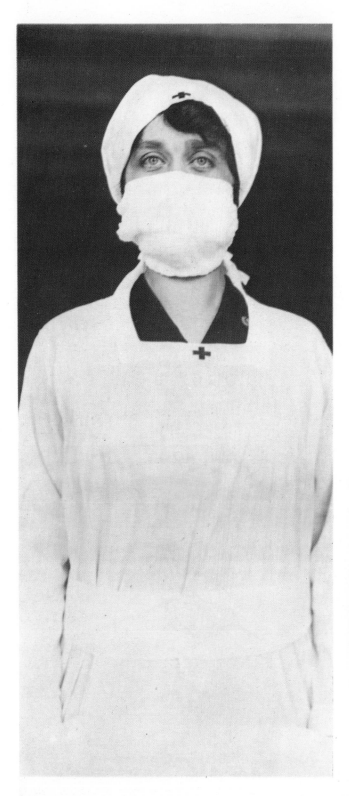

Above: a Red Cross nurse wearing a mask during the 1918–19 influenza pandemic that killed an estimated 21,500,000 people throughout the world.

On October 1, 1918 William Hill sat in the engine house, gripping the controls of a machine that raised a steel cage up a mine shaft in the Witwatersrand, South Africa's great gold-field region. The 40 Africans crammed inside that cage had just finished a shift deep underground. Suddenly sweat soaked Hill's skin. His muscles seemed to lose their power. Firework-bright flashes blurred his vision. Hill tried to grab the levers that would halt the lift. As in a nightmare, though, his arms and hands seemed paralyzed. The cage zoomed upward past the shaft's rim, or collar, soared high above the ground, crashed into the head-gear, then plunged 100 feet to crash upside down on the collar. Inside the wrecked cage 24 of the African miners lay dead. In the following investigation officials cleared Hill of blame. The true cause of the tragedy, they agreed, was Spanish influenza – an infection that could fell a man almost as swiftly as a bullet.

In the course of one year – between 1918 and 1919 – this new strain of influenza swept the globe. The pandemic afflicted more than half the total human population, killing more victims than all the guns of World War I, which ended as the disease reached its climax. One medical historian has described it as "the greatest outbreak of pestilence that the human race has ever experienced."

Yet there was little hint of future carnage in the first, mainly mild, epidemics that almost simultaneously struck China, North America, and Spain. Where the disease originated has never been decided. From February 1918, thousands of Spaniards began

Above: young boys in New York in 1917. They wear bags of camphor around their necks in the hope of escaping the influenza virus. In the absence of any medical cure such home-made remedies were ordinary people's only hope.

Left: British troops embark for France during the First World War. Influenza took a heavy toll of troops, who were mainly in the age group that proved most vulnerable to the disease.

taking to their beds, suffering from high temperatures and aching bodies. Three days after falling sick most were up again. As an epidemic it seemed quite mild contrasted with the severe "Russian" influenza of 1889–90. By early summer mild influenza had reached most corners of the world.

Then, in early September, a second, far more deadly outbreak started. It was a new strain of influenza virus originating possibly in Africa or Russia. Like the earlier mild outbreak, the fatal virus spread around the world much faster than the pandemics of the past.

Trains and steamships – products of industrial progress – were ironically the vehicles that helped to spread destruction. It took only a few hours for trains to spread the disease from the northern British trans-atlantic ports of Liverpool and Glasgow to London in southern England. A few days was enough for a train-load of infected troops to bear the virus across the breadth of Canada. Transoceanic voyages admittedly took longer. The *SS Niagara* spent three weeks transporting influenza from western Canada to New Zealand; its arrival on October 12 foredoomed almost 6700 citizens to death.

The second influenza wave died down as 1918 closed. But early in 1919 a third and final wave occurred.

Although less severe than the second wave, it nonetheless killed countless thousands of people.

Because of the speed with which influenza spread no one could determine its point of origin. Different nations got the blame for starting it. In Western Europe, Spain became the major scapegoat. The Russians blamed nomads from Turkestan in Central Asia. The Germans believed the virus came from Chinese serving with the British troops in France. An American officer claimed that German submarines had loosed influenza on North America as a secret weapon.

What no country disagreed about was the grim effects of the pandemic that had gripped the world by late autumn 1918. Many cases came on with sudden violence. At embarkation camps in North America, troops collapsed in droves. In Rio de Janiero a man waiting for a street car casually inquired about its destination and dropped dead. An off-duty Cape Town streetcar driver reported six deaths among the

sufferers gasped for air at twice their normal respiration rate, and adults' pulses raced like those of healthy infants. Purple blisters on back, chest, and limbs were other ugly signs. Most of the discolored patients felt no great discomfort. But doctors quickly discovered that blue lips and face were usually followed by death within two days.

In normal influenza epidemics the old are always vulnerable, but Spanish influenza seemed to strike most harshly at the fit and young. Half of those who died were in the 20- to 40-year-old age group. Soldiers were one of the groups worst hit. From as early as the first, spring wave, Italian troops began to choke to death, lungs clogged by mucus, blood, and foam. By October 8, influenza had immobilized 16,000 US troops entrenched in the Argonne Forest area of France. Meanwhile, back home in North America, pneumonia was killing up to one in five of troops awaiting embarkation. As one doctor claimed, it had become more dangerous to be a soldier in the peaceful

passengers and crew in one three-mile journey.

Pneumonia was one of the complications of the disease and struck one in five afflicted individuals – often with no warning. Lips, face, and sometimes the whole body of some victims took on an unnatural purplish-blue tinge, revealing a massive viral attack upon the lungs that starved blood and body of the oxygen they needed. One New York doctor grimly described patients newly admitted to his hospital as "blue as huckleberries and spitting blood." Many

United States than to have been on the firing line in France. In southern England, 1000 of a group of 3000 German prisoners of war succumbed.

The world over, influenza crippled social and economic life as World War I had never done. By the second week in October, Montreal had shut all schools, cinemas, dance halls, and theaters to try to halt the spread of influenza. In other nations other cities took similar action. Vital tasks were interrupted. As farm laborers sickened and died, neglect affected crops around the world. In northern India, countless fields of grain remained unharvested. In Poland potatoes rotted in the ground. Similarly, there were few fit enough to harvest the coffee, rubber, and other cash crops of the tropics.

Industry and business lost momentum. Staff shortages forced a temporary closure of banks in Brazil and New Zealand. Major copper mines in the Belgian Congo and Peru stopped operating. Trade and travel faltered. Trains no longer ran between Germany and Sweden, or between Spain and Portugal. Some ports lay idle. Even organized government began to crumble. New Zealand's Parliament temporarily shut down for lack of members.

Many places tried a variety of futile efforts to halt the spread of the infection. Policemen patrolled in gangsterlike masks, against the risk of breathing germs. In Dublin, water carts swilled disinfectant through the gutters. In New Zealand a teacher used a shovelful of hot embers and formalin to fumigate her school. At Bilbao in northern Spain, officials forced people to breathe fumes from burning sulfur.

Superstition flourished widely. Japanese tried fooling the disease demons by pinning up notices declaring that no one was at home. Traders in voodoo charms did brisk business in New Orleans.

Some bids to ward off influenza were actually dangerous. The world over, terrified people shut doors and windows and blocked draughty chinks to shut out the agents of disease. Deprived of oxygen, scores of householders suffocated in Jamaica alone.

There were countless stories told of individual tragedies. Rich and poor, famous and obscure, no one escaped the terrible disease. But individual deaths were merely drops in the swelling ocean of mortality. In Australia one woman counted 26 funerals passing in a mere three hours. By October 1918, 700 people were dying of the disease every day in Bombay. By December death was daily diminishing Barcelona's population by 1200. By the time the third flu wave

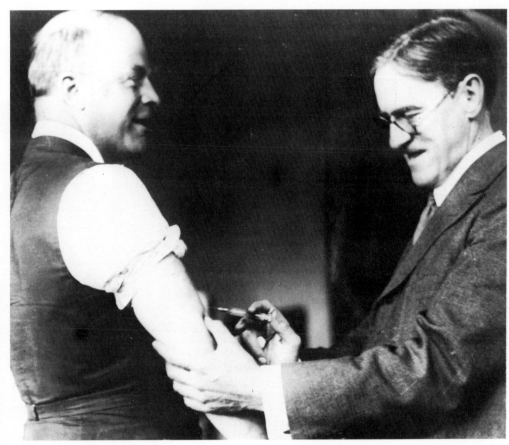

Above left: enrolling nurses for the "Women in Emergency Aid Corps" in the USA. A graph on the wall gives the mortality rate. **Above center:** a street cleaner wearing a mask to check the spread of influenza. **Above right:** the Mayor of Boston, Mayor Peters, being inoculated against influenza in 1918. The inoculations were not, however, very effective.

subsided some estimates put the worldwide toll at over 21,500,000. Probably three quarters of all deaths occurred in Asia, with Europe the next worst affected continent, then North America, and Africa.

Mercifully, by 1920 the supply of fresh victims was exhausted and the lethal strain of influenza vanished (although we know that pigs carry influenza virus). It was to be many years before scientists learned to isolate an influenza virus and produce a vaccine to protect a population from attack.

Preventing and Eradicating Disease

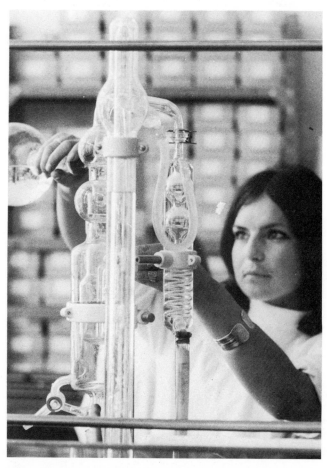

Above: all man's medical skills are being summoned in the fight against worldwide diseases. Rehydration fluid to fight Cholera outbreaks is being manufactured in Geneva. One firm produces about 15 tons daily.

For most people in the Western world widespread pestilence is unknown. Modern medicine and a high standard of hygiene have numbed any awareness to the dangers of global killer diseases. Elsewhere, though, most of the old killers are still busy. Already in the second half of the century true plague has flared up on the Saudi Arabia–Yemen border, in Brazil, and in Vietnam. Meningitis epidemics in which the linings of the brain and spinal cord are attacked by bacteria have erupted across sub-Saharan Africa every six to eight years, killing thousands. Epidemic typhus spread by lice and fleas and causing fever, coma, and death has been active in eastern-central Africa. West Africa has suffered yellow fever outbreaks. The Indian subcontinent has annually lost up to 200,000 lives from cholera and well into the middle of this century 1,000,000 people were dying every year from malaria, while the once high hopes of eradicating

malaria – found in North and Central America, all countries bordering on the Mediterranean, and central and eastern Asia – have withered.

Far from being eradicated some of these diseases still send their scouts out into parts of the world where they are not naturally endemic. In the 1970s, for instance, 500 imported cases of malaria were diagnosed annually in the United Kingdom. Modern high-speed travel assists the spread of infection, adding a new dimension to the threat of epidemic outbreaks. Someone incubating plague could fly from Southeast Asia to Europe unaware of disease organisms multiplying inside his body. With hundreds of millions of passengers annually flying around the world the risk of rapidly spreading lethal virus diseases has never been greater.

Of course health regulations ensure that most long-distance travelers are immunized against the commonest epidemic killers. But sometimes obscure and potentially highly dangerous viruses emerge spontaneously, especially inside the tropics. One of these was Machupo virus, which causes severe bleeding and fever, and hundreds of people have already died in Bolivia. In Nigeria in 1969 and 1970 a mysterious sickness broke out at Jos and Lassa, killing Africans and Europeans alike. American researchers had to

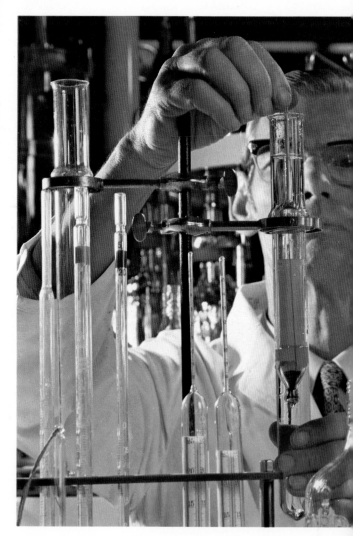

abandon studies of so-called Lassa virus because it proved so fiercely virulent. What is perhaps most disturbing is that its host is a rodent common in West Africa.

In 1967 an unknown disease infected some 30 laboratory workers at Marburg and Frankfurt in West Germany with fever, diarrhea, and bleeding. Seven died. The virus that killed them was traced to green Vervet monkeys imported from Uganda for use in medical experiments. The Marburg virus or "green monkey disease," which was unaffected by antibiotics was quickly contained in the sterile laboratory conditions. An outbreak of the same fever in Zaire and the Sudan in 1976, however, killed about 300 Africans.

"New" diseases do not emerge only in the tropics, of course. In July 1976 an outbreak of a strange illness appeared in the United States among ex-servicemen at a Philadelphia convention. At first some of the legionnaires felt just generally ill, with muscle pains. A high fever quickly followed, with shivering, coughing, chest pain, and breathlessness. Of the 183 veterans affected 20 (roughly one in nine) died of the disease. Its cause at first baffled doctors. Then tests revealed it to be a new type of pneumonia. Later, it was proved that "legionnaires' disease" in fact had been erupting

Left: improved vaccines have controlled many diseases that were once widescale killers. **Top right:** part of a World Health Day procession in 1975, when India started its mass smallpox eradication campaign. **Right below:** part of the Ethiopian campaign to eradicate smallpox was to visit rural areas for mass vaccination.

sporadically at least since 1965. Luckily, there is an antibiotic available to help fight this first new bacterial disease to be identified in years. Fortunately, too, occurrences seem so far small and scattered.

Some "new" diseases liable to cause pandemics are really old diseases that have passed unrecognized. But well-established viruses can sometimes evolve new strains more lethal or infectious than their predecessors. Among these germs none changes faster or more quirkily than the influenza virus. A new form emerges to sweep the world about once every decade.

Following the deadly 1918 pandemic, doctors have long kept watch for the reemergence of that lethal strain, or the evolution of another. Early in 1976 just such an outbreak seemed about to strike. The first signs were 12 influenza cases – one fatal – among

Above: enormous precautions are taken when handling a phial of the deadly Lassa fever virus at the microbiological Research Establishment in Wiltshire, England.

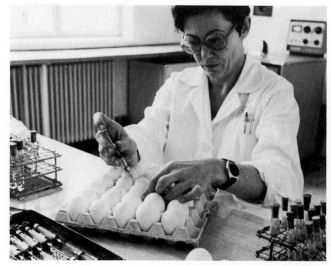

Above: two technicians wearing protective clothing carry a Lassa fever victim from the plane in Hamburg to a special isolation hospital. **Left:** the greatest venture in public health ever undertaken was the WHO's drive against malaria. Here workers in Kabul, Afghanistan, kill mosquito lavae by spraying pools where they breed. **Below:** preventive measures against influenza in Hungary begin in this laboratory, where some 100,000 eggs are used to culture the anti-influenza vaccine.

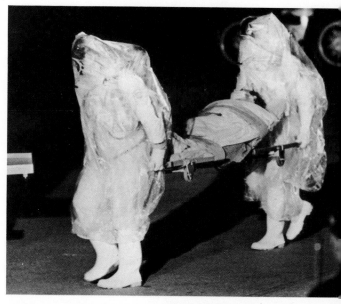

recruits at a New Jersey military camp. Tests showed that 500 US troops had been infected with a hitherto unrecorded strain of Influenza. Antibody in the troops proved similar to that built up by survivors of the 1918 outbreak. Medical authorities accordingly alerted the 95 World Health Organization influenza centers located around the globe. Inside America, a mass vaccination program started. Meanwhile the epidemic, contained among well-fed people with expert medical care, tamely petered out. It is perhaps worthwhile speculating on what might have been – and might yet be in years to come if the disease spreads among the millions of people in the world who are both hungry and lack any kind of medical care.

There is no shortage of likely sources of pandemics and epidemics in the future. One source is old disease organisms that could gain resistance to drugs that now destroy them. Another danger is our own complacency. Vaccines have so successfully suppressed diphtheria and poliomyelitis that parents increasingly forget that these were once-feared killing or crippling diseases, and it has become fairly common among parents to omit the vaccinations required to keep their children safe. Then, too, war, earthquake, famine, flood could release a Pandora's Box of typhoid, cholera, plague, or other germs. Only the constant vigilance of the developed countries, and their awareness of the problems of the less fortunate in the world holds down the lid on plague and pestilence.

Above: the speed with which man can travel to any part of the globe also means that deadly diseases can be transported with equal speed. **Below:** these outside lavatories in Dacca, Bangladesh are another example of insanitary conditions that help spread diseases such as cholera.

139

Chapter 8

Tragic Accidents

Man is an inventive animal and the steps of his technical development are accompanied by an increasing mastery over his surroundings. In no other area have his inventions brought such resounding changes as in his means of transport. Only 150 years ago man was unable to move across the land faster than a horse could carry him, nor could he travel over the seas swifter than the wind blew the sails of his ship. Since that time great technical advances have carried him with increased speed, safety, and comfort over land, over sea, beneath the sea, into the air, and finally beyond the earth to other worlds.

But man's ambition can sometimes tragically outstrip his technical knowhow. The terrible accidents that result ultimately lead to greater knowledge but at the time inevitably the fear is voiced that man has reached the frontier of his achievements.

Opposite: searching the wreckage of an aircraft for survivors. Although statistics may prove that air travel is as safe as, or safer than, other means of transport, the loss of many passengers in a single accident can often produce a deep sense of shock to a whole nation with repercussions throughout the whole field of international travel.

The Tay Bridge Disaster
Scotland 1879

There were no first-class passengers traveling on the 5.20 pm mail train from Burntisland to Dundee but the second- and third-class carriages were moderately well filled. Not full, for this December 28 was a Sunday, and in 1879 few Scottish people approved of travel on the Sabbath. Furious westerly winds were keeping all but the most determined travelers at home. The girders of the impressive new bridge across the Tay estuary trembled and sang in the gale like a giant's harp.

Shortly after 7 pm the train pulled in to Wormit station at the south end of the two-mile-long bridge. The train had a four-man crew and about 80 men, women, and children passengers. At 7.13 the Wormit signalman, Thomas Barclay, gave the train permission to cross the single-track bridge. The gale was now blowing violently as Barclay and another railwayman, John Watt – who had expressed doubts about the safety of the bridge – stood watching the train steam slowly onto the bridge at three miles an hour. Barclay and Watt remained watching until the red tail lights disappeared within the high girders of the central spans. At this moment "a fearful blast, with a roar resembling a continuous roll of thunder, swept down the river." The lights of the train did not reappear on the curve down to Dundee, and when Barclay tried to telegraph Dundee the line was dead.

Left: the two-mile-long Tay Bridge before the 1879 disaster.

Right: steam launches and a diver searching for survivors and bodies after the Tay Bridge disaster. Three of the 12 central cast iron piers that collapsed can be seen in the picture.

Below: one of the two North British Railway trains that operated on the Dundee to Burntisland line, using the Tay Bridge crossing.

"There is something wrong with the train," said Watt and went down to the beach. There was indeed something wrong. All 13 of the central high girders and 12 cast-iron piers had crashed into the River Tay carrying with them the train and all its 80 passengers.

At Tay Bridge Station on the north end of the bridge the tremendous gust had blown down part of the station roof. While the Stationmaster was preoccupied with this, some people hurried into the station saying they had seen a red flash on the bridge. The train was four minutes overdue and the stationmaster hastened to the signal tower where he found the signalman very anxious because his line across the bridge to Wormit was dead. A station foreman and a waitingroom attendant set off to walk onto the bridge fighting their way through the blinding storm until within six feet of the gap. There was nothing beyond but black emptiness.

There were no survivors of the Tay Bridge Disaster. Two mail bags were washed ashore during the night and the following morning some of the dead came floating in, with small articles of luggage and fragments of broken coachwork. A team of naval divers went down through the mass of twisted metal and located the train lying in a tangle of girders. The bridge had been open for barely 18 months.

The North British Railway Company, who for some years had wanted to bridge the Firth of Tay, entrusted the design to Thomas Bouch, a construction engineer. Bouch said of the Tay Bridge project, "It is a very ordinary undertaking," and designed a structure of 85 spans of wrought iron lattice girders and in midstream 13 high girders, 11 of them with a span of 245 feet. This section of the bridge rested on piers of wrought iron caissons lined with brick and filled with concrete. The bridge was opened in June 1878; a year later Queen Victoria traveled over it and created Thomas Bouch a knight.

But the Court of Inquiry into the disaster found that Bouch had not allowed in his design for the notorious winds of the Tay Valley, and had failed to supervise the work of his contractors, Hopkins, Gilkes, & Company. In reply to questioning, this firm's foundry foreman said evasively, "I wouldn't like to say that it was the best, but . . . it was not what you would call terribly bad iron." In fact, it was discovered that the quality of the iron was appalling and that the collapse had probably begun in one of the piers, weakened by unequal expansion of the cast iron and the concrete, poured into the caissons while wet.

The disaster broke Sir Thomas Bouch. He was dead within six months. The disaster train was raised from the river bed, repaired, and returned to service but it is said it was never allowed to cross the Tay again.

The "Unsinkable" Titanic
Atlantic: 1912

Only one ship has been proudly called "unsinkable" and on its maiden voyage it sank. At 2.20 in the morning of April 15, 1912 the *SS Titanic* went down in the northwest Atlantic, taking with it 1513 of the 2224 people on board. It was a sea disaster without equal, not so much because of the appalling death toll, but because it seemed to pass a damning comment on the ability and aspirations of man. The British ship was the newest and most luxurious ship in the world, nearly 900 feet long, 11 decks high, and a marvel of technology and science. Yet a 10-second scrape against the submerged shelf of a drifting iceberg turned all this achievement into mockery.

When the White Star Line's *Titanic* sailed from Southampton on April 10 bound for New York its passenger list included many millionaires and members of British and American fashionable Society, all bent on enjoying a carefree week's voyage on the latest miracle of the sea. Far below, on levels ignored by the first-class passengers and in conditions far less privileged, hundreds of emigrants were crossing the Atlantic to a new life in a new land.

The first days were uneventful but on the fourth day the radio operator began receiving alarming messages from ships ahead. Icebergs were drifting unusually far south. Throughout Sunday April 14, in the gaps between the innumerable personal cables sent out by the first-class passengers, the messages continued to come in. The first was forgotten about for several hours. Two later messages never arrived at the bridge. By early evening the air temperature fell sharply but despite this indication that ice was in the vicinity the *Titanic* never changed its direction nor reduced its speed even slightly.

As night fell Captain Edward Smith posted lookouts to watch for ice and at 11.40 pm the crow's-nest lookout caught a glimpse of an iceberg ahead. The officer on the bridge ordered the *Titanic* to turn hard to starboard. It was too late – the ice cut a 300-foot slice along the plates of the ship's hull. Ironically, if the ship had continued on course and collided with the ice head-on it might well have emerged from the encounter scarcely damaged.

Most passengers, aware only of a faint jarring sensation, thought no more about it. But to the engineers anxiously examining the damage it was clear the ship was doomed. The "unsinkable" could keep afloat if four of its 16 watertight compartments were flooded but the iceberg had sliced the walls of five. Already third-class passengers had awoken to find the floor of their cabins awash. The radio operator sent out the new SOS call – the first time it had been used by a ship in distress – and at 12.05 the order was given to launch the lifeboats.

Left: the newly completed White Star Line's *SS Titanic* leaves Belfast in Northern Ireland.

Right: an artist's impression of the "unsinkable" *Titanic* at the moment it struck the iceberg that sank it. In fact had the *Titanic* struck the iceberg head-on (as is depicted here) it might not have sunk. By turning to avoid the iceberg, the undersea part of the ice holed five watertight compartments – and the ship was doomed.

Below: Captain Edward Smith, Commander of the *SS Titanic* on its first – and last, voyage.

Unknown to the passengers the lifeboats held no more than 1178 people, half the number of people on board – and even this was generous by the legal requirements of the day. At first there was no panic. Passengers simply refused to believe the ship could be in danger – after all, it was the "unsinkable." Only when it began to list alarmingly did they lose their complacency. Women and children were given priority and husbands and fathers said farewell to their weeping families. There were also shameful displays of selfishness by people who thought only of themselves. Number One lifeboat, with a capacity of 40, was lowered with only 12 people in it – Sir Cosmo and Lady Duff Gordon, her secretary, two Americans, six stokers, and one of the ice lookout men. First-class

Above: an illustration from a British newspaper showing Captain Smith in the water and one of his crew offering to rescue him. Smith refused, telling the men to look after themselves. He was never seen again.

passengers were looked after in preference to those of other classes. Only four women from the first class died, three of them by choice because they prefered to remain with their husbands. But of the 272 women in second and third class only 96 survived – and for a time the doors leading down to the third-class levels were locked to prevent people surging up.

The ship's band played ragtime tunes on the sloping deck, their last number being the hymn "Autumn" with its hopeful line, "Hold me up in high waters." As the ship tilted further, millionaire Benjamin Guggenheim and his valet went to their cabins and reappeared on deck in evening dress. Howard Case, a London oil executive, was last seen leaning against the top deck calmly lighting a cigarette. At 2.20 am the *Titanic* stood almost vertical in the water and then slid down, nose first, to bury itself in the soft Atlantic ooze two miles below. The emigrants who had been unable to find their way along the dark companionways were carried down with the ship. Those on deck were washed into the freezing sea where their cries for assistance were largely ignored by those in the lifeboats. The most disgraceful feature of the appalling tragedy is that out of approximately 1500 people in the water only 13 were picked up by 18 lightly laden boats.

The Last British Airship
France: 1931

Sweat was pouring down the height coxswain's face. "It's as much as I can do to hold her up," he gasped. The British airship *R101* was on display at the Royal Air Force airfield at Hendon, a few miles northwest of London, and something was seriously wrong with its stability. Either it nosedived or it tried to rise steeply nose-up and it was as much as the sweating crewman could do to pull the airship back. An officer

from the rival British airship *R100* was a guest on the flight and he commented afterward that it was the first time he had ever been alarmed in an airship.

This instability was never fully cured but it was only one of the many faults that dogged the *R101* until it crashed in flames on its first commissioned voyage in October 1931. Rivalry between the two airships lay at the root of the poor performance and this dated back to 1923 when the government of the time ordered two airships to be built, one by the commercial firm of Vickers, another by the Air Ministry at the government airship works at Cardington, Hertfordshire.

The two teams of designers worked independently and in the five years it took to make the airships neither team conferred with the other on problems both had to solve. There was much duplication of

Above: luncheon being served aboard the *R101*. Several of the people in the photograph were later killed when the airship burned out over France.

Left: the British airship, the *R101* circling St Paul's Cathedral in London.

Right: an aerial view of the wreckage of the *R101* which crashed and caught fire near Beauvais, France, burning 48 passengers to death.

effort as a result and enormous wastage of money, chiefly from the Air Ministry team. Both airships were made buoyant by hydrogen gas, which, though the lightest gas available, also explodes violently when mixed with oxygen and ignited with a spark – an extremely hazardous character in view of the almost inevitable slight accidents such large craft were exposed to. The design chosen for the *R101*'s 777-foot hull was beautifully streamlined, and the finish and probably the workmanship was better than its rival. But power and steerage were complicated and far less efficient. The *R101* was powered by diesel engines instead of by lighter petrol engines, its tail fins had a tendency to stall at small angles and most serious of all, the gas valves were so sensitive that they opened automatically if tilted more than three degrees. As the *R101* rolled considerably more than three degrees in the air, it was always losing gas and becoming heavier instead of steadily becoming lighter through burning fuel.

After the *R100* had taken successfully to the air in 1930 and flown safely to Canada and back, the Air Ministry urged their own team to finish the government ship. The designers had had to put up with constant interference by government officials. Morale was low. After its unsatisfactory Hendon flight it was cut in two and a new bay inserted with extra gas bags to increase its height.

The Air Minister was a former army general who, on being created a baron, had taken the title Lord Thomson of Cardington, as though to emphasize his

for its first scheduled stop, Ismailia on the Suez Canal. The airship managed to cross the Channel but over northern France the winds increased and its instability worsened. At 1.30 the *R101* passed so low over the village of Saint-Valery-sur-Somme that the inhabitants scrambled from their beds, certain it would scrape the roofs off their houses. Slowly – too slowly – the airship roared on into the pitch-dark night. Just before Beauvais the steadily leaking airship hit the ground. It righted itself and there was apparently no panic on board.

A few seconds later the airship hit the ground again, this time in a wood. Probably it was a spark from some broken electrical circuit that set light to the leaking gas. A huge flame lit the area like daylight and a roar sounded through the valley as 5,000,000 cubic feet of

identification with the success of the *R101*. He had ambitions to become Viceroy of India and for this personal reason as well as for other political considerations he insisted that the *R101* be available to fly him to India and back in October 1931. The airship was far from ready. Tests had not been completed and it had never flown at full speed nor in bad weather. When Lord Thomson and his party of Air Ministry officials boarded at Cardington the airship had not been certified as airworthy. The crew were tired and strong winds with rain were forecast.

Still too heavy – the dining room was fitted with heavy carpets and potted palm trees were arranged in the lounge and smoking room – four tons of water ballast had to be dropped before the *R101* could set off

hydrogen exploded. Of the men aboard the airship, 48 were burned to death at once, including the designers, and those who had ordered it to fly before it was ready. Two others died later of their injuries and the six men who survived, all in the rear gondola, owed their lives to the water from the emergency ballast tank that had been emptied over them in a last desperate attempt to gain height. This gave the men just enough time to make their escape.

The crash of the *R101* put an end to British interest in airships. The wish to dismiss all thought of them was taken to such an extreme that the *R100*, which had worked admirably, was taken to pieces and the remains flattened with a steamroller and sold for scrap.

The Hindenburg's Last Voyage
Lakehurst, USA: 1937

The vast silvery bulk of the *LZ129 Hindenburg* approached the airship station at Lakehurst, New Jersey, for the third time in three hours. Lightning still flickered on the horizon but the rain clouds had moved away westward. After the two delays the airship's commander, Captain Max Pruss, decided it was safe to bring the ship in to the mooring mast. He gave the necessary orders.

The *Hindenburg* came over the airfield at a height of 590 feet. Down below the ground crew, reporters, cameramen, and relatives waiting to greet the passengers watched the "great floating palace" slowly descend. At 7.21 on this evening of May 6, 1937, two lines dropped from the nose of the ship to the ground 200 feet beneath and were seized by the waiting line handlers. At the rear of the ship, in the lower vertical fin, four crewmen were preparing to pay out the mooring cables. At 7.25 they heard a "pop," a sound like the firing of a small gun, and looked up to see a brilliant flash where the central catwalk passed through Gas Cell 4. Seconds later the hydrogen gas,

cause of so many airship disasters in the past, was a mass of flame.

After a moment's horrified disbelief the waiting crowd screamed and scattered. In the control gondola Captain Pruss had felt only a slight shudder and did not realize what had happened until he glanced out and saw the ground below glowing redly. Flames from the blazing tail leaped forward bursting one gas cell after another to fuel more hydrogen to the already white hot inferno. People 15 miles away heard the explosions as the dying ship sank to the ground beneath an enormous mushroom of fire and smoke. In 32 seconds the *Hindenburg* was dead and so were 35 of the passengers and crew aboard her. Dead also was the era of airship travel. There would never be another commercial airship flight.

What started the fire on the *Hindenburg?* The commission of inquiry set up at Lakehurst to discover the cause of the tragedy considered various possibilities – a spark from an engine, an electrical fault, a sticking gas valve. Dr Hugo Eckener, considered after Count von Zeppelin to be the greatest figure in airship development, believed that an internal stay wire had broken and pierced a gas cell while at the same time creating static electricity that ignited the escaping hydrogen. The commission wanted to consider the possibility of sabotage but those crew members well enough to be called to give evidence were curiously unhelpful on this point. Not till after

World War II was it learned that Hermann Goering, chief of the Nazi air force had sent orders to the officers and crew of the *Hindenburg* that "they should not try to find an explanation." The destruction of the airship was a serious enough blow to the pride of Nazi Germany. If it had become known that an enemy saboteur had managed to elude the strict security surrounding the airship, the anger within Germany – and perhaps also the flickering powers of resistance – might have become uncontrollable. So nothing was said. No suspicions were voiced. One of the *Hindenburg's* officers later quoted their instructions: "Give no opinions. Answer questions. No more."

Until this last voyage of the *Hindenburg* there had never been a passenger fatality in any of Germany's commercial airships. The *Graf Zeppelin*, most successful airship ever built, entered the passenger service in 1928 and in nine years flew 590 flights, carrying over 16,000 passengers and covering a distance of 1,053,389 miles. Work on the even larger *Hindenburg* began in 1931. Designed specifically for the North and South Atlantic run it could carry 70 passengers and 13 tons of freight and mail. The cabins, promenade decks, and state rooms were all elegantly and simply decorated. The spacious lounge even contained a small, lightweight piano made of aluminum.

The obvious weakness of the *Hindenburg* was the 7,000,000 cubic feet of inflammable hydrogen that filled the 16 vast gas cells. Dr Eckener's original design for the ship specified the noninflammable gas helium. But at that time the United States held the monopoly of helium production and with Hitler's rise to power in 1933 refused to grant an export permit for this strategically important gas. Only by airship could the cities of America be bombed. So the gas cells were altered and stringent fire precautions introduced. The crew wore hemp-soled shoes and antistatic asbestos overalls without buttons or any kind of metallic surface. All matches and lighters were removed from passengers before they boarded. The smoking room was especially insulated, pressurized to prevent hydrogen entering, and fitted with a double door. A steward lit cigars and cigarettes from a special lighter and ensured that no fire left the room.

The *Hindenburg* went into passenger service in May 1936 and safely performed several journeys to Lakehurst and to Rio de Janeiro. In March 1937 it began the first of the season's South American crossings, fully booked in both directions, and on May 3 left Frankfurt-am-Main on the first of 18 flights to North America scheduled for the year.

This flight however was not fully booked. For appearance's sake, so that the airship should not fly three-fourths empty, the authorities offered complimentary tickets to certain privileged persons. Even some of these had been politely declined. It was very puzzling. It was almost as though the flying public had become aware of a fact the Nazi authorities wished to

Left: the 240-ton airship *Hindenburg*, the pride of Nazi Germany, seen here at Frankfurt airfield before its last flight.

Right: the luxuriously appointed lounge of the *Hindenburg*.

Below: Captain Pruss (left) the ill-fated *Hindenburg's* commander in the control gondola.

keep secret: that there had been several threats to blow up the *Hindenburg* if she landed in America.

Accordingly, the day before the passengers boarded the airship, security police had searched it. Crew members, too, had checked as best they could, though they knew only too well how easily something could be hidden in the folds of material in the cavernous interior – and none more so than the three riggers, the only crew members permitted to use the central catwalk that ran from nose to tail high up through the center of the airship. This catwalk was a recent innovation and one of the riggers, the quiet and secretive Erich Spehl, had helped to cut and sew the tunnels through the 16 gas cells to make the catwalk possible. The other two riggers on the *Graf Zeppelin* at the time had not acquired Spehl's intimate knowledge of the catwalk.

Nothing suspicious was found. The following day 36 passengers embarked – about half the capacity –

and the greatest of the zeppelins took to the air. Two and a half days later it crossed the North American coast at Boston and moved south toward New Jersey, arriving above Lakehurst at 4 pm but not able to commence landing until 7.10. Supporters of the sabotage theory argue that it may not have been intended to blow up the *Hindenburg* while it was in the air but after all the passengers and crew had disembarked. It may have been that the delay caused by the storm threw out the timing. Whatever the cause, by 7.25 the airship was a blazing inferno.

When Captain Pruss realized his ship was doomed he knew the only hope of escape for the passengers lay in getting the airship down to the ground as quickly as possible. Even before it touched ground some of the passengers jumped from windows, doors, any opening they could find, and hurtled to the ground. Miraculously, there were some survivors. Once on the ground, others were saved. One or two stepped off without a singed hair on them. Captain Pruss repeatedly ran into the flaming wreckage to help until he was forcibly prevented from reentering. A 14-year-old cabin boy Werner Franz saw a mass of blazing wreckage falling toward him, then a burst water tank soaked him and saved his life. The four men in the tail section emerged from it virtually unscathed.

The crew in the interior were not so lucky. In the most forward section electrician Joseph Leibrecht, hung onto his overhead hand grips with a desperation born of terror. The airship sank to the ground tail-first and as Leibrecht swung from the handgrips he

Left: the moment of the explosion aboard the *Hindenburg*.
Above: within seconds the whole airship was ablaze.
Below: it took only some 30 seconds for the highly inflammable hydrogen-filled airship to burn out. In the spectacular disaster 36 of the passengers and crew died, bringing to an end regular airship services from Germany.

observed a fearful sight: "the other 11 men in the nose of the ship falling in rapid succession back into the raging crucible that had been the interior of the *Hindenburg*."

One of these 11 was the tall, fair-haired rigger, Erich Spehl. A moody and reserved young man, his hobby was photography. He had full access to the interior of the airship and could have placed an explosive device in the crevices of a gas cell on many occasions. His last watch ended one and a half hours before the explosion, and it is significant that at the time of the blast he was as far away from it as possible. Before the *Hindenburg* left Frankfurt he had been seen in the company of an older woman suspected of having Communist sympathies. She called at the Zeppelin company's offices three times during the airship's flight to ask about its position.

One other piece of evidence, overlooked by the Commission of Inquiry, could link Spehl with the disaster. A small metallic object was removed from the wreckage and identified as the remains of a small dry battery – not powerful in itself but when connected to a photographic flash bulb able to produce in it a flash of dazzling brilliance and a temperature briefly of 6400 degrees Fahrenheit – six times the temperature required to ignite hydrogen. The men in the tail fin who saw the start of the fire said it began with the sort of flash that could be produced by a photoflash bulb.

A battery, a bulb, a pocket watch to set the time of the explosion – that would be all that would be necessary to destroy the airship. Spehl died in the inferno so it will never be known for certain whether it was an inferno of his own making.

Trapped in a Submarine
Liverpool Bay: 1939

"You see . . . how easy . . . it is," gasped Lieutenant Harold Chapman. From within the trapped British submarine *Thetis* he had watched two men safely make their escape to the surface. After 17 hours with the submarine's bow held in the soft mud 160 feet down in the strong tidal waters of Liverpool Bay, sufficient water and fuel had been pumped out to raise the stern until it was several feet above water. The submarine had been located by the surface ships and the two men who had just successfully made their way through the aft escape chamber were at this moment being picked up. But after so many hours submerged the concentration of carbon dioxide within the submarine was becoming painfully high. Two more men would escape. They were to be the last – 99 stayed and died.

On June 1, 1939, *HMS Thetis* had left Birkenhead on her final acceptance trials. Officers and crew numbered 53 in all but on this occasion there were also 50 passengers aboard – Admiralty personnel, representatives from the various firms involved in building it, and two men from the firm of Liverpool caterers who were supplying the celebratory lunch.

Thetis was escorted by the tug *Grebecock* to its diving position 38 miles out of Liverpool. A slow dive had been planned for 2 pm but the *Thetis* proved to

have far too little ballast and, despite the 50 extra people aboard, was too light. It was half an hour before the bow could be made to go down. But after another half hour it descended, very quickly, and disappeared from the *Grebecock's* sight.

What had happened was that, in trying to account for the submarine's failure to dive, Lieutenant Frederick Woods, the torpedo officer, went to examine the six torpedo tubes in the bows to discover whether they were filled with air or water. The first four he examined were filled with air. When he reached the fifth tube it, too, appeared to be filled with air. In fact an inspection hole had been blocked with paint. Other tests were thwarted by a mechanical fault. The tube was in fact filled with water – and far more serious:

Left: the ill-fated British submarine *HMS Thetis* being launched.

Right: a salvage vessel alongside the upended stern of the *Thetis*, which had sunk in Liverpool Bay while undergoing acceptance trials. Soon after the picture was taken more water was let into the submarine which, combined with strong tides, snapped the cable and the submarine and its 99 passengers and crew sank to the bottom.

someone had left the seaward end of the tube, the bow-cap, open. When the rear door of No. 5 tube was opened, sea water surged in.

Woods and the other crewmen present scrambled back frantically into the next compartment but as the boat was now rapidly tilting downward they were unable to pull tight and close the heavy bulkhead door. They retreated to the second watertight door, which they did manage to close. But with two compartments flooded the submarine lost its buoyancy and within moments it was down on the sea bed.

Three attempts were made to go out through the forward escape hatch into the flooded compartments to close the tube door. All failed because the Royal Navy had trained submariners to work at pressure in a tank that was only 15 feet deep. The difference in pressure between 15 and 150 feet had never been taken into account.

In the strong surface tides *Grebecock* drifted four miles from where *Thetis* had sunk and it was not located until 7.50 the following morning. The tug was not equipped with a strong wireless and when its messages were received they were delayed on shore. The Admiralty was slow to bring divers and suitably strong vessels to the scene, and when they finally arrived the divers were able to work only in the 30-minute interval between tides.

With twice the normal complement of men aboard the *Thetis*, the air became deadly after 20 hours. Woods and another senior officer went out through the aft escape chamber carrying details of a plan to pump air into the submarine and draw the carbon dioxide out. Another successful escape followed. Two sub-

sequent attempts failed because a safety clip on the escape hatch was not fully withdrawn, making it impossible to open the hatch from inside the escape chamber. This error was not noticed by the increasingly drowsy submariners. Equipment for introducing the two-way air tubes did not arrive and at 3 pm, 24 hours after its fatal dive, the hawser holding *Thetis* to the salvage vessel *Vigilant* snapped and the submarine was gone. Its weight had suddenly increased after the last couple in the escape chamber opened in error the forward door into the engine room. Water rushed in and spread rapidly through the boat, drowning those men who had not already succumbed to oxygen starvation.

The Admiralty Report drew attention to the errors of certain individuals but ignored their own failure to organize adequate inspection, proper training, and swift rescue work. Presumably it was thought unwise

to criticize the Admiralty in 1940 once war had begun.

Thetis was finally salvaged and beached in October 1939, repaired and renamed *Thunderbolt*. It spent three years at sea before being sunk off Sicily by an Italian sloop in March 1943. For the second and final time it sank with a full crew – although on this occasion the deaths of the men aboard were quicker.

Above: one of the divers shown during salvage operations.

Below: the *Thetis*, raised and beached after five months at the bottom of Liverpool Bay.

153

Disaster Underground
London: 1975

"His eyes seemed to be staring straight ahead. They seemed to be larger than life." This is how an eye-witness standing on London Underground's platform at Moorgate station described the driver of the six-coach train that hurtled past him at an estimated 40 miles an hour on February 28, 1975. Moorgate station, near the heart of the City of London, is the terminus of a short branch line but the driver in his cab at the front of the leading coach did not slow the

construction the tunnel was 16 feet high and not the more usual 10 feet. The difference of six feet saved many lives in the third coach and even in the second. John Ryder, a survivor from the second coach, recalled, "After we stopped there was a long silence and then people started moaning but there was nothing we could do to help them. One woman was lying across me and I was holding her head in my hand . . . On either side the roof had squashed down to the floor." A fireman reported that some bodies appeared to have been forced through the floor. He added, "You could tell when somebody was alive; when you touched them they screamed."

Rescuers worked all day in the heat, dust, foul air, and cramped conditions to free the injured from the telescoped wreckage of the front coaches. Temperatures reached 120°F at times and rescuers required

Left: the view outside the London Underground tube station at Moorgate after the train crash on February 28, 1975.

Right, above: the interior of one of the tube-train compartments.

Right, below: one of the wounded passengers being brought out of the wreckage between the train and the tunnel wall.

train as he approached. To some witnesses and survivors it seemed to gather speed as it raced through the station and into the short blind tunnel at the far end. The leading coach smashed through the buffers, plowed through a barrier of sand, and crashed into the end wall of stone and brick backed by the solid earth. The second coach telescoped into the first, compressing it into less than half its original 50-foot length. The third coach rode up on top of the second, embedding its front in the roof of the tunnel. The three rear coaches came to a stop alongside the platform. The time was 8.46, the peak of London's rush-hour.

The London Underground safety record was so good that no annual casualty reports had been issued for many years. The 1975 Moorgate accident in which eventually 43 people died was by far the worst since the system was opened in 1863. By a peculiarity of

salt tablets to keep going and could only work shifts of 20 minutes with breaks of 40 minutes. Doctors and rescue workers had to crawl through a hole three feet by two feet bored into the second coach where it had been forced into the first. One doctor briefly emerging to take some breaths of clear air was barely able to describe the scene below. "It is so ghastly I just can't explain. There have been terrible injuries and people very badly mutilated." A senior police officer commented. "It is like working in a sardine tin; it is just a lump of consolidated metal."

It was 13 hours before the last two survivors were brought out, and another four days before the body of the driver, Leslie Newson, could be recovered, after breakdown gangs had smashed through the metal and winched out the heavy wheels of the third coach suspended above the other two. The driver's cab was

crushed to a depth of only six inches against the end of the tunnel and it was not possible to determine the position of the driver's hands at the time of the crash. Underground trains are equipped with two emergency braking systems and a safety device known as the "dead man's handle," designed to stop the train in the event of the driver's collapse or death. All these systems were discovered to have been effective when the crash occurred and there was no indication that the driver had relaxed his hold on the "dead man's handle."

In view of the description of Newson's staring eyes there were suggestions that he had gone into a trance, or was even committing a bizarre form of suicide. But other photographs show him to have had rather staring eyes anyway. He was 56 and described as a careful and conscientious man who loved his job. There were only six stations on the run to and from Moorgate which makes it very dull for the driver and it is possible that on this particular morning – in spite of many years successfully driving the run – Driver Newson became fatally mesmerized. The public inquiry ended with no positive reason having emerged for the crash – except that no attempt had been made to apply the brakes.

The World's Worst Air Crash
Tenerife: 1977

to be dealt with by the three air traffic controllers. At 1.45 pm a KLM Boeing 747 flew in from Amsterdam and 90 minutes later a Pan American 747 from Los Angeles joined it on the crowded airfield. The KLM jumbo carried 235 passengers and a crew of 14, the Pan American jumbo 364 passengers and a crew of 16.

Los Rodeos has long been known to pilots as a

Ever since the era of the jumbo jets began in 1969 the airlines of the world have dreaded the day when one of these giant planes would crash loaded with passengers. That day finally came on March 27, 1977, but the accident involved not one but two jumbo jets. They collided and exploded on the runway of Los Rodeos airfield on the island of Tenerife, largest of the Spanish Canary Islands off the west coast of Africa. Over 570 people were killed in the blast and raging fire that followed. It was the world's worst disaster of the air.

Sundays were always busy days at Los Rodeos. On Sunday, March 27, air traffic was exceptionally heavy. In the morning a bomb had exploded in a shop at Las Palmas on the island of Grand Canary and all the planes that would have normally landed there were diverted to Tenerife. Normal Sunday traffic was doubled, with nearly 400 landings and takeoffs having

difficult airfield. Narrow and windswept, with only one main runway, it lies 2000 feet up in the mountains. During the afternoon mist rolled over the airfield and by 5.0 pm a light drizzle was falling. Horizontal visibility was 300 feet but vertical visibility was almost zero, conditions just on the margin of safety. After waiting three hours 15 minutes the KLM was given instructions to prepare for takeoff. From the terminal buildings it proceeded across a short linking runway to the single takeoff runway. It turned left into the main runway, taxied to the far end, and made a 180 degree turn in readiness for the takeoff flight back along the route it had come. The Panam plane was to follow it and make the same maneuver with one important difference: as it taxied to the far end of the main runway it was to turn left off it down a diagonal runway that would eventually bring it to

156

the takeoff position – but behind the KLM plane, which would by then be taking off.

The Panam copilot Robert Bragg vividly recalled what happened as his plane approached the diagonal that would take it off the main runway. "We saw lights ahead of us in the fog. At first we thought it was KLM standing there at the end of the runway. Then

ing with all except their shoes burned off them. "They were walking singly, mechanically," he said, "without any sort of reaction, like puppets."

How could the collision have occurred? Both Captain Grubbs and the KLM pilot, Captain Veldhuizen van Zanted, were senior and experienced men. One suggestion is that the Panam was making for the

Above: Spanish soldiers searching among the wreckage after the crash between a KLM jumbo jet and a Boeing 747 at Tenerife on the Canary Islands in March 1977.

Left: the scene of the crash on the Los Rodeos airfield.

we realized they were coming toward us." In the three seconds left to them the Panam flight crew turned the nose of their plane left, off the runway. The pilot, Captain Victor Grubbs, called the control tower – "We're still on the runway!" Bragg remembers shouting, "Get off, get off!" But the KLM plane was already lifting its nosewheel and could neither stop nor swerve nor get high enough to miss the Panam plane, which it hit amidships, ripping the top off. The KLM then hit the ground, and bounced along for a further 600 yards, before finally exploding, killing everybody on board.

The Panam plane did not catch fire immediately and 54 people managed to jump from the gaping holes in the hull before the fuel tanks exploded and enveloped the remaining 326 in flames. Mr Asger Smith, a Danish travel agent, saw some of the survivors emerg-

wrong diagonal, too far along the main runway. Flying conditions on that foggy, crowded Sunday were dangerously complicated by the fact that two of the airfield's three radio frequencies had been out of action for six months. All planes had to use the same frequency and it is thought this may have led to a fatal misunderstanding on the part of the KLM flight crew. The last exchanges between the planes and the control tower were recorded on the flight data recorders – the "black boxes" – and recovered after the explosions. According to a report in the London *Sunday Times* the exchanges that took place went as follows:

"KLM: We are now ready for takeoff.
Tower: Ok. Stand by for takeoff. I will call you.
Panam: *Clipper 1736.*
Tower: *Papa Alpha 1736*, report runway cleared.
Panam: We'll report runway cleared.
Tower: Ok. Thank you."

Did the KLM flight crew believe they had been cleared for takeoff, having heard the words "runway cleared" without realizing it was a message to the Panam plane? Nothing further is recorded on the black boxes and within seconds 575 people were dead.

Space Age Catastrophes

"Fire – I smell fire!" the frantic voice suddenly shouted over the intercom. The date was January 27, 1967. A full-dress rehearsal was under way at Cape Kennedy for Apollo 4, a manned earth-orbit test planned for later that year. It was 6 pm. The astronauts, Gus Grisson, Edward H. White, and Roger B. Chaffee had been strapped into their seats since noon, working their way through the countdown as if it were the real thing. The big Saturn rocket contained no fuel, so there were no fire crews or doctors standing

Chaffee: "We're on fire – get us out of here!" After that there was a deadly silence.

Investigation into the tragedy, the worst in American space history, suggested that a faulty wire near Grissom's couch sparked the fire. In seconds the 100-percent oxygen atmosphere turned the tiny, cramped command module into a blast furnace. The three astronauts never stood a chance. They died from smoke inhalation within 15 or 20 seconds after the fire started – the first fatalities of the space age.

In an unhappy coincidence, the Soviet space program too was struck by tragedy later that same year. On April 24 cosmonaut Vladimir Komarov was in earth orbit in Soyuz 1 spacecraft when Soviet ground control ordered him to end the mission ahead of schedule. At the re-entry stage of his flight the lines of his single parachute became snarled and failed to open properly. Komarov in his spacecraft plunged to

by when the frightened shout came over the intercom at the discovery of fire. Instruments in the control center flickered as the astronauts began groping to force open the sealed hatch of the command module. "Fire in the cockpit" shouted White. Instruments showed that the temperature in the cabin was rising sharply. Then came the sounds of unintelligible shouting as the trapped astronauts clawed and pounded on the hatch. Then a last desperate cry from

his death. He was the first spaceman ever to die in flight, but not the last.

Perhaps the most appalling space disaster of all occurred in June 1971. The Soviet cosmonauts Georgi Dobrovolsky, Viktor Patsayev, and Vladislav Volkov made a dramatic link-up between their spacecraft Soyuz XI and Salyut, the 24-ton space laboratory already in earth orbit. For 24 days they worked on numerous experiments and broadcast regular TV

crew landed alongside the spacecraft, and, rushing across, the ground personnel eagerly opened the hatch. All three crew members were lying lifeless in their seats.

What had gone wrong? A Soviet commission of inquiry set up immediately announced that sudden decompression, due to a hatch seal fault in the crew module, had been the cause of the cosmonauts' death. This was later changed to a faulty valve that had caused the fatal decompression.

In any case, Dobrovolsky, Patsayev, and Volkov had died in seconds at the very moment of their triumphant return to earth. It was a disaster that was to prove a stunning blow to the Soviet space program and no further activity took place for two years.

Giant bridges that collapse, unsinkable ships that go down on their maiden voyage, airships whose tragic failure end an era – all these present obstacles to man's

Above: an artist's impression of a capsule reentering earth's atmosphere.

Left: the interior of the Apollo 4 space rocket after the fire that killed astronauts Gus Grisson, Edward White, and Roger Chaffee.

Right: the crew of Soyuz XI, a decompression fault killed them in their moment of triumph.

Below: Colonel Vladimir Komarov, whose capsule parachute-brake failed on reentry to earth and he was killed.

bulletins to the Soviet people. On June 29, their mission successfully concluded, Soyuz XI separated with all systems functioning correctly and early on June 30, the spacecraft re-entered the earth's atmosphere. As usual, all radio communication with the crew ceased while the normal re-entry procedure of braking, parachute deployment, and soft-landing engines continued faultlessly. The spacecraft touched down exactly on target. A helicopter carrying a recovery

technological progress. But with the one exception of the airship, they have never prevented men from trying again. Once the will is there, once the ever-ingenious human mind is set upon an objective, it is generally only a matter of time before that objective is achieved. Only two years after the Apollo 4 disaster, United States astronauts Armstrong and Aldrin became the first men to walk on the moon's surface. It was a triumph of human technology.

159

Chapter 9

Economic Disasters

Most people dream of sudden riches, whether by chance, by the swift exercise of skill, or by divine favor. They dream of being suddenly freed from the uncertainty and all too often the boredom of laboring for their daily needs. Lotteries and the numerous variations of gambling have catered for this need down the ages, and add the spice of danger inseparable from all speculations. The alternative to sudden riches is sudden loss.

Sometimes whole communities have been overwhelmed by a speculative mania. Everyone wants to buy, resell, and take a quick profit. Prices soar dizzily until the bubble breaks. Those who took their profits in time are left very wealthy. Those who held on are ruined. It is the classic boom-crash situation. But occasionally a whole nation miscalculates. Warning signs go unheeded and the economy slumps. Governments try to prevent these damaging setbacks but crises come in many forms, sometimes hard to foresee.

Opposite: an unemployed man with his wife and baby from a 1920s poster. Rarely, it seems, do governments run their economies smoothly. Employment ever since the Industrial Revolution can be charted as a series of peaks and depressions. High birthrate, excessive wage demands, government mismanagement of the economy are all contributing factors. Whatever the cause, the effects in human terms are always hardship and poverty – sometimes destitution – for millions of people.

Profit-and Loss

A hole in the remote desert of Western Australia hit the world's headlines in September 1969 when a mining company named Poseidon brought up an ore sample rich in nickel. Such was the world shortage of nickel at the time that this essential component of stainless steel was fetching £7000 a ton against the official price of £985. In the Australian stock exchanges a savage scramble for shares in Poseidon sent

100 shares in September and watched a modest £25 outlay soar to £12,300 in five months. The fall took rather longer. Shares came down to £66 in March, halved again by May and at the end of the following year were valued at £6. The company went bankrupt and was acquired by Shell Oil but the difficulties of extraction – and the fall in nickel prices – led to the closure of the mine in February 1978. The shares are not entirely valueless, the nickel is still there to be mined, but "not in the foreseeable future." Those who held on to shares bought during the boom will never see a return on their money.

The rise and fall of Poseidon is a classic example of a speculative venture that goes wrong but there are many other ways of losing money. As well as such obvious causes of decline in the fortunes of individuals

Left: this tiny construction in the remote desert of Western Australia is all there is of the Australian Poseidon mining company, whose discovery of nickel-rich ore here in 1969 led to a phenomenal boom in the price of the company's stock.

Right: the nickel mine at Kambalda, Western Australia, proves there is more to mining than hysterical share-speculation.

their value rocketing from £0.25 to £10 in a week. Financial journalists urged caution, pointing out the inaccessibility of the region and the huge expenditure needed before the company could show a profit. Speculators paid no attention and amid scenes sometimes of near hysteria drove the few available shares up to £95 by the end of the year. The wonder share reached a peak of £123 on February 11, 1970, by which time the usual legends were circulating about the errand boy or the cleaning woman who had bought

or communities as war, famine, and plague are others rather less apparent. Scarcity of money leads to stagnation of trade but, paradoxically, too much money leads to the same thing. Incredible riches poured into 16th-century Spain from America but they brought about an inflation that priced Spanish goods out of the international market. The treasure poured out to pay for imported goods. King Philip II went bankrupt in 1575 and again in 1596. American treasure ruined Spain.

Debt-ridden kings have tried to restore their fortunes by debasing the coinage but this expedient always proved disastrous. Philip the Fair of France was a notorious offender and so was Henry VIII of England. As prices rose trade shrank, small merchants were ruined, and beggars swarmed the land.

"Put not your trust in princes," was a wise general rule. The mighty Florentine bankers who lent money to peasants and popes alike, also lent to foreign kings. The two leading banking houses of the Bardi and the Peruzzi had the misfortune to lend considerable sums to Edward III of England. In 1343 he calmly defaulted, owing them 1,400,000 golden florins – a colossal sum, five times the ordinary annual income of the English crown. The resulting bankruptcies spread a wave of panic through the financial centers of Europe.

weavers. Such ups and downs were inevitable consequences of the interplay between politics, trade, and economic growth. The same process can be seen at work today in the varying price of oil.

The modern stock-exchange originated 400 years ago in marine partnerships, where a number of small merchants split the cost of a ship and its cargo and later divided what profits there were. In time shares in these "venturing companies" came to be sold for cash in certain exchanges, notably those in Amsterdam and London. Man's compulsion to gamble led him to start speculating in commodities such as grain, spices, and whale oil where the supply was unpredictable but demand constant. Soon he was speculating in all manner of companies and by the middle of the 17th century stockbrokers and their clients were

Defaulting kings were one of the risks a banker of the time had to take but another of King Edward's actions wrecked the economy of a whole region. The cloth-making cities of Flanders – Bruges, Ghent, and Ypres – bought their wool from England. Edward cut off supplies. Within 50 years Ypres was a shrunken town and her manufactures were down to 15 percent of their former level. By a fortunate piece of timing a draper of Arras invented the art of woven tapestry, which re-employed hundreds of the impoverished

regularly congregating around one of the 46 marked pillars in the courtyard of the Amsterdam Exchange. Many of the features of the modern stock exchange were already in evidence, the "bulls," the optimists who try to raise the price of certain shares, the "bears," the pessimists who do the reverse. Also present were all the risks of sudden fortune and sudden ruin, and it is not surprising that Tulipomania, the first great boom-and-bust in the Poseidon style, occurred in the Netherlands.

Tulipomania!
The Netherlands: 1630s

In 1636 in the Netherlands a single tulip bulb was sold for the incredible sum of 4600 florins (£380) plus a new carriage and a pair of dapple gray horses. For comparison, a sheep at that time was worth 10 florins. This was Tulipomania, a frenzy of speculation that involved every class of Dutchman from prince to road-sweeper in a get-rich scramble.

Tulips were still new to Western Europe. The plant originated in Turkey, and the name is said to come, because of the shape of the flower, from the Turkish word meaning "turban." Tulips first appeared in the Netherlands in the 1590s and were at once in great demand because they possess a quality unique in the

floral world. A plant grown from seed will produce a flower of uniform coloring season after season, and all the bulbs that grow from it – offsets – will do the same, until after an indefinite time some plants will "break" or change into a striped form. The broken plant continues broken and so do the offsets from it. Botanists do not know why this phenomenon occurs

Above: a 17th-century Dutch flower-painting. Flowers have always been widely grown and admired by the Dutch.

but the gardeners of the Netherlands were quick to exploit its potentialities.

The broken varieties with the delicate feathering were the tulips collectors wanted. "Semper Augustus" – for which the carriage and pair had been paid – became the most coveted of all. It was basically white, feathered with scarlet, and tinted with blue underneath. In 1624 there were only 12 bulbs in existence and the price was 1200 florins each. The following year 3000 florins were offered for two of them but the owner refused to sell. People now realized that bulbs were a perfect investment. The offset was the interest while the capital remained intact. Bulbs could be grown in the smallest garden. Anyone could plant

Left: "Flora's Fool's Cap" a 1637 satirical Dutch print of tulipomania.
Below: drawing of four famous Dutch tulips (from left to right) Admiral Liefkins, white with crimson stripes; Viceroy d'Orange, white striped with violet: Brabanson, white with crimson stripes; and Anvers, white striped with violet.
Below right: an illustration from *The Black Tulip*, by the French novelist Alexandre Dumas. One of the themes of this novel of political intrigue, is the passionate interest shown by Dutch horticulturalists in tulip breeding and the offer of 100,000 guilders prize for a "grand black tulip."

were taken out of the ground, to September, when they were planted again. But now trading went on throughout the year, for delivery of purchases in the summer. Not only merchants but noblemen, sailors, farmers, turf-diggers, chimney sweeps, maids, and washerwomen, all joined eagerly in the trading. Artisans sold their tools, businessmen raised money on their houses. Some of the poorest people in the land gained in a few months houses, coaches, and horses and dressed in the finest clothes.

Bulbs that used to be sold at so much each or by the dozen came to be sold by individual weight, and weighed in goldsmith's scales as though they were jewels. Some were more precious than jewels. For one "Viceroy" bulb the following items were assembled in exchange: 2 loads of wheat, 4 loads of hay, 4 fat oxen, 8 fat pigs, 12 fat sheep, 2 hogsheads of wine, 4 barrels of beer, 2 barrels of butter, 1000 lbs of cheese, a complete bed, a suit of clothes, and a silver beaker – the whole valued at 2500 florins.

The crash came in February 1637 when suddenly everybody wanted to sell and no one wanted to buy. Contracted buyers could not meet their obligations on a falling market. Thousands of transactions were brought to a halt and the law courts crowded with people trying to make one another pay their debts.

bulbs or seed and if luck went his way he might find himself the fortunate owner of a uniquely beautiful and valuable tulip.

Tulip speculation reached fever pitch by 1634. Clubs were formed, tulip auctions held in inns. Soon the physical presence of the bulbs ceased to be neces- sary. At first they had been sold from June when they

The courts could not decide what to do and eventually most people agreed to cut their losses and accept 5 or 10 percent rather than hold out for the huge profits that would now never come. Tulipomania made a few people very rich, others became beggars. The first national involvement in commodity speculation had ended in disaster.

The John Law Affair
Paris: 1716-1720

John Law of Lauriston, Scottish-born gambler, duelist, and escaped murderer, was the unlikely savior of the fortunes of France after the country had been left virtually bankrupt at the death of Louis XIV. Law's system of finance, involving the liberal use of paper money, seemed to contain the secret of eternal wealth. Everyone made fortunes. The nobility repaid the debts of generations of reckless ancestors. A duchess was seen publicly to kiss Law's hand. The Regent's mother commented, "If a duchess will kiss his hand, what will not other women kiss?"

Above: John Law, Scottish financier and speculator. He founded the first bank of any kind in France and eventually controlled French finance. His financial empire collapsed through over-issue of paper money.

Law was born in Edinburgh but as a young man migrated to London where his mathematical skills brought him success as a gambler. After killing a rival in a duel he was sentenced to death, pardoned, imprisoned again, and finally escaped from the Tower of London after drugging his guard. For the next 20 years he led a roving life throughout Europe, supporting himself and his wife by his winnings at the gaming table and studying the intricacies of banking. He was the most successful gambler of the age and

often had to carry with him 100,000 or more livres in gold (about 10,000 dollars), an inconvenience that led him to invent gaming counters. All this time he was working on the details of his plan for stabilizing national finance. In 1715 he was in Paris and the time was ripe.

Louis XIV's wars had bled the French Treasury white and left a national debt of 3,500,000,000 gold livres. The interest on this alone was a crippling burden. Several provinces were refusing to pay taxes. Vast quantities of money had left France and throughout the country there was an acute shortage of cash. Law explained his economic theories to the Duke of Orleans, ruling as Regent for the boy-king Louis XV. "Money is to the State," he said "what blood is to the human body. Without the one, we cannot live. Without the other, we cannot act. Circulation is necessary to both alike."

Law convinced the Regent that the kind of money man used was unimportant and that as paper was lighter than gold, the ease with which it would be passed from hand to hand must accelerate trade. The flaw in his otherwise sound and modern theories lay in his failure to relate the quantity of his paper money to his bank's gold reserves. He refused to consider the possibility of a run on the bank and in the heady early years of success his confidence seemed justified. His banknotes were payable on demand in the value of the coin current at the time of their issue. This stroke of genius on Law's part made his notes immensely more popular than the continually debased coinage; they soon virtually replaced it. Deposits poured in to Law's bank, and as he had forecast, trade flourished.

Within a short time the bank had become the *Banque Royale* and Law had acquired the profitable tobacco and shipbuilding monopolies and the right to gather taxes. Next he set up a company for developing the Mississippi Valley, recently claimed for France by the explorer La Salle. The "Mississippi Scheme" was followed in 1719 by Law's acquisition of sole rights to trade with India, China, and Africa.

The unprecedented magnitude of these operations dazzled the public who scrambled to buy shares in his companies. The Regent and other nobles possessed so many shares that relatively few were available to the public. This sent the price sky-high and the street where the stock exchange was situated was continually blocked with frantic speculators. Immense fortunes were made. One servant, sent by his master to sell 250 shares at 8000 livres each, found on arrival at the stock exchange that the shares had meanwhile risen to 10,000. He pocketed the 500,000 difference, speculated further, and retired to the country. Rent for offices in the neighborhood was so phenomenal that a hunchback let out his hump at an enormous fee to speculators who needed a desk. Speculators waiting to enter Law's office were sometimes crushed to death but were borne along wedged between their neighbors until they dropped at the counter.

By January 1720 the 500-livre shares stood at

Above: "covetousness tries either to overtake or to outrun fortune" is the caption to this Dutch engraving satirizing the share mania of the years leading up to 1720, when the shares of the Mississippi Scheme, which John Law set up to finance the settlement of New Orleans, became greatly inflated through wild speculation. The company went bankrupt when the expected profits did not materialize.

Left: Madame Law, John Law's wife. She remained loyal to her husband through all his varying fortunes.

18,000! At this point the more prudent investors started to sell. Among the first was the Prince de Conti, a relative of the Regent and an enemy of Law. He cashed in his vast holding of stock and insisted on converting the banknotes he received into gold. Three wagons were required to remove it from the bank. Confidence was shaken. Prices started falling. People fought to sell as once they had fought to buy. There was panic to convert from Law's shares and banknotes into coin – and not enough coin in France to go around. Trade came to a standstill. Law tried every expedient to shore up his collapsing empire but was swept away in the general ruin. People starved with their pockets stuffed with the worthless paper money. Grimmest of all the discoveries after the crash was a certain house where a man had hanged himself, his wife was found stabbed to death and their children with their throats cut. In the same room lay half a dozen copper coins and 200,000 livres in notes.

The South Sea Bubble
London: 1719-1720

A company for making square cannon balls for use against the Turks. . . . A company for importing large jackasses from Spain to improve the breed of British mules. . . . A company for making butter out of beechnuts. . . . These harebrained schemes were just three of the countless promotions dangled before the eyes – and purses – of Londoners in the dizzy, desperate, money-made summer of 1720. Coaches choked the streets around Change Alley, where the stockbrokers did their business, clamoring to buy stock. Any stock would do. Prices were rising all the time and fortunes had been made by those who bought early. Some even bought shares in a mysterious "Company for carrying out an undertaking of Great Advantage, but no-one to know what it is." The ingenious promoter of this scheme took £2000 in share deposits on the first day of business and prudently left town.

Above: the Dividend Hall of South Sea House in 1810. Long before this date the original South Sea Company had crashed through wild speculation in its stock.

The market leader and initial cause of the whole frenzied boom was the South Sea Company, formed eight years earlier to trade with South America and revitalized in 1719 by a certain John Blount, son of a shoemaker but now a prosperous London merchant. Hearing of the sensational rise in Paris of government-backed Mississippi stock, Blount decided to embark on an even more grandiose scheme in London. The South Sea Company would take over from the British Government nothing less than the National Debt, swollen to £51,000,000 as a result of the recent French Wars.

The success of this bold plan depended on being able to persuade the government's creditors to exchange their state annuities for South Sea stock. Blount first bribed the king's German mistresses and

selected ministers to get his proposals through Parliament. The Chancellor of the Exchequer, Lord Aislabie, received £27,000. With the mixture prepared, it was time to inflate the bubble.

Blount and a small group of his friends carefully spread rumors of huge discoveries of gold and silver in South America. South Sea stock issued at £100 a share rose to £128 on January 1, 1720, then to £184 in February, and £280 in March. On April 14 the South Sea directors opened a public subscription for an issue of two million units of stock, 20 percent of the value to be paid on application. A large percentage of the state annuities were exchanged and so great was the public demand that two weeks later a second issue was offered at £400 a share. Investors borrowed from all sources and stampeded to buy. Soon South Sea had passed £500.

The historian Lord Erleigh wrote, "it would be wrong to regard all those who subscribed to the mythical projects of the day as positive imbeciles; many of them were only comparative imbeciles who hoped to unload upon superlative imbeciles at a handsome profit the worthless paper that they had acquired. Their hopes were more often than not promptly realized; when everyone was struggling to buy, the man in the strong position was he who had something to sell."

On June 24 the individual shares in the stock touched £1050, the highest point reached. The value of Lord Aislabie's bribe was now £270,000, though since then he had been secretly allotted more stock. His final profits were a stupendous £794,481. Other men had made remarkable gains. The Prince of Wales (the future George II) made £40,000. Lord Castlemaine's doorkeeper accumulated £4000. By judicious buying and selling of South Sea and other stock a bookseller named Thomas Guy amassed such wealth that at his death he founded a hospital; it bears his name to this day.

In July Blount decided the time had come to dispose of his holdings – discreetly, so as to maintain the price. At the same time the Company took action against three of its rivals who had made patently false claims. The three were closed down, at a loss to their shareholders of several million pounds. At once, and to the amazement of the directors, the South Sea Bubble burst.

It burst because people who had lost money in the other companies were forced to sell South Sea stock. As the price fell, those who had bought at an inflated price hastily tried to get out. Panic set in and the market was swamped with unwanted stock. Fortunes melted away. The portrait painter Sir Godfrey Kneller lost all the profits of his life's work. Banks closed, goldsmiths defaulted. Ruined men cut their throats and so many went mad it was impossible to find room in the private sanatoriums. The Directors (and Aislabie) were imprisoned in the Tower of London and later stripped of their profits. No action could be taken against the king's two mistresses, a fact that aroused much popular wrath. "We are ruined by Trulls [prostitutes]," one journalist cried "Nay, what is more, by old ugly trulls." (King George I liked his women middle-aged and fat.)

Ruin was widespread. The Government salvaged the South Sea wreck to some extent but the restored annuities retained only half their former value. It took all the political courage of Robert Walpole, the new prime minister, to restore the country's credit, and many years were to pass before the public at large would put their trust in stock markets again.

Above: a scene in Change Alley, the London Stock Exchange of the 1700s. So great was the stock-gambling fever that charlatans were able to make fortunes by shares in non-existent companies.

Below: the British artist William Hogarth's satirical comment on the South Sea Scheme. The monument on the right commemorates the South Sea Company's debacle in 1720. In the center speculators are scrambling to be "taken for a ride."

Inflation Out of Hand
Germany: 1923

For the Germans in 1914 one mark bought a dozen eggs. By the summer of 1923 a single egg cost 5000 marks. In November 1923 the price of one egg had reached 80,000,000,000 marks. To cope with such astronomical prices the printing presses of the Reichsbank poured out mountains of paper money. Some 30 paper mills were engaged full time in making the paper, and 132 private printing firms had been brought in to help the national bank turn out the wagon loads of money that would become valueless within a matter of days, sometimes in a matter of hours.

Before the war the highest denomination banknote had been the 1000 mark note, equivalent to 250 dollars. The mark began its downward slide in 1922 and the first 10,000 mark notes were then issued. These were soon insufficient except for tiny purchases – a single match was eventually to cost 900 million marks – and the Reichsbank added more and more zeros to the figures shown on the notes. After the 200,000 mark note came the 500,000 and the 1 million mark note. This was followed by notes for 10, 100, 500 million; then by notes for 1000 million, 10,000 million, 100,000 million. Often these were produced by stamping a higher value on notes of lower denomination that had become worthless by the time they were printed. Finally, 1 million million mark notes were issued, the largest being for 100 million million marks or 100,000,-000,000,000 – sufficient to buy 1200 eggs.

Inflation of this sort was unparalleled and the speed with which the mark sank brought a terrifying insecurity. A man going into a café with 5000 marks for a cup of coffee would call for his bill an hour later and find the price had gone up to 8000. Prices of durable goods went up daily, sometimes several times a day. Objects in shop windows were given a basic figure, which remained fixed for that object at say 18 or 20 or whatever it might be. In the middle of the window was the multiplier, a number by which the basic figure had to be multiplied to arrive at the current price. The multiplier might be 25,000,000 one morning, but if you delayed too long in getting the money from the bank you might find that it had

gone up to as high as 50,000,000 by the afternoon.

How had this insane state of affairs come about? The cost of the war and the problems of postwar recovery had imposed severe strains on the German economy. Reparations were a crippling burden and any hope of meeting them became impossible after the French and Belgians occupied the industrial Ruhr in January 1923. Unemployment was low but foreign currency soon became expensive. Prices that had been mounting steadily since the end of the war began to go up fast. The government increased the circulation of notes and soon too much money was chasing too few goods. Prices shot up faster, the exchange rate of the mark dropped rapidly, yet more notes were issued and the vicious spiral of inflation was well under way.

Above: a 2,000,000,000,000, German mark note issued in 1923.
Top left: German postage stamps at the height of the inflation the center stamp has been overprinted with an even higher denomination.
Below: customers queueing in a bank in 1923 with hampers and sacks to collect money that would later become valueless.

Right: a queue outside a butter store in 1923. Goods for sale were scarce during the worst inflationary period because the value of money dropped so rapidly that most stores operated at a loss.

Below: free meals being given out by German welfare authorities.

Below right: a group of homeless waiting for entry into a shelter. The old and the poor were particularly badly hit by the runaway inflation.

The harsh effects of inflation were distributed unequally, and this left a legacy of bitterness. The collapse of money ruined pensioners and members of the middle class whose capital assets were in marks (cash or annuities). The life assurance policy of one wealthy man, intended to provide amply for his family and the education of a daughter proved to be just sufficient, after inflation had eroded it, to buy a loaf of bread. Three months' pension for a policeman's widow with four children bought three boxes of matches. Such people and others such as doctors, and teachers who provided service were cruelly hit. To obtain food they resorted to barter, a pair of socks for a sack of potatoes. People parted with their furniture, their clothes, their wedding jewellery. When they had nothing left they starved.

Manufacturers, on the other hand, did well out of the inflation. So did farmers whose products were always in demand. They sold at high prices and bought property cheaply from men who were ruined.

People who had access to foreign currency were luckiest of all. In Munich the hotel porters, receiving tips in foreign money, could afford private boxes at the Opera. A cook in service with the eminent publish-

ing firm of Ullstein was presented with a dollar. The dollar had then become worth so many untold millions of marks that a trust fund was set up to administer her dollar. So ludicrous was the economic situation that such stories abounded.

Paper money became useless. Only things had value. The story is told of two women carrying a vast quantity of paper money in a laundry basket. They put it down for a moment and when they turned round the money was still there but the basket was gone.

Anarchy threatened and on November 9, 1923 Hitler staged his unsuccessful putsch at Munich. One week later the government introduced the Rentenmark, a new currency supposed to be backed by the agricultural and industrial strength of the nation. People turned to it like drowning men who see a lifebelt. The "miracle of the Rentenmark" worked because the Germans desperately needed it to work. By 1924 the mark was steady again – but the ruined middle class had lost what faith they had placed in the Democratic government of Weimar. It needed only another economic crisis, such as a Depression, and they might well be inclined to support a "strong man" – Hitler for instance.

171

The Great Crash
1929-1931

"Stock prices have reached what looks like a permanently high plateau." This confident statement was made on October 15, 1929 by Professor Irving Fisher, a distinguished economist at Yale University. Exactly two weeks later, on Tuesday, October 29, the New York stock market had crashed with a thud that had repercussions in the stock markets around the world.

In the months before the collapse a few voices had

broker only a small portion of the cost of the share, the difference being made up with money borrowed by the broker from a bank and loaned to the buyer. As collateral for this loan the buyer left other securities with his broker on the understanding that if the value of the securities should happen to fall the broker would call upon him to increase the cash margin. So long as prices rose, of course, these calls never came. Buyers had to pay interest on the loan but the increase in share values covered this handsomely. Shares were bought on margin and sold later at a profit; then more shares were bought, on margin again, for later resale, again at a profit. It hardly mattered what the share was – General Motors, Radio, United States Steel, Woolworth – they were all climbing. It is an unhappy fact of speculative buying that when prices are rising

warned that the unparalleled boom under Presidents Coolidge and Hoover could not go on for ever, that what went up had an ugly tendency to come down. But these pessimists were few and went unheeded. Ever since the spring of 1927 the stock market had been climbing higher and higher. Why should it stop?

In fact, the good years went back even further. Ever since 1923 life for a greater number of Americans than ever before was one of prosperity and plenty. Wheat farmers were a community that did not share in the general upsurge but for factory workers and businessmen – especially businessmen – the bandwagon rolled ever onward. Factory production was high, money readily available, and the stock market was booming.

This availability of money was one of the reasons for the boom. Shares in the climbing market could be bought *on margin* – that is to say, the buyer paid the

fast, whether the rises occur in land, or shares, or even tulip bulbs, people cease to look for the reason why they are rising. The items may be intrinsically worthless but what counts is that they can be resold at a profit – sometimes a very great profit. In 1928 and 1929 Americans became dazzled by the real possibility of becoming very rich very quickly.

During 1927 the New York Times average of the price of 25 representative stocks rose from 181 to 245. By 12 months later it had risen a further 86 to 331. Brokers had once spoken in awe of the possibility of 5 million shares being traded in a single day. By November, 5-million-share days were a frequent occurrence. In December the market sagged unnervingly. Shares in Radio that had climbed since the spring from 150 to 400 hurtled down to 296. But the market steadied and the upward rise resumed.

Another "shake-out" occurred in March 1929. The fall sharply reduced the value of loan collateral and thousands of investors had the novel and unpleasant experience of receiving telegrams from their broker calling for more margin. The brokers sold the shares of those who could not provide the necessary cash. A "shake-out" technically describes a strengthening of the market at a lower level – but in individual human terms it can mean a disaster. Those who were "shaken out" abruptly woke from the rosy dream of easy riches as the shares they had bought with hard-earned savings were sold for less than the purchase price.

The man credited with stopping the fall was Charles E. Mitchell, Chairman of the powerful National City Bank, who announced that his bank was prepared to lend 20 million dollars "to avoid any dangerous crisis

would choose their moment to sell at a profit, and one of the arts of speculation that summer was to know someone who could tip you when to get in early on a forthcoming movement. The American writer Frederick L. Allen, who witnessed the crash and wrote an account of it in *Only Yesterday*, described the general involvement:

"The rich man's chauffeur drove with his ears laid back to catch the news of an impending move in Bethelehem Steel; he held fifty shares himself on a twenty-point margin. The window-cleaner at the broker's office paused to watch the ticker for he was thinking of converting his laboriously accumulated savings into a few shares of Simmons. Edwin Lefévre [a knowledgeable journalist] told of a broker's valet who had made nearly a quarter of a million in the

Above: a cartoon of a speculator from a 1927 New Yorker, "Say Doc, do me a favor. Just keep your eye on Consolidated Can Common, and if she goes bearish tell my broker to sell and get four thousand shares of P & Q Rails Preferred on the usual margin. Thanks."

Left: concerned crowds gather outside the New York Stock Exchange during the Wall Street Crash.

Right: Wall Street clerks computing gains and losses long into the night during the weeks preceding the crash.

in the money market." Mitchell, who was speculating heavily, had strong reasons for wanting the boom to continue, and his words rallied the market. (Five years later Mitchell was arrested and tried on charges of tax evasion.)

In the crazy summer of 1929 all thoughts of caution fled as the market went soaring up to levels few had even dreamed of. Between the end of May and the end of August it went up an astonishing 100 points. The movement of shares was frequently manipulated by members of the stock exchange working together. A group would combine to buy a certain share and send its price up. This increase would be observed by investors watching the ticker tape in boardrooms and brokers' branch offices across the country. Suspecting something big in the offing they would hurry to buy and increase the price further. The manipulators

market, of a trained nurse who cleaned up thirty thousand following the tips given her by grateful patients."

On September 3, 1929, the speculative, or Big Bull Market, reached its peak. The *New York Times* Index stood at 469; US Steel was at 262, Anaconda Copper at 131, Radio at 505. What led to the loss of confidence that followed no one knows for certain. The market did not immediately go into reverse. Over the next seven weeks shares rose and fell without noticeably altering the position. Professor Fisher made his historic pronouncement about the permanently high plateau, adding, "I expect to see the stock market a good deal higher than it is today within a few months." And on Monday October 21, people began to sell. Sales totaled over 6,000,000 and there were some alarming plunges. Selling was less on Tuesday but increased on Wednesday. October 24 was "Black Thursday." As soon as the stock exchange opened large blocks of shares were put on the market and prices descended rapidly. But this was not panic selling. It was forced selling, the dumping of hundreds of thousands of shares held in the name of wretched investors whose margins were exhausted. For these people, their paper profits and money lost, their collateral gone to make what it could, "Black Thursday" shattered the dreams and hopes of a good future. As the forced selling continued, panic selling joined in. Prices fell further and faster. The ticker soon lagged far behind. The pyramid of high prices, honeycombed with margin loans, was collapsing under its own weight. By 11 am traders on the floor of the Stock Exchange were stampeding to unload. A weird roar could be heard by the crowd gathering outside. It was the death-cry of the Bull Market.

Above: the former head of the New York Stock Exchange, Richard Whitney testifying about the collapse of his brokerage firm. He was sentenced on two accounts of Grand Larceny for juggling the accounts of his firm.

Incredibly, the market rallied again. Richard Whitney, Vice-President of the Exchange (later to be tried and sentenced for misappropriating Stock Exchange funds) walked onto the floor as representative of the bankers' pool and bought heavily in 20 assorted stocks. Again the volatile market recovered. On Friday and Saturday the market remained steady but the weekend gave people time to think. The falls of the previous week had eliminated most of the small investors; now it was to be the turn of the wealthy.

Monday was bad enough with the *Times* Index

dropping 49 points in the day. But Tuesday October 29, was the most devastating day in the history of the American Stock Exchange – the day the market went over the edge of Niagara. From the beginning of the session the storm to sell raged in full force. Vast amounts of shares were flung onto the market for what they would fetch. Men who had called themselves millionaires a week before were now irretrievably ruined. Large fortunes, small savings, all wiped out. The cry was sell at any price. The stock of the White Sewing Machine Company had fallen from 48 to 11

and at that point somebody – said to be an astute messenger boy for the Exchange – had the bright idea of putting in an order to buy a block of shares at 1. In the absence of any other bids he got his stock at a dollar a share!

By the end of the day sales totaled 16,000,000, three times the business of a normal heavy day, and the Big Bull Market was dead. Billions of dollars worth of profit – some real, some paper – had vanished, and the office clerk, the chauffeur, the window-cleaner, the salesman had lost all their capital. In every town of the United States families dropped suddenly into debt. The number of suicides told its own dismal story. Few people took what legend records as the popular way out – jumping from a high window. Most shot themselves, like the financier J. J. Riordan who went to his bank on November 8 and took a pistol from a teller's cage, returned home and shot himself.

Even after October 29 the market went on falling. It reached its lowest level of the year on November 13. At 224 the *Times* Index was now less than half its position a bare two months earlier. US Steel had

Above: unemployed at the New York Municipal Lodging House during the depression in 1930 that followed the crash of 1929.
Left: a man tries to sell his car after losing all his money in the Stock Exchange Crash.
Below: one of the many poor being fed during a cold spell in New York under the orders of Mayor La Guardia in 1934-5.

fallen to 150, Anaconda Copper to 70. General Motors halved from 73 to 36. But these levels would come to seem high by later standards. The Crash was followed by the Slump and the Slump turned into the Depression that wound on and on for year after hopeless year. Investors who bought at the prices of November 13, believing the bottom had been reached, saw the value of their purchases dwindle inexorably through 1930 and 1931 until in July 1932 US Steel had dropped to 22, General Motors to 8 and Anaconda Copper, from a high of 131, to 4. Ruin could go no further.

The Great Depression
The 1930s

"I'd get up at five in the morning and head for the waterfront. Outside the Spreckles Sugar Refinery, outside the gates, there would be a thousand men. You know damn well there's only three or four jobs. The guy would come out with two little cops: 'I need four guys.' A thousand men would fight like a pack of Alaskan dogs to get through there. Only four of us would get through."

It was 1931. Ed Paulsen, later to hold an administrative job with UNICEF, was just out of High School and there was no work. His experience was in San Francisco but it was repeated in thousands of cities throughout the United States. And not only in the USA. The Stock Market Crash of October 1929 exposed the gaping holes in national economies throughout the world. The Australian economy was heavily reliant on the export of a single product, wool. The slump sent world demand for wool right down and set off a chain reaction through all the occupations and industries that were dependent on the prosperity of the wool trade. The number of unemployed rose to 25 percent of the Australian work force and spread acute distress throughout the country.

Economists differ as to the relative importance of the various factors that caused the slump and the Great Depression that followed it. There is agreement, however, that well before the Stock Market Crash of 1929 all the signs of an economic downturn were present. Incomes were very unequally distributed and the significant investment money was concentrated in the hands of a relatively small group. When this group could no longer afford to invest, industry was deprived of the new plant and funds it needed for recovery. Heavy American investment abroad proved to be another hazard. Early in 1929 this money was called back to the United States to fuel the rising stock market. It never returned to Europe and the crash had disastrous consequences there, particularly in Germany, which plunged immediately into a severe slump, less than five years after emerging from the trauma of hyper-inflation. The result was widespread disillusion with the democratic forms of government that seemed to permit such crises.

There had been slumps before but never one that lasted so long. In the United States it lasted right through the 1930s until the start of World War II. Throughout the industrial world factories cut their workforces by 50 percent, 80 percent, or closed down completely. In July 1932 steel production in the USA was down to 12 percent of capacity. Men found them-

selves out of work and without any prospect of finding work in the foreseeable future. Without a job, without money, they joined bread lines and soup lines, shuffling along wearing shabby clothes that had once been good suits, their expressions flat and vacant.

In Britain the heavy industries most affected – coal-mining, iron and steel, shipbuilding, cotton textiles – were concentrated in Wales, Scotland, and northern England. It was to force the other parts of the country to take note of the sufferings of these "industrial graveyards" that the hunger marches were organized. Money was collected to supply boots for the marchers and in September 1932 huge contingents of workless men converged on London. The shipbuilding town of Jarrow became a by-word for poverty and suffering.

Malnutrition there was widespread; death from tuberculosis was double the national average and so was child mortality. The British novelist J. B. Priestley described a visit to the town: "Wherever we went there were men hanging about, not scores of them but hundreds of thousands of them."

By the end of 1932 Britain's unemployed totaled just under 3,000,000. Germany's jobless totaled 6,000,000, and, at its worst, the United States figure reached 15,000,000 and no headway was made in reducing this shocking total until Franklin D. Roosevelt became President in 1933. In the week of his Inauguration he took the unprecedented course of closing all banks in the country for a week. During this long Bank Holiday the finances of each were examined and only those considered sound were allowed to reopen. Following this, the Federal Deposit Insurance Corporation was established, guaranteeing all bank deposits up to $10,000. This removed from the small investor the specter of total ruin.

Roosevelt and his advisers launched a vigorous program of legislation to cure the country's ills. Tens of thousands of men were recruited to work on such projects as reforestation and construction jobs as various in scale as the huge Tennessee Valley dams and the Children's Zoo in New York's Central Park. But despite the real achievements of Roosevelt's New Deal there were still 10,000,000 unemployed in 1939. It had been a grim and terrible decade, never to be forgotten by those who lived and suffered through it.

Above: the Jarrow Crusade, one of many marches in which unemployed British miners and factory workers trudged to the City of London to impress the central government with their plight.

Left: two contestants in a "dance marathon" during the Great Depression, one of the many bizarre "entertainments" by which people hoped they could forget about the poverty and uncertainty of the times.

Right: Fort Loudoun Dam, part of the United States Government drive to lift the nation out of the Depression. Huge projects like this were started to give paid work to thousands of unemployed.

The Poverty Gap

nations, and the gap between them and the richer ones becomes wider each year. One of the problems economists have to solve is how to spread affluence more justly throughout the world, yet the problem has been from the start bedeviled by the very existence of the gap. European countries and countries originally peopled by Europeans – the USA, Canada,

"Shoot us now, we're starving anyway!" This was the cry of the Egyptian mob on January 18, 1977, when the Cairo riot police were given their orders to fire over their heads. The 30,000-strong crowd had raged through the city all day, inflamed by the government announcement that a wide range of essential goods was about to be raised sharply in price. Rice, for instance, was to go up by 16 percent, petrol by 31 percent. About 90 percent of Cairo's 8,000,000 people exist on the poverty line, in conditions made worse by chaotic transport, high unemployment, and bureaucratic inefficiency. The 1977 riots were the most severe since the revolution that had swept King Farouk from power 25 years before. For two days the acrid blue smoke of the tear gas used to disperse the crowd drifted across the city. Elsewhere in Egypt cars, which only the rich can afford, were smashed and police stations set alight. Faced with the real prospect of anarchy the government of President Sadat canceled the price increases and the hungry crowds dispersed.

The price rises were a desperate last resort by a government whose country was heading toward economic collapse. Because of the long dispute with Israel, one quarter of the national income was having to be spent on keeping the economy on a war footing. Foreign debts were believed to total $15,000 million and every year the United States provided $250 million worth of food grants. Egypt has just enough oil to be self-sufficient but none to export. The foreign aid that was enabling the country to survive was becomingly increasingly hard to obtain. Tourism and the Suez Canal provided virtually the only sources of foreign currency. Sadat's predecessor as President, Gamel Abdel Nasser, had tried socialism and a nationalized economy to cure his country's ills. Nasser failed. Sadat reversed this strategy by opening Egypt to Western industrialization and investment. But the chief imports that arrived were luxury goods that only increased the envy of the poor. By the beginning of 1977 inflation stood at a crisis 50 percent and the International Monetary Fund, negotiating another loan to Egypt, had made the price rises one of the conditions for the loan.

Sadat's dilemma highlights the problem facing many of the world's poorer nations and incidentally helps to account for his courageous offer to Israel later in the year to end hostilities between the two countries. Prices have in general been rising throughout the world since 1934 but, if the cost of living has gone up, so also, in the wealthier countries, has the standard of living. This has not been the case in poorer

Australia, New Zealand – enjoy a head start of a century and a half of industrialization and technical expertise. Only Russia, China, and Japan have been able to join this fortunate group. Unrestricted free trade – by which the first industrialized nations gained their head start in the 19th century – would now prevent underdeveloped nations from ever reaching a competitive position. To help them with their economies and to produce the goods that can be sold profitably to the industrialized nations, various international bodies have been established since World War II to supply financial and technical aid.

One of these is the International Bank for Reconstruction and Development, commonly known as the World Bank. Eight months after the Cairo riots of January 1977 came news of ambitious programs drawn up by the Bank to assist the Egyptian economy from within. Meanwhile, the worldwide increase in the cost of food made the earlier figure of $250 million for food grants look very small, and with the aim of reducing the need for costly food imports, technical experts from a number of industrialized nations worked out plans for creating canals and irrigation systems in Southern Egypt in order to grow such crops as tea, coffee, wheat, and sugar cane. If the agricultural development succeeds, some industrial settlements may follow – and in all these schemes the World Bank will be playing an active part.

Such remedies as these are admittedly partial but in the complex and sensitive field of international aid economists have to grope their way toward the best remedy. A high proportion – 99 percent possibly – of all wars have trade disputes as their initial cause. Trade disagreements are probably inevitable, but to avoid economic disasters in the future the short-term interest of some nations has to be subordinated to the long-term interest of the whole world.

Three totalitarian regimes that rose to power through economic and social chaos.

Left: a May Day Parade in Moscow's Red Square. Communism in the Soviet Union, as in China (below left, Mao Tse-tung surrounded by ecstatic crowds), certainly meant a better deal for the peasants, but the price was that power must remain in the hands of only one political party.

Below: Hitler with Nazi party leaders at a rally. Disillusioned with democracy the German people were hypnotized into believing that they had only to follow him in order to accomplish any ambition.

Chapter 10

The Horrors of War

Some wars have been brief. Others have dragged on for decades. The Hundred Years' War between France and England actually overran a century by 15 years. But wars are rarely, if ever, fought without casualties. Many early wars killed relatively few. In this century, however, some 9,700,000 people perished in World War I and in World War II the toll was probably around 55,000,000.

Whatever their scale, most wars bring death or misery not only to soldiers but to civilians caught up in the fighting. This is particularly true in siege and civil war. Many of the 1,500,000 Russians killed in the siege of Leningrad, which lasted from September 1941 to January 1944, were civilians. In 1871 many thousands of unfortunate Parisians died in a brief but bloody civil war.

The famous Prussian military theorist Karl von Clausewitz blandly defined war as an extension of foreign policy. This chapter reveals the terrible inadequacy of that definition.

Opposite: this painting by the British artist Sir William Orpen depicts the desolation and horror of war and also the human angle — a point too often overlooked by those who direct wars — as this French soldier in World War 1 carries his wounded British comrade.

The Seeds of War

"And Abel was a keeper of sheep, but Cain was a tiller of the ground . . . and it came to pass, when they were in the field, that Cain rose up against Abel his brother, and slew him."

This story from the Book of Genesis holds clues to the immediate cause of many wars in early history – those waged between nomadic shepherds and herdsmen of steppe and desert on one hand and the settled farming peoples in the richer plains and valleys of the lands around. The Jews themselves, after 40 years nomadic wandering burst upon and conquered the settled farming lands of Canaan. Indo-Europeans, Huns, Arabs, and Mongols between them overran Europe, North Africa, the Middle East, India, and China.

War probably evolved as a result of man's increased numbers after the discovery of farming about 10,000 years ago. Agriculture filled more mouths than hunt-

struggles helped successful war leaders to unite city states into the world's first nations. Eventually, militant Assyria engulfed surrounding nations to build one of the world's first empires – a precedent for the larger empires successively carved out by Persian, Greek, Roman, and other armies.

From very early on, then, war had become a way of life. There were always new pretexts for people to fight one another. War was the unthinking solution to many problems such as overpopulation, or emigration, or differences in religious or political ideology.

As social units grew in size, the scale of war was also magnified. First hundreds, then thousands, and eventually millions grappled on the battlefields. Meanwhile, man's ingenuity improved the range and destructive capability of his weapons until they could annihilate not just the fighting men but the inhabitants of cities far behind the lines of battle.

What has made man such a ruthless killer of other members of his species? Biologists, psychologists, anthropologists, and others have come up with a variety of explanations. Many social scientists see war as part of man's genetic inheritance. Some argue that he naturally pursues death as compulsively as he seeks life. Others say war stems from man's craving for excitement – a psychological phenomenon that

Left: by the time of the great city-states man had already developed and institutionalized his aggressive instincts into organized warfare. These highly mobile Assyrian warriors expanded the state to its greatest extent between the 800s and the 600s BC.

Below: Roman soldiers fighting barbarians. Roman methods of warfare depended on mobility to defend the borders of its ever-growing empire, won by conquest.

ing had. As populations rose and farming villages proliferated, rival settlements began competing with each other and with nomadic tribes for the same tracts of fertile ground. So war was born.

Apparent evidence for this theory appeared from excavations at Köln-Lindenthal, a Neolithic village near Cologne in Germany. The first occupation showed no sign of war weapons or defenses. But later rebuilding revealed weapons buried with the dead, as well as a defensive ditch and a palisade. Flint daggers and stone battleaxes figured importantly in later Neolithic Europe in general.

Meanwhile in Bronze-Age Mesopotamia, trade and manufacture supported towns and rival city-states that warred for land or local supremacy. In what is now Iraq, Sumerian soldiers with metal armor and weapons were fighting 5000 years or more ago. Such

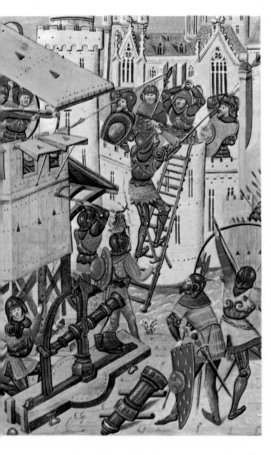

leads men actually to enjoy the risk of death. A third view sees war as a transitory phase in human evolution. War is also seen as an environmental phenomenon – a product of "social learning gone awry."

An interesting explanation for the phenomenon of war is argued by the British zoologist Desmond Morris in his book *The Naked Ape*. Morris claims that man's animal origins hold the secret of his aggressive urges.

Man's relatives the apes usually resolve a conflict bloodlessly by threat and counterthreat, and tend to fight only when overcrowded. Even then, each usually seeks his enemy's submission, not his death. Once a vanquished ape makes certain submissive signals the victor stops attacking.

Man, Desmond Morris believes, acts somewhat similarly. War springs primarily from man's group defense of territory, and – because his species is now so badly overcrowded – from efforts to enlarge that territory at the expense of other human groups. As with apes, man originally fought to force the enemy's submission, not to kill. But cringing and other gestures of appeasement that would stop a fight between two foes in punching range of one another no longer operated in an age of long-range weapons.

According to this line of thought, even a superhuman global effort at disarmament could not stop further wars from breaking out. For, under pressure, man would always make more weapons. Morris believes that massively depopulating the world by contraception or abortion is the only way to end the overcrowding at the root of war.

Above left: medieval warfare largely consisted of siege-tactics as opposing armies attacked or defended walled castles or towns.

Above: trench warfare, often leading to stalemate, during World War I.

Below: Atlas Intercontinental Ballistic missiles blasting off. Modern weapons will carry war to every corner of the globe.

Genghis Khan
"The Wrath of Heaven"

Genghis Khan 1167–1227.

and embracing parts of what are now Afghanistan, Iran, and the USSR. The murder of a Mongol envoy in the Khwarizmian border town of Utrar supplied the pretext for a Mongol onslaught that devastated Khwarizm's major cities in three years of planned annihilation.

Mustering 200,000 troops, Genghis Khan sent his sons Chagatai and Ogadei to besiege Utrar. They soon avenged the Mongol emissary's murder by pouring molten gold down the local governor's throat; or, according to another story, tipping molten silver in his ears and eyes. Meanwhile, Genghis Khan himself besieged Bokhara – the largest and richest city in the region. The garrison was cut down trying to escape, and in February 1220 the citizens submitted.

Entering the city's leading mosque, Genghis Khan proclaimed himself "the wrath and flail of heaven." His Moslem hearers soon believed it as Mongol troops ransacked Bokhara, tortured wealthy citizens to find their hidden wealth, and fired the city's buildings. A Moslem chronicler wrote: "It was a fearful day. One heard only the weeping of men, women, and children, who were to be separated for ever; women were ravished by the barbarians under the eyes of those who had no resource save sorrow; some of the men, rather than witness the shame of their families, rushed upon the warriors and died fighting."

Mongols then forced thousands of Bokhara's citizens to march in military formation ahead of them to make their army seem far larger than it was. Outnumbered by the garrison of Samarkand the Mongols nonetheless subdued this splendid city, too, killing indiscriminately and deporting 30,000 craftsmen to Mongolia.

Some of the most hideous attrocities occurred at

In 1167 the wife of a Mongol sub-clan chief gave birth to a son named Temujin. Legend says the right hand of the infant clutched a knucklebone-sized clot of blood – an omen of the slaughter he would one day cause. By 1206 Temujin had forged a union of nomadic Mongol and non-Mongol tribes in eastern central Asia. With the title *Genghis Khan* ("Universal King"), this fierce and crafty warrior now led barbarian hordes of mounted archers in onslaughts on the settled lands around. Calculatedly he wielded terror as a weapon to win an empire stretching from Armenia to Korea.

North China was the first cultured area to suffer from his ravages. Its emperor tried buying off the Mongols with gifts including 500 youths and 500 slave girls. But Genghis Khan mercilessly murdered all his captives, and in 1215 his forces stormed the northern Chinese capital, Peking, looting palaces and butchering inhabitants.

Genghis Khan then halted his attack on China to crush enemies in Central Asia. First he defeated the Kara-Khitai peoples south of Lake Balkhash. This victory pushed his territories' western rim against Khwarizm, a Moslem kingdom south of the Aral Sea

Merv in February 1221, as retribution for the killing of 1000 of the khan's imperial guard. After an unsuccessful siege, Genghis Khan's son Tolui deceitfully invited the city's governor to dine, then strangled his companions. Seizing Merv by a trick, the Mongols beheaded its military leaders. They then forced male citizens to lie with arms behind them, and hacked and

Souboutai, Mongol war general.

Below: Mongol Warriors demonstrating their skill.

strangled all of them to death. Women and children died separately. One account says 700,000 perished, and only 80 craftsmen were spared.

In April, Nishapur endured perhaps the worst bloodbath of all. Mongols massacred the citizens, cut off their heads, and heaped them up in pyramids by sex and age. (Beheading ensured that no intended victims could escape by feigning death.)

To Genghis Khan, success lay less in empire building than in plunder and destruction. He once supposedly declared that what brought the greatest happiness was "to crush your enemies; to see them fall at your feet – to take their horses and goods and hear the lamentation of their women." Thus he was happy merely to desolate Khwarizm and fill its ruined cities with the stench of death. These deeds accomplished, the Mongol leader abandoned warfare from 1222 to 1226. In 1227 the aging khan fell sick and died in China while besieging Ningsia, the capital of the Tangut peoples.

His army and his legacy of cruelty lived on, however. Successors enlarged the Mongol empire as brutally as Genghis Khan had forged it. In 1240 they blotted out the Russian city of Kiev and in 1241 wiped out a German-Polish army in Silesia. After the battle troops supposedly filled nine sacks with ears lopped from the dead. In 1258 Genghis Khan's grandson Hulagu smashed the dikes on which Iraqi farms relied, burned the major buildings of Baghdad, rolled the last Arab caliph in a carpet, and had him kicked to death by horses.

Surprisingly, when the conquests ended, the vast Mongol Empire enjoyed unprecedented peace. In time, too, its barbarian rulers embraced the very cultures they had done so much to crush.

The Thirty Years War
Central Europe: 1618-48

From 1618 to 1648 war ravaged Central Europe. It began in the Bohemian corner of the Holy Roman Empire when local Protestants rose against their Catholic overlord. It eventually became a struggle for the balance of power in Europe. Before it ended, Protestant Denmark, Holland, England, and Sweden, and Catholic Spain and France were all involved. The chief battleground was the area that comprises Germany which was then split into 300 principalities and cities whose loyalties were largely divided between two rival Protestant and Catholic leagues.

Some historians claim that the resulting war razed countless German towns and farms, slashed the

with its attendant horrors. In the first, Bohemian, period of 1618-20, Bohemians were championed by the German Count Ernst von Mansfeld's small mercenary army, supported by Prince Gabor Bethlen's Hungarian forces. Ill-disciplined and brutal, Gabor's troops murdered prisoners, burned farms, and even fought their allies in the search for food. The superior Catholic forces of Duke Maximilian of Bavaria, under the command of the Flemish Count of Tilly, had problems too, as a typhus epidemic struck troops of the Catholic league.

On November 8, 1620, both armies clashed decisively near Prague in the Battle of the White Mountain. The Catholic forces were victorious, and dissident Bohemia suffered a reign of terror as its masters brought the land to heel. Imperial troops rounded up and executed 27 leading rebels (12 heads and a hand were skewered for diplay upon a bridge in Prague). Many nobles forfeited estates and crippling taxes were imposed. Imperial mercenaries rampaged at will through Prague, tearing doors and windows from the

Left: the capture of the Protestant capital of Prague by Catholic forces of the Duke Maximilian of Bavaria.

Above: Count Ernst von Mansfeld, whose mercenary forces entered the service of the Protestants against the Emperor.

Right: the barbaric execution of leading rebels after the capture of Prague.

German population by three quarters, and generally did damage that took 200 years to repair. Other historians argue that these claims are wild exaggerations. But all admit that certain regions suffered heavily.

Civilians were the major victims of the war. The reason lay in mercenary armies made up of hired ruffians. Like swarms of locusts on the move, troops plundered town and countryside for food and clothing, and, in their wake, brought typhus, plague, and dysentery.

The war passed through four major periods, each

houses to loot what lay within, extorting money from the citizens, and plundering the countryside so ruthlessly that peasant farmers lost buildings, fields, and livestock and left the land entirely. Combined with religious persecution, such horrors forced large-scale emigration from Bohemia.

Meanwhile, Tilly's victorious troops were so loaded down with booty that they hired men to carry it around. His army's size became inflated, too, by such hangers-on as beggars, peddlers, prostitutes, quacks, children seized for ransom, and women kidnaped from the fields and farms. On the march, several new-born babies would be added to the army's hungry numbers every week.

Camp followers similarly swelled Mansfeld's army – defeated but not disbanded. In 1621 his troops were spreading war through Germany – and bringing with them typhus, plague, and devastation. By winter, refugees huddled behind Strasbourg's walls counted up to 16 spears of flame at night, where Mansfeld's foragers had fired village properties they could not bodily cart off. Within a 15-mile radius of nearby Haguenau, they reportedly set alight to every house and in many of the Catholic churches they tore down the images of Christ and hanged them from trees. "God help those where Mansfeld comes!" became a saying of the day in Germany. By 1623 Mansfeld's Protestant troops and forces of the Catholic League had between them helped spread epidemic typhus through much of western Germany.

In 1625 the war entered its Danish Period, which lasted until 1629. It was named for the intervention of the King of Denmark whose Protestant army fought

met up with a wedding celebration in Vienna and "cut down the bridegroom and the wedding guests, violated the women, looted all the table and silver ware, stripped the women of their clothes, and carried off the bride. . . ." In Thuringia, central Germany, drunken soldiers in Wallenstein's army sat in a basement eating-place, shooting at the feet of passing citizens. In Brandenburg, troops tied hostages to horses' tails. The German author Hans Jakob Grimmelshausen wrote a novel based on his personal experiences of the havoc wrought in Germany by the war. The novel, *Simplicissimus*, graphically describes brutalities Grimmelhausen may have actually witnessed – for instance tying prisoners in a row to see how many toppled to one charge of shot; pouring filth in victims' mouths; roasting them above a fire; using a pistol muzzle as a thumbscrew.

There were, however, even wider repercussions from the war than direct brutality. They were the inevitable famine and disease. In 1627 Danish and Imperial troops destroyed the harvest on the Havel's

the Imperial troops in Saxony. At the beginning of the Danish Period, though, the formidable Austrian general Duke Albrecht von Wallenstein was given government command of the Imperial armies and went on to win a chain of victories that forced the Danes from Saxony and ended armed resistance by the Protestants.

By 1630, western and eastern Germany and nearby lands had been embroiled in 10 years' fighting. Throughout, the impact of the troops upon noncombatants was horrifying. Typical of their behavior was an account that describes how in 1620 Polish troops

banks. In 1628 Tyrolean peasants were forced to grind beanstalks to make bread. In 1630 the inhabitants of Nassau used roots and acorns. In usually fertile Bavaria the corpses of emaciated famine victims lay along the roads.

Spread by soldiers, typhus, plague, and dysentery ran riot. From 1625 to 1630 epidemics raged through much of Germany: 28,000 died from various "plagues" in 1626 in Württemberg alone; 9000 in Augsburg two years later.

In 1630 peace still eluded Germany, for now the war began its Swedish period, in which King Gustavus

Adolphus led a Swedish army on to German soil and fought the Catholics until killed in 1634 at Lützen.

The Swedes arrived too late to lift the siege of Magdeburg by Tilly's forces. In May of 1631 the Protestant city was fired by its defenders but burned both defenders and attackers. The death toll has been estimated at 25,000. For two weeks, wagons carted blackened corpses to the nearby river. Pope Urban VIII rejoiced in the "wicked" city's smoking ruins as "eternal monuments of God's mercy."

In 1635, after nearly six months' siege, the Swedes

Cologne to Frankfurt "all the towns, villages, and castles have been battered, pillaged and burned," and in the Rhineland village of Bacharach starving people had perished "with grass in their mouths." In 1638, foodless Imperial troops besieged at Breisach ate their dead comrades' flesh.

The frequent floods of refugees endured appalling hardships. Thousands of Germans lost homes when brutal commanders systematically burned villages. After the Swedes' defeat at Nördlingen in 1634, droves of fugitives died of plague and hunger in a refugee

Above: Frederick V, the Elector of the Palatinate, whose election to the throne of Bohemia sparked the 30 Years War.

Right: the coronation of Frederick V as King of Bohemia. Because of his short reign he was known as the "Winter King."

themselves surrendered Augsburg. Famine and pestilence had cut its population from some 70,000 to only 16,000. People had survived by eating rats and chewing hides; in one reported case a woman dined upon a soldier who had perished in her home.

Meanwhile the Swedes' defeat at Nördlingen in southwest Germany in September 1634 marked an Imperial Hapsburg victory that had drawn Catholic France into the war to help the German Protestants fight France's Hapsburg rivals. The war now launched out on its last, Swedish-French, period. But soon disease and hunger more than military strategy dictated how and where the armies moved. In the winter of 1635 there were many tales of starving people eating human flesh. According to these stories, the famished inhabitants of Alsace tore down and ate the very bodies on the gallows. In the Rhineland, meat from newly buried dead became a saleable commodity. Near Worms, someone found half-cooked feet and hands in a gipsy's cauldron. The English ambassador's traveling entourage was horrified to find that from

camp at Frankfurt, and in overbrimming hospitals elsewhere. Swiss cities drove out those seeking sanctuary there. In midwinter 30,000 slept out in the streets of Strasbourg until many died of cold, disease, or hunger. Then the magistrates expelled the rest.

Peace came at last in 1648. The Treaty of Westphalia handed lands to France and Sweden, and gave Germany a new measure of religious toleration. But some say the war's chief legacy to Germany was more than half the population killed, heavy emigration, two-thirds of all property destroyed, and commerce, industry, and culture blighted. Probably this paints too black a picture: depopulation was often only due to refugees who later returned. Much of Germany enjoyed long spells of peace when daily life ran on unbroken. Certain cities actually thrived. Astonishingly, while the war raged on, much-battered Leipzig became a major German trading center, with trade fairs attracting merchants from all over Europe. But such achievements stood out as isolated monuments to man's resilience in times of great uncertainty.

Above: a contemporary print of the capture of the Castle of Entschinn in Bohemia in 1620 by Catholic Forces.

Right: the siege of the city of Magdeburg by the armies of the Holy Roman Emperor Ferdinand II.

Below: the signing of the peace treaty of Westphalia in 1648, brought to an end the 30 Years War. It took almost 200 years for Germany to recover from the ravages of the war.

The American Civil War 1861-65

From 1861 to 1865 the United States tore itself apart with a loss of more American lives than any other conflict before or since. In the American Civil War, 1,500,000 Union (or Federal, or Northern) troops confronted nearly 900,000 Confederate (or Southern) forces. The 2400 listed skirmishes and battles cost 364,511 Union casualties, and 258,000 Confederate dead and injured.

The war began when 11 of the 15 slave-owning states tried seceding from the Union. Outnumbering

eventually triumphed, historians have called this the first modern, or total, war. In weaponry and tactics it was in many ways a dress-rehearsal for World War I. New and frightful tools for long-range mass slaughter made obsolete the cavalry charge and bayonet attack. Infantry equipped with muzzle-loading, percussion-capped rifles could open fire at 400 yards – up to eight times the old flintlock musket's range. Rifled cannon, mortars, machine guns, grenades, rockets, trenches, wire entanglements, mines, booby traps, and armored battleships – all these, and more, foreshadowed warfare in the century ahead.

At first, many of the fighting men measured up less well in battle than the weapons in their hands. Regiments marched into war a mere two weeks after being raised. At the Battle of Shiloh in April 1862 a Confederate brigadier admitted that before then he had never heard a gun go off. A gray-faced Union colonel

Above: the largest gun made during the American Civil War. It was used by Union forces at the beginning of 1865.

Left: a trench scene after the Battle of Spotsylvania Court House, Virginia in 1862. Some 19,000 men died during the battle, which ended in stalemate.

Right, above: the Battle of Fredericksburg in December 1862 resulted in a terrible defeat for the Union forces.

Right, below: Union victory at the naval battle at Memphis in June 1862 gave the North control of a large part of the Mississippi River.

the South by more than two to one in people and railroad miles, and far wealthier in mines and factories, the antislavery North and West seemed set for easy victory. It hatched a plan to crush the Confederacy by sea blockade, and a two-pronged invasion, east and west of the Appalachian Mountains: their north-south axis naturally created two Southern battlefronts. Yet four years passed before the North could force submission.

Because the North's superior industrial strength

hid behind a log, then ran for his life. But swarms of braver men surged to and fro behind their battle flags, contesting ground at a colossal cost in manpower to both sides. Afterward, the victorious Union General Ulysses S. Grant said one field was "so covered with dead that it would have been possible to walk across the clearing in any direction, stepping on dead bodies, without a foot touching the ground." This was the price Confederates had to pay to defend the "backdoor" to the Mississippi.

Troops grew battle-hardened quickly – as at Antietam, five months after Shiloh. The Union General George B. McClellan fed his 70,000 men in driblets to Robert E. Lee's 40,000 Confederates, and lost 12,500 casualties in the process. On both sides, as one man put it, commanders saw "green regiments go to their graves like beds." After this hollow Union success, Lincoln decided that granting McClellan's plea for reinforcements would be like "shoveling flies across a room" and sacked the General instead.

McClellan's errors paled beside General Ambrose E. Burnside's bullheaded uphill Union assault on a Confederate army entrenched upon the hills overlooking Fredericksburg. Advancing in parade-ground ranks toward the hills, the Union troops dropped like dominoes beneath a hail of artillery and rifle fire. Of the 5000 that charged, 2000 toppled in 15 minutes. A force of 4000 then tried a bayonet assault; 1700 fell before the rest reeled back. Modern weapons fired from well prepared positions had cost the Union side more than twice as many casualties as they themselves inflicted.

Many Civil War encounters resulted in heavy loss of life without bringing any measurable gain. But the Battle of Gettysburg was an undoubted turning point. In July 1863, Robert E. Lee's Confederate army forced General George G. Meade's Union army to entrench itself upon Cemetery Ridge, a two-mile elevated "fish-hook" south of the sleepy farming town of Gettysburg in Pennsylvania. After two days of indecisive fighting, Lee planned to batter down the Union center.

More than 100 guns pounded the target area. Then 14,000 Confederate troops led by General George E. Pickett moved out of woods and charged in ordered columns across a mile of open, undulating ground that

was exposed to the still formidable Union artillery. At 700 yards' range the Union artillery firing grape and canister shot began blasting lanes in the approaching mass. At 200 yards' range, Union infantry stood up and fired volleys into their attackers. The battered line pressed on and took the ridge – but only for 20 minutes. They eventually fell back against a wall of bayonets and clubbed rifles.

Picket lost two brigadiers, eight colonels and three lieutenant colonels killed. He wrote: "Only one field Officer of my whole command was unhurt." Of the 14,000 who had marched out to attack, 5000 came back. At Gettysburg, the Confederates lost 22,000 killed and wounded – the Union side probably 4000 fewer. Lee's hope of carrying the war into the North was finished, and the next day Vicksburg fell to Northern troops.

191

As in most past conflicts, more soldiers expired from the effects of wounds in the Civil War than died in battle, and far more died of infectious diseases than both these groups combined. The Northern States listed some 110,000 killed or died from wounds, but deaths from disease swelled the numbers to more than 360,000. Typhoid was among the biggest killers, followed by infections grouped as dysentery and diarrhea, then smallpox, measles, and malaria. Figures for the South are similar. Of the 258,000 men lost in the war, only 94,000 Confederate troops died on

ing sides. The Confederate Navy's commander lost a son serving with the Union fleet. Two brothers fought as major-generals with hostile armies. While Abraham Lincoln led the North, three brothers of his wife died fighting for the South. When a bullet felled the dashing Union general James McPherson, his fiancée heard someone in her Southern family describe his death as "the most wonderful news."

As war progressed, government contracts helped Northern manufacturers and businessmen to get rich fast. Bribery and graft were rife, producing sand in

Above: the interior of a Union prisoner of war camp. Conditions in both Northern and Southern prisons were appalling.

Left: a proud pose from a Union soldier who was killed later.

the battlefield. Death from disease reached its frightful climax in the concentration camps for prisoners of war. Almost one quarter of all captured Southern troops perished in Northern prisons. In the South mortality among imprisoned Northern troops was even worse. At one time, inmates of Andersonville Prison in Georgia were perishing at an annual rate of three in every four. Confederate General John H. Winder vindictively built this insanitary camp's stockade without leaving shade trees or erecting sheds for shelter "so as to destroy more Yankees than can be destroyed at the front." Sergeant-Major Robert H. Kellogg, who was sent to the camp two months after it had opened, wrote: "As we entered the place, a spectacle met our eyes that almost froze our blood with horror and made our hearts fail within us. Before us were forms that had once been active and erect, stalwart men, now nothing but mere walking skeletons." Disease, malnutrition, and sadistic shootings by the guards killed nearly 13,000 of Andersonville's 49,000 inmates.

For many families of North and South the war brought heartbreak as different members took oppos-

sugar casks, rye in coffee bags, and uniforms that fell apart in the rain. But things got done and the North's economy began to prosper.

The story in the South was different. Hemmed in by the North's naval blockade, the tobacco and cotton growing states ran short of manufactured goods and of imported luxuries. In February 1864 one diarist wrote: "I have not tasted coffee or tea for more than a year." Metals grew so scarce that manufacturers melted down church bells for guns; window weights for bullets; rings and jewelry for money. The daily news appeared printed on wallpaper or brown wrapping paper. Molasses served as sugar; roasted corn as coffee.

Railroad decay brought many fatal accidents and there were too few food trains to keep all Southern regions fed. By the war's end parts of the South were in real distress. Many troops deserted for lack of food and pay. Confederate paper money slumped in value. Flour cost $1000 a barrel, and in winter wood sold for $5 a stick.

The South's western states suffered horribly from the plundering of Northern troops. After guerrillas had attacked a Union regiment at Athens, Alabama, Colonel John Basil Turchin told his men to take the town apart. In northern Mississippi, one soldier writing home announced that "chickens, fences, swine, etc., are entirely unseeable and unfindable within 15 miles of where our camp has been this week."

But it was the east that suffered worst of all, when in 1864 General William Tecumseh Sherman launched his famous march from Atlanta through Georgia to the sea. For some 300 miles his 60,000 troops devastated crops, mansions, towns and railroad yards

Above: General George Pickett leading 14,000 Confederate troops into battle at Gettysburg, 1863. Altogether 22,000 Confederate troops perished in the battle that marked the turning point of the war in the North's favor.

across a 60-mile-wide band of countryside. He was not looking for an enemy army, Sherman's mission was to wreck an economy and to destroy a faith.

War ceased in April 1865. It had repaired the Union, smashed slavery, and crushed the South's slave-based rural economy. But the memory of his own cruel part of this accomplishment led General Sherman to declare to a graduating class of officers: "I am tired and sick of war. Its glory is all moonshine. It is only those who have never fired a shot nor heard the shrieks and groans of the wounded who cry aloud for blood, more vengeance, more desolation. War is hell."

Below: ruined mills on the waterfront at Richmond in 1865. The residents burned their own city before retreating rather than allow it to fall into Union hands.

Paris Under Siege 1871

The weary, hungry citizens of Paris were dumb-founded with rage and humiliation as the guns around Paris ceased firing on January 28, 1871, and the forts were handed over to the Germans. It was the final blow in the most disastrous war in French history. The anger and humiliation felt by the volatile, proud Parisians smoldered on for three months, eventually to boil over into a brief but desperately bloody civil war against the government they considered had betrayed them.

Only the year before, in the Summer of 1870, the cosmopolitan capital had been the world's most glittering city. By mid-September, the German forces under the Prussian Otto von Bismarck had crushed the French army at Sedan, captured the emperor, and surrounded Paris. For nearly 19 weeks Parisians had endured the increasing ravages of hunger. Then cold and indiscriminate shelling had added to their misery.

At the start of the German siege of Paris the new Republican government felt confident of holding out indefinitely. There were 400,000 troops, 3000 heavy

guns and a massive system of defenses, including a high outer wall, a moat, 94 bastions, and 15 forts. There was food and fuel for 12 weeks. But for a population of close on 2,000,000 the supplies of food and fuel were not enough.

As traditional foods ran low people turned, reluctantly, to substitutes. Candles were eaten instead of butter, and by October horse masqueraded as beef in restaurants (where the wealthy always found some food to eat). By mid November skinned cats displayed with paper frills and labeled "gutter rabbits" appeared in butchers' shops. By the end of December zoo animals had found their way onto the dinner plate. All told, Paris ate an estimated 65,000 horses, 5000

cats, 1200 dogs and 300 rats. But only citizens with cash ate well. By December food prices had rocketed – up to 9 times the prewar level for butter, 13 times for eggs, 15 times for cheese and 18 times for turkeys.

Officially, everyone got certain basic rations. But October's daily 3.5 ounces of meat per person was later cut to a minute 1 ounce. Every day shops ran out of food and shut early. By late December an eyewitness noticed "half starved" women and children. Women sold themselves for crusts of bread, and infants were now dying every day for lack of milk. By late January, the French writer Edmond de Goncourt observed, "You see nothing but thin, drawn, pallid features, faces as pale and yellow as horse-flesh."

Meanwhile a bitter winter had brought other hardships. By January, 1000 troops had suffered frost-bite, and some froze to death on sentry duty. Lack of coal for fuel forced the Government to cut down avenues of trees for firewood. Disregarding private property, poor people, thinly clad, grabbed anything that burned.

To crown the miseries of cold and hunger came

Left: German and French troops engaged in battle at Champigny, a southeastern suburb of Paris in November and December 1870. The battle was part of the German siege of Paris that lasted until January 1871, when the city surrendered.

Right: a German gun emplacement showing the bombardment of Paris. In three weeks 1200 missiles were fired into the city.

bombardment by the Germans. Outlying fortresses suffered first, but by early January shells were falling nightly in the city. Nonetheless, in three weeks, a total of 12,000 projectiles killed fewer than 100 people. Far more deaths occurred in failed military sorties, and from disease and hunger. Children suffered most; someone wrote "at every step you meet an undertaker carrying a little deal coffin." The beleaguered government in Paris now had to choose between deaths on a massive scale from famine, or the humiliation of surrender. It chose surrender. Paris won peace and food in return for handing over to Germany Alsace, northern Lorraine, a huge cash payment, and temporary occupation of the capital by German forces.

The armistice began on January 28, but the peace that followed was uneasy. Many Parisians resented the victory parade of German troops through their city and the largely royalist French National Assembly that had let them in. They resented even more the humiliating terms of the surrender and were convinced better terms could have been obtained from

Above: a butcher selling "gutter rabbits" (cats) in the St Germain market during the 19-week siege of Paris.

the victors. Adolphe Thiers' bourgeois government then insensitively bankrupted Parisian workers and small tradesmen by calling in all rents and debts suspended during war, and it enraged the National Guardsmen (largely composed of workers, enrolled during the siege) by canceling their pay.

Aware of the anger boiling up against him, Thiers tried to disarm the National Guard. But on March 18 rebels prevented government troops removing cannon

Above: the triumphant entry of German troops into Paris, March 1, 1871.

from Montmartre. A blood-hungry mob unhorsed General Lecomte and seized General Thomas. Rebellious soldiers shot both down inside a garden, and pumped bullets in their corpses while frenzied women urinated on them.

Reading the signs, Thiers' government immediately fled to Versailles, and Paris organized municipal elections through the central committee of the Guard which led to the formation of the Commune of Paris, dominated by extremists who demanded violent action. The governing body of the Commune set up its headquarters in the Hôtel de Ville (town hall). A long wrangle began among its members who were divided in their aims between, among other things, a national federation of communes and a Parisian dictatorship of France. It lost 13 precious days in argument and dissention after the Thiers government had fled Paris. Thiers, meanwhile, had not wasted his time and had organized "one of the finest armies possessed by France" as he declared to the Versailles Assembly on April 1, 1871.

On May 8, after skirmishes around the city and the forts, Thiers warned the Parisians that he was opening a general attack on the city. But the city was as secure against the Versailles troops as it had been against the Germans. For 13 days the military stalemate dragged on. Then, on May 21, a government sympathizer found an undefended city gate and let in Thiers' army. There followed the terrible *semaine sanglante,* or "bloody week," in which Thiers'

130,000-strong army crushed Communard resistance street by street.

As government troops began to press in on the Communards, rebel leaders took desperate defensive measures. On May 23 sniper fire from the Rue Royale led Paul-Antoine Brunel to fire buildings that had put his soldiers' barricades at risk. Soon, jewellers' shops and cafés were ablaze. Meanwhile, another Communard military leader had heaped barrels of gunpowder in the historic Tuileries Palace, daubed its fine hangings with petrol and tar, and set the splendid buildings explosively alight. Next morning, the Communards burned down their own seat of government, the great Hôtel de Ville. By nightfall on May 24, the Prefecture of Police, Palais de Justice, the Palais-Royal, one wing of the Louvre, other major buildings, and whole streets of houses blazed like fireworks in the dry May air, or lay reduced to glowing ash. "It seemed literally as if the whole town was on fire and as if all the powers of hell were let loose upon the town," observed one Englishman. Only the risk to wounded fellow Communards lying in a nearby hospital led arsonists to spare Nôtre-Dame Cathedral. As the rumor grew that women were swarming the streets with bottles of petrol firing the buildings (although there was never any proof of the story), government troops summarily shot anyone found carrying bottles. It will never be known how many innocent old women or children met their deaths while returning empty milk bottles to the dairy.

Burning buildings had become the vengeful "scorched earth" policy of men who knew their cause

was dead. The same destructive urge now caused the Communards to murder six of their prisoners. In the evening of May 24, troops hauled their hostages from prison cells at La Roquette: Monsignor Darboy the Archbishop of Paris, the ex-Empress Eugenie's 75-year old confessor, Abbé Deguerry, three Jesuits, and Judge Bonjean. The Archbishop blessed the other five. Then ragged shooting from a National Guard firing squad cut down all six. Troops bayoneted the Archbishop's body to make sure he was dead.

By next day only eastern Paris remained in Communard control and, with German troops cutting off Communard escape eastward, by May 26 government troops were mopping up the last stubbornly defended barricades. Pinned down in the 20th Arrondissement, men, women, and children died fighting fiercely in the web of narrow streets and alleys.

An English medical student claimed that one women's battalion "fought like devils, far better than the men; and I had the pain of seeing 52 shot down, even when they had been surrounded by the troops and disarmed."

This incident typified a new and ghastly wave of horror in which victorious troops took summary revenge upon the enemy that had burned much of Paris and (as they later found) murdered its archbishop. Wickham Hoffman of the American Legation claimed: "Any lieutenant ordered prisoners to be shot as the fancy took him, and no questions were asked." A local preacher reported "the execution of 25 women who were found pouring boiling water upon the heads of the soldiers."

Savage treatment awaited the convoys of prisoners that were now marched to Versailles. Before they started, a cavalry general, the Marquis de Gallivet, inspected them, selecting some at random for immediate execution. Stragglers died too. The novelist Alphonse Daudet saw two mounted troopers drag one man until he was "a mass of bleeding flesh," then fire two shots "into the moaning and kicking parcel of meat" before it died. Lewis Wingfield, an American assistant surgeon, told how he saw an old couple among the stragglers, the woman, who was crippled said, "shoot me; I cannot walk any further." It took 30 revolver shots to cut her and her husband down.

On May 26, Wingfield's friend Colonel John Stanley computed "Five thousand people have been shot (after being made prisoners) today." He thought that the worst was over, but there was worse to follow. All over Paris shots rang out for days as prisoners were led out and shot. People died of suffocation in overcrowded prisons at Versailles. Mass shootings took place there and back in Paris. Disposing of so many corpses led to hasty shallow burials in streets and squares, and there were grisly tales of people interred alive, and of arms sprouting from the ground.

All told, in this second Siege of Paris, fewer than 900 Government troops had perished compared with more than 20,000 Communards, sympathizers, and those killed in error with them – about 10 times as many as had perished in the infamous Reign of Terror. The worst civil war in 19th-century Europe was finished, but the social wounds it left are not yet healed.

Left: Paris during *le semaine sanglate* – "bloody week" – May 1871. The Tuileries can be seen ablaze.

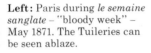

Right: Honoré Daumier's comment on the outcome of the war between the communards and the government, that ended in the deaths of more than 20,000 Parisians – communards, sympathizers, and those killed in error.

War of Attrition
Verdun: 1916

More than a year after the start of World War I, stalemate gripped the Western Front. Allied French and British troops fought the German forces from opposing lines of trenches that cut across Europe from the English Channel through Belgium and eastern France to neutral Switzerland. Barbed wire entanglements and machine guns turned infantry attacks into mass suicide. In 1915 scores of thousands of Allied troops perished in their efforts to win back just a few square miles of territory. Erich Von Falken-

by three groups of massive forts upon the wooded hills above the River Meuse. His calculations took these forts into account.

By early 1916 the Germans were funneling a huge mass of men and munitions into the Verdun sector. Big guns rolled in around the clock on 10 purpose-built railway lines, until more than 1200 menaced a front eight miles long. Ammunition and troops arrived by the trainload, and 140,000 soldiers were spread out to occupy whole villages. Immense secrecy cloaked the vast operation. Concrete tunnels burrowed deep underground to hide assault troops, leaving above ground what seemed a thinly held line. German warplanes patrolled the front to stop French aerial observers spotting the military build-up.

It was the digging sounds heard by a French listening post and reports from captured prisoners that convinced French Intelligence that there would

Above: the Prussian general Erich von Falkenhayn, chief of the general staff of the German Army from 1914 to 1916. He planned the offensive at Verdun.

hayn chief of the German general staff, believed that such butchery would help him win the war. Quite simply, he proposed to make the French army "bleed to death" beneath a rain of German shells upon a killing ground selected by the German army.

The battlefront he chose hinged on the famous fortress city of Verdun. There, some 130 miles east of Paris, the French line bulged out vulnerably. Verdun's historical importance and position as a door to central France convinced Falkenhayn that France would throw in every man it could to save Verdun from falling. He knew that Verdun itself was guarded

soon be a major attack on Verdun. Joseph Joffre, commanding the French army, dismissed the idea. He even sacked Verdun's military governor for saying that Verdun's defense was weak. In fact, Joffre himself had weakened it. He had stripped more than 4000 guns from Verdun's outlying forts, believing these too vulnerable to big German guns.

Deprived of their main firepower, most of Verdun's defenders left the forts and crouched instead in a weak line of trenches, where they were cold, wet, and unprotected from enemy shells. They were also outnumbered by three divisions to six. Almost too late

Joffre awoke to the danger. He sent in two more divisions nine days before the enemy struck.

On February 21, 1916 the German Fifth Army attacked on the east bank of the River Meuse. But first came the heaviest artillery barrage in history. Rapid-firing field guns placed at 150-yard intervals began pounding the French trenches. Meanwhile heavier mortars and the giant Big Bertha mortars blasted away at the forts. One large naval gun shelled Verdun itself. Another joined smaller field artillery guns in knocking out supply lines. Other guns known as "whizz-bangs" fired shrapnel shells and more than 500 mine throwers hurled cans laden with scrap metal and high explosive. Both these types of missile tore men apart.

The whole French front thundered, convulsed, and was lost to view in smoke and churning soil as the Germans sprayed it with 100,000 shells an hour. In

Above: trench warfare at Verdun. In spite of terrible bombardment by German guns, the French soldiers charged from their trenches offering fierce resistance to the advancing waves of German infantry.

Left: a column of German troops advancing into France in 1914.

Below: the death of a French soldier during the Verdun battle in 1916. So great was the German bombardment of the French entrenchment area that the ground resembled a lunar landscape. Heavy winter rains turned the battlefield into a sea of mud. Fighting under these conditions was an added nightmare for the troops.

one day, 2,000,000 shells screamed down on Verdun, Ornes, and Brabant; gouged deep, raw craters everywhere, and blotted out the French front line.

In the afternoon the German guns fell silent. Then German infantry patrols dashed forward. Jets of flame leaped from their flamethrowers – a terrible new weapon that at first unnerved the French.

For Germany a victory at Verdun seemed certain. Yet the French fought back like tigers. On 23 February, French machine guns leveled waves of German assault infantry in what went down in German archives as a "day of horror." But by that night two

French divisions totaling 26,500 men had suffered more than 16,000 casualties.

The French line began to crumble. Next day the Germans quickly overran the second French position. Scared by the artillery inferno, and miserably cold, Algerian and Moroccan reinforcements fled the field. A day later, a handful of Germans gained the mighty fort of Douaumont without a shot. Many of the French were now petrified. The Germans seemed about to seize Verdun itself. Terror gripped the city, and refugees began to block its exit roads.

Above: French war heroes, generals Petain and Joffre, from World War I calendars. Philippe Petain was commander at Verdun during the German attempt to overrun the city.

Right: this painting by the French artist Georges Leroux, entitled *L'enfer*, was inspired by the special hell of a World War I bombardment.

Philippe Petain was the man who stopped the panic. Powerful reinforcements helped his task as the new Commander at Verdun. Petain began blasting German troops north of Douaumont with flanking artillery fire. He also organized "The Sacred Way." Kept open by hordes of laborers, this narrow road from Bar Le Duc became the only lifeline of Verdun. Along it wound an endless snake of trucks containing men, food, guns, and ammunition. Six thousand trucks could pass by in a day and night. All told it fed 500,000 soldiers and 170,000 draft animals into the inferno.

By the end of February, the German push had halted. Now it was their turn to suffer at Verdun as 500 heavy guns pounded them. Streams of mangled soldiers began to stagger from the front "like a vision in Hell." The German painter Franz Marc wrote home of the frightful scenes that he had witnessed. A day later he himself was dead.

Both sides were now inextricably locked in a monstrous battle of attrition. The next act in this tragedy began on March 6, after the German commander-in-chief Erich von Falkenhayn had approved an onslaught on hills above the west bank of the Meuse. Some of the bloodiest battles in the whole

campaign sprang from this German bid to crush French flanking fire. Once more, German infantry gained ground. But the hill named Mort Homme ("Dead Man") proved to be well named. Each time the Germans launched themselves against its barren slopes, French guns chorused from Hill 304 and the Pois Bourrus ridge on either side and the German onslaught withered. The Germans then made Hill 304 a new, additional, objective. As March ended, the French had lost 89,000 men, the Germans 81,607 at Verdun.

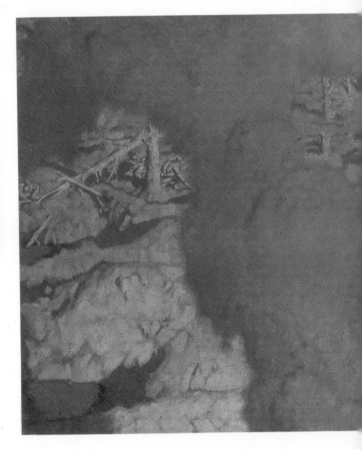

The battle for the western hills raged on into April and through May. On April 9 German troops tried rushing both the Mort Homme hill and Hill 304. This time they reached a lesser ridge upon Mort Homme. As each side's artillery blazed away at an opposing ridge the hilltop erupted like a volcano. A French machine-gun sergeant on Hill 304 described the pounding as "continuous, and terrifying." He felt the earth heave and saw men tossed about. Explosions had filled his trench with soil, so he crouched in a crater, caked by mud splashed up with each new blast and nearly suffocated by the acrid, smoke-filled air. Later he told how: "Our blinded, wounded, crawling, and screaming soldiers kept falling on top of us and died drenching us with their blood." Suddenly, the enemy artillery ranged farther on. As someone cried out that the enemy were coming, the sergeant saw the weary infantry come magically to life and grip their rifles, ready to repel the next assault.

Weather conspired to make the wretched troops'

conditions even worse. After this German onslaught rain set in immediately and lasted for 12 days. Sodden troops sloshed about in water above their knees. No trench or crater offered infantry escape from the pervasive damp. Many soldiers fell sick.

By May Verdun had cost the Germans 120,000 men, the French 133,000. Worse followed, as German forces renewed their attacks. Before June they had overrun Hill 304 and Mort Homme. On Hill 304 two days and a night of incessant bombardment had robbed French defenders of food, water, sleep, and reinforcements.

through the Verdun slaughterhouse. At this time too, the Germans had to face the Somme offensive, launched farther north by British troops on July 1 largely to take pressure off the French at Verdun.

By August, Verdun had lost the French 315,000 men, the Germans more than 280,000. The new German military leaders Paul von Hindenburg and Erich Ludendorff were sickened by this senseless slaughter. German attacks stopped and the battleground grew strangely quiet. But in late October the monster roared again. This time a mighty French attack dis-

One battalion lost all but three men, and altogether 10,000 French troops had died vainly defending this shell-pulped moonscape.

Meanwhile, east of the Meuse river, troops of the French Fifth Division were mauled fearfully trying to retake Fort Douaumont, in late May. On June 1 a new phase opened in the slaughter on this flank. Five German divisions began blasting a path to Verdun. They won Fort Vaux in days of unlit fighting, underground. Flamethrowers, machine guns and grenades at last silenced the fort's defenders. By June 22, German shells firing lethal phosgene gas paved the way for an assault that brought German troops within machine-gun range of Verdun.

Suddenly, the German effort faltered. The need for troops on other fronts robbed it of much-needed reinforcements. The troops already at Verdun were battle weary and dispirited. French troops, on the other hand, had been kept fresh by rotation: Petain eventually fed two thirds of the entire French Army

lodged the Germans from forts Vaux and Douaumont, and one day's assault clawed back land that the Germans had spent more than four months winning.

By the year's end the French had saved Verdun, and with it France's military honor. But the cost was hideous. More than 377,000 French troops were casualties – almost half killed or missing. Germany lost 40,000 fewer. Half Verdun's houses had gone, and nine villages had been pounded to oblivion by some of the 40,000,000 shells unleashed in this campaign. Meanwhile, in the Somme Valley battlefields, 1,100,000 British, French, and Germans were wounded, killed or missing.

These titanic struggles of 1916 dwarfed any battles of the past for carnage. They also branded disillusionment deep in the minds of the survivors. For as the future German chancellor Prince Max of Baden declared: "we and our enemies had shed our best blood in streams, and neither we nor they had come one step nearer to victory."

201

The Destruction of a City
Dresden: 1945

On February 14, 1945, British prisoners of war at a camp in eastern Germany awoke to see a huge pall of dirty brownish-yellow smoke. It towered 3 miles high above the city of Dresden, 25 miles to the northeast. The strange phenomenon persisted for three days. For a long time afterward a rain of blackened shreds of paper and clothing continued settling gently on the camp, and sooty rain fell in the valley of the Elbe river. Meanwhile the smoke pall drifted south toward Czechoslovakia. People glancing up at it were seeing what the British writer David Irving has called "the last mortal remains of a city which twelve hours earlier had sheltered a million people and their property." For, overnight, Allied bombers had transformed the heart of Dresden into a massive crematory oven and killed more people than have died in any other air attack in history.

Dresden was not in fact the first German city to suffer massive incendiary attacks in World War II. In

Above: an artist's sketch of the ruins near Hamburg docks after a bombing raid by British planes in 1945.

July 1943, the most densely populated part of Hamburg turned into a raging bonfire after British planes had showered it with a concentrated hail of incendiary bombs. The mass of fires heated the air above, the hot air rose, and cool air rushed in to take its place as though pumped in by some gigantic bellows. The

result was the first man-made fire storm – an artificial tornado with flames of furnace temperatures. One eye-witness reported "Scenes of terror. . . . Children were torn away from their parents' hands and whirled into the fire. People who thought they had escaped fell down, overcome by the devouring heat, and died in an instant." Kitchen pots and pans just buckled, slumped, and liquefied. Coal stored in basements blazed, and underground air-raid shelters were transformed from sanctuaries into ovens roasting anyone who sheltered there. When rescue workers at last broke into one bunker they found that the 250 inmates had been reduced to soft, grey ash. The four Hamburg districts struck by fire-storm respectively lost 36, 20, 16, and nearly 38 per cent of their entire populations. Altogether nearly 50,000 people perished. In 11 days bombs killed almost as many people in Hamburg as died throughout the war in all of Britain.

More fire storms followed. In October 1943, 8000 people died at Kassel. In August 1944, 134,000 people lost their homes at Königsberg. In September, more than 250,000 fire bombs struck Darmstadt, killing probably 12,000. Streets were strewn with naked, brightly colored corpses, and small, charred, log-like forms. Bremerhaven, Brunswick, and Heilbronn suffered similar attacks.

Allied air commanders justified such sorties as part of "the progressive destruction and dislocation of the German economic and industrial system" – the goal laid down in their leaders' so-called Casablanca Directive. Admittedly, most of the urban targets involved ports or factories essential to the German war effort. The cruellest blow of all was different.

Popularly called "the Florence on the Elbe," Dresden was world famous for its fine old buildings and splendid art collection. True, marshalling yards and factories had already drawn two air attacks upon the Saxon capital by early 1945. But any assault upon the old, inner city seemed too barbaric to be contemplated. Anyway Dresden was remote from Britain's bomber bases. Thus the city kept its reputation as the safest air-raid shelter in Germany. Children were evacuated there from cities more at risk. By early February 1945, women and children refugees from eastern Germany were pouring in by road and rail, escaping from the westward thrust of the Russian armies. Dresden brimmed with hospitals and military dressing stations for troops wounded at the Eastern Front. Then, too, thousands of forced Belgian, French, and other foreign laborers, and thousands more Russian, British, and American prisoners of war were kept in the vicinity. On 13 February, Dresden probably held 1,200,000 people – nearly twice its normal population.

This was the moment chosen by the British and Americans to launch a massive triple blow against the city's very heart to spread terror, disrupt the flow of German troops and refugees, and to impress and aid the Russian allies. Snow had fallen but the sky was largely clear when the first wave of 244 Lancaster

Above: the burned-out ruins of the city of Dresden after a massive air attack by British and American bombers.

Right: a porcelain figure from the Royal Saxon Factory at Meissen, center of Dresden china manufacture. Dresden, known as the Florence of the Elbe, was a cultural center regarded as relatively safe from air attack because of its non-industrial character.

Far right: the Altmarkt, or Old Market in Dresden before the allied air attack. Hundreds of people jumped into huge water tanks in the market to escape the terrible heat. All perished in the deep waters before the heat evaporated the water.

bombers droned in unopposed at 10.15 p.m. Below them, war-weary Dresdeners had tried to raise their spirits with a carnival, and the city's opera, circus, and many cinemas and theaters had all been open. Soon after 10 pm red flares lent an added atmosphere of gaiety. But minutes later the Lancasters began shedding bombs around these markers. High explosives tore the roofs off black and white half-timbered houses – some dating back perhaps 1000 years. Largely wooden buildings struck by fire bombs burned ferociously. Whole streets began to blaze. Soon a segment of the city was twinkling with scores of fires. Three hours after this attack began, 529 more Lancasters arrived and began stoking up the fires lit by their colleagues.

Above: some of the thousands of bodies laid out in the rubble after the Dresden air raid of February 1945.

Above right: war-weary Germans clearing rubble from the remains of their home after the Dresden holocaust.

Between them, both groups dropped 650,000 incendiary bombs (apart from other types) upon the city.

Even before the second blow fell, a fire storm had gripped the city center. Pilots saw the blaze from 200 miles away. A flight engineer found the night sky so bright that he could even see the vapor trails of other aircraft. Looking down, a navigator saw that "Dresden was a city with every street etched in fire." The pilot of the last Lancaster above the target could actually feel the heat inside his cockpit.

Even as this second bomber wave flew back to England, 450 Flying Fortresses were being readied for a third assault upon the stricken city. Some 14 hours after the first attack, the American bombers were pounding Dresden, and accompanying Mustang fighters swooped down and machine gunned groups of people moving in or out. The second and third raids had been accurately timed to smash the rescue services at work among the ruins.

The impact of the three attacks upon the city almost beggars imagination. Overnight, Allied planes had flattened nearly three times the urban area that London lost throughout the war, and lit perhaps the greatest fire in history, which burned on for a week. Taken with lesser raids that hit the city the night's work destroyed 90,000 homes and apartments or made them uninhabitable, and created 11 lorry-loads of rubble for each inhabitant. Dresden's priceless paintings had luckily been stored in safety, but more than 150 major works of art on their way through Dresden were destroyed when the trucks bearing them were caught up in the conflagration. Famous landmarks such as the circus, opera house, and cathedral dome were gutted and collapsed.

Property could be rebuilt, but nothing would restore the lives of those who perished. The likely toll was 135,000, or roughly one in 10 of all the citizens and refugees accumulated in the city.

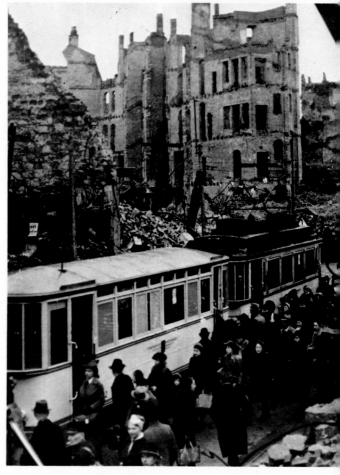

Most died in the fire storm that began about 45 minutes after the first attack, and enveloped the colossal area of some 11 square miles. As temperatures reached and passed 1000°C, bricks melted, heated air rushed upward and a gale of unbelievable ferocity raced in with a waterfall-like roar. Trees snapped like twigs, or were torn up bodily, and railroad trucks blew over. A railway worker saw a woman pushing a perambulator seized and hurled along a street into the giant jets of flame. Crowds of people running into the streets for safety were plucked up and dashed into the white hearts of infernos. Countless weak, old people who might otherwise have escaped, died inside a ring of fire.

There was no escape even for those who fled below ground. In some places up to 90 people were crammed inside the cellars under the houses. As choking fumes billowed down the stairs, inmates burst down the weak partition separating their cellar from the next. In this way poisonous carbon monoxide gas spread from house to house.

When hundreds of fire bombs cascaded through the glass roof of the Central Station, 2000 refugees lay huddled in a subterranean baggage tunnel. One hundred were burned to death, and 500 more died by breathing hot gases, smoke, or carbon monoxide fumes. The bombs struck just as a trainload of children had arrived. Workers soon had the dismal job of

Left: a year after the fire-raid, citizens attempt to go about their business amid scenes of devastation.

Right: the Altmarkt in Dresden today. Much of the city has been faithfully restored to its pre-war designs by the East German government.

piling up their bodies at the station entrances.

In another part of the city a telephone operator later told how she saw a dozen of her colleagues crushed beneath a collapsing "red-glowing glass roof" while trying to escape from a courtyard. Scores of legless soldiers and expectant mothers were incinerated when their hospitals burned down.

Refugees crowding the city's open spaces suffered particularly heavily. Thousands perished in a big park called the Grosser Garten, and blazing oil escaping from an army transport depot killed hundreds on the Exhibition Site.

To dodge the flames, hundreds of men and women leaped into water tanks in the old market square, only to find the water more than 8 feet deep. Sloping sides made escape impossible. Non-swimmers dragged swimmers down, and everyone was drowned before intense heat caused the water to evaporate. When the holocaust subsided, rescue workers found more than 200 people seated around the rim of a shallower tank in the Seidnitzerplatz. All of them were dead.

Death came in many ways. Most people died relatively painlessly from carbon monoxide poisoning or lack of oxygen. Others were roasted, or boiled alive when burst pipes poured scalding water into basements. Director Voigt, of the Dead Persons Department later set up to identify the corpses, found victims "burned, cremated, torn, and crushed to death."

Forced laborers and prisoners of war had the grisly task of clearing up the bodies. Some were scarcely recognizable. One Dresdener recalls the street remains of what must have been a mother and child. "They had shriveled and charred into one piece, and had been stuck rigidly to the asphalt. . . . The child must have been underneath the mother, because you could still clearly see its shape, with its mother's arms clasped around it." In one cellar an exploding bomb had liquidized 200 people, leaving a calf-deep swamp of blood, flesh, and bone.

At first men buried lorryloads of bodies in mass graves. But the huge task of disposal took weeks. In the end workers had to burn decaying corpses in layered pyres constructed in the city center.

Of all the European war's atrocities, only the Germans' annihilation of the Jews surpassed this massacre in scale.

Nuclear Holocaust
Hiroshima & Nagasaki: 1945

The people of Hiroshima were puzzled by their city's luck in World War II. By early August 1945 American air raids had pounded Tokyo and other major centers in Japan. Yet Hiroshima's regional army headquarters, port, rail terminus, war industries, and warren of flimsy wooden homes spread out across the islands of the Ota River delta remained almost untouched. Optimists thought that the Americans

believed Hiroshima too beautiful to bomb, or that they lacked the heart to devastate a city from which so many Japanese had emigrated to the United States. But pessimists suspected the Americans were reserving some new and terrible destruction for Hiroshima. Soon after 8 am on August 6, the pessimists proved right.

No one took much notice of the B-29 Superfortress that flew in high above Hiroshima that hot, glittering morning. The Japanese radio reassuringly diagnosed its purpose as reconnaissance. People went about their daily tasks: housewives performing after-breakfast chores, while workers walked or rode to factory and office, or were already busy there. Meanwhile, far above their heads, a bombardier aboard the B-29

Enola Gay was arming and releasing Little Boy – a bomb the like of which had never been dropped upon an enemy before. The 10-foot long, 9000-pound bomb fell to an altitude of 1850 feet, then a radar echo triggered a small explosion in the bomb that drove one uranium wedge against another. The result was a nuclear explosion equal to a blast from 17,000 tons of TNT. Probably about 75,000 people were killed or fatally injured – some put the figure as high as a quarter of a million. Either way, no single bomb before or since has killed and maimed so many, or so totally destroyed a city.

Only people standing far off could see what actually happened. Nearer, a history professor three miles away just managed to glimpse a blinding blue-white flash before he flung himself down. He felt the searing heat. Then he heard a boom like thunder and sensed a crushing rush of air, followed by a chain of crashing sounds. Looking up, he saw a vast pillar of cloud boiling up into the sky until the top overflowed to form a giant mushroom. Although the sunshine made the boiling cloud seem many hued, it was black with dust and ash and shed black rain.

Above: a Little Boy atomic bomb – a replica of that dropped on Hiroshima on August 6, 1945.

Left: The Los Alamos atomic-energy laboratories where the atom bomb was made and then tested in July 1945 in the desert region of western Sierra Oscura, New Mexico.

Right: the mushroom-headed cloud from the Little Boy atomic bomb photographed after the Hiroshima explosion.

Below the cloud Hiroshima had vanished. A city of some 390,000 inhabitants had turned into a ragged desert of tiles, bricks, and shattered glass, with here and there stumps of trees and poles. Nothing stood within a radius of two miles of the explosion. Within three miles, two thirds of Hiroshima's 90,000 buildings had been devastated.

This urban desert was almost immediately ablaze. Many fires began when blast-shattered houses fell on charcoal stoves. Other fires resulted from the scorching heat of the explosion. Near the point over which the bomb had exploded, stone and metal had melted, and people had turned to blackened crisps. Air sucked in by the inferno fed fires that raged within a two-mile radius.

Apart from the crackling of flames, the city was enveloped by a deathly hush. Thousands of citizens had perished instantly from blast or burns. Others drowned as they crowded into rivers to escape the flames. But thousands more now dragged themselves in stunned processions to the suburbs. Many had had the clothes blasted from their heat-seared bodies. Some trudged with arms held out from painfully burned torsos. Some had hideously bloated faces. A girl's parents failed to recognize her, until she started crying. A grocer described people burned so black and hairless that "you couldn't tell whether you were looking at them from the front or the back." Shreds of skin dangled from faces, hands, and torsos. Anyone within two and a half miles of the center of the blast had been liable to suffer flash burns from the heat energy released in the explosion. People even farther out had suffered injury from splintered glass, or falling timbers, or masonry. Many of the wounded refugees died along the roads into the countryside.

A few people near the center had had miraculous escapes from blast and burns, when rubble fell protectively around them. But even those without a mark were often doomed. For besides emitting blast and heat, the bomb had showered the area around with invisible but deadly gamma rays capable of penetrating brick and wood. Anyone unshielded from these rays and caught within about one and a quarter miles of the center of the blast was liable to die from damage to their body cells. Even rescue workers entering the city became contaminated by radio-active dust and ash.

Any time from minutes to weeks after the explosion, people who had been within the radiation area began to vomit, lose appetite, and suffer diarrhea. They felt weak and feverish. Mouth and gums became ulcerated. Blood leaked from mouth, throat, rectum, urinary tract, and into the skin, where purple spots appeared. Hair fell out. Even the slightest wounds turned septic. Tests showed severe lack of white blood cells. Many victims lost much of their stomach linings, Unable to absorb food, they grew emaciated. Death soon followed.

One man later told how his daughter seemed fit for almost a month, then began coughing up small clots

center. Hundreds eventually died. By the early 1950s the leukaemia rate was dropping. But cancers of the lungs, stomach, thyroid, ovaries, and cervix became unusually common. People are probably still dying in Hiroshima from diseases that date back to that August day in 1945.

Even robust individuals became hypochondriacs, fearing not only for their own health but their future children's. The fate of babies born soon after the bomb had certainly been grim. Women pregnant when the bomb fell aborted, or bore dead or sick babies, or imbiciles with stunted skulls. However no trend of abnormality has appeared among babies conceived by survivors after the disaster.

Surprisingly, the bomb that smashed Hiroshima

Above: an aerial view of Hiroshima looking very much as it might have done to the crew of the B-29 superfortress *Enola Gay* on that fateful August 6, 1945.

Right: Hiroshima after the atomic bomb explosion. It is estimated that some 75,000 people were killed or fatally injured in the single-bomb blast.

of blood, showed other signs of radiation sickness, and died "after 10 days of agony and torture." Another individual described how patients in hospital perished daily in their beds around him. Of 35 sufferers isolated on an island, only two survived.

Rumors said that everyone in Hiroshima would die within three years, that trees would never grow again, and that the city would be uninhabitable for 75 years. But grass soon sprouted in the ruins, and thousands recovered from the sickness, albeit often aging early and displaying sexual impairment or ugly scars. Time showed, though, that no one could feel ultimately safe. By 1948 up to 50 times the normal incidence of leukaemia began emerging among survivors who had been within 6560 feet of the blast

failed to force war-weakened Japan's capitulation. But this catastrophe was swiftly followed by two even more decisive hammer blows. On August 8 Russia declared war. Next day, America dropped a further atom bomb, this time upon the major industrial city of Nagasaki. This bomb was a 10,000 pound plutonium device called *Fat Man*. At 11.02 am *Fat Man*'s explosion struck a Nagasaki suburb and seared it with a fireball like the flame of a gigantic blowtorch. Deaths and damage were less widespread than they had been at Hiroshima because Nagasaki is shaped like a two-pronged fork, with intervening ridges that helped to block off heat and blast. But a heat wave launched at 300,000°C and a shock wave moving at 9000 miles an hour destroyed 20,000 of Nagasaki's 55,000 buildings and killed at least 40,000 citizens – possibly more – with as many wounded.

Within 1000 yards of the center of the blast every living thing was scorched to death. Metal roofs and girders buckled, bubbled, and sagged like chewing gum. Schools, a Roman Catholic cathedral, hospitals, a prison, steelworks, arms factories, and shipyard plants were totally wiped out.

When numbed rescue workers moved into the shattered area they found stark scenes. Children who had been performing calisthenics lay dead in rows in a school courtyard. A row of cremated passengers sat in the window seats of a gutted streetcar. More than 40 inmates of an institute for the blind and deaf, and 95 prisoners and their 15 guards in Ukrami Prison had

Equally remarkable were the survivals. Some of those who lived had hidden in deep air-raid shelters. A kneeling man weeding sweet potatoes below a wall missed the wave of heat that killed his wife who stood behind him. Inhabitants in a block of buildings a mere 1000 yards from the center of the blast escaped relatively lightly, thanks to a hill that acted as a buffer. But a carpenter had the most amazing luck of all. He was running for shelter on a rooftop five stories high when the blast whirled him off and dumped him, safe and upright, on the ground 53 feet below.

Thousands of Nagasaki's "survivors," though, faced a brief, bleak future of radiation sickness and painful death. The next day it opened the peace overtures that ended what had been the bloodiest war in history.

Above: Hiroshima in September 1945 viewed by an Allied War Correspondent. The only building standing is the Industrial Promotion Hall, still preserved in the re-built Hiroshima (below).

been annihilated. People struggling home through debris found death and desolation. One woman returned to discover she had lost four of her five children, her husband, a brother, and her mother. As searchers moved farther in from the safe outer areas the cries of injured people gave way to moans. These ceased where everyone had been incinerated.

The bomb had had bizarre effects. Heat rays passing through their clothing had reddened peoples' skins, etching patterns made up of labels, straps, and buttons. Rays from the bomb had also printed the "shadows" of objects onto the ground. A stripe stood for an incinerated telephone pole; a row of bars, for the railings of a bridge. One shadow showed where a man had scorched to death, megaphone in hand.

A Balance of Terror

From 1954 to 1973 the United States plunged deeply into a guerrilla war in Indochina, and although American planes showered Indochina with three times the weight of bombs dropped by all Allied planes in World War II, the United States failed to halt Communist North Vietnam from absorbing South Vietnam.

The horrors of Vietnam, in which thousands of uninvolved civilians died, are a reminder that atrocities did not cease with World War II. Vietnamese peasants caught up in the fighting suffered dismally from both sides. American troops massacred 500 men, women, and children at My Lai in 1968. Elsewhere, an eyewitness saw US helicopter gunners shoot at farmers for fun "as if in a hunting mood." Prisoners interrogated by South Vietnamese troops met death "under

Almost as soon as World War II came to an end, nations began squaring off in new, mutually hostile groups: the USSR, China, and their Communist satellites confronting the United States and lesser "Western democracies."

What followed was the Cold War – a propaganda conflict with incidents when a third World War between the superpowers seemed almost unavoidable.

Above: Vietnamese children on crutches and (left) a wounded Vietnamese soldier. Civilians bear the brunt of suffering in modern warfare both as hastily recruited and barely trained soldiers and the young and old left defenseless between the conflicting armies.
Right: a soldier passes a victim of crossfire on the road.

Happily, the serious incidents were resolved even as the threat of war loomed yet again. The West's airlift of supplies, for instance, peacefully broke a Soviet blockade of West Berlin, and United States pressure forced the Soviet Union to dismantle its rocket sites in Cuba where they had been threatening America.

But Communist and Western powers were almost always fighting somewhere. From 1950 to 1953 2,000,000 perished in the Korean War in which United Nations troops successfully prevented Communist North Korea and China overrunning South Korea.

the tracks of armored vehicles, by decapitation or by bleeding to death after both hands have been chopped off, or by a bullet in the head." The Communists were just as bad. In 1967 Dak Song villagers were burned to death. At Hue, many victims including women were tied together, tortured, mutilated, then – some still alive – tossed into mass graves. Altogether, the Vietnam War probably killed 3,000,000, wounded 5,500,000 more, and spawned 9,000,000 refugees.

Vietnamese peasants burned to death by flaming napalm jelly would have found no consolation in the fact that only "conventional" weapons have been used since World War II. Meager though it is, most people are thankful for this mercy. The superpowers now have tools of death able to erase all major cities and kill scores of millions of people, in literally minutes.

Today a single bomber can carry enough nerve gas to asphyxiate 3 in every 10 people in an area of 100 square miles. But chemical and biological agents of destruction are less generally feared than the nuclear devices invented since atomic bombs flattened Hiroshima and Nagasaki in 1945. In 1951 American scientists announced the test explosion of a hydrogen bomb with an explosive force 1000 times that of the atomic bombs dropped on Japan, and a colossal capability to kill by searing heat and radioactive fall-

out. Now China and the Soviet Union have this weapon, too. By the late 1970s several nations were also capable of making neutron bombs designed to spray lethal radiation without destroying buildings.

Meanwhile the USSR, China, and America had been developing missiles able to deliver nuclear devices with pinpoint accuracy to targets half way around the world. There is almost no place in the world that is not in range of an American or Soviet nuclear warhead housed underground or under water, or circling above inside an artificial satellite.

We live in the shadow of a global war more terrible than we can imagine. Can anything be done to stop it happening? Some hope must rest with the United Nations, the international body set up in 1945 to work for peace and world security. The Korean War involved United Nations' action. Since then, UN troops have helped defuse explosive situations in Africa and Southwest Asia. But the United Nations has failed to halt the arms race between the superpowers.

It has been a popular argument that to avoid a future holocaust nations must strike a balance of terror, then both sides would be too scared of reprisals to unleash the doomsday devices already pointed at one another.

But the peace is frail. Conceivably some military madman's finger could press the first button of destruction. Then, too, old habits of national aggrandizement and new threats to world stability produced by shrinking energy supplies bode ill for everyone. The editors of *War* (an anthology of war's psychology, sociology, and anthropology) believe that "the combination of human irrationality and the existence of super-weapons constitutes the greatest danger ever faced in the history of man."

Only unblinking awareness of this danger can save us from the ultimate catastrophe, and only a change in human attitudes can draw the world back from the brink of the abyss.

Above: a Soviet army display in Red Square, Moscow in 1977. Such displays are meant to serve both as morale-boosters to those in power and as a warning to would-be aggressors. In spite of assurances that such power has been accumulated for "defense," weaker countries interpret such displays as a threat to their own independence.

211

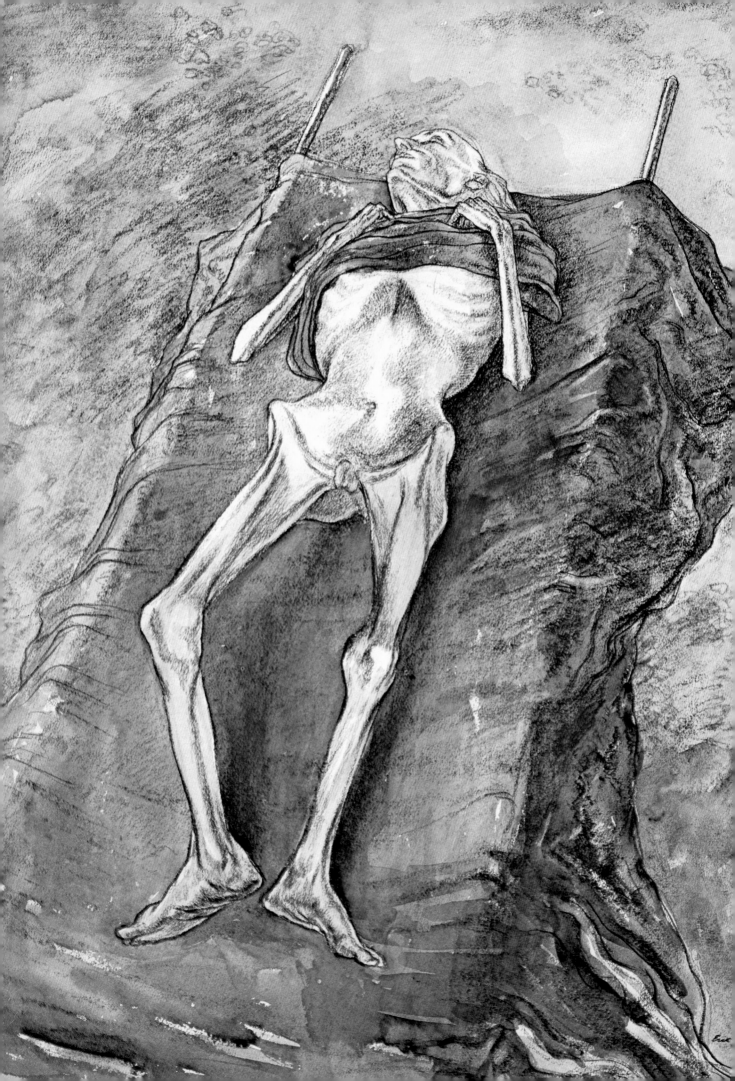

Chapter 11

Man's Inhumanity to Man

From the earliest times, the persecution of defeated enemies and despised minorities has been a feature of world history. The Romans persecuted the early Christians, the Church in its turn persecuted the heretics. When Europeans founded empires across the sea they took with them the same appetites for atrocities – as the Mayas, Aztecs, and Incas in Central and South America, and the Indians in North America found to their cost. These and the later horrors of the transatlantic slave trade all bear witness to the truism that absolute power over one's fellow men is a great corruptor. No one has a monopoly of cruelty. Many "civilized" peoples have sloughed off the moral code by which they lived and turned on national minorities and other helpless groups as fiercely as a cat destroys a mouse. The difference is that when a cat plays with a mouse before killing it, the cat is oblivious of the pain it inflicts on its prey. Man's cruel, often sadistic, behavior toward his fellows is all the more culpable because he can fully comprehend the pain he inflicts upon his victims.

Opposite: the skeletal remains of one of the many inmates of Belsen Concentration Camp in Germany. The cold, brutal decision by a so-called civilized government of a large nation in mid-20th century Europe to degrade and exterminate 6,000,000 fellow Europeans between 1939 and 1945 still has the power to shock and horrify after several decades.

What Makes Men Cruel?

who actually enjoy causing pain to others – bullies like Vlad Tepes, a 15th-century ruler of Walachia (now in Romania). Vlad's idea of real enjoyment was sitting down to dine to the groans of scores of captured enemies impaled on stakes. This prototype for Dracula shared such tastes with his Turkish contemporary Sultan Mohammed II ("Drinker of Blood") who

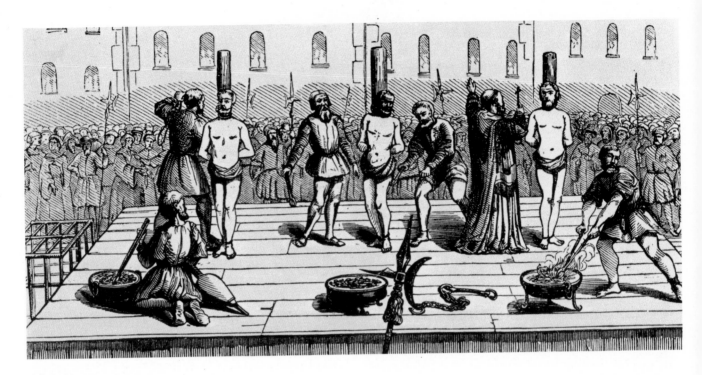

nailed turbans to the heads of captured prisoners.

Stories of massacres, tortures, and cruel exploitation of people are always difficult to comprehend. How can human beings bring themselves to act like beasts? One answer is that, biologically, man *is* just another kind of beast, and reacts in an aggressive, animal, way to real or supposed threats against the group he lives in. When such threats arise from outside groups, war follows. When a splinter group within his own appears to threaten it, the consequence is often persecution of the political, racial, religious, or other minority concerned. Black slavery and Amerindian servitude fall into a different category of cruelty. In such cases a powerful white minority callously exploited a weak majority of alien peoples regarded by their captors as subhuman and not fit to receive humane treatment.

In many cases of repression persecutors have gone to work with what they felt was righteous zeal. Crusaders fought the Albigenses of medieval France. Inquisitors, religious and civil, rooted out the witches throughout Europe – and America. SS camp guards exterminated Jews in death camps. Propaganda led many of these murderers to believe that they were purging their society of a dangerous, erosive canker. Sometimes subordinates detested their own bestial work but feared punishment for not performing it. Through cowardice or lack of concern, it seems, people can be cruel to fellow men to whom they bear no malice.

Most persecutions, however, attract individuals

No age lacks such human monsters. In 1930 Peter Kürten combed the streets of Düsseldorf for women and children whom he stabbed for the perverted sexual pleasure that he gained by making them bleed. Still in prison are a young British couple who tortured children to death, recording their screams for future listening pleasure.

Sadism, as such perversion is now known, takes its name from the 18th-century Marquis de Sade, who argued in obscene novels that sexual pleasure is *best* achieved by inflicting pain on others. De Sade held that there is no God, but a Goddess, Nature – a creative yet destructive force. In such a context human cruelty is a manifestation of impersonal energy, and personal guilt is irrelevant. It is an attitude that strikingly recalls Adolf Hitler's claim that he was "freeing men from the restraints of . . . the dirty and degrading self-mortification of a chimera called conscience and morality. . . ."

To most psychiatrists such amoral attitudes merely mask a major abnormality of personality, often rooted in some traumatic childhood experience that warped the individual's future emotional development.

There is no doubt that such psychopathetic individuals are responsible for many atrocities committed during times of persecution – especially when the psychopaths wield power as policemen, soldiers, or prison guards. Worst of all, such evil men have some-

214

Opposite: the leaders of the German and Dutch Anabaptists being tortured to death in Münster. Persecuted by both Lutherans and Catholics, the Anabaptists gathered at Münster where they controlled the city and held off an army drawn from the surrounding states for over a year. Eventually the city fell and the authorities exacted a terrible retribution against the Anabaptist defenders.

Right: a scene from the 1932 movie of Dr Jekyll and Mr Hyde, showing Dr Jekyll's evil other self the malignant Mr Hyde about his murderous business.

times held government positions enabling them actually to launch massacres or pogroms.

Yet are most of us so very different from these human monsters? Many of us who believe ourselves incapable of inflicting pain on others are fascinated by stories of pain being inflicted. People react to a headlined atrocity by crying out, "How terrible!" But they buy a newspaper to learn about it. Tales of massacre and genocide are nauseating – yet they attract a wide public.

The fact is that all of us are complex beings. Each combines something of the goodness of fiction's Dr. Jekyll with something of the bestiality of Mr Hyde, the evil other half of Jekyll's personality. The "Hyde" in most of us is no more than the selfishness that in infancy we learn to subordinate to the good of the community we live in. Yet, conditioned by a certain kind of propaganda, millions of docile, law-abiding citizens are capable of brute behavior against some racial, religious, or other group within their midst. Ganged together in this spirit, individually loving husbands, fathers, even wives and mothers – have been transformed into a raging rioting mob bringing terror to the objects of its spite. "Normal" man has too many times proved himself to be potentially a monster.

Above: a satisfied mob stand beneath the bodies of two men lynched by members of America's Ku Klux Klan.

Right: an elegantly gowned and coiffured torturer contrasted with her gory victim.

Early Christian Martyrs

The crowd seized Stephen, drove him from Jerusalem and pelted him with stones. Stephen fell to his knees, praying to God to forgive those who were killing him. He soon lay dead – the first of thousands of martyrs to perish for preaching or just admitting their belief in Christianity. In all ages Christians have died for their faith. But perhaps at no time or place were they so ferociously degraded, tortured, and murdered by non-Christians as in the Roman Empire in the first three centuries of what we now call the Christian Era.

From early on, Jesus' apostles – his closest followers – endured humiliation or torment. Saint James the Greater became the first apostle to die for his faith. In 44 AD (nine years after Stephen's murder), King Herod Agrippa I had James beheaded in an effort to curry favor with the Jewish leaders. Some 20 years later Saint Peter perished at Rome, reputedly crucified upside down after declaring himself unworthy to die like Jesus. According to legend most of the other apostles were also martyred – one by stoning, another flayed alive, others crucified. The sites claimed for their deaths – Egypt, Ethiopia, Cyprus, Palestine, Greece, Armenia, Persia, India, and Rome – suggest that the Christians were spreading their message far through the civilized world from an early period, and that they were also dying for it.

It was inevitable that Christians should meet aggressive resistance wherever they went. Their beliefs clashed with old faiths. They also seemed to call for an allegiance rivaling that due to established political rulers. Christianity preached a new kingdom. It condemned all other religions as false. Its meetings barred unbelievers yet welcomed women, and even slaves – inferior beings whose encouragement by Christians suggested subversion. Then, too, people hinted that Christians were guilty of worse things. Did they not eat someone's "body" and drink his "blood" at their services? (Small children were the victims, it was claimed). Christians also seemed anti-social. They despised the popular theaters, festivals, sports, schools, hospitals – because all in some way involved acknowledging the pagan gods of Rome.

Left: the stoning of Saint Stephen, the first Christian martyr. One of those responsible for the punishment of blaspheming "Christians" under Jewish law was Saul of Tarsus (at bottom right of picture) who later joined those he persecuted and became Saint Paul.

Right: Saint George, who refused to sacrifice to Apollo is tortured on a cross by having his flesh scraped with iron combs. The story is from *The Golden Legend*, a popular source of saints' lives in the Middle Ages.

It was no wonder that many people looked on the local Christian minority with suspicion. Christians became scapegoats – they were blamed for earthquakes, volcanic outbursts, famines, plagues or other natural disasters. In places a small incident would be enough to turn distrust to hatred and physical attack.

Persecution began in Palestine. As the rift with Judaism deepened the Orthodox Jews turned on the Christian Jews, who had opened their ranks to non-Jews – a shift of policy largely due to Saint Paul, himself a former persecutor of the Christians. In Asia Minor, the Pagan authorities soon joined in Christian baiting. Orgies and cannibalism were among the charges that laid a legal basis for torture and execution.

As Christianity continued to gain ground, Roman emperors saw a mounting threat to the empire's cohesion in the Christians' rejection of the official and unifying cult of emperor worship.

It was the Emperor Nero who carried out the first organized brutalities against the Christians. It was not their refusal to worship him that was Nero's declared objection to the followers of Christ. When a six-day fire razed most of Rome to ashes in 64 AD, Nero claimed that Christian arsonists had caused the

Above: the Apostle Peter, who was crucified upside down because he considered he was unworthy to die like his master.

conflagration. Although no hint of guilt emerged from those arrested and interrogated, Nero nonetheless damned these innocents as "enemies of the human race" and deserving punishment. Some were sewn into the skins of animals and set upon by bloodhounds. Some were tied to oxen. Many were mangled, others crucified. People also wrapped Christians in cloths previously soaked in pitch and then set fire to them, to burn as living torches. These "entertainments" took place in Nero's own imperial gardens while the emperor, in charioteer's dress, drove or walked among the watching crowd. Saints Peter and Paul traditionally perished in the general slaughter.

To the Romans' astonishment, many Christians almost seemed to welcome such barbaric treatment. In the Gospels of Matthew (Chapter 24), Mark (Chapter 8), and Luke (Chapter 21), Christ himself had warned them of the difficulties they would encounter in preaching the Gospel. The persecutions they were to expect were the necessary pains that would accompany the birth of the kingdom of God on earth. From early on, then, Christian teaching schooled the followers of Christ to glory in suffering and a death of martyrdom as a path to immortality.

From Nero onward they often had the opportunity to tread that path. Not every persecution of the Christians was organized at imperial level. Most were localized or started by political concern at the Christians' refusal to toe the official line in worshiping the emperor. Nonetheless, when persecution came, it was often hideously brutal.

About 110 AD, in northern Asia Minor, the Roman legate Pliny executed people merely for admitting accusations that they held the Christian faith. The first Christian record of a martyrdom is a letter from Asia Minor telling how Smyrna's aged bishop Polycarp was killed in 155 or 156 during the reign of Antoninus Pius. Betrayed by a servant the 86-year-old ecclesiastic was led into a crowded stadium and there refused to deny this Christian faith. To the roaring of the spectacle-hungry mob the saint was burned alive:

"and the flames made a sort of arch, like a ship's sail filled with the wind, and they were like a wall round the martyr's body; and he looked like . . . gold and silver being refined in a furnace."

During Marcus Aurelius's disaster-ridden reign (161-180) Christian scapegoats suffered horribly. The worst massacres occurred at Lyons and Vienne in southern France. Non-Christian slaves falsely confirmed rumors that their Christian masters practiced incest and ate children. A mob began to seek out Christians. Some were thrown in jail to die. Others perished publicly in agony. The 90-year-old bishop of Lyons, Pothinus, was kicked, punched, and dumped insensible in prison, where he died. According to one story, the Christian slave girl Blandina had her body mangled, and was then hung upon a cross for wild

In spite of persecutions, by 200 AD Christianity had put down roots throughout the Roman world – from France to Syria. For the next 50 years or so there was relative relief from harassment as Christianity shared in the growing popularity of Eastern mystery religions. Local, sporadic persecutions did occur, however – especially when emperors Septimius Severus and Maximin issued anti-Christian edicts. The most poignant story of this period deals with six Christians condemned to death at Carthage in North Africa in 203 in the reign of Septimius Severus. Four were men. The fifth was Felicity, a slave girl who gave birth in prison. The sixth victim was Perpetua, a young married noblewoman with a baby. A contemporary writer describes how in the amphitheater of death the women helped each other fend off a ferocious cow, but

beasts to devour. They would not eat her and she perished on a bonfire. Crowds seated around an arena watched Christians roasted in a red-hot iron chair. Any Christians who were Roman citizens were lucky to be beheaded. Their executioner heaped their severed heads upon the remains of carcasses of other victims and burned the pile to ashes, which were scattered in the River Rhône.

In vain did Christian writers seek to improve the public image of their faith. Justin, the leading apologist of the 2nd century, resolutely refused to sacrifice to idols when examined. He was beheaded at Rome, with six disciples – a woman and five men.

a bear, boar, and leopard were unleashed upon the men. Then all six martyrs were finished off with sword thrusts at the throat – Perpetua herself guiding the second blow when the first had failed to kill her. Under Maximin (235–238) the state clamped down on Christian clerics and men threw Christians to the lions as scapegoats when earthquakes shattered towns in Asia Minor.

In 249 Decius launched an empire-wide onslaught against the new religions. Anyone refusing to make sacrifices to the Roman gods was liable to suffer jail, torture, or death. The bishops of the three major centers of the Christian faith, Rome, Jerusalem, and

Antioch all perished in this pagan inquisition. Some Church leaders fled. Thousands of Christians at least temporarily denied their faith to save their skins.

Another burst of savage persecution followed under Decius' successor Valerian. By exiling Christian clergy and seizing the property of other Christians, Valerian hoped to impoverish the now rich and relatively powerful Church. He failed and harsher measures followed. One victim was Rome's bishop, beheaded while teaching in the catacombs – the burial caves of Rome that had become the Christians' secret meeting place.

For 40 years after Valerian Christians were unmolested. Then in the year 303, Diocletian launched the most terrible attack of all. His first edict decreed smashing down all churches, burning all sacred books, socially degrading all high-ranking Christians and enslaving Christian servants. Severer edicts followed, and self-acknowledged Christians became automatically liable for death.

The 300-year-old Church was far too strong by then to be subdued. By 320 Christianity had even gained a footing in the army. A contemporary Greek account exists of the story of 40 members of the Emperor Licinius' army stationed in Armenia who were stripped naked and kept on a frozen pond until they died because they would not renounce their faith.

In 323 Licinius, Roman Emperor of the East, was defeated by his western counterpart Constantine, a sympathizer with the Christians. Constantine later became the first Christian Emperor of Rome. The persecution of the early Christians was over.

Left: a romanticized view of Christian martyres in the Colosseum in Rome during the persecution by the Emperor Nero in the 1st century AD.

Below: an ivory plaque showing Christians herded together to await death in the arena. Above them Christ, surrounded by angels waits to present them with the crown of martyrdom.

Above: the catacombs, or rock-hewn burial chambers in Rome. It was here that Christians met to hold their services in secret during the years of persecution under the Roman Emperors.

Below: a portrait bust of the Roman Emperor Nero, who first made persecution of Christians official state policy.

219

The "Albigensian Crusade"
France: 1180-1270

The citizens of the southern French city of Bèziers gazed from their walls at the besieging army camped below. Impregnable inside their fortress, the citizens were outnumbered but not undaunted. On this July day of 1209, they confidently settled down to sit out a siege that they expected might last several weeks. Then, a small foolhardy group of burghers made a

Above: medieval engraving of an Albigensian heretic being burned.

sortie from one city gate and skirmished with the pilgrims who had gathered with the hostile army to gain the blessings promised by the pope on all who witnessed the defeat of the Church's enemies. The ferocious mercenary troops from the besieging force quickly came to the pilgrims' rescue and swiftly turned the burghers' surprise attack to their own advantage. Thousands pursued the burghers through the gate and swarmed into the city walls. Then began one of the worst massacres in a war where French

killed French, and Catholics slew Catholics. Cruelties inflicted on early Christians by their pagan persecutors pale beside the mass butchery of Christians by Christians in the war against the Albigensian heretics, known as the "Albigensian Crusade," that wracked the region of Languedoc in Southern France early in the 13th century.

The Albigensian Crusade takes its name and, indirectly, origin largely from a peaceful event that took place near the town of Albi, northeast of Toulouse. Disturbed by tales of local heresy, in 1165 Roman Catholic religious leaders questioned local men and women accused of being heretics about their faith. With dismay they heard these people reject the Old Testament, deny the need for baptism by priests, and speak evasively about their attitude to marriage and confession. They saw Jesus merely as an angel, whose suffering and death had been illusory. The Albigensians or Cathars ("pure ones"), also rejected the Catholic sacraments, laws, and priesthood.

They lacked church buildings but organized their members into the "Perfect" (clergy) and "Believers" (laymen). The Perfect observed celibacy, fasting, strict vegetarianism, poverty, and pacifism as the price for everlasting life, secured by a spiritual baptism called the Consolation. Believers were allowed to marry – even though marriage and the begetting of children was considered evil – to possess property and even outwardly to remain members of the Catholic Church. They received their Consolation on their deathbeds. In certain circumstances, ritual suicide was encouraged.

As with all heretical movements, the Roman Church at first tried squashing such sects by selective actions such as flogging, exile, and heavy fines and finally excommunication. But as heresy persisted, and began to win support from nobles, the fabric of both church and state seemed threatened. In 1179 the Third Lateran Council offered rewards for catching heretics. In 1181 the Abbot of Clairvaux launched the first crusade inside a Christian country against those who denied the sacraments and the authority of popes, cardinals, and bishops, and also against those protecting such heretics. The Abbot successfully besieged the fortified town of Lavaur between Toulouse and Albi, persuading the heretical Roger Trencavel II to submit to the authority of the Church and to renounce his beliefs.

In 1184 the papal bull *Ad abolendum* decreed excommunication for Cathars and other heretics, and their protectors; ecclesiastical trial of heretics; and punishment by secular authority of those refusing to recant. The heresy of Catharism had begun to generate the powerful machinery of Papal Inquisition. Even so, the Church preferred peaceful persuasion to force. But many years of striving by Catholic missionaries to the French Cathars won relatively few back to orthodox Christian beliefs.

Then in January 1208 came the crisis that provoked war – the murder of a papal ambassador, or legate, in the county of Toulouse. The legate had recently excommunicated Toulouse's ruler Count Raymond VI, the greatest feudal lord of southern France, for doing nothing to check the heresy then rampant in his domain. Pope Innocent III understandably blamed Raymond for the murder and called on all Christian states to launch a crusade to crush the Cathar heretics

The plan of campaign was simple: besieging each hostile fortress and walled town until the place submitted. The first major objective was Béziers – reputedly a rich nest of heretics, under one of Raymond VI's leading vassals. The storming of Béziers set a hideous precedent for later sieges. Mercenaries rampaged through the streets, hacking at anyone

Above: a 19th-century version of the massacre at Beziers, when crusader troops burst into the city – a stronghold of the heretical Albigensians – and slaughtered 20,000 of its inhabitants.

Left: Saint Dominic presiding over the burning of books belonging to the heretical sect of Albigensians. One "pure" book rises, untouched from the flames consuming the rest.

and to confiscate the lands of their protector Count Raymond. In June 1209 an army gathered at Lyons, many of them enthusiasts untrained in war and loosely styled pilgrims. This force consisted of contingents supplied and led by barons, largely from northern France.

Frightened by troops lined up against him, Count Raymond made a public apology to the Church. At St Gilles, he accepted a beating with birch twigs as an act of penitence. The crafty count then actually joined the crusade about to invade his own country.

they met. Bursting down doors, they looted houses and slashed the throats of all who resisted. Ahead of this terror, hundreds of citizens abandoned their homes and streamed through the narrow streets. Catholics and Cathars alike sought shelter in churches where priests tolled the bells as if for a burial. Clanging bells, clashing weapons, war whoops and the screams of the dying combined in a dreadful cacophony. Then the enemy burst into the churches, and transformed what had been sanctuaries into slaughterhouses. Priests, cripples, women, infants – mercenaries hacked all to death indiscriminately. In the church of St Marie-Madeleine alone, 7000 people reputedly perished. Altogether, it is said that 20,000 Cathars and Catholics died in the bloodbath of Béziers, the former for being heretics, the latter for harboring heretics.

Between 1209 and 1215 slaughter and pillage struck many centers sympathetic to heretics as the crusaders criss-crossed Languedoc. Besieged Carcassonne's surrender prevented a second massacre. Then from 1209 the famous walled city served as a base from which the crusaders' leader Simon de Montfort brutally assaulted other centers. Chilled by the fall of Béziers and Carcassonne, some quickly submitted, and escaped the worst excesses. But in 1210 came fresh atrocities – this time at Bram and Minerve. Bram survived only three days resistance. Simon de Montfort then gouged the eyes from the entire 100-strong garrison and lopped off their noses and upper lips. He left one man one eye in order to guide the rest to the hostile castle of Cabaret. Cabaret took the hint and offered no resistence. At Minerve, came the first selective mass execution of heretics. Scorning to recant and thereby save themselves, more than 140 of the Cathar Perfect cast themselves voluntarily onto a huge bonfire lit near the castle.

In 1211 de Montfort took two months to batter down Lavaur's defenses. Then his men hanged its leader and 80 knights, slitting their throats when the gibbet collapsed beneath their combined weight. Here, too, 400 Cathars perished on a giant pyre erected in a field. Troops also seized the Cathars' noble protectress, Guirade de Laurac, hurled her down a well, and buried her beneath a hail of stones.

Above: a carved stone cross found over the 13th-century grave of one of the Albigensian "elect."

Above: an illustration from a 13th-century French manuscript that cites Albigensians as heretics and "people to avoid."

Left: part of a 13th-century stone carving from the church of St Nazaire in Carcassone showing the siege of the Albigensian city of Toulouse by the forces of Simon de Montfort.

VII sued for peace, and in 1229 the Albigensian Crusade was over.

Southern France still had its heretics. But in 1233 Dominican inquisitors began to smell them out in operations that became a model for the Papal Inquisition everywhere. Meanwhile missionary Franciscans converted many Cathars to orthodox Catholicism.

It was the massacre of an inquisitorial group of Dominicans and Franciscans near Toulouse that unleashed the last great blow against the Cathars in southwest France. For the murderers had come from Montségur, a major refuge for the Cathar Perfect. In 1243 a French force attacked this fortress eyrie perched among the northern foothills of the Pyrenees. Unbelievably, its small garrison held out for nine months before surrendering. The terms were astonishingly generous: liberty or light punishment except for heretics. But legend tells that 200 Cathars refused the amnesty and perished on a bonfire built inside a palisade below the fortress. Whatever really happened, the loss of so many leading Cathars struck deeply at their sect. By the 1270s the Inquisition had crushed the Cathar leadership in southern France. The movement lingered feebly for another century before disappearing into history.

Above: the castle of Montségur, perched in the rocky foothills of the Pyrenees, was the last stronghold of the Albigensians. A small force held out for nine months against a state army.

Right: the Inquisition, under the direction of the Dominican Order, was formed to root out heresy.

Even terrorism on this scale failed to wipe out the heresy. Lands once subdued flared up behind de Montfort in revolt. Support revived for Raymond VI and his son (later called Raymond VII). For more than eight months they withstood de Montfort's siege of Toulouse. On this occasion the defenders' bestial treatment of prisoners matched anything previously suffered by their colleagues. Captured beseigers had tongues and eyes torn out; or were burned, dragged along by horses, or chopped up alive. Suddenly, de Montfort himself was killed by a "stone-gun" catapult and the siege soon collapsed.

The interval from slaughter was brief. Exhausted by 10 years of fighting, Languedoc now suffered a new crusader invasion including 10,000 archers, led by Prince Louis of France. A year after Simon's death, Louis joined Simon's son to capture the town of Marmande, southeast of Bordeaux. Their troops cold-bloodedly put to the sword 5000 innocent citizens. But once more Toulouse withstood siege, the new crusade foundered, and by 1225 most of Languedoc's old ruling houses were re-established.

Then in June 1226 the French king himself led a major invasion with an army twice as large as that of 1209. This time most lands submitted. Toulouse held out until crusaders crippled its economy by wrecking crops, uprooting vines, and burning houses, Raymond

The Great Witch Panic

"Now, dear child, here you have all my confession, for which I must die. And they are sheer lies and made-up things, so help me God. For all this I was forced to say through fear of the torture which was threatened beyond what I had already endured. For they never leave off with the torture till one confesses something: be he never so good he must be a witch." So wrote the Mayor of Bamberg to his daughter in July 1628. He wrote painfully; his hands had been crushed by presses "so that the blood ran out at the nails and everywhere." This was to be his last letter. Soon after composing it secretly in gaol, the mayor suffered execution for witchcraft. It was a punishment that

uncounted thousands shared in Europe during what has been called the Great Witch Panic – a panic that reached its peak in the 15th and 16th centuries.

No one had been much bothered with witches before the late Middle Ages. This was not because there were no such people. Before the beginnings of written history there had been wizards and sorcerers, supposedly able to make things happen by magic. By the Middle Ages, belief in such powers lingered in Europe as part of a belief in the supernatural shared with the Christian religion.

At first when authority acted against witchcraft and sorcery it attacked only individuals accused of bewitching people or crops. What put persecution of witchcraft on a savage international basis was the Papal Inquisition, established in the 13th century to stamp out the Albigensian heresy. In the 13th century, roving Dominican investigators authorized by the Pope attacked the Albigensians in the south of France so successfully that the Inquisition worked itself out of a job until it redirected its onslaught at witches.

What exactly did witches believe in and do that made them obnoxious to the Church? The answer is that they had supposedly joined Satan in a diabolical plot to overthrow Christendom. Some idea of the full range of their crimes emerged in 1335 in the Inquisition held at Toulouse. Trial records quoted the accused women's belief that the Devil was God's equal and

Above: Waldensian witches flying on broomsticks, from a 15th-century manuscript. Witchcraft has been added to the sect's other heretical beliefs.

Opposite: a witches' Sabbath (left) and its consequences (right), from a 16th-century Swiss manuscript.

Right: the death of some of the 54 Knights Templar, who were accused of witchcraft by Philip IV of France, who was anxious to acquire the great wealth accumulated by the Order.

Below: Witches using a magic spell involving a cock, snake, and a fiery cauldron to conjure a shower of rain. They were accused of being able to conjure storms to wreck crops on land, and ships at sea.

reigned over the earth. The women said they had made a pact with Satan and had had sexual intercourse with him in the guise of a goat. Upon Satan's instructions they had behaved sacriligously at Holy Communion. They used to meet at witches' Friday-night sabbats – licentiously Bacchanalian frolics. They had cast spells. Mixing bits of dead people and beasts with

225

scraps of clothing from hanged corpses, and with poisonous herbs, they had made a deadly brew. They had stolen and eaten newly born babies. They had caused neighbors' sheep to fall ill, blighted crops, and killed people by melting wax figures wearing bits of the victims' dress.

There is no doubt that some people were justly accused of foul practices. A notorious example was Gilles de Rais, Joan of Arc's noble comrade in arms. After losing a fortune, Gilles tried to get rich by Black Magic acts that involved shedding the blood of innocent virgins. He sadistically attacked and killed more than 50 children before being discovered and burned at the stake. But apart from the gullible and those with a thirst for notoriety, most so-called

Above: Gilles de Rais, the 15th-century French nobleman on whom the Bluebeard legend is based, watching with delight the murder of a child.

witches were doubtless just old and confused, or people wrongly accused by people hoping to settle an old score against them or by those seeking scapegoats for such natural disasters as plague.

Accusation of witchcraft often meant automatic torture and death. In theory the death penalty was imposed only by civil authority. When they handed over the guilty to the local secular power for punishment, inquisitors asked that punishment should exclude bloodshed or risk to the prisoner's life.

An early instance of large-scale legalized torture and murder for Satan worship came in the early 1300s when France's Philip IV smashed the Order of Knights Templar so that he could seize its great wealth. The Grand Master and 54 Knights of the ancient religious brotherhood were burned to death after rigged trials. In 1459 began a major trial resulting in the burning of many poor people of Arras accused of heresy and witchcraft, watched by curious thousands.

But the Church's assault burst into full, ugly bloom in the 1480s and 1490s. In 1484 a papal Bull issued a fierce condemnation of witches, magicians, and sorcerers and forbade clergy or laymen from hindering the Inquisition's attack on the "heretical depravities" of the witches.

Among the judges appointed to reinforce the Bull were two Dominicans: fathers Heinrich Krämer, formerly inquisitor in the Tyrol, and Jakob Sprenger, of Basel. Although both were of dubious honesty, they now became Chief Inquisitors for Germany. They also jointly produced the *Malleus Maleficarum* ("Hammer of Witches") – a 250,000 word "handbook for witch hunters." For two centuries zealots in various countries followed its hideous rules for catching, trying, interrogating, and murdering witches.

Mere ill repute was sufficient to bring a person to trial. Outwardly virtuous behavior gave no immunity. Indeed, the ascetic were especially suspect as subtly concealing a devotion to evil. There was almost no chance of an accused clearing her or his name. A test sometimes permitted was casting the victims in water: witches supposedly floated, while the guiltless sank (and some no doubt drowned). But most cases had a predictable outcome, for accused witches were held to be guilty until proved innocent. "Not guilty" was a verdict almost unheard of in trials where defendants lacked legal aid and never knew who had borne witness against them.

Trials nearly all followed the same course. Hauled into court, the defendant would face a barrage of questions about his or her magic, about a pact with Satan, and sabbat activities. The inquisitor would demand a confession of heresy and the names of association. If a "witch" denied all accusations, questioners stripped and shaved the prisoner's body, and sought for telltale marks. Any wart, mole, or birthmark might serve as the "Devil's mark"; while an extra nipple or vague bump might be a "witch's mark," a diabolical teat suckled by a familiar (personal demon). People thought some Devil's marks invisible but detectable as areas of skin insensitive to pin pricks. Unscrupulous witchhunters "found" invisible marks by tools with retractable blades.

After this search, the defendant was once more commanded to confess. Refusal meant torture. First came the thumbscrews, then the rack, next the stretching ladder. If these failed there were leg-screws, red-hot pincers, and *strappado* – in which the naked victim had heavy weights tied to the feet and was suddenly hoisted high in the air.

After the Reformation, torture procedures were zealously adopted by Protestant countries. In Calvinist Scotland in 1594 Alison Balfour spent 48 hours having her arms crushed in an iron vice called the "caspie claws." Meanwhile 700 pounds of iron bars were bearing down on her octogenarian husband; 57 blows with a wedge pulped her son's leg bones, trapped in the "Spanish Boots"; and thumbscrews tormented her daughter, aged seven. In the course of such unsubtle persuasion, "witches" had limbs torn from sockets, and bones crushed. Few lasted long without gasping out the required confession.

The more zealous the local inquisitor, the larger the death toll. Around Treves (now Trier) in West Germany, 368 women from 22 villages perished as witches in six years. In the early 1600s the Bishop of Wurzburg in southern Germany burned more than 900 "witches" of both sexes including children of seven and from all social ranks. In Bamberg his equally cruel cousin murdered many hundreds of men, women, and children.

During the 17th century, new, more rational attitudes were astir. The Netherlands, for instance, stopped executing witches after 1610, but it was not until nearly the end of the century before other countries followed suit, and the Great Witch Panic abated. By then many thousands of innocent people had gone to a brutal death. It is known that at least 100,000 were slaughtered in Germany. The figure for France and Scotland combined is in the region of 10,005. England's total was something like 1000. No one knows the full figures. Some put the total at 200,000. Others believe that it ran into millions.

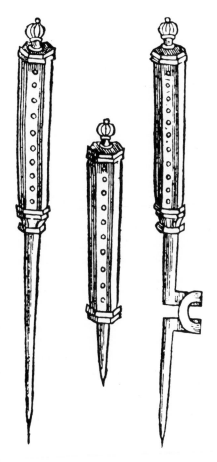

Above: prickers used by witch-hunters to find the Devil's mark – the patch on the skin insensitive to pain. The one in the center has a retractable blade to find so-called proof of guilt.

Right: *strappado,* a method used by the Inquisition to extract confessions from witches. The accused, often naked, has heavy weights tied to his or her feet and is then hoisted into the air.

The Conquistadors

Less than a lifetime after Christopher Columbus had discovered America, Spain had forged a mammoth New World empire. The men who made it were self-seeking adventurers – the ruthless soldier-explorers called *conquistadors*. By 1522 Hernando Cortes had overrun the capital of Aztec Mexico. Francisco Pizarro had crushed the Inca Empire of Peru to the south by 1535. Long before, the larger Caribbean islands had been conquered. In each case a few score Spaniards with the help of treachery and firearms cowed thousands of Stone Age Amerinds. No one could withstand the European invaders, driven on by lust for gold and land. After them came missionaries determined to convert heathens to Christianity.

In the ensuing scramble for the souls and bodies of the conquered Amerinds, humanity was trampled underfoot, and ancient cultures brutally demolished.

Ill-treatment of the vanquished began in the West Indies – the first region to be discovered and exploited. Columbus observed that the first islanders he met were timid, peace-loving, and intelligent. Soon, though, he was seeking to enslave them, for he discovered also that they practiced cannibalism which, the Spaniards decided, made the Caribs natural candidates for slavery.

Back in Europe, Pope Alexander VI (a Spaniard) was less sure. Indeed, he urged Spain's royal rulers to offer kindness to the Amerinds and convert them to the Catholic faith. Accordingly, Ferdinand and Isabella decreed that Amerinds who willingly embraced Spanish rule were Spanish subjects and so immune from slavery. But this was taken by the conquistadors to mean also that Amerinds resisting Spanish rule might be enslaved. Ignorant of the Spanish tongue, hostile islanders would listen uncomprehendingly while a Crown official read out a royal *Request* to accept the Christian faith and the sovereignty of the Spanish crown. Faced with superior Spanish weapons, the Indians lost most of the encounters that followed. Mounted Spanish troops with tracker dogs hunted down their fleeing enemies. When they had subdued large areas, the Spanish then demanded heavy tribute payments: up to two ounces of gold or 100 pounds of cotton per person annually. Rather than submit, many natives left their crops to rot, and starved to death in mountain hiding places.

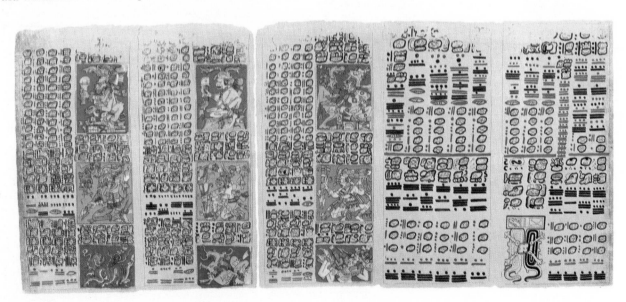

Top: a Peruvian gold toucan and (**above**) the Dresden Codex, a pre-Mayan manuscript of elaborate astronomical calculations on the planet Venus, illustrate the heights to which pre-Spanish culture had risen.

In the late 1490s, islanders who had not fled faced a fresh disaster when Columbus parceled out their lands among his followers – together with the labor of the natives living on them. Discovery and settlement were what had led the Spanish to America, now Spanish feudal culture was being imposed on the

Caribbean. Acknowledging the Spaniards' need for labor, yet wishing to protect the Amerinds from exploitation, the Spanish Crown approved *encomienda* a system that gave temporary responsibility to a Spaniard for the physical and Christian welfare of a number of Amerinds. In return they made him tribute payments. In theory they were free: in fact, in

1498 Columbus reported that unskilled Spaniards shipped in as laborers and scullions refused to stir outdoors unless carried (by Indians) on a palanquin. Many poor Spaniards abandoned work for theft and womanizing. Before Hispaniola's native population vanished, dealers even prowled the land for girls as young as 9 or 10.

Above: Aztec warriors defending themselves against an armor-clad Spanish horseman. The Indians are armed with wooden swords edged with volcanic glass.

Below right: Indians being massacred by Spanish soldiers. The Indians, struggling under the heavy burden of the Spaniards' luggage, were murdered by Cortes' orders in reprisal for a supposed plot against the Spaniards.

Above: a drawing made in the 1500s of the Spanish conqueror of Mexico, Hernando Cortes.

Hispaniola and Cuba, they toiled as slaves. Thousands died from overwork and undernourishment and in a generation Hispaniola's several hundred thousand Amerinds dwindled to 14,000.

Meanwhile, the poorest fortune-hunting Spaniard treated the Amerindian islanders abominably. By

The same contemptuous attitudes colored some Spaniards' treatment of the Aztecs in Mexico. To the Spaniards, these beings were strange, inferior creatures that worshiped idols, practiced mass human sacrifices, and sometimes ate human flesh. They were fit only to serve the Spaniards as serfs or slaves.

229

Once more, Spain's *encomienda* system lent respectability to brutal exploitation of the local population. In Mexico, Spanish overlords used Aztec Indians unsparingly for every kind of labor. They fed, clothed, and housed their masters, and served as beasts of burden. They yielded tributes including textiles, grains, and precious metals. Thousands of unpaid Aztec carriers and masons toiled to rebuild the Aztec capital, destroyed in Cortes' conquest. As the 16th century progressed, the costly ambitions of Spain's Hapsburg rulers kept up the pressure on their New World colonists to squeeze more gold and silver from the natives. Exhaustion, lack of food, and accidents killed many. It is said that more than 200 Aztec porters died bearing heavy loads of tribute to Veracruz for the ruthless conquistador, Gonzalo de Salazar.

But few men used the Indians of Mexico more cruelly than Cortes' rival Beltrán Nuño de Guzmán.

three Spanish riders forged ahead, keeping up some semblance of morale by cutting down and hiding more than 500 Amerinds who had hanged themselves in despair on roadside trees. When Guzmán ruled, anarchy and pillage reigned in Mexico.

In Peru the Incas fared no better than their northern Aztec, Maya, and Carib fellow Indians. In November 1532, Pizarro set the tone for what would follow by massacring thousands of unarmed Incas at Cajamarca. There he seized their king, Atahualpa, and held him to ransom. For months Atahualpa languished in captivity while his subjects scoured the land for gold. They piled a large room high with superbly crafted golden statuettes, goblets, plates, and other treasures – a ransom such as history had never seen. But instead of freeing Atahualpa, the Spaniards treacherously strangled him for trumped up "crimes" including treason. Then they melted

Appointed governor of Pánuco (northeast Mexico) in 1525, Guzmán enslaved the entire population, then branded them and shipped them off in thousands to their deaths in Caribbean mines and fields. Guzmán made slave-trading big business. He even kept it up after 1527 when he became president of the court of judges of New Spain – the highest tribunal of Spanish Central America. In Nueva Galicia, New Spain's northernmost province, Guzmán's raiders herded Amerindian men, women, and children inside a large corral, and plundered and burned the lands around. By treachery, his raiders slaughtered thousands, and force-marched others for 12 days in which all the children of the mothers present perished. Meanwhile,

down their priceless loot to manageable ingots – a task that kept nine forges glowing for a month.

A year later, Pizarro and 480 Spaniards stormed the Inca capital, Cuzco, and stripped temples, palaces, homes, and royal tombs of treasures, such as life-size gold and silver figures. Once more the furnaces were put to work. By the time conquistadors had finished with Peru a priceless heritage of individual works of art had been reduced to metal bars.

Pizarro's troops then began a ruthless exploitation of the country's people and resources. One report claims that thousands of high-ranking women and their maids were turned out on the streets and driven into prostitution. Another writer claimed "I have seen

the Spaniards, long after the conquest, amuse themselves by hunting down the natives with bloodhounds for mere sport." Spaniards worked Indians to death, mining precious metals high in the cold, thin air of the Andes. They also recklessly used up national reserves of grain and livestock – destroying whole flocks of llamas merely for the brains, a special delicacy. Deprived of meat, and fleeces for clothing, the Indians suffered horribly from cold and hunger.

While such excesses were darkening the name of Spain throughout its New World Empire, missionaries devoted to the welfare of their Indian flocks began to press for government reform. None proved more influential than Bartolomé de las Casas, the first Catholic bishop actually consecrated in America. Las Casas' arguments convinced the Spanish Crown that overexploitation was un-Christian and destroying the very people whose labor made the New World empire pay. Accordingly in 1542 the Emperor Charles V published his New Laws for the Indies. These specifically forbade slavery, severely punished overexploitation of Indians, and ended the *encomienda* system. The laws proved hard to enforce, and came too late to save the Caribbean islanders from extinction. But they marked a turning point in Spain's dealings with the peoples it had colonized.

In the long run, though, the Spanish struck their hardest blows against the Amerinds not through deliberate bullying but accidentally. By 1570 imported smallpox, measles, and other Old World ailments had cut the population of the Valley of Mexico to less than one quarter of its pre-Conquest total. Elsewhere, Old World epidemic diseases similarly decimated towns and villages. For most of Spanish America, these diasters proved far more damaging than the cruelties of colonial misrule.

Above: the Spanish conquistador Gonzalo Pizarro setting his dogs on the Indians who refused to tell him where he could find gold.

Left: Spanish soldiers guard the entrances to the main square at Tenochtitlán while others brutally attack Aztecs taking part in a ceremony.

Below: Indian laborers erecting a building under Spanish supervision.

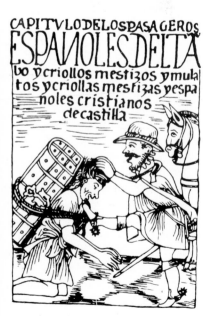

Above: this Inca drawing of a Spaniard ill-treating his Indian servant sums up the brutal reality of the conquest of the Americas.

231

St. Bartholomew's Eve
Paris: 1572

Above: Catharine de Médicis, mother of the French King Charles IX and the brain behind the St Bartholomew's Day Massacre.

The day before the Feast of St Bartholomew was known as St Bartholomew's Eve, and it dawned hot in Paris in 1572. After a stifling summer, the water of the river Seine was warm, and Charles IX of France was bathing. Armand de Clermont, Seigneur de Piles, helped him learn to swim, by holding up the royal chin. Few people witnessing this amicable scene on August 23 could guess that overnight Piles would perish on a royal guard's halberd while the king looked on approvingly. By the early hours of August 24, not only Piles but dozens of his fellow Protestants were being felled by Catholic troops in a massacre planned as a coldblooded political act to keep the reigns of power in royal hands. As killing spread, and got out of hand, thousands were wiped out across the land of France.

The brain behind the massacre was that of Charles's mother, Catherine de Médicis, granddaughter of Lorenzo the Magnificent, the unscrupulously power-

ful ruler of Florence. Catherine herself was an authoritative, crafty politician, determined to keep the mastery of France within her family, at whatever cost.

This promised to be difficult. Charles IX, though only 22, was sickly and doomed to an early death. Catherine had other sons. But she saw two rival forces jockeying for power in France. One was the Guise family of extremist Catholic nobles. The other force was that of France's emergent Protestant minority (named Huguenots, for Besançon Hugues, a Swiss political leader). The royal family itself was Catholic, but Catherine sought to forge a united kingdom through a third, royalist, force that placed king before religion. So far she had failed. In 10 years the Guise family had forced three Religious Wars between Catholics and Huguenots. Since the last clash in 1570 the stability of France rested on an uneasy peace. Now, in 1572, the Huguenot leader Gaspard de Coligny, Admiral of France and Seigneur de Chatillon, was threatening Catherine's personal position as Charles's chief adviser.

Catherine de Médicis remained undismayed. Her confidence was rooted in the cynical teachings of Niccolò Machiavelli, the pioneer of political realism, whose masterpiece *The Prince* had actually been inscribed to Catherine's grandfater. Machiavelli taught that "A prince's job is to keep his realm by any means." No one absorbed this lesson better than Catherine, a woman skillful at pretending friendship to a victim while she had her agents thrust their daggers in his back. She now sought to regain her position as chief adviser to her son, as well as seek peace and personal security, by setting the Huguenot leaders and the Guises at one another's throats. The chief scene for this slaughter was to be Paris (where leading Huguenot nobles had assembled for the wedding of the leading Huguenot, King Henry of Navarre to the French King's sister). Catherine planned to use royal troops to smash whichever side emerged on top.

The match to light the fuse of conflict was to be the murder of Coligny by a henchman of the Guises. But this plot misfired. Coligny survived two assassin's bullets shot at him on August 22. Charles IX blamed the Guises for the deed. Further probing threatened to implicate Charles's mother. Anticipating this event, Catherine and her noblemen saw Charles on the evening of St Bartholomew's Eve. Between them they persuaded him that nothing short of slaughtering the leading Huguenots could save France and the throne from an imminent Protestant uprising. Some of Charles's closest friends were Huguenots, but the weak-willed, sadistic king was soon convinced that leading Protestants must die. "Kill them! Kill them all. . . ." he cried.

Late that evening, the King's mother and her supporters drew up a list of killers and their victims. The king himself arranged for leading citizens to lock the city gates, for chain boats to prevent escape across the Seine, for the arming of citizens at the crossroads,

232

Above: scenes like this were repeated all over Paris when the royalists and Catholics turned on the Huguenots in the capital gathered to celebrate the wedding of the Protestant Henry of Navarre to the French King's sister.

Below: *St Bartholomew's Day Massacre* painted by a Huguenot who survived the butchery. When the news spread to the provinces similar massacres followed there, too.

and generally to turn Paris into a huge trap for Huguenots. Troops and citizens who would do the killing were to tie white crosses to their hats to help show friend from foe. City lodgings occupied by Huguenots were marked by crosses.

Three centers were singled out for slaughter: the Louvre – the king's own palace – where many Huguenot noblemen and their servants were staying; houses in the Rue de Béthisy, where Coligny was still recovering from gunshot wounds; and the Faubourg St Germain on the left bank of the Seine.

To deceive their doomed guests, the royal family went to bed as usual. But at 2 am the king, his mother, and other royal conspirators dressed secretly. Soon afterward, the great bell of St Germain l'Auxerrois

and swords. From his window the king looked down upon an orgy as hideous as any organized by Nero.

Inside the palace, alerted Huguenots darted down passages like rabbits in a warren suddenly invaded by a pack of stoats. Pursued by four archers, the Viscount de Léran sought sanctuary by bursting into the bedroom of Queen Marguerite, Henry of Navarre's Catholic bride. De Léran then clung to the frightened woman as she lay upon her bed. In a rare gesture of mercy, the chief of the guards permitted him to live. Less fortunate was another Protestant who was stabbed to death within three paces of Queen Marguerite as she later made her way into her sister's room.

Meanwhile killers had been busy in the Rue de Béthisy. The Duke of Guise arrived there, with scores

boomed out the signal for the killing to begin. The king and his younger brother the Duke of Anjou personally supervised the murders in the Louvre. The royal Swiss guards, well plied with drink, performed the actual "executions" in the palace. As spluttering torches lit up the Louvre, they rounded up and disarmed the bewildered Protestant lords and their servants, secretaries, and tutors. They drove them through a courtyard gate; struck them down with clubs, halberds, and lances; then hacked or stabbed the injured Huguenots to death with daggers

of troops, to settle an old personal debt by supervising the murder of Coligny. A spy admitted them to the statesman's house, and Coligny's guards were cut down or shot before they could resist. The murderers thundered up the stairs and found Coligny praying in his bedroom. According to one story, a Swiss guard stabbed him as he pleaded for his life. The badly wounded man was tossed down from the window, still alive, for Guise's personal inspection. Coligny's corpse was later beheaded, dismembered by a mob and hanged upon a gibbet.

Above: the murder of Admiral Coligny, leader of the Huguenots. He was attacked and thrown from the window of his lodgings, where he was recovering from an earlier attempt to assassinate him by his enemy the Duke of Guise.

Left: Huguenots being massacred at Tours.

Below: Charles IX and his mother Catharine de Médicis watching the slaughter of their Protestant guests from a palace balcony.

Nearby, other Protestants were dying – some murdered in their beds, others as they clambered out onto the roofs in their night clothes. Grooms, pages, valets, perished with their masters. A personal friend of Charles IX, La Rochefoucauld, thought he had awoken to some royal prank when six masked men burst in upon his room. "Not so hard, my little master!" he exclaimed before he died, believing that the man who struck at him was Charles, disguised.

One thousand militiamen were supposed to pin down Huguenots already outside the city walls in the Faubourg St Germain, across the river. But a swimmer reached them first and warned them of their likely fate. About 90 got away on horseback. Hampered by a sick son, the great Huguenot noble La Force remained behind. Promise of a huge ransom payment saved him and his two sons from being immediately spitted on a soldier's sword. (Father and elder son were nonetheless murdered later.)

As St Bartholomew's Day advanced, the nature of the killers underwent a monstrous change. The mob joined in – a horde drawn largely from the beggars, tramps, and thieves who teemed in 16th-century Paris. What had supposedly begun as the selective murder of leading Protestants and their servants, became a far wider, wilder massacre. At first murderers had looted from the victims they had killed; now they actually killed to loot. Wealth as much as heresy or political opposition invited death. Many jewellers and money-changers perished, hurled from their own upstairs windows. Joining in the greedy scramble, nobles had rivals murdered to secure their wealth or position. As one writer put it, "If a person had money, or a well-paid office, or dangerous enemies, or even hungry heirs, then he was deemed a Huguenot."

As the massacre accelerated, the Seine became a major killing ground. Ferrymen dumped bodies in midstream. Assassins tossed corpses off bridges, especially the downstream Pont-aux-Meuniers. Thugs vied with one another to find the most ingenious ways of bringing death. Some threw victims in alive, or made them walk the plank. Two women who had stayed afloat and clung to piles, were stoned by laughing louts. Having killed a couple in their home, one murderer bore their tiny children to the river in a basket, then let them roll into the water from his back. The King himself reputedly took pot shots at those slow to drown.

By midday the alarm of the leading citizens of Paris caused Charles to try to halt the slaughter. But days passed before the killing stopped in the capital. Meanwhile it spread into the provinces. Meaux, Troys, Orléans, Bourges, Lyons, Rouen, Toulouse, Bordeaux and other centers suffered massacres as Protestants were gaoled and then cut down in the prisons.

No one knows how many died before the killing petered out in October. One murderer alone boasted of butchering "more than 400 gentlemen." A Catholic defender of the massacre later put the national toll at a bare 2000. Another writer estimated 50 times that many. Several reports suggest 3000 deaths in Paris, and 10,000 for the rest of France.

Outside France, Protestant powers looked with dismay upon the massacre. Pope Gregory XIII however, struck a medal to celebrate it as a crusade for the one true faith. In fact, the slaughter was entirely politically motivated. The dissension it was meant to crush, only deepened. The Huguenots acquired new leaders and the rivalry with the Catholic party continued until they were given complete religious and political freedom 200 years later.

The Black Slave Trade

"The Negroes are so wilful and loth to leave their own country, that they often leap'd out of the canoes, boat and ship into the sea, and kept under water till they were drowned, to avoid being taken up and saved by our boats, which pursued them; they having a more dreadful apprehension of Barbadoes than we can have of hell. . . ."

It was 1694 when Captain Thomas Phillips recorded the tiresome problem of suicide among the black slaves that his ship *Hannibal* bore from West Africa for sale to the European planters in the West Indies. By then, nearly two centuries had passed since Spain launched the transatlantic slave trade. No less than 10 states in Europe and America eventually soiled their hands

labor to work the plantations in South, Central, and North America. But cruel conditions and imported Old World diseases soon decimated the available Amerindian labor force. Within a generation of Hispaniola's discovery, for example, its 1,130,000 population of Indians had pined, sickened, and shrunk to 11,000 according to one Spanish writer. On the other hand, Africans proved relatively durable in the hot climates needed to grow such crops as rice and sugar cane. The Europeans soon found that West African chiefs gladly bartered their own countrymen in return for cloth, gold, or rum. So started a three-cornered trade, begun by Spain but perfected by Britain. Loaded with trade goods from England, a ship would sail to Africa. Exchanging goods for slaves, the slaver then sailed on toward the West Indies. This was the Middle Passage, or second leg of the triangular voyage. The captain sold his human cargo in the Caribbean for cash or bartered it for sugar. Then his ship sailed back to England again. In time New England joined the trade, using American rum made from West Indian sugar to buy slaves in Africa.

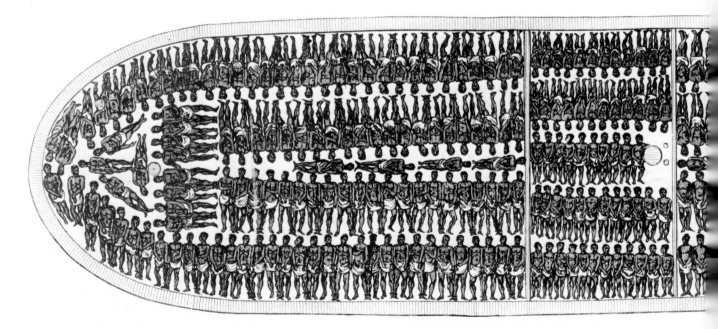

with it. By the time it came to an end late in the 19th century, some 20 million Africans had been torn from their homelands and probably as many as half of them had perished before reaching the New World.

Even high losses failed to deter the slave traders, for their profits were huge. This traffic in human flesh was known as the most lucrative business in history, and helped build the wealth of the English ports of Bristol and Liverpool, as well as Boston and Newport in New England. Indirectly, slavery helped support the industrial growth of England and the young United States.

The roots of this inhuman commerce lay in simple supply and demand. The Portuguese, Spanish, and (later) British, Dutch, French, Swedish, and other north European colonists needed plenty of cheap

The source of most slaves was a narrow 3000-mile long coastal belt of West Africa from Senegal southward through southern Angola. At first slave-ship captains haggled with the local chiefs for a few slaves at a time. But by 1700 far larger numbers were required to supply the 249 ships possessed by England's Royal African Company alone. Encouraged by the lure of traded wealth, tribal chiefs went to drastic lengths to satisfy the white men's needs. Prisoners of war, debtors, wife stealers – under tribal custom all might be enslaved legitimately. But greedy chiefs found ways to get more human livestock. Some sold their own wives and children. Some issued social invitations with a view to kidnap. Some launched wars and raids to seize large numbers of prisoners from neighboring tribes. When short of enemies, the

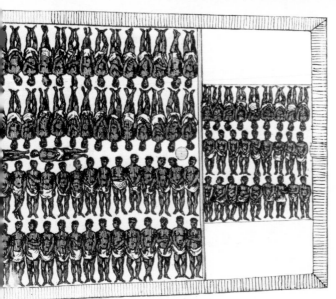

Above: a gang of captives met by the explorer David Livingstone in Africa in 1865. The black drivers armed with muskets seemed to feel that they were "doing a very noble thing."

Left: a plan of the arrangement of a cargo of slaves in the holds of a ship.

Below: an advertisement for a slave auction, a regular feature of Jamaican life in the settler days. As well as outright sale, slaves could be "let" or hired.

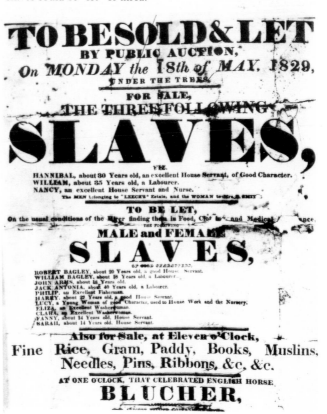

powerful King of Barsally treacherously ravaged his own towns for slaves.

Once seized, the luckless men and women had their arms pinioned behind them. They were then strung together by thongs or chains to form a line, or "coffle." Goaded on with whips and guns, the wretches trudged up to 900 miles to reach the coast. There, they would be herded in an airy, palm-roofed prison known as a *barracoon*.

The next indignity was a kind of rough and ready medical inspection. Male and female prisoners were forced to stand stark naked while ships' surgeons examined them for defects, like cattle in a market stall. Those with gray hair, or faulty eyes, lips, teeth, or venereal disease, were set aside as rejects. The rest were branded on the breast with red-hot irons,

237

to prove which shipping company had bought them. But the worst – and for many slaves last – part of their lives began with the Middle Passage to America.

At first, when slaves were few and relatively highly prized, ships' captains took care to house and feed them adequately. Later, though, they tried to maximize their profits by packing in as much black "merchandise" as they could. Hundreds of male slaves lay side by side in rows, feet facing the ship's sides. One captain claimed he packed them in so that "They had not as much room as a man in his coffin." Some captains favored stowing slaves on their sides, "spoon fashion"; others seated them in rows like bobsled riders. Women and children traveled separated from the men, but unpinioned. The lower decks of most slave ships lacked room for any adult to stand upright. The ships sailing from Liverpool were five feet deep between decks – but captains used the extra space to cram in extra slaves, laid on racks in tiers between the decks.

Feeding slaves was easier than keeping their quarters clean. In theory slaves defecated in big metal pots. In practice, men chained to the lower deck could scarcely reach them. Moreover, many would be violently seasick where they lay. Each morning the crew hosed down the night's accumulated filfth, but the stench was always stupefying. Sailors claimed that they could smell an English, French, or Portuguese slave ship from five miles away. Dutch slave ships were more humane, because better ventilated and less smelly.

Under normal conditions, the slow transatlantic voyage was bestial. When storms broke out, however, conditions became much worse. Captains battened down the hatches, and the filth and misery of those below became unspeakable. If a storm lasted several days the whole human cargo perished. Becalming was another hazard, for the slaver might run short of food and water. In 1781, Luke Collingwood used the threat of water shortage as a pretext for throwing overboard 54 sick slaves from the overcrowded *Zong*.

Sickness was a risk to crew as well as slaves. Both

died from dysentery, spread by filfth. In one slave ship, the *Britannia*, more than half the 450 slaves succumbed to smallpox. Sometimes a form of blindness struck a ship. All but one member of the *Rodeur's* crew reportedly went blind. He hailed a passing slave ship for help but learned that everyone aboard was sightless. The second ship was never seen again.

Slaves faced a new danger on the Middle Passage when humane and economic motives drove Britain to outlaw the slave trade in 1807. Rather than pay a fine of up to £100 for every slave they carried, captains

collars, and face muzzles were some of the instruments of punishment.

Not all slaves went passively to their doom. Some tried fighting back. Mutinies broke out on slaving ships; rebellions flared up on the sugar plantations. Countless slaves just ran away. But the whole ugly system ended only when governments brought in enlightened legislation. In Cuba and Brazil slavery persisted till the 1880s. Now slavery is dead. But in places where it flourished a deep social and economic gulf still divides black and white.

Left: one of the methods of controlling slaves was this head frame to prevent eating. Another cruel punishment meted out for the least offense was the treadmill (right). Slaves were tied by their wrists to a rail above a sharp revolving cylinder with sharp projecting boards. If they failed to keep step, their legs were lacerated.

Left below: a slave auction.

drowned whole human cargoes if threatened with search by ships on antislavery patrol.

Few slave ships docked in the ports of North or South America without deaths from disease, starvation, brutality, or "melancholy." Sometimes a tiny fraction of the cargo survived. For the survivors, the last and longest phase of slavery began when they were sold by auction, previously advertized in the local press. On June 4, 1772, for instance, the *Virginia Gazette* proclaimed "Two hundred very likely African Slaves will be sold at Petersburg, on Thursday."

Most slaves ended up in gangs working beneath an overseer's lash, toiling on plantations of sugar, cotton, rice, or tobacco. Many were continually underfed. A report from one Jamaican plantation, stated "Each slave had a pint of grain for 24 hours, and sometimes half a rotten herring. . . ." Their homes were wretched. A Polish visitor to those on George Washington's Mount Vernon estate in 1798 declared, "They are far more miserable than the poorest cottages of our peasants."

Slaves in domestic service had better treatment than field laborers. But these too were liable to punishment by professional floggers known as Jumpers. The fear of rebellion by the human chattels who outnumbered them was one reason why their owners suppressed their slaves so harshly. Stocks, iron

Above: successful black competitors at the Olympic Games give a "black power" salute. Success in the Games gave American Negroes a platform to demonstrate against the prejudice that still exists in their country.

239

The "Final Solution"
Nazi Germany: 1941-45

By 1945 nearly 5,000,000 Slavs and other European peoples had been kidnaped for forced labor in Germany, where thousands died under cruel conditions. None suffered a harsher fate, however, than Europe's Jews. Nazi leaders declared them "human animals," "vermin," and "parasites." Adolf Hitler rode to power in 1933 largely through blaming the Jews for Germany's economic problems. Before World War II began, the persecution of the Jews in Germany was in full swing.

It grew by stages. In 1935 the Nuremberg Laws deprived German Jews of German citizenship and forbade Jews to marry Germans. By 1938 the German government had driven tens of thousands of Jewish doctors, lawyers, civil servants, journalists, and actors from their jobs. In 1938 the government seized Jewish businesses; forced German Jews to carry identification cards; and barred Jewish children from schools. By 1939 Jews who had not fled from Germany were thrown into concentration camps at Buchenwald, Dachau, and Mathausen. As one writer puts it, in Germany "Everything relating to the Jewish question, it seemed, had been disposed of, except the Jews themselves."

But there were plans to solve that problem, too; not just in Germany, but in the rest of Europe – especially in Eastern Europe, where Hitler claimed the "Jew-

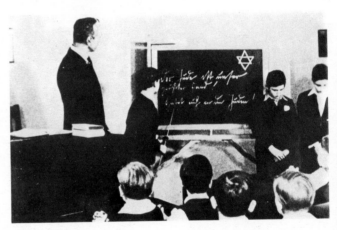

Above: Jewish schoolchildren are forced to stand next to a blackboard that declares "the Jew is our worst enemy! Beware of the Jew!"

Left: a special streetcar for Jews in Germany.

In 1939 nearly 9,000,000 Jews were living in the roughly 20 European states soon to be overrun by Nazi Germany. By 1945 almost 6,000,000 of those Jews had perished in a planned program of annihilation. With them also died millions of other peoples – chiefly Russians, Poles, and Gypsies. The reason lay in the ideology of the totalitarian Nazi Party who ruled Germany between 1933 and 1945. The Nazis declared that all these peoples were "racially degenerate" and therefore expendable – fit only for providing slaves for a more superior "Aryan race" as represented by their German conquerors.

Bolsheviks" to be the Germans' mortal enemies. In 1941 began the "Final Solution" to the Jewish problem. Behind the German army thrusting east from Poland into Russia came four heavily indoctrinated special-duty groups recruited largely from the Gestapo, the secret state police, and the SS (the Nazi "Elite Guard"). Each group was subdivided into units. One unit would round up 500 Russian Jews, march them out of town, and make them dig their own mass grave. Stripped naked, they were then slaughtered with machine guns or hand grenades. Each murder unit could carry out five such "actions" in a week.

The method was extravagant with bullets, however. By spring of 1942 mobile gas vans made killing cheaper. But by then Adolf Eichmann, head of the Gestapo's Jewish Office in Berlin, had had the Germans' slaves build big permanent gas chambers for massacre upon a truly lavish scale. These chambers mostly stood in death camps purpose-built in Poland

Above: Jews arriving at Auschwitz Concentration Camp in southern Poland. Behind them are the cattle wagons that were used to transport them.

Below: wooden boards and straw make up the sleeping bunks in Auschwitz.

where Jews accounted for one tenth of the population.

At first the Germans had terrorized the Polish Jews by arbitrary killing and deportation. By 1940 Jews were being segregated in city ghettos where 500,000 died from famine, starvation, sickness, and forced labor. In 1941 mass deportations were shifting ghetto populations to the killing camps.

Soon, Jews from all over German-occupied Europe were being funneled to these sinks of death. A bait of bread and a promise of "resettlement" persuaded thousands of starving Polish Jews to step into the box cars that would roll them to the crematory ovens.

Unwilling Jews were simply terrorized into the journey. Millions faced days of travel packed in cattle or freight cars without food, water, or proper sanitation. Sometimes half a trainload reached its destination dead; the rest in coma.

For many, journey's end was Auschwitz in southern Poland, the biggest of all the extermination camps. When the cattle cars stopped and guards slid back the doors, the wretched prisoners glimpsed a bleak landscape – a great grid of streets framing hundreds of huts in regimented rows, hemmed in by electrified barbed wire strung between concrete pylons that marched off to the skyline. SS guards leaned on machine guns mounted in watch towers planted at frequent intervals. From huge, square, red-brick "factory" smokestacks belched flames and black, greasy smoke. The all-pervading stench of burned flesh and hair hung in the air.

Bewildered families fell from the trucks, Dr Mengele, chief physician at Auschwitz, divided them into two main groups. In the first group were the active women and men, in the second, the old, weak, and disabled, and women with young children. The first group would be worked until they dropped and then exterminated; the second group were massacred at once.

So bad were camp conditions that many of the first group lived for only a few weeks. Up to 1000 Jews were crammed into each barracks, where lack of space

Above: Jews being made to dig their own graves before being executed by their guards, standing above them.

241

forced men to sleep crosswise above their fellows. Before dawn, guards wielding rubber truncheons beat them from their huts and made them line up for inspection; the living propped up those who had died in the night, for everyone had to be counted.

Food was poor and scanty. The prisoners ate bread made from chestnuts and sawdust, margarine based on soft brown coal, and a scrap of horseflesh – all washed down by nettle soup.

Thousands were undernourished. Filthy prisoners broke out in sores and died from dysentery. Others perished in a month or so from hunger, overwork, and blows delivered by the SS guards or barracks leaders (men selected from convicted criminals).

But for most of those who entered Auschwitz death came much faster. Two thousand men, women, and

menstrual blood, and feces – discharged involuntarily as death occurred.

The mess was soon cleared up by a squad of prisoners. This "special task commando" hosed down the heap and loaded bodies onto elevators for disposal in huge incinerators. Incidentally, upon appointment, each squad's first task was disposing of the corpses of its predecessor, machine gunned after four months' grisly work. The Nazis wanted no one left to tell the tale.

Before the dead were burned the Germans made them yield their last remaining assets (a squad had already gathered up the corpses' clothes and shoes). Men shaved the cadavers for their hair, for stuffing mattresses or to be used in time-bomb detonators. Then an eight-man team of dentist-prisoners prized

Left: the compound for women in Belsen concentration camp and (right) SS Guards taking bodies to the Death Pit at Belsen, both paintings by the artist Leslie Cole.

children at a time trudged from the train straight into one of the huge basements labeled "Baths and Disinfecting Room." There, all were made to strip stark naked and hang their clothes on pegs. Then doors were shut and lights switched off. Instead of a refreshing shower, the prisoners received a lethal dose of Cyclon B – a gas produced by prussic acid crystals. They did not die at once. The killing usually took 20 minutes, sometimes half an hour. Meanwhile, as the lower air in the chamber became unbreathable, people of both sexes and all ages trampled on each other as they screamed and fought to rise above the acrid fumes. When fans eventually expelled the gas a mass of bodies lay piled to the ceiling. Sometimes the victims had been so tightly packed that all died standing. Either way the scene was always the same: a mound of blue corpses, soaked in sweat, urine,

open jaws and plucked out gold teeth and fillings.

Meanwhile, twins and deformed Jews had been separately shot, or murdered by a chloroform injection in the heart. Doctor-prisoners in a dissecting room were then forced to carry out autopsies on their bodies in unsuccessful bids to prove Nazi theories of racial degeneracy, and to unlock the secret of multiple births so that German mothers could quickly people Germany's new East European colonies.

Back inside the crematorium a squad of prisoners laid the hordes of bald, naked corpses in threes upon a metal pushcart and sent it into an incandescent oven. Some 20 minutes later, lawyers, doctors, musicians, businessmen, factory hands; wives, mothers, babies, children, fathers, grandparents, uncles, aunts – all had merged anonymously in a heap of ashes to be tipped into the river Vistula.

At Auschwitz there were 15 ovens in each of the four crematoriums. Thus thousands of people could be killed and burned in hours. In one busy seven-week spell in 1944 an average of about 6000 Hungarian Jews died daily. Altogether 2,000,000 Jews, Gypsies, and other "undesirables" perished in the Auschwitz holocaust.

To most of us it seems incredible that millions of people walked obediently to their deaths like cattle in a slaughterhouse. But then to most of them the sheer enormity of such a fate itself seemed unbelievable. In Auschwitz, Jews daily witnessing the smoke and stench of the crematoriums refused to believe what their senses told them. The long history of Jews as an oppressed minority deceived them into thinking that their best chance for survival was to submit meekly

to each fresh demand imposed upon them by their persecutors. Conditioned as they were to oppression they saw their last steps to the gas room or the muzzle of a gun simply as a continuation of the degradation already endured when they lost first jobs, then homes, and lastly clothing.

Almost as astonishing as the submission of the victims was their captives' inhumanity. Admittedly some SS mass murderers suffered nervous breakdowns. But almost to a man the 3000 SS guards at Auschwitz stifled conscience to embrace the attitude expressed in 1943 by secret police chief Heinrich Himmler to his SS group commanders: "Whether nations live in prosperity or starve to death interests me only in so far as we need them as slaves for our *Kultur.*"

Above: a photograph of a Jewish girl taken on the morning she was deported to a concentration camp. She was one of the rare lucky ones who survived and returned to Czechoslovakia.

Left: the special rail spur to the arrival point at Auschwitz, where 4,000,000 people died. The Camp remains today as a grim memorial.

Many death-camp guards gained sadistic pleasure from torturing and murder. Irma Gresse, in charge of 30,000 women at Auschwitz, used whip, walking stick, top boots, and rubber truncheon to beat or kick her victims senseless. She often shot prisoners for sport. Josef Kramer, Camp Commandant of Bergen-Belsen, kicked children toward the gas chambers and set dogs on prisoners to force them into the flames. When British troops reached Bergen-Belsen in 1945 they found 40,000 living skeletons: starved, filthy, racked with dysentery and typhus. Around the camp 13,000 corpses lay unburied and as many more survivors died within the next six weeks.

Thus, by calculated degradation and brutality, a modern Western power committed acts of barbarism on a scale and of an ugliness almost unparalleled in history.

243

Post-War Persecution

In 1945 the world recoiled at the abyss of barbarism that was revealed by the atrocities of World War II. Never again, the newly formed United Nations vowed, should it be possible for nations to find a pretext for such persecution of minorities as had almost annihilated the Jews of Nazi-dominated Europe. In 1948 member nations agreed on a Universal Declaration of Human Rights that would apply to all people in all stages. According to this document everyone has the right: of unhindered travel; of fair trial; to form associations; to hold meetings; and to worship as he pleases. These words have since rung

Officially, at least, black people no longer toil as white men's slaves. In places, though, they suffer harshly as his underdog – especially in South Africa. Hundreds of black Africans died in the summer of 1976 alone, when South African police crushed black unrest fomented by the white government's repressive *apartheid* policy.

A novel horror to emerge in that year was a report of black slavery inside a black African nation. The Anti-Slavery Society in Britain alleged that more than 20,000 citizens of Equatorial Guinea on the West African coast had been impressed as slaves for cocoa plantations on the island of Macias Nguema (formerly Fernando Po). The same society has shown that chattel slavery, debt bondage, serfdom, servile types of marriage, and pseudo adoption are violations of human rights widespread around the world.

In and after the 1960s the thrust to open up the remote interiors of Brazil and Paraguay brought misery to tribes of forest Amerinds who had escaped

Left: Indians from the forests of Brazil. The callous attitude of officials appointed to protect them and the indifference of government has meant wholesale destruction of tribes and their homelands.

Right: segregated African settlement at Modderdam in South Africa. It seems that little has been learned from history when civilized peoples show such indifference to conditions of their fellow men in the Third World.

mockingly for millions. Among the minorities most harshly bullied, some live among certain of the very nations that drew up the rules designed to guarantee their safety. Christians, "heretics," Amerinds, black Africans – all victims of past persecution – figure in new waves of inhumanity, together with countless individuals hounded for political or cultural ideals at odds with those of their totalitarian rulers.

the first repressive wave of Spanish conquest 800 years before. A French medical attaché reportedly found proof that between 1957 and 1963 Brazilian landowners and Indian agents had deliberately spread influenza, measles, smallpox, and tuberculosis germs among Mato Grosso Indians. Thousands may have perished. In 1968, Brazil's Figueiredo Report apparently revealed that corrupt, sadistic members of the Indian

244

Protection Service had dynamited, machine gunned, and poisoned whole tribes of Amazonian Indians in their care. In spite of government reforms, the Amerinds are being dispossessed of their lands at an increasing rate, and accidentally imported epidemics continue to decimate tribes.

South of Brazil the Amerinds of Paraguay have suffered just as savagely. Reports in the late 1970s spoke of quasi-official manhunts in which male Indians were shot, and women and children herded into camps and used as prostitutes and slaves.

Prisoners of conscience have suffered terribly in autocratic left- and right-wing states. In Stalin's Russia, conditions in hard-labor camps had killed millions of potential dissidents by the end of World War II. As late as 1948, 1949, and 1950, three waves of fresh arrests put thousands into jail with standard 25-year sentences. Alexander Solzhenitsyn's monumental record of persecution inside Stalin's Russia lists the kind of victims who are alleged to be spies:

gious prisoners were languishing in Soviet captivity.

In 1973 a right-wing coup destroyed Salvador Allende's democratically elected Marxist government in Chile. Amnesty International calculated that in the next four years 100,000 people were arrested and held in jail, more than 500 were "executed", and tens of thousands driven into exile. Scores of people simply disappeared, including the 67-year-old leading communist Bernardo Zuleta, whose grandchildren saw him "hanging by the hands and moaning" following arrest by DINA (the government security service).

In 1975 new hope for an end to repression came with the European Security Conference at Helsinki. The USA, Canada, the USSR, and all European states except Albania signed a long document, part of which proclaimed that: "The participating states will respect human rights and fundamental freedoms, including the freedom of thought, conscience, religion or belief, for all without distinction as to race, sex, language, or religion."

Christian believers; geneticists rejecting the unscientific theories that Stalin favored; and "just plain ordinary thinking people" sympathetic to the West. Since Stalin's day Soviet repression has become less crudely brutal. But in the 1970s there was proof that dissidents had been shut up in mental hospitals to be brainwashed or mentally destroyed. In 1975 Amnesty International reckoned that 10,000 political and reli-

By the late 1970s there were signs that world opinion and political expediency were having some effect upon barbaric treatment of minorities. The communist USSR began expelling leading dissidents instead of making them disappear. Right-wing Chile began to free political prisoners. But there remained plenty of abuses. Beneath man's new humanitarian mask, his old bestial nature is still alive and snarling.

Chapter 12

Murders That Changed History

War, pestilence, and earthquake hit whole populations. In contrast, assassination is selective. Usually the victim is one individual – a king, dictator, president, or other figurehead, or a representative of those in power. Such individuals always have their enemies – madmen convinced their leader persecutes them; fanatics bent on murder for reward or revenge; idealists determined to end tyranny.

Sometimes the victim's death is merited. Sometimes he dies a martyr. Either way his killing makes a wider impact than any ordinary murder, for it represents a blow against authority. Thus assassination may appear to benefit a people, or to rob them of a statesman they can ill afford to lose. But in both cases confusion or anarchy may follow as the murder rocks or overturns the ship of state. Once, a world war started. Then the murdered leader paralleled the first plague victim in some terrible pandemic. An assassination's aftermath is always unpredictable. There is always the strong possibility that it will bring about a catastrophe upon a devastating scale.

Opposite: Cain murders his brother Abel, from a panel in the great bronze door of the Florence Baptistery. Each had offered a ritual sacrifice to God for the fertility of crops and herds but the farmer Cain believed that God's benevolence was directed toward Abel alone. The Bible tells the story to explain both how the two types of community came into being and how the crime of violent murder first entered the world.

Motives for Murder

There is a long history of murders of important individuals for political, religious, and other motives that stretches back at least to ancient Athens, where the removal of tyrants by assassination was made respectable. In 514 BC two young noblemen, Harmodius and Aristogeiton led a band who tried to kill the dictator Hippias and his brother Hipparchus. Hipparchus died but Hippias survived and the noblemen and their friends were put to death. Although the tyrant's power was left intact, he embarked on a reign of terror that indirectly led to his expulsion from Athens. Tradition has since hallowed the assassins as Athens' deliverers from tyranny.

Rome, too, had early precedents for tyrannicide – precedents that were taken by Caesar's murderers as justification for their act. Caesar's death in turn helped to set a fashion for the murder of successive Roman emperors by ambitious heirs and disenchanted bodyguards.

But the actual word "assassin" has a medieval, Eastern origin. It comes from hashshashin ("hemp-eaters") – the Arabic name for a Syrian branch of a Persian-based Moslem sect founded about 1090 by Hasan ibn-al-Sabbah. From mountain strongholds in Southwest Asia the sect's successive grand masters – each known by the title of the Old Man of the Mountain – waged terror on established Moslem states. Upon their orders, fanatics drugged with *Cannabis* suicidally assassinated leading Moslem generals and statesmen. In the 13th century, invading Mongols smashed the sect, but its reputation for slyly killing off political opponents had meanwhile reached Europe with crusading knights returning from the Holy Land.

No European country more diligently sought to solve its problems by assassination than 15th-century Italy. Split into petty states and independent cities, Italy became a hotbed of intrigue and murder, as tyrants and those they tyrannized killed for fear, revenge, or power. Naples led the field for hired assassination, and by the 1490s Rome itself swarmed with licensed and unlicensed assassins. The most industrious murderers were members of the Spanish Borgia family, Pope Alexander VI and his evil son Cesare. To seize the revenues of various church offices or properties, Cesare simply murdered their holders. In 1500 the Venetian ambassador at Rome noted that four or five "bishops, prelates, and others" were found dead every night. Cesare's own brother, brother-in-law, other relatives, and any courtier who blocked his path to power were liquidated. Some he

killed with the sword, others died by poison. Cesare and Alexander joined their many victims in 1503 when both accidentally tasted a poisoned sweetmeat meant for a rich cardinal. By then few people believed that any powerful Italian died naturally.

Cesare's successful ruthlessness had wider repercussions, for it influenced Niccolo Machiavelli's *The Prince* – a widely circulated ruler's guide justifying treachery and murder if used as stepping stones to power.

Soon after the Borgias' deaths, the religious Reformation provided a new motive for assassinations inside Europe. Religious fanatics killed France's Henry III in 1589 and his successor Henry IV in 1610. To some exponents of the Counter Reformation assassination of Protestant monarchs seemed a godly act. This attitude undoubtedly encouraged Spain's Philip II publicly to urge the killing of his rebel enemy William the Silent, who fell to an assassin's gun in 1584.

William died a victim of an absolutist monarch. But by the 17th century, Europe's absolutist kings themselves began to fall victim to their subjects' clamor for a voice in government. In 1649 the English judicially murdered Charles I. In the next century, the French beheaded Louis XVI. In the 19th century the surviving autocratic monarchies in Eastern Europe became a target for political killers who wished to sweep away the whole of the existing order. In 1881 a bomb planted by one of these nihilists killed Czar Alexander II. Meanwhile unrest by national minorities within great European states expressed itself in bombs and bullets aimed at royal heads of government. In 1914 it was a young Serb who killed the heir to Austria-Hungary and started World War I.

By then, democratically elected premiers and presidents had begun replacing absolute hereditary rulers. But there were always some disgruntled subjects prepared to kill such leaders for real or imagined tyranny or other reasons. No fewer than four United States presidents died by assassins' hands within a century. In 1865 the actor John Wilkes Booth killed Abraham Lincoln to avenge the South's defeat in the Civil War. In 1881 a crank named Charles J. Guiteau shot James Garfield as "an act of God." In 1901 the young anarchist Leon Czolgosz shot William McKinley. In 1963, Lee Harvey Oswald, a communist sympathizer, shot John Fitzgerald Kennedy in Dallas.

The half century from 1865 to 1914 could be called, for want of a better term, assassination's golden age. Besides those already mentioned, kings, queens, presidents, and prime ministers of several other countries also fell victim to various assassins. But the next half century – ending with the death of Kennedy – reaped its crop of leaders: men as different from one another as the exiled militant Russian communist Leon Trotsky, and India's frail old, saintly pacifist, Mohandas Gandhi. The later pages of this chapter examine some post-Kennedy patterns of assassination, and look closer at the whole phenomenon.

Left: an illustration from a Persian manuscript showing the founder of the Assassins, Hasan ibn-al-Sabbah. His sect challenged the right of the caliphs of Baghdad to rule the Moslem world. He established a series of strongholds in inaccessible, mountainous areas from where his followers could descend on their secret missions to murder the ruling Turks. So successful were his followers that the word *assassin* has passed from Arabic into English and French to mean a political murderer.

Right: a Persian manuscript illustration of one of Hasan ibn-al-Sabbah's followers murdering a leading official.

Julius Caesar
100-44 BC

Near noon on March 15, 44 BC, Julius Caesar stepped into his litter and was carried through Rome to Pompey's Theater. Someone in the crowd pressed a paper into his hand – a warning of a plot to kill him. People were always badgering Caesar with petitions. He entered the chamber with the papers still unread.

Above: a marble bust of Julius Caesar. It was carved six years before his assassination in 44 BC when he had just subdued the British and German tribes.

Within the hour he was lying at the base of Pompey's statue, a mangled bleeding corpse. The enemies of Caesar considered they had rid Rome of an uncrowned emperor, whose autocratic rule they had come to distrust. But the effects of the assassination were far-reaching – for them, for Rome, and for the Western world.

The reasons for the murder of Julius Caesar lie in the gulf that existed between two sections of the Roman people and in the undemocratic nature of the Republic. Republican Rome was largely run by two annually elected military leaders, or consuls. They presided over the Senate, a council of elders which at first consisted only of *patricians* – descendants of the old upper class. The other Roman citizens – the *plebeians* – eventually gained spokesmen in the Senate. These men were *tribunes*. In law, plebeians became the patricians' equals in 287 BC. In fact, rich landowners and nobles dominated the government, for most other people lacked the cash to stand as unpaid senators or consuls. Rome's wars made matters worse for the underprivileged majority because they enriched the wealthy, but impoverished the peasants, forcing them to sell their holdings.

Vested interests crushed attempts at land reform begun in 133 BC, and a century of civil war and riots followed. Not all the rich or noble Romans took sides with the establishment. At the time of Caesar's birth, about 100 BC, the consul Gaius Marius opposed Rome's few ruling families. Marius recruited troops from landless peasants and started popular reforms. Lucius Cornelius Sulla raised another army but used his troops to crush Marius' forces. Ruling as dictator from 82 to 79 BC, Sulla abolished Marius' reforms, destroyed the tribunes' power, then returned authority to the wealthy members of the Senate.

This was the atmosphere under which Caesar reached manhood – a republic ruled by and for a rich minority that clutched power by stifling popular unrest. So divided, the Republic – and its empire overseas – was set for certain civil war and probably disintegration. Caesar learned to exploit the first to stop the second.

In some ways this aristocrat's rise to power as a

people's champion seemed unlikely. His clan – the Julii – lacked wealth and influence. But it had traditionally sided with the popular party. Indeed Sulla hounded the young Caesar for marrying the daughter of a friend of Marius. Caesar escaped abroad, and fought for Rome in Asia Minor, winning fame for bravery and daring.

When Sulla died in 78 BC Caesar returned to Rome to launch his own political career. By his early 40s he had held increasingly important offices eventually becoming a consul in 59 BC. He joined Marcus Licinius Crassus and Gnaeus Pompeius (Pompey) in the First Triumvirate. The three men embittered the conservatives by forcing reforms through the Senate.

But a consul had only brief, limited, elective powers. Caesar wanted more time to rule, with more authority. He knew he could win supreme power only with military fame and the backing of a loyal army. He gained both. Becoming proconsul of provinces north of Italy, he began nine years of brilliant cruel campaigning that brought Gaul (France) within Rome's orbit. Caesar's troops and the masses back at home learned to adore this tall, black-eyed, pale-faced conqueror of Celts. Caesar was vain and profligate, but he shared his soldier's hardships, fought bravely, rode and wrote skillfully, administered his territories wisely, and brimmed with energy. What is more, he backed the people's aspirations.

Above: a relief carving showing Roman soldiers in pitched battle against a Germanic tribe. A brilliant general, Julius Caesar showed his considerable skill in subduing the peoples of Europe.

Right: *The Ides of March,* by the 19th-century British historical painter Sir Edward Poynter. Caesar's wife Calpurnia was upset by the warnings of the fortune-tellers and by a warning dream she had before the fateful Ides (15th) of March.

251

Of the two other members of the triumvirate, Crassus had died fighting the Parthians and Pompey, fearing Caesar's growing power, had sided with conservatives seeking to undermine Caesar's popularity at home. But Pompey lost face because he failed to end factional fights that racked the capital. Meanwhile loot from Gaul helped Caesar buy Roman politicians to secure his interests inside the Senate.

Crisis between the leaders broke in 49 BC. Refusing to relinquish his military command when ordered by the Senate, Caesar marched on Rome. Pompey fled, and in nine weeks Caesar held all Italy. Outside Italy he enlarged his power by crushing opposition in Egypt, Asia Minor, North Africa, and Spain. By his mid-50s Caesar was master of the Graeco-Roman world.

He now spent lavishly to celebrate his victories, and curry favor with the masses. He feasted Rome's citizens at 22,000 tables and staged a mock-naval battle, and a hunt involving 400 giraffes and lions. Detached and cynical, Caesar nonetheless planned

for our own. In all this, Caesar's will was law. For he now ruled as dictator for life, supreme commander of Rome's armies, and master of a Senate packed with his nominees.

Ahead lay even greater power and authority. People began to set up statues to him as a god. In public, he appeared dressed in royal purple, and seated on a golden chair. In fact, though not in name, he ruled as emperor, and planned to found a dynasty. Clues to his intentions appeared early in 44 BC. Caesar downgraded two tribunes who had arrested a man for hailing him as "king." He also allowed his friend Mark Antony to try to crown him at an important public festival.

But while Caesar kept the favor of the masses, his autocratic attitude was building enemies. Senators and tribunes seethed at personal rebuffs and at Caesar's alteration of the Roman constitution. The aristocrats saw governments slipping permanently from their hands. Ambitious nobles watched Caesar's monopoly of power with growing envy.

overdue reforms postponed by previous leaders. His planned innovations included enabling more people to vote; a vast public buildings program; creation of a police force and municipal councils; land grants to army veterans; an imperial tax based on a projected census; strict supervision of provincial tax-gatherers and governors; and a corrected calendar – the basis

Above: the 19th-century German historical painter Karl von Piloty's version of the death of Julius Caesar. Caesar is brushing aside Tillius Cimber's request for him to recall Cimber's brother from banishment. Behind Caesar, Publius Servilius Casca prepares to strike the first blow with a dagger.
Right: the body of Caesar lies bleeding beneath Pompey's statue. His murderers expected that the death of Caesar would free Rome of tyranny and restore the Republic. But Caesar had concentrated so much power in his own hands that his enemies had simply destroyed any real governing authority.

By March of 44 BC Caesar's enemies had conceived a plot to kill him. Its prime mover was probably Gaius Cassius, a patrician military leader who had discreetly surrendered Pompey's fleet to Caesar when he saw his former leader's cause was lost. But he had been overlooked for high promotion, and nursed the affront as a private grudge. He also believed that killing Caesar would free Rome from a tyrant.

Marcus Junius Brutus held high office under Caesar, and rumor had it that he was Caesar's illegitimate son. Like Cassius, Brutus had fought for Pompey, but evidently joined the plot disinterestedly. He detested tyranny and admired an ancestor who had killed a would-be king of Rome.

Others in the plot had been consistent followers of Caesar. Decimus Junius Brutus, a soldier of patrician background who trained gladiators, joined for rewards above anything that Caesar had given him. Gaius Trebonius, whose promotion had stopped short at tribune, completed the core of the conspiracy. It was soon joined by the tribune Publius Servilius

Casca, and the pro-praetor-designate Lucius Tillius Cimber, and perhaps several other senators. Within two weeks more than 60 Senators knew of the plan to murder Caesar. Several schemes had been put forward. One was to set upon him at a polling station as he supervised a consular election. Another proposed killing Caesar as he traveled on the Sacred Way, or reached the Theater. Finally, Caesar himself unknowingly provided the ideal opportunity. He called a Senate meeting for March 15 – the Roman Ides of March. Fittingly for the conspiracy the venue would be the portico attached to Pompey's Theater. The conspirators could gather unsuspected at this function. Anyway they knew they must act soon, for Caesar was about to travel east to fight the Parthians.

Considering how many knew about the plot it seems incredible that Caesar did not get to hear of it. He guessed that there were secret enemies among his close lieutenants. When warned that Mark Antony planned mischief he said he did not fear the 'sleek, long-haired fellows . . . but the pale and lean" – a

description of Cassius and Brutus. Even so, Caesar refused to think that Brutus – a man whom he admired and loved – would go as far as murder. Roman historians relate that supernatural omens warned Caesar of his impending death. Some were probably invented afterward. But a fortuneteller named Spurinna apparently told Caesar he faced danger on the Ides of March. Caesar rejected such portents as superstition or out of sheer complacency. He had dismissed his bodyguard because the Senate had offered him protection. When friends declared his life at risk, Caesar said that he preferred to die than skulk in daily fear of death.

As Caesar entered the Chamber of Pompey's Theater the scores of waiting senators stood in his honor. He little guessed the preparations some had made for just this moment. At dawn Brutus had left home with a dagger. The other plotters had gathered at Gaius Cassius' house, with daggers hidden in their stylus cases – the holders for the pointed instruments with which the Romans wrote on wax. Near Pompey's Theater a band of Decimus Brutus's gladiators stood by in case of need.

Caesar sat down in a recess below a statue of Pompey, his former enemy. Some of Brutus' supporters sat behind him. Deferentially, a group of conspirators

But two events almost saved the great dictator's life. One was a distressing dream experienced by his wife Calpurnia. Two versions of her dream are that she saw a mark of honor torn down from the gable of the house, or pictured Caesar's bleeding body in her arms. Calpurnia begged Caesar not to travel to the fateful meeting. Impressed despite himself, and feeling rather ill, Caesar agreed. But before he could cancel the meeting, Decimus Brutus arrived and talked him into attending. According to the historian Plutarch Decimus used as bait the Senate's promise to vote Caesar king of all provinces outside Italy.

approached. Tillius Cimber pretended to petition Caesar for a banished brother. Caesar waved the plea aside, but Cimber insistently seized him by the shoulders. "This is violence!" cried Caesar. At the same time Casca slipped behind, then stabbed him just beneath the throat. Caesar grabbed Casca's arm and jabbed back with his stylus. He was rising as another dagger pierced his chest. Now all the killers closed in, surrounding Caesar with a ring of knives. One version of the story tells how Caesar glimpsed Marcus Brutus among his enemies and said, "You, too, my child?" Then Caesar drew the top of his toga over his head, and fell beneath a rain of dagger thrusts. The plotters wounded one another in collective frenzy, for all had planned to share the guilt and glory of this act.

The deed done, the murderers and other senators fled as if pursued. One moment the place was noisy, violent, and crowded – the next, still, empty, lifeless. For a while Caesar's bloody corpse lay beneath Pompey's statue. Then three of Caesar's slaves crept in and bore away his body on a litter.

Caesar's death achieved the opposite of what his murderers intended. Instead of celebrating a tyrant's death, the masses mourned and worshiped Caesar as a martyr and a god. Instead of putting back the clock to old-style republican rule, his assassinators plunged Rome into 13 years of civil war. From this his nominated heir and great-nephew, Octavian, emerged as Augustus, the first Roman Emperor. Imperial rule patterned upon Caesar's now gave Rome a continuity of government it badly needed. Under the old-style republic, which nominated leaders annually, Rome would have quickly foundered. As it was, the Roman Empire lasted 400 years – long enough to set its stamp upon world history. Caesar's martyrdom had sealed and authorized the autocratic brand of rule that made this possible.

Above: the first invasion of Britain in the summer of 55 BC. Caesar landed 10,000 legionaires but after fierce fighting with the Britons, he was forced to retire. His second, better planned invasion the following year was completely successful and he defeated the Britons in a battle near what is now Canterbury.

Left: slaves remove the body of Caesar after the murder.

Right: the first Roman Forum. It stretched from the Senate House, or Curia, to the Temple of Venus and Roma. It was the oldest of the city's public squares and was a complex of government buildings, temples, stores, and open spaces. It was the center of Rome and the center of the empire. From the Forum all roads fanned out across Italy although its own main road was closed to chariot traffic while officials, priests, businessmen, shoppers, and sellers wandered through the area on foot. It was in the Forum at a meeting of the senate that Caesar was killed.

William the Silent
1533-1584

On March 18, 1582 William I the Silent, Prince of Orange, champion of liberty, and founder of the modern Netherlands, left the dining room of his residence in Antwerp and crossed the crowded ante-room. A man stepped from the throng, pulled out a pistol and squeezed the trigger. There was a bang, and a smell of singeing hair. Flames spurted from the ruff around the prince's neck and blood began to fill his mouth. Swordsmen instantly cut down the assassin and servants helped their stricken master from the room. Surgeons found that a bullet had plowed through his cheeks and palate, but left the brain intact. The Prince of Orange had escaped King Philip II of Spain's revenge this time. He was not to be so lucky when the second attempt was made.

When, two years later, a bullet from the pistol of Balthazar Gérard ripped through the body of the Prince of Orange his murderer posthumously won a cash reward. But Philip of Spain who paid it hoped to reap far larger gains. By having William killed he aimed to smash the brain and backbone of a revolt that was robbing Spain of its richest European provinces. Had William died years sooner, Philip indeed might have brought the Netherlands to heel. As it was, Philip lost the seven northern provinces, though the murder did make sure that William's greatest hope remained unrealized and two nations, Belgium and the modern Netherlands, emerged instead of the one large state that the prince worked and died for.

Chance made William a champion of rebels. He grew up in the simple, Lutheran household of his father, the Count of Nassau-Dillenburg, a minor German nobleman. When he was 11 William inherited a cousin's lands: the principality of Orange in southern France, the vast Nassau estates in the Netherlands, and other holdings. Overnight, he had become one of Europe's richest noblemen. William's new importance led the Emperor Charles V to summon him to the imperial court at Brussels and to raise him in the official, Catholic, faith.

Likeable, self-confident, worldly, William seemed set for a conventional courtier's career. But beneath his sociable exterior, he hid inner thoughts and feel-

Left: William the Silent, first stadholder of Holland. He was brought up in the court of the Emperor Charles V, and later made governor of northern Holland provinces. He clashed with Charles' successor Philip II of Spain over Philip's persecution of the Dutch Protestants and from then on William sought to end Spanish rule in the Netherlands.

Right: Spanish troops enter a Dutch town. Revolution in the Netherlands was sparked off by Philip II's determination to stamp out Protestantism in this richest and most prized possession of the Hapsburg empire. The more ruthlessly Philip tried to suppress the independent-minded Netherlanders, the more determined they were to secure their freedom.

ings with a skill that later earned him his title "the Silent." In particular, he felt a deep sense of justice and of moral obligation to the peoples of the Netherlands. The Netherlands in the 1500s comprised not only what are now known as the Netherlands but also Belgium, Luxembourg, and part of northeastern France. In theory all belonged to the Duke of Burgundy who – as Charles V – happened also to be Holy Roman Emperor. In fact, the Duke's power was limited to naming the stadholders (governors of provinces) and grand pensionaries (chief magistrates of cities).

In 1559 Charles's successor, Philip II of Spain, made William stadholder of the northern provinces of Holland, Zealand, and Utrecht. (William's own hereditary lands lay chiefly farther south.) But William soon found his loyalty to Philip clashing with his own interests and sense of duty to the people of the Netherlands. He found that Philip was insensitively bent upon curtailing nobles' powers and provincial rights and privileges. Philip wanted to impose Spanish-style Catholic, centralized autocracy upon his diverse northern lands, where many Protestants were living. William saw a different need. Successful government, he felt, consisted of cooperation between the sovereign, the leading nobles, and the separate provincial estates, or parliaments.

Above: the proud and ruthless Duke of Alva, the man sent by Philip II of Spain in 1566 to subdue the Netherlands. His "Council of Blood" sentenced thousands of Dutch people to death.

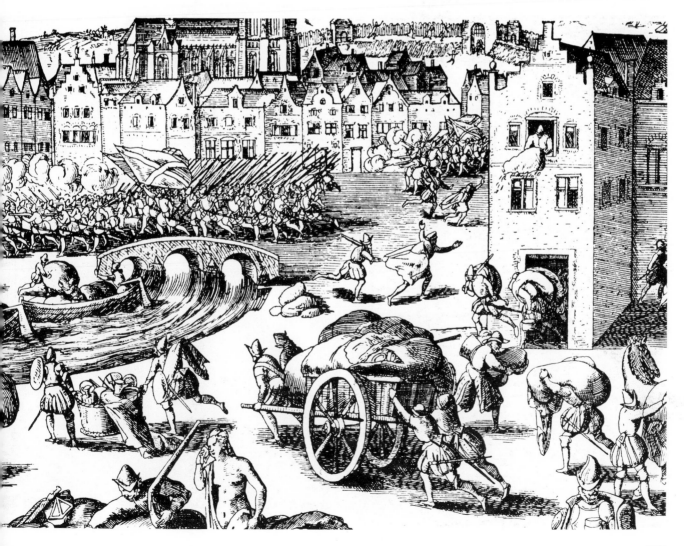

Philip set up court in Spain in 1559, leaving Margaret, Duchess of Parma to govern the Netherlands. A council of advisers headed by Cardinal Granvelle was appointed to enforce Philip's new repressive policies. In 1564 three major nobles – the Prince of Orange, the Count of Egmont, and Count Horn – forced Philip to withdraw the hated Granvelle. But they failed to stop a threatened persecution of the Protestants. Lesser nobles, both Calvinist and Catholic, opposing Inquisition methods reacted by forging the confederacy of the Gueux or "Beggars." William tried to calm the hotheads, but fighting started.

In 1566 Philip responded with a Spanish army led by a new, brutal governor general of the Netherlands, the Duke of Alva. The Duke's Council of Troubles punished heretics, arrested troublesome nobles, and seized their estates. In 1568 Alva beheaded Horn and Egmont, and outlawed William, who had fled to Germany. Alva's atrocities and taxes enraged the people of the Netherlands and they began looking to the exiled Prince of Orange as a potential champion in their bid to end Spanish occupation. Because the north – a stronghold of the Calvinists – became the core of the resistance, William eventually adopted Calvinism, too, although his goal was always a united Netherlands where men were free to choose their own beliefs.

Resistance really started in 1572. William invaded the Netherlands with 20,000 troops but the support he hoped for from France failed to materialize and the revolt failed. Meanwhile the Sea Beggars (Dutch pirates) seized the port of Brille, and the northern coastal provinces now called on William as their stadholder for an independence struggle. By 1573 his forces held some of Friesland and Zealand, and one third of Holland. For four years he led the north's tenacious fight for survival.

By 1576 the death of the Spanish governor general, and ravages by mutinous Spanish troops in the disunited south gave William a chance to use his statemanship – the field in which he excelled. Acting for the north he negotiated the Pacification of Ghent, by which south and north agreed to share resources under William's leadership to drive the Spanish out and reach a religious settlement. Of the 17 Netherlandish provinces, 16 seemed close to union, with only Luxembourg remaining in Spanish hands.

In 1577, faced with a united stand by north and south, another governor general, Don John of Austria, pretended to agree to take out foreign troops and to respect provincial liberties. Then he rashly seized Namur, and the Catholic south invited William to Brussels to unite Catholics and Protestants against their common enemy. But religious issues soon divided the states and into this divided land in 1578 marched 20,000 troops under the Duke of Parma, who succeeded Don John as governor. Parma's sweeping victory at Gembloux effectively won back the southern provinces for Spain. In 1579 the Treaty of Arras

proclaimed a southern union. The north responded with the Union of Utrecht. Religion had irreparably split the Netherlands. William nonetheless toiled grimly on to reunite them.

By summer 1580, Philip decided that ridding the Netherlands of their champion was the shortest way to crush rebellion. Already he had given assassination plots his unspoken approval. Now he openly condoned them. To encourage would-be murderers, Philip offered a large reward for the death of William, as well as noble status and free pardon for any old offenses for the man who did the deed. The reward was great but scarcely in proportion to the risk of winning it. Short of poisoning, a man would have to bludgeon,

258

stab, or shoot at close range as there were no effective long-range rifles then. Any assassin would face almost certain death from William's followers.

The Spanish murder threat discredited Philip in popular opinion and showed the Dutch how vital to their cherished freedom their enemies knew William to be. His popularity increased. In December 1580, William published an *Apology*, justifying his rebellion against Philip as a ruler unworthy of his people's loyalty. Next May the Estates General of the United Provinces signed an Act of Abjuration, deposing Philip. No republican, William planned a simple transfer of Netherlands allegiance from Philip to Francis, the Duke of Anjou. William believed that a

French figurehead could win his nation-in-the-making the vital help of France. But the treacherous and autocratic behavior of the Duke alienated most of the states.

In 1582 a Portuguese merchant equipped a clerk, Juan Jauréguy, working in his Antwerp warehouse with a pistol and new French suit, and sent him off to shoot the Prince of Orange, expecting to pocket the reward himself. It was after dinner on March 18 that Jauréguy made his attempt on William's life. Although the bullet ravaged the time-scarred face of the Prince still further, it did not kill him and after a week William seemed on the mend. Then the wound burst open and bled uncontrollably for hours. Doctors

A contemporary Dutch print of *The Murder of The Prince of Orange in Delft in the Year 1584*.

259

Above: King Philip II of Spain who devoted his reign to stamping out Protestantism throughout his vast possessions, especially in the Netherlands.

Left: the tomb raised by the Dutch people over the body of William the Silent.

Right: the special assembly of the States General meet in the Great Hall of the old palace of the counts of Holland at The Hague. It was the outstanding ability of its stadholders, or leaders, who ruled the federation of states more or less as kings, which preserved the union.

despaired. William called his family around him and faintly said: "All is over with me." But pressure stopped the hemorrhage and he recovered.

Anjou eventually lost the people's confidence by plotting to seize Antwerp and take over supreme power in the Netherlands. Divided and disillusioned, the south drew closer once again to Spain. William left Antwerp in order to rally the four northern provinces and to argue for alliance with the south.

Meanwhile would-be murderers still tried to kill him. None reached striking distance of their victim until July 1584 – more than two years after William had recovered from the first attempt. This time the gunman was a cabinetmaker's apprentice and fanatical Catholic named Balthazar Gérard. At Dôle in France, Gérard had once plunged a dagger into wood to show how he would kill the Prince of Orange. A bystander reprovingly declared that small fry like

Gérard did not assassinate great princes. But although Gérard lacked a plan, he had determination.

In May 1584 he arrived – unarmed – at Delft. There William welcomed all petitioners at the red-brick Prinsenhof. Gérard introduced himself as Guyon, a Protestant whose father had been martyred for the cause. Gérard pretended that he sought to serve William, as the greatest Protestant leader of the day. William sent him off with letters for the Duke of Anjou. Gérard returned with detailed news of Anjou's death. Then, for days, he hovered by the Prinsenhof. When told to go away to seek work from the French commander, Gérard pleaded lack of cash. William gave him 12 crowns for traveling expenses. With this he bought a pair of pistols from one of William's guards, explaining that the roads were dangerous.

William spent the morning of July 10 on official business with Leeuwarden's burgomaster. The burgomaster stayed to lunch. Just as the two men and four ladies walked to the dining room, Gérard shoved forward, and in a strangely hollow voice asked for a passport for his journey to France. William promised to prepare one. While William moved on, Gérard quickly scanned the building for escape routes. He already wore hidden waterwings to help him swim a canal. Then Gérard mingled with petitioners waiting in the corridor between the stairs and dining room. He had to wait some time, for, after lunch, officers arrived to talk military business.

At last, William emerged. He had just touched the bowed head of a kneeling veteran soldier when Gérard fired his pistol. Its charge ripped through William's lungs and stomach, and lodged in a wall. "My God have pity on me, I am gravely wounded," William cried in French. He staggered. For a moment he stood. But he knew this wound was mortal. He gasped "God, have pity on my soul; God have pity on these poor people." Then he slumped down on the staircase in his equerry's arms, lost consciousness and shortly afterward died.

Gérard got not farther than the garden wall before men seized him. He at once admitted guilt, and duly suffered public execution, glorying in death as a religious martyr. The King of Spain kept his bargain and paid the reward to Gérard's family. It cost the monarch nothing, for the cash came from revenues seized from William's imprisoned eldest son.

William's death robbed the northern provinces of the man who had shown them how to work together for their mutual good. William's second son Maurice – a better general than William – went on to make the young Dutch state secure. But Maurice lacked his father's statesmanship and charm. William's death had snuffed out the last weak hope of winning back the south from Spain and building a united Netherlands. But had William been shot down when Philip first put a price upon his head the consequences might have been far greater. For William had time to sever the north's links with Spain. By doing so he helped to forge a nation with influence far greater than its size – a trading power whose vessels plied the oceans and built an empire in the east; a state whose art and intellectual freedom enriched the culture of a continent.

Abraham Lincoln
1809-1865

Above: the log cabin in Hardin – now Larne – County, Kentucky, where it is believed that Abraham Lincoln was born. From such humble beginnings, this son of poor, uneducated parents became the 16th president of the United States of America.

A few minutes after 10 pm on April 14, 1865, during a performance of *Our American Cousin* at Ford's Theater in Washington, a shot rang out through the crowded house. President Abraham Lincoln slumped mortally wounded in his theater box. His assailant, John Wilkes Booth, one of the best-known actors of the day, dropped the single-shot pistol, and leaped from the presidential box. Although he had broken his leg in his fall, Booth limped across the stage and cried out "Sic semper tyrannis" (Thus ever to tyrants), the motto of the Southern state of Virginia.

Lincoln's death seemed to be the work of one misguided individual: the revenge killing of a stern father figure from the North who had chastized the rebels of the South. His murder was only part of a larger death plan, however – some say of a deep political plot engineered by high officials in the United States government. The reason suggested for the plot was Lincoln's post Civil War aims of "malice toward none. . . . charity for all" – aims that were anathema to Northern capitalists intent on legalized plunder of the beaten South.

One sure consequence of Lincoln's death was to create a martyr and a legend. It also set an ugly precedent for future presidential killings. No leader of the United States since Lincoln has felt safe from sudden death. And as it grew to be the West's most powerful nation, assassination of the United States president also became a threat to shake the very bedrock of world peace.

Lincoln was tall, large-framed, gangling, and

walked bent at the knees. At 56 he looked considerably older. His suit flapped loosely on an emaciated body. Above his scraggy beard his craggy face was sallow – almost jaundiced, and big creased bags underhung his eyes. Some days, he found getting out of bed an effort. Some medical historians now believe that he was suffering from a fatally progressive ailment.

Abraham Lincoln's doctor blamed the President's poor physical shape on exhaustion. By 1865 he had spent almost four tiring years leading the North against the South in the American Civil War. By the time spring came around, victory was close. Lincoln could feel justly proud of his achievements – not just for steering the United States through the worst years of its history, but for becoming president at all. Lincoln had been born in a Kentucky log cabin. He spent a tough frontier boyhood on his father's farms and later worked as a laborer, clerk, storekeeper, and surveyor.

Less than a year's formal schooling had helped him learn to "read, write, and cipher to the Rule of Three." Otherwise he was self taught. In 1834 Lincoln was persuaded to study law, and in 1836 received his license to practice. By then he was building a reputation as a leader and for plain, pungent, honest oratory. In 1834 he won election to the Illinois legislature. From then on politics and law became his life.

Above: the first known photograph of Abraham Lincoln. He was nominated for the United States Senate in 1858 after a speech in which he stated that "I believe that this government cannot endure permanently half slave and half free." His stand against slavery eventually won him the presidency.

262

In 1847 he entered Congress as a Whig, but in 1856 joined the antislavery Republican Party. Lincoln gained national fame in 1858 running for the United States Senate against the Democrat Stephen A. Douglas. At that time the Northern States had outlawed slavery, but it was still legal in the South. Douglas favored introducing black slavery to states newly admitted to the Union. Lincoln objected. He opposed slavery as a "moral, social, and political evil." The two clashed in much-publicized debates at seven Illinois cities. Douglas won the Senate seat for Illinois. But Lincoln went on to gain Republican nomination as presidential candidate for 1860. His plain speaking and humble background helped. So did divisions that split his rivals' votes. Late in 1860 Lincoln was elected President of the United States.

The Southern states at once saw Lincoln as a threat to slavery – the institution that underpinned the farming South's prosperity. By the time of Lincoln's inauguration in early March of 1861, seven Southern states had seceded from the Union. Four followed later. In his inauguration speech Lincoln declared that he had no wish to meddle with slavery in states where the Constitution upheld it. He knew that Civil War would follow such interference. Lincoln put preservation of the Union before abolishing an ugly institution in one section of the country. The South distrusted his intentions, and Civil War began on April 12, 1861.

Lincoln fought ferociously to save the Union. His forceful conduct of the war made many enemies. In spite of the Constitution, he hurled thousands of suspected traitors into jail untried. But he also wooed the rebel states, eventually promising to readmit them unpenalized provided only that they freed their slaves. This enraged hard-line "Radical" Republicans who wanted to impose harsh penalties upon the South. It also angered some of the North's big businessmen who hoped to slice large profits from a crushed and beaten South.

When the South surrendered on April 9, 1865, several factions had good reason to wish the newly reelected President out of office. When he perished five days later, 80 letters threatening his life lay on his desk.

His assassin, John Wilkes Booth, was by birth a Southerner but lived in the North. He was the son of one of America's greatest actors, and brother of two more. At 26 John was also well established on the stage. Dark-haired, handsome, and athletic, he overacted with absurd flamboyance. But audiences loved him and he won big money and a flock of mistresses. Riled when critics compared his acting unfavorably with his father's and his brothers', John determined to eclipse their fame by some histrionic deed of truly national proportions. In 1864 he planned to kidnap President Lincoln, and hand him to the Confederate government. Booth believed that the Confederacy would then bargain for a favorable peace or improve its fading hopes of victory by freeing Lincoln in

Above: a torchlight procession in the campaign for Lincoln's nomination to the presidency. Lincoln was regarded as a moderate candidate on the sensitive slavery issue, but even so, six weeks after his inauguration as President, the southern states seceded from the Union.

exchange for Confederate prisoners of war. Booth built a gang of co-conspirators and tried two kidnap bids in Washington.

First, Booth aimed to seize the President at Ford's Theater on January 18. Unexpectedly, Lincoln changed his published plan and the plotters scattered, fearing betrayal. Later, they reassembled. This time they planned to grab Lincoln's carriage as he rode out to a matinee at the Soldiers' Home on Seventh Street. On March 20 six men on horseback waited in futile ambush under trees. Again the President had changed his mind. Once more the gang broke up and fled. Weeks later, peace had been declared, making the kidnaping of Mr Lincoln pointless. Instead, Booth changed his object to revenge. He was determined to kill not just the President but two more key men in the Washington administration. He would personally gun down Lincoln, while Booth's associate Lewis Powell would murder Secretary of State William Seward, and another plotter, George Andrew Atzerodt, would kill Vice President Andrew Johnson.

In early 1865 hints of bids to kill the President resulted in a four-man bodyguard of armed, plain-clothes police. Two worked by day – one from afternoon until midnight, one from midnight to morning. Secretary of War Edwin McMasters Stanton –

responsible for Lincoln's safety – also organized an escort of light cavalry to ride with Mr Lincoln when he left his big, shabby presidential residence. Lincoln smiled tolerantly at these precautions. He knew that anyone sufficiently determined could kill him at any time.

The time that Booth in fact selected was the evening of April 14 – Good Friday. Booth's choice of Ford's theater as the place for the assassination was sound. He had played at Ford's and knew the staff and layout well. Luck sided with him, too. On March 7 a ticket seller had smashed a lock on a box door to let some patrons in. That box and the next, with the partition removed, became a single presidential box for Lincoln's visit. By then the lock was still broken.

About 6 pm on the day of the President's visit, Booth lured the Ford Theater stagehands to a tavern. He left them drinking and slipped back inside the now empty theater. He prepared a board to jam a foyer door to stop anyone chasing him from the Mezzanine into the nearby state box. He found that the box door opened easily, and drilled a peephole in it to get a

view of Lincoln's rocking chair. Booth gathered up the dust and shavings created by his work, and slipped back to his hotel.

That evening the presidential party left the White House for the theater after several disappointments. First, Edwin and Mrs Stanton would not come: Stanton disliked theater going. Also General and Mrs Grant had been unable to attend. Then too, the usually fatalistic Lincoln had tried but failed to get a special guard to join them.

The party that drove up to the theater at 8.25 consisted of the Lincolns, a Major Henry Rathbone and his fiancée Clara Harris, Charles Forbes, a footman-valet, and Lincoln's personal bodyguard, an unreliable policeman named John Parker.

The comedy, *Our American Cousin*, had already started when the President arrived. But the play stopped briefly as the theater band struck up "Hail to the Chief" and the audience, some 1700 strong, stood to applaud. Lincoln sagged in his haircloth rocking chair, next to Mrs Lincoln, half hidden from the audience by a curtain and a wall. Major Rathbone and Miss Harris sat farther forward in the box. Forbes sat at the back, then left to join the coachman. Parker sat in the corridor behind the box.

More than half the play passed uneventfully. Then, about 10 pm, Booth entered the foyer leading to the boxes. He found John Parker's seat conveniently empty. Bored because he could not see the stage, the bodyguard had slipped off for a drink. Booth walked through the foyer door and jammed it. He now stood in the dark corridor leading to the State box. Peeping through his peephole in the box door, he glimpsed Lincoln's silhouetted head, Booth listened for lines that told him one actor stood alone upon the stage. Then he pushed the box door open, and crept up

Above: an escaped American slave wearing a punishment collar is hunted by his owners. Strong feelings against the degradation of slavery forced the rift between North and South.

264

Left: the Union-held Fort Sumter in Charleston Harbor (on right of picture). The first shots of the Civil War were fired on April 12 1863 from the Confederate Fort Moultrie (at left). Cut off from supplies and reinforcements Fort Sumter surrendered after 34 hours.

Below: the Battle of Gettysburg in Pennsylvania, the bloodiest and largest-scale battle of the Civil War lasted from July 1–3, 1863. It marked the turning point of the war when an invading Confederate force under Robert E. Lee met a Union force under General George Meade. So heavy were the Confederate losses that they were unable to launch any major offensive during the rest of the war.

behind the President, a single-shot vest-pocket pistol in his hand.

Booth fired a lead ball into the back of Lincoln's head. Laughter half-drowned the noise of the shot. The President stopped rocking. His companions turned. They saw a wreath of smoke and a man who brushed past the Lincolns toward the front of the box. Major Rathbone leaped up and grabbed. Booth slashed down with a knife, cut Rathbone's left arm to the bone, and pushed him back, crying: "Revenge for the South!" Next moment, Booth was hanging from the lip of the box. Dropping to the stage, he fell heavily and broke a leg, but staggered off, half running.

The puzzled audience and single on-stage actor watched him go. Then Mrs Lincoln unloosed a scream. The audience buzzed uneasily. Someone in the State box shouted: "He has shot the President!" Audience and actors milled about in confusion. Doctor Charles Leale forced a way into the box where Lincoln lay, unconscious. At first the wound eluded him. Then he found matted, bloody hair behind the head and saw that neither eye responded to the light. Leale knew then that the President would die.

silver pennies on his eyes, Stanton said "Now he belongs to the ages." Once more a murder had ennobled the victim and made his memory imperishable.

Meanwhile the hunt was on for Lincoln's killer and his henchmen. Despite his broken leg, Booth, with collaborator David Herold, galloped clear of Washington. Incognito, Booth had his leg attended by a Dr. Samuel Mudd. Booth's own diary then records a week of "being hunted like a dog through swamps, woods and . . . chased by gun-boats. . . ." On April 26 he was cornered and shot in a burning barn near Bowling Green, Virginia. Men dragged him from the flames before he died. Atzerodt, Powell, and Herold were all caught and hanged. So was Mary Surratt, the almost certainly innocent mother of another plotter. Other individuals involved – including the unlucky Dr. Mudd – got prison terms. As with the Kennedy assassination almost a century later, writers have argued that Lincoln's killer was a front man for a deep political conspiracy – a scheme to crush Lincoln's conciliatory plans for the South and throw it open to the North's big business exploiters. Some even hold that War Secretary Stanton was behind the

Lincoln was not the only victim of Booth's plot. Lewis Powell had bluffed his way into the house where William Seward lay recovering from a carriage accident. Powell stabbed or bludgeoned several people including Seward, then made off. But the Secretary of State survived. George Atzerodt, the third plotter, did not attack Andrew Johnson as planned. Instead he got disconsolately drunk and threw away his weapon.

Lincoln lingered on into the morning, and died at 7.22 am. A day before he had simply seemed a strong-willed, controversial president. But as a doctor laid

Above: the murder of Abraham Lincoln in the presidential box at Ford's Theater, Washington, April 14, 1865, from a contemporary print.

Left: John Wilkes Booth, an actor and a sympathizer of the Confederacy. He assassinated Lincoln at Ford's Theater during a performance of *Our American Cousin.*

Above: the last photograph of Abraham Lincoln.
Below: the unconscious Lincoln was taken to a house across the street from the Theater, where he died early next morning.

murder. Certainly he stood to gain politically. With Lincoln, Seward, and Andrew Johnson dead, he might in fact have ended up as President and virtual dictator of a Southern Empire. In many eyes, his crafty, scheming manner, and perfumed beard made him seem an ideal villain. Quite possibly, too, he knew of the impending plot yet took no useful action. John Surratt's room-mate had told the authorities of over-hearing incriminating talk at Mrs Surratt's rooming house. His warning may have worked its way up to Stanton. But although detectives supposedly watched the rooming house for weeks, none of the suspects was arrested.

Andrew Johnson's survival at first dimmed the Radical's hopes for new repressive laws against the South. Nonetheless Congress began to override the presidential veto, and Radicals subverted presidential power. New black governments established in the South became the stooges of salesmen and business-men who swarmed down from the North with appetites like locusts' to batten on the land.

Had Lincoln lived, corruption might not have gripped the South so cruelly. His forceful personality might have won Congressional support denied to Johnson. But in a nation where the chief of state cannot enforce his will against a hostile Congress, Lincoln too may have left office with his work largely frustrated and discredited. Instead he died a hero at his hour of victory.

Archduke Franz Ferdinand
1863-1914

As the royal car drew to a stop in Franz Josef Street on June 28, 1914, a young man in the small crowd that had gathered drew a revolver and fired twice. Inside the car the Archduke Franz Ferdinand of Austria and his wife slumped back in their seat. Within minutes they were dead. Two months later Europe was plunged into war.

Above: the Archduke Franz Ferdinand with his wife and their children. His children were excluded from succession to the throne because his wife was not of royal blood.
Right: Franz Ferdinand photographed in Bosnia, 1914.

Croatians, Slovenes, Bosnians, and Serbians. He toyed with the notion of granting them a parliament like Hungary's, thus making the Empire a three-state nation. At heart, though, he believed in the supremacy of the Austrian element represented by his own Hapsburg Dynasty. Franz Ferdinand came to detest the Hungarians and the Slavs. One story half seriously blames his hate for Hungarians on a rumor in one of their newspapers of his impending death in the mid 1890s, when he was gravely ill with tuberculosis. His loathing of the Empire's Balkan subjects dated from the early 1900s when nationalist unrest revealed just how much the southern Slavs detested the central government at Vienna. A cold reception awaited Franz Ferdinand when he visited Dubrovnik, near

Many people had reason to dislike Franz Ferdinand, the heir to the aging emperor of Austria-Hungary. The 50-year-old Archduke was a dour man with a biting tongue. He had the knack of making people in his presence feel uneasy. His unendearing appearance and manner did not commend themselves to those around him, either. He was paunchy and bull necked, with cold grey eyes, a ferociously bushy moustache and a mouth that seldom smiled. Occasionally he would break out in a rage that terrified his wife. Some people actually thought him mad.

He made enemies more readily than friends. Franz had already broken court etiquette by marrying a woman not of royal blood. But it was members of the creaking Empire's South Slav minority who most sincerely wished him dead.

At one time he looked almost liberally on the

the borders of the independent Serbian State. In 1906 a strike for better conditions by the deprived peasants and industrial workers of Bosnia-Hercegovina further alienated the heir-apparent from his future South Slavic subjects. Franz Ferdinand came to see the introduction of a democracy and the national expressions of minorities as the ruin of the Empire. He dropped plans for reform and was determined instead to impose centralized rule under himself in Vienna. In 1913 he became Inspector General of all the armed forces. Now he had the power to help him execute his program of repression.

Franz Ferdinand and the Hapsburg policies he represented earned the especial enmity of those Serbs within the Empire who dreamed of a federation with the independent South Slav nation of Serbia. By 1911 secret revolutionary societies of South Slavs collectively called Young Bosnians had been set up within the Empire. These had links with like-minded revolutionaries outside the Empire, such as Serbia's Black Hand group, dedicated to a union of all Serbs. The more sophisticated of the revolutionaries sought a broad-based revolution. Less sophisticated groups saw no further than the slaying of the leaders who oppressed them – and in particular Franz Ferdinand, the heir to the Hapsburg throne.

One of the revolutionaries, Gavrilo Princip, was a Serb from a West Bosnian family of poor peasant-serfs. Gavrilo grew up small, slightly built, and intelligent. When Austria-Hungary formally annexed Bosnia-Hercegovina in 1908 he became a determined revolutionary, and was dismissed from school for his activities. March 1914 found Princip across the border in the Serbian capital of Belgrade, where he learned that Franz Ferdinand planned in June to visit Sarajevo, the provincial capital of Bosnia.

At once the 19-year-old revolutionary began to plot the archduke's assassination. His friends Nedjelko Cabrinović and Grabez agreed to play a part. Another friend obtained six bombs and four revolvers, probably from "Apis" – the codename of Colonel Dragutin Dimitrijevic. (Apis was the leader of the Black Hand, former head of Serbian military intelligence, and the most formidable individual in Serbia.) A week's intensive revolver practice in a quiet Belgrade park made Princip a tolerable marksman.

Meanwhile Franz Ferdinand's intelligence service urged him not to go to Sarajevo as planned on the Feast of St. Vitus, which was the anniversary of two major Serbian battles, and a symbol of the Serbs' resurgence. The Archduke ignored all warnings. In a sense he *had* to go. By inspecting army maneuvers in Bosnia and visiting its capital, the heir to Austria-Hungary would be warning the war hawks in nearby Serbia not to meddle with imperial possessions. Also the trip allowed his much-snubbed wife Sophie, Duchess of Hohenberg, to appear with him in public. Above all he would assert his personal authority in a particularly fractious corner of the Empire. But he knew the risk, and only half in jest supposed that people would throw bombs at him.

By late June the Archduke and his would-be slayers had converged upon the killing ground. No hint of tragedy emerged on June 26, when Franz and Sophie drove in informally to visit the bazaar. Sarajevo's citizens crowded around the royal pair in greeting. Next evening at dinner, Sophie smilingly told a worried local dignitary that his fears had been unnecessary.

The official drive through Sarajevo began on Sunday morning, June 28 (St. Vitus' Day). It was already hot by 10 am when the six cars of the royal motorcade drove fairly quickly into town. The royal route to the Town Hall led down the Appel Quay, a street on an embankment above the Miljacka river. Spaced out along a 330-yard section of the crowd that lined this road, seven men were waiting with more than ordinary

interest. Besides Princip, Cabrinović, and Grabez, were three more killers and Danilo Ilić who had organized this second team in case the first one failed. By a stroke of luck jealousy between Sarajevo's chief of police and the provincial military governor meant that no police cordon separated the attackers from their prey.

At 10.10 am the Archduke, wearing a splendid uniform crowned by a feathered helmet, rode into view seated in the second open car. Beside him sat Sophie in white dress and gloves with a white parasol, and flowers in her belt.

The royal car rolled safety past the first two killers. Mehmed Mehmedbasić dithered, and Vaso Cubrilović

Above: three of the young Serbians who were enlisted by the Black Hand organization to murder the Archduke Franz Ferdinand of Austria and his wife. Left to right: Milan Ciganovic, Nedelko Cabrinović, and Gavrilo Princip.

held his fire from pity for the Duchess. Then Cabrinović hurled his grenade. It struck the hood of the royal car, rolled beneath the next, and exploded, wounding members of the royal escort and spectators. The fuse cap slightly grazed Sophie's neck. Cabrinović swallowed cyanide and leaped into the river, but vomited, and lived to be seized and beaten by police.

After halting to discover what had happened, the Archduke continued safely on his way. Popović, a schoolboy member of the gang, did nothing. Grabez could not bring himself to throw a bomb liable to injure people in the crowd. Princip failed to recognize the royal vehicle in time. The bid to kill Franz Ferdinand had flopped. Or so it seemed. But luck soon veered to favor his assassin.

At the Town Hall the mayor delivered his speech of welcome. Then Franz Ferdinand changed his schedule. Instead of going to the museum by way of Franz Josef Street as planned, he decided to visit his injured officers in the military hospital – a safe drive back along the Appel Quay, now cleared of crowds. At 11.15 the cars set off again. But through treachery or error, the first two cars turned into Franz Josef Street. The military governor shouted at the leading driver to stop and take the other road. Among the crowd watching from a corner was Princip, who had just stepped from a nearby coffeehouse. A mere three yards now separated Princip from his almost stationary quarry. The Serb drew his revolver. A policeman moved to jog his arm, but was deliberately jostled by a bystander.

Princip fired twice. His first shot struck the heir to Austria-Hungary in the chest. The second bullet

caught Sophie in the abdomen. Both remained sitting upright. Then their car jerked forward, and Sophie's inert body fell against her husband. Blood trickling from his mouth, he stammered "Sopherl, Sopherl, dont' die!" Count Franz Harrach, Franz's aide, asked him how badly he was hurt. "It's nothing," he replied, repeating it six times, in ever fainter tones.

A gipsy had once told Franz Ferdinand that his

Hungarian affair calling only for internal action. This came quickly. Danilo Ilić and two more conspirators were condemned to death. Princip – now just 20 – escaped that penalty because an error in the civil register had made him still officially 19, and by law too young to die. Instead he got 20 years' hard labor. But he was so badly beaten that he lost an arm, and in under two years tuberculosis had killed him.

Above: the bloodstained jacket worn by the Archduke Franz Ferdinand when he was assassinated by Gavrilo Princip (far left).

Left: Gavrilo Princip arrested by Bosnian police immediately after the murders of the Archduke and his wife.

Below: the trial after the murder of Franz Ferdinand. Princip is in the middle of the first row of the accused. The young assassins thought the murder would bring the union of Slav peoples closer. It did, but only after sparking off one of the bloodiest wars in history.

destiny would be "to unleash a world war." In death he now began to make her words come true.

News of the Archduke's assassination left the Austrian capital remarkably unruffled. Most Viennese had never seen the man, and his death spawned no succession crisis. The rival royal faction felt secretly delighted. Prince Albert Montenuovo, Grand Master of the Imperial Court, arranged a deliberately obscure funeral, and the 83-year-old Emperor Franz Josef sorrowed only for his newphew's orphaned children.

At first sight, the assassination was a purely Austro-

271

Meanwhile the assassination gained international dimensions. Within days of the murder came evidence of Serbian involvement. Interrogation of the conspirators revealed they had had help from a Serbian army major and an Austrian employee of the Serbian State Railways. Their weapons had originated in the Serbian army.

There was no proof of official Serbian involvement.

Archduke's assassination, and a crackdown on arms smuggling. Austria demanded to know how Serbia would fulfill all these demands, and insisted on an answer within 48 hours.

The Austrians felt confident that Serbia could not accept these terms, some of which meant surrender of national integrity. Yet Serbia's reply, delivered on July 25 just two minutes after the allotted deadline,

But Franz Josef told his ally Kaiser Wilhelm II of Germany of his determination to isolate and diminish Serbia as a threat to peace while "this hotbed of criminal agitation in Belgrade is allowed to exist unpunished." Proof of Serbia's innocence left the emperor unmoved. He had made up his mind to use the conspirators' Serbian links and Serbia's new strength and known hostility to Austria as a pretext to crush Serbia in war. Austrian territorial ambition was of course an underlying motive.

Franz Josef knew that such a war bore heavy risks. The Serbians had powerful friends in their fellow Slavs the Russians. War with Serbia might mean war with Russia too. Then Russia had potential allies in the United Kingdom, France, and Italy. Thus any move against Serbia would be unthinkable without the backing of Austria-Hungary's powerful ally Germany.

Wilhelm II assured the Austrian ambassador that Austria-Hungary could count on German aid, should Russia intervene. Austria then presented Serbia with an ultimatum demanding that Serbia suppress anti-Austrian propaganda, and dissolve the Black Hand and other groups that advocated the incorporation of the South Slavs into Serbia. It demanded that anti-Austrian officials be sacked, that Austrian police should be allowed into Serbia to crush subversion and help catch the remaining conspirators involved in the

Above: in the famous Unter den Linden in Berlin an officer reads an imperial proclamation declaring war on Russia, August 1, 1914.

Right: two transport trains meet with soldiers on their way to the front in the first days of the war. Once the "war machine" had been put into action, there was nothing anyone could do to stop it. After the euphoria of the first days of marching bands and the high hopes of an early victory, came the killing and the bloodshed and the misery of all-out war (far right).

proved remarkably accommodating. Only by refusing to let in Austro-Hungarian police and to dismiss officials on Austro-Hungarian instructions did it fall short of what the Austrians demanded.

But by now probably no answer would have slaked the thirst for war in Austria. The Austrian ambassador in Serbia had packed his bags before the note from Serbia arrived. He read it, snapped out a brief "Unsatisfactory!", and left at once for Vienna.

World leaders might still have stopped the drift to war. On July 27 Sir Edward Grey, the British Foreign Secretary, begged Germany to pull Austria-Hungary back from the brink. Through his chancellor, the kaiser passed Grey's message to Franz Josef. But the German chancellor deliberately watered down its content to remove the veiled threat of British intervention.

On July 28, Austria-Hungary declared war on Serbia, and war fever sent Vienna wild with joy. In last minute messages that crossed, the kaiser and the Russian czar appealed to each other to help stop the fighting.

But by then the war machines were on the move. On July 29 Austro-Hungarian troops bombarded Belgrade. Russia mobilized against Austria-Hungary. Austria-Hungary responded by mobilizing against Russia. By August 1 Germany had declared war on Russia, and, on August 3, on Russia's ally France, as well as Belgium. On August 4 the United Kingdom declared war on Germany. Next day, Austria-Hungary was formally at war with Russia, and on August 12 the United Kingdom declared war on Austria-Hungary. Soon, almost all Europe, and European colonies beyond the seas, were sucked into the holocaust.

World War I destroyed the Hapsburgs and forged Yugoslavia ("Land of the South Slavs"). Franz Ferdinand's death had brought about all that his assassin could have hoped for. But it did much more besides. It killed perhaps 10,000,000 people. It also created new nations with German national minorities. Their grievances later gave Nazi Germany pretexts for aggression that helped to pave the way for World War II.

Admiral Yamamoto
1884-1943

The Japanese naval leader Isoroku Yamamoto was not particularly well known outside his own country in the years leading up to 1941. Yet it was this man's surprise attack upon Pearl Harbor that brought the United States into World War II on December 7, 1941. Events on what President Franklin Delano Roosevelt called "a date that will live in infamy" earned Yamamoto the Americans' deep hatred. Revenge was one of

Above: Isoroku Yamamoto in 1934. As commander-in-chief of the Japanese combined fleet in 1941, Yamamoto planned the destruction of the United States navy at Pearl Harbor.

several motives behind an American plan for Yamamoto's assassination some 16 months later that was unique in military history.

Born in 1884 of Samurai descent, Yamamoto was destined for a warrior's career. In 1904 he graduated from the Japanese Naval Academy and next year fought aboard the battleship *Nisshin* at Tsushima. In this battle the young Japanese Navy smashed Russia's Baltic Fleet, bringing to an end the Russo-Japanese War and establishing Japan as a major naval power. Promotion followed promotion over the next 35 years,

then in 1940 he became an admiral, and in August 1941, commander-in-chief of the Japanese Combined Fleet.

By then Japan had been at war with China for four years, and in July had just seized French Indochina. That act triggered the events that led to Yamamoto's greatest triumph, and culminated in his death. First, the Americans, Dutch, and British reacted to Japan's invasion of a European power's colonial possession by freezing Japanese assets and launching a trade embargo. This blocked the flow of oil desperately needed by Japan for crushing China. To get essential oil the Japanese conceived a daring series of invasions. They would push south, seizing oil-rich Java and Sumatra in the Dutch East Indies, and at the same time overrun British-ruled Malaya, then the world's chief source of tin and rubber.

Only the United States Pacific Fleet seemed near enough and strong enough to wreck this daring scheme, which depended largely on seaborne landings. As Yamamoto put it, this United States' Fleet was potentially "a dagger pointed at the throat of Japan." He argued that unless that dagger's blade could be snapped or blunted any move against Malaya or the Dutch East Indies was liable to fail. He rejected an existing plan to draw the United States gradually into battle by attack upon the Philippines (then largely under American supervision). Instead, Yamamoto urged a sudden savage blow to paralyze the United States Pacific Fleet. Somewhat reluctantly, the Japanese Naval Staff agreed.

Yamamoto aimed to strike his blow at America's mid-Pacific naval base of Pearl Harbor on the Hawaiian island of Oahu. Trained intelligence officers working in the Japanese consulate at Honolulu had told him that the United States Pacific Fleet lay in port each Sunday, never fully manned. A moonless night and other weather conditions made early Sunday morning, December 7, particularly favorable for attack. To assure secrecy, the Japanese fleet took a roundabout route via the Kurile Islands northeast of Japan. The force included two battleships, three cruisers, nine destroyers, three submarines, and five midget submarines. But most of these ships were there chiefly to defend the six aircraft carriers. For Yamamoto had planned a sea-based air assault. The attackers were 135 dive bombers, 40 torpedo bombers, 104 conventional bombers, and 81 fighter planes.

At 7.55 am 145 bombers and 45 fighters launched from the carriers out of sight over the horizon swept south across Oahu and for 30 minutes pounded the unsuspecting battleships, cruisers, and destroyers at anchor in Pearl Harbor, as well as port installations, and island airfields. Fifteen minutes after this attack subsided 134 bombers and 36 fighters were launched in another attack. The combined devastation was dramatic. Three torpedoes split open the battleship *Oklahoma*, which turned turtle. Fighter planes then machine gunned crewmen who managed to leap overboard. A bomb plunged down the *Arizona's* smokestack, blasting her apart and killing 1000 sailors. The *California* and *West Virginia* also sank, and the *Maryland, Nevada, Pennsylvania*, and *Tennessee* were badly damaged. Besides this loss in battleships, three destroyers and four smaller craft foundered, and three light cruisers suffered heavy damage. One report lists 349 aircraft crippled and more than 4000 soldiers and civilians dead or injured. This carnage cost the Japanese a mere 29 aircraft and fewer than 100 lives. Only his failure to catch American aircraft carriers at anchor marred Yamamoto's triumph.

What horrified Americans, apart from the force of Yamamoto's blow, was the fact that it arrived before Japan had declared war on the United States. The Japanese had actually sent a cabled ultimatum to

Midway Island at the western end of the Hawaiian group, and to trap the Pacific Fleet's aircraft carriers between his Midway task force and a northern force attacking the Aleutian Islands. Unhappily for Yamamoto, United States Intelligence aided by IBM tabulators had cracked his naval code. As his ships bore down on Midway from the northwest, carrier-borne American aircraft fell upon them in a flank attack. The Battle of Midway cost Yamamoto 330 planes and all four of the big aircraft carriers he used for Pearl Harbor. The Americans lost only one carrier and 150 aircraft. The Japanese Navy never fully recovered from what Admiral Chester Nimitz later called this "victory for intelligence."

American code-breakers had delivered Yamamoto's first defeat. Soon they would take his life.

Right: Vice-Admiral Yamamoto in 1937 announcing what retaliatory plans the Japanese navy were taking against the Chinese for the shooting of a Japanese officer in charge of a landing party. Japanese aggression against China erupted into full scale war in 1937 as military leaders began to take over control of Japanese government.

reach Washington just before the attack, but a problem of decipherment delayed delivery until too late. In the months that followed, Americans had further reasons to hate Yamamoto. From December 1941 to June 1942 his ships swept from victory to victory. Yamamoto rightly believed that only rapid, swift assaults could keep America subdued while Japan tightened her stranglehold upon the Southeast Asian archipelago.

In June 1942 he struck again, this time at the rebuilt American Pacific Fleet. Yamamoto planned to seize

Even after Midway, the Japanese continued island-hopping across the southwest Pacific until they almost reached Australia. But by early 1943 their tide of victory was ebbing. The Allies were destroying their Solomon Islands garrisons and endangering the major Japanese base of Rabaul on New Britain Island, just east of New Guinea.

The Japanese were able to strike back with air attacks, however, and Yamamoto arrived at Rabaul to direct operations personally. He decided to inspect Japanese positions in the Solomon Islands, southeast

of New Britain. On 13 April his headquarters broadcast to the islands' Japanese garrisons. The coded message announced Yamamoto's scheduled visit five days later, specifying flight times and giving details of his aircraft and its fighter escorts.

Also listening in and deciphering this information was the Hawaii-based United States cryptanalytic unit FRUPAC (Fleet Radio Unit, Pacific Fleet). Washington's top brass was soon alerted and urgently debated what to do about this communications windfall. Should they seize a unique chance to ambush Yamamoto? Revenge for Pearl Harbor and elimination of Japan's ablest naval leader were compelling arguments in favor. Against, stood the moral stigma of assassination – albeit in a brutal war – and fear that the Japanese would guess – and mend – their breach in code security. Washington optimistically decided that the Japanese would blame the ambush on information leaked by local spies. They felt that the psychological victory of killing Yamamoto mattered more than any moral qualms about how they did it. The plot was on.

Early on April 18, Admiral Isoroku Yamamoto stepped abroad his aircraft as punctual as ever. He wore full formal uniform complete with ceremonial samurai sword. At 6 am his aircraft left Rabaul and headed southeast, aiming to arrive in southern Bougainville, about 330 miles away at 8 am.

Thirty-five minutes before Yamamoto left Rabaul, 18 American Lightning aircraft took off from Guadalcanal Island 700 miles on the other side of Bougainville. Skimming the waves to hide from Japanese radar, they flew to intercept the admiral. The chance of finding him seemed slim to Captain Thomas Lanphier, of the US Army Air Force leading the

Above right and left: the destruction of the United States Pacific Fleet at Pearl Harbor December 7, 1941. The horror of the attack was made worse because the Japanese had not at that time officially declared war on the United States. American revenge came next year when code-breakers uncovered Japanese plans to attack Midway Island. The attack was repulsed with heavy losses to the Japanese including 300 planes, all four aircraft carriers used in the Pearl Harbor attack and the heavy cruiser *Mogami* (below).

assassination mission. Surveying the vastness of the ocean he felt doubtful that a prediction based upon intelligence could bring both sets of planes together at a precise time and place.

Yet this is just what happened. Above the Shortland Islands just off southern Bougainville the Japanese pack of aircraft came in view. The Lightnings set upon the escort fighters. Lanphier himself chased the Mitsubishi bomber containing Yamamoto.

"I fired a long steady burst across the bomber's course of flight from approximately right angles. The bomber's right engine, then its right wing, burst into flame. . . . As I moved into range of Yamamoto's bomber and its cannon, the bomber's wing tore off. The bomber plunged into the jungle."

All but one of the American attackers flew safely back to base. Yamamoto, too, had come down almost at his destination. But he was dead, his body still sitting in its seat, the chin resting on the samurai sword. Men carefully removed and cremated Yamamoto's corpse, and the Japanese deeply mourned his loss. Admiral Koga, his less formidable successor, justly said: "There was only one Yamamoto, and no one is able to replace him." With Yamamoto's death the Americans indeed avenged Pearl Harbor and struck a blow at Japanese morale. By gunning down this able leader they may have even helped speed up their final victory.

John F. Kennedy
1917-1963

In 1960 there were two men powerful enough to keep the world at peace or push it into war. One was the premier of the Soviet Union, Nikita Krushchev. The other was the newly elected Democratic President of the United States, John Fitzgerald Kennedy. At 43, Kennedy was the youngest-ever candidate to be elected president and few people doubted that he would complete his four-year term as vigorously as he had campaigned for it. But superstition cast a cloud: all six presidents elected at 20-year intervals since 1840 had died in office – three of them assassinated. "That's one jinx I'll break," laughed Mr Kennedy. He failed – and perished in what the American press called the crime of the century.

"Jack" Kennedy emerged as a golden boy of US politics. He was a member of a large, rich, and powerful family of largely Irish origin. His father, Joseph Kennedy, had been US ambassador in London and Jack too, was groomed for a major role in politics. People liked his tall, well-built figure; his strong, open boyish face; and charming, honest manner. They admired his young and beautiful wife, Jacqueline, or "Jackie", and their attractive children.

People knew that Jack had won awards for wartime bravery. But what largely lifted him to power was his

Above left: John Fitzgerald Kennedy campaigning for the presidency in 1960.
Below: the inauguration of Kennedy as 35th President of the United States.
Right: opposition to the "New Frontier" program, and a series of crisis in foreign affairs brought heavy responsibilities and cares to the new president.

"New Frontier" program to reduce poverty and racial discrimination, and to gain ground in the Cold War with Communist Russia.

Yet despite his personal appeal, Kennedy became president by one of the slimmest majorities in US history. Many Americans distrusted his relative youth, wealth, inexperience in foreign affairs, or else his Catholic religion. So from his first day in office he already had his enemies. He soon made more. Big business disliked much of his reformist legislation. Others reviled his efforts to improve the position of the blacks. Black Power movement itself condemned these efforts as inadequate. Communists blamed him for the Bay of Pigs fiasco of 1961, when Fidel Castro's left-wing Cuba crushed an invasion supported by the CIA (Central Intelligence Agency) of the United States. In 1962 Kennedy's brinkmanship scared people of all persuasions when he risked world war to force the USSR to remove Cuban-based strategic missiles threatening the USA. Then, as relations with the Soviets improved, extreme right-wing politicians and their supporters vilified him as a communist sympathizer.

There was, and is, always someone ready to attempt to kill the president. No fewer than 870 cranks wrote to threaten Kennedy in his first presidential year. To keep such enemies at bay, 170 uniformed police guarded all White House entrances, X-rayed incoming parcels, dunked those that ticked, and destroyed confectionary gifts untasted. About three dozen special agents acted as the president's bodyguard on all journeys. Some even supervised the preparation of his food.

The President's security men faced a special problem in November 1963, when he planned to visit Texas – a state notorious for sudden deaths. Its Democrats were deeply split between liberals, conservatives, and ultra-rightists. John Kennedy believed a personal visit would help heal divisions and secure the Lone Star State's electoral votes – a quota crucial to his reelection in 1964. San Antonio, Houston, Fort Worth, Dallas, and Austin were cities that he planned to see in a crowded two-day airborne tour.

Few doubted that the trip was dangerous. Death threats flowed in before the President started – four of them to Houston alone. Hostile advance publicity appeared in Dallas – a city of a million inhabitants, a hotbed of extremist factions, and a bastion against Catholicism. At that time, the annual murder rate exceeded that for the whole of Britain, and people could buy guns as easily as bread.

Of a former President, the head of the Federal Bureau of Investigation had once said: "If anyone really took it into his head to shoot the President, I guess there's not a lot we could really do about it." The Kennedy bodyguard perhaps uneasily recalled these words as the Texas trip began.

But the first day's visits to San Antonio and Houston in southern Texas went well. The Kennedys flew on to spend that night at Fort Worth in the northeast. Next morning they were to drive through nearby Dallas.

It was raining at 7.30 am on November 22 when the President was wakened. Since Dallas was a mere 13-minute air-hop from Fort Worth, the weather there was almost certain to be wet as well. If so, a plexiglass bubble top would be added to the open presidential limousine, keeping out the rain – and, incidentally,

ings commanded such a double view of the procession.

As the time for the presidential motorcade drew near, Oswald's co-workers gathered on the fifth floor to watch. On the floor above, he put his gun together and loaded it.

Air Force One had touched down at Love Field, Dallas, at 11.38. Airport rooftops bristled with police, and a fence penned back spectators. Security officials took few chances, although the crowd seemed largely friendly. One batch of school truants waved the slogan *"We love Jack."* But another group came to hiss. More dissidents brandished placards voicing such sentiments as the mis-spelt *"Your a traitor."*

deflecting any missiles hurled by demonstrators as the presidential motorcade passed through the city.

After breakfast the presidential aircraft, *Air Force One,* took the Kennedys on to Dallas. In flight, Kennedy rehearsed the luncheon speech he would deliver at the Dallas Trade Mart – its themes: peace, equal rights, and social justice.

Meanwhile a 24-year-old filing clerk had been getting ready too. Lee Harvey Oswald rose early at the Dallas house where he had spent the night. He took a dismantled high-powered rifle with telescopic sight and a clip of four bullets and hid them in a brown paper sheath. Then an unsuspecting colleague drove him to their workplace. It had stopped raining in Dallas by 8 am when Oswald reached the Texas School Book Depository. Somewhere there he hid his weapon. Near noon, workers left the upper floors to take their lunch break. Oswald ascended quickly to the sixth floor, where stored cartons lay heaped along one side while another section was refloored. Oswald rearranged cartons to build a sniper's nest in the southeast corner of the building. This nest would hide him from the rear, but give a bird's-eye window view of the President's car as it approached up one street, then turned left sharply down another, past the book depository. Apart from Dallas Jail, few other build-

Undeterred, Jack Kennedy touched fingers with the enthusiastic horde behind the fence. Then a secret serviceman ushered him aboard the presidential car. The big blue Lincoln convertible had no bubble top. The weather now was hot and sunny.

At 11.55 the motorcade and its police escort of motorcycle outriders moved off. The first car contained police and security officials. Then came three motorcycle escorts. Five lengths back lay the Presidential car. A secret serviceman sat in front beside the chauffeur. Behind them were two jump seats occupied by John B. Connally, Governor of Texas, and his wife Nellie. The President and Mrs Kennedy rode in the rear. Four motorcyclists flanked the back of the President's car. Behind it drove a convertible bulging with 10 security agents, two standing on the running boards. Following two and a half lengths behind, Lyndon B. Johnson and his wife traveled in the Vice-President's car. Then came a hardtop with more agents. Other vehicles held politicians, journalists, and photographers.

The motorcade headed south toward the heart of Dallas and to his agents' discomfort the President twice stopped the convoy, once to shake hands with a line of children, once to greet a group of nuns.

The crowds were sparse at first, but thickened as

the cars approached the city center. The sidewalks were 12 deep in people while hordes of secretaries leaned enthusiastically from windows. The crowd surged out into the street, forcing Kennedy's chauffeur to drive almost at walking pace. One of the agents leaped from the next car's running board to shield the President's wife with his body, a maneuver he was soon repeating often.

At 12.21 the motorcade reached Dallas City Jail and turned right into Main Street. It was gay with bunting and Christmas decorations, and clamorous with cheering. Supposedly unfriendly Dallas was giving the President one of the warmest welcomes of the tour.

bullet tore off the right rear part of his skull, spattering his car with blood and blue-gray bits of brain. Jacqueline turned, saw Jack's dazed expression, and watched him raise his hand toward his forehead. Then he fell into her lap as she cried out "Oh, my God, they have shot my husband!" A third shot flew wide.

A bodyguard scrambled up onto the back of the Lincoln, pulled Mrs Kennedy down into her seat and lay on its back, shielding her from any further bullets with his body. Then the car accelerated, leaving wild confusion behind.

At the Parkland Memorial Hospital doctors did what they could. They dripped blood and saline fluid

Left: a sequence of pictures taken as President Kennedy is struck by an assassin's bullets while riding in a motorcade through Dallas, Texas. The first bullet struck the president in the back of the neck and plunged on to wound the Governor of Texas, also in the car, in the chest and wrist. The second tore into the President's head, a third shot flew wide. John Kennedy slumped unconscious and died in the hospital next morning.

After Main Street, the lead cars passed into the greenery of Dealey Plaza and began to skirt it in zigzag turns: right into Houston Street, then left down Elm Street before heading toward the Trade Mart. As the President's car turned into Houston, continuing applause led Nellie Connally to remark: "You surely can't say Dallas doesn't love you, Mr President." "No, you can't," he answered. His car made the difficult 120-degree turn left into Elm Street, and passed the book depository's tan brick front at a slow 11 miles an hour. It was now 12.30. Glancing up, the chauffeur uneasily glimpsed workmen on the railroad overpass ahead. Security had required this to be cleared. But the real danger lay behind.

As the President raised his hand to wave, several sharp cracking sounds came in quick succession. Some people heard two, others three. Some thought they were firecrackers, or backfiring motorcycles. Others recognized rifle fire.

The first 6.5 millimeter bullet struck the back of John Kennedy's neck, punched through his windpipe, and plunged on through Governor Connally, breaking ribs, puncturing a lung, smashing his left wrist and stopping in his left thigh. Connally was momentarily unaware of what had happened. But Kennedy grabbed at his own throat and gasped. Seconds later, the next

into the President's emptying veins, and gave oxygen through a slit cut in his windpipe below the wound that blocked his breathing. But his brain had been irreparably shattered. For a while an occasional breath and heartbeat gave signs of life. Then both stopped. Heart massage yielded no response. At 1 pm the hospital's chief neurosurgeon officially declared John Fitzgerald Kennedy dead.

The world received the news in shock. US forces went on the alert around the globe. Wall Street panic selling slashed share values. Theaters closed in Broadway. The UN General Assembly was adjourned. Even Russian television shut down as a sign of respect.

Meanwhile, in Dallas, police were tracking the assassin. Oswald had escaped from the depository, but left his rifle and ammunition clip behind. Soon patrolmen had his radioed description. At 1.15 pm a police officer stopped his patrol car to accost a suspect. The man whipped out a .38 caliber revolver and shot him dead. Someone saw the killer dart into a cinema. Police moved in. This time Oswald's revolver misfired. He was seized and charged with double murder.

Oswald never lived to stand trial. Two days after Kennedy's assassination, detectives took Oswald to a basement garage to transfer him from police court to county jail. Among the watching crowd stood a

52-year-old stripclub operator named Jack Ruby. As Oswald approached, Ruby produced a revolver and killed him, leaving unexplained Oswald's role and motive in the President's assassination.

Public disquiet and puzzlement followed Kennedy's and Oswald's deaths. The new President, Lyndon B. Johnson, accordingly set up a commission to investigate his predecessor's murder. Chief Justice Earl Warren headed the inquiry. Nine months, 25,000 FBI interviews, and 26 volumes of evidence later, the Warren Report concluded that Oswald was the sole assassin.

But rumors persisted that he had had accomplices, and that Oswald's murder and the commission's find-

Above: John Kennedy's funeral procession entering Arlington National Cemetery. Leaders from all over the world came to honor him for his integrity, courage, and his forward-looking domestic and foreign programs.

Left: members of the president's family at the funeral. Left and right are the president's brothers Edward and Robert and between them the president's widow Mrs. Jacqueline Kennedy.

Right: assassin assassinated. Lee Harvey Oswald, alleged killer of President Kennedy was himself shot by a Dallas night-club owner as he was being transferred from the city jail to the county jail.

ings were a cover-up. Right-wing political opponents, the Mafia, the CIA, the Russians, and others have all been variously cited as powers that had been using Oswald as a pawn. Late into the 1970s newshounds were still digging up evidence suppressed or missed in the original inquiry. Some of it suggested that the FBI had stifled facts betraying its laxness in not guarding the President against a known communist and former defector. Nonetheless proof still points to Oswald as the only murderer.

The picture so far pieced together is that Oswald was a withdrawn, lonely, hostile individual with communist sympathies dating from the age of 15 when he read Karl Marx's *Das Kapital*. He entered the Marine Corps and became a sharpshooter and a qualified radar technician. He was later posted to a US airfield in Japan. From there U2 aircraft took off on high level spying missions over communist terrain – flights the Russians dearly sought to learn about.

Oswald later defected to Moscow, offering to pass on military secrets. He was reportedly refused Soviet citizenship, but allowed to wed a Russian girl. Both returned to the United States after two and a half years. Oswald then drifted in and out of modest jobs. His marriage crumbled. In New Orleans he got involved with pro- and anti-Castro Cuban communists; in Mexico, with Soviet intelligence; in Dallas, with White Russians. He clearly played some kind of double game whose cloudy purpose is still a subject for lively debate.

Any notion that Oswald killed Kennedy on Russian orders seems absurd. His death left the American machinery of government intact. President Johnson continued pushing through reforms that Kennedy had started. Under Johnson, the major change in US policy was deepening involvement in wars against the Indochinese communists. In the long term, this indeed weakened and discredited the US government. But John F. Kennedy's assassin could not have guessed that outcome.

Political Assassination
The Two-edged Sword

Less than five years after President Kennedy's death, assassins killed his brother Senator Robert Kennedy, and the Negro civil rights leader Martin Luther King. It was enough to make the London *Times* newspaper view gloomily the "prospect of a return to political assassination as a resort for the political extremist." If this view suggested that until then would-be assassins had been meekly sheathing knives and holstering their guns, it was not so. But the killing of three major figures in the leading Western nation brought home to millions who had never pondered it the risk endured by men in public life. And, in a sense,

the *Times* proved right. By the late 1970s numbers of political and nationalist assassinations had soared high enough for journalists to talk of a new age of the assassin.

New sects appeared and were prepared to kill to press aims that differed little from those of past extremists. But some of the methods they used were different. Features of the new wave of assassinations included international cooperation between left-wing and nationalist terrorist groups from different countries and the use of kidnap and hijack and the threatened death of hostages used as a lever to extort release of terrorists already jailed.

Many killings had a nationalist basis, as in Canada in 1970 when Quebec separatists kidnaped and killed Quebec's labor minister Pierre Laporte.

Inside Europe three nationalist groups – Basques, Irish, and South Moluccans – repeatedly made news with terrorist acts in which assassination played a part. In northern Spain, Basque-speaking Spaniards

who want a separate Basque nation repeatedly gunned down police and officials. In 1973 they tunneled under a Madrid street, and with a bomb blew up the Spanish premier as his car passed overhead.

In 1975 South Moluccans exiled in the Netherlands seized a passenger train at Beilen and killed three hostages. Their aim was to force the Dutch government into pressurizing the Indonesian government to grant autonomy to the South Moluccan group of islands. This incident proved the first of several in which South Moluccans took Dutch hostages by seizing trains and public buildings.

By far the largest list of nationalist assassinations in Europe built up during and after the late 1960s in Northern Ireland – a United Kingdom province whose Catholic minority had long considered themselves oppressed. By 1976 1000 civilians had perished in six years. British troops sent in to maintain order were also ambushed and shot. In the Irish Republic, bombers ambushed and killed the British ambassador.

In Israel and elsewhere, Palestinian Arabs displaced by the Jewish state created in 1948 have often used assassination as a tool to publicize their cause. It was an Arab's bullet that killed Senator Robert Kennedy – some believe for the Senator's friendly attitude to Israel.

Murder became an everyday occurrence in the political life of countries around the world. Killings by left- and right-wing extremists reached savage proportions in Latin America. In 1970 alone terrorists assassinated Argentina's former President Pedro Aramburu and the West German ambassador to Guatemala – where 8000 assassinations had happened in a five-year reign of terror. By 1974 on average one person was dying daily in Argentina.

In Europe, the Mediterranean area was a frequent area of politically motivated murders, continuing a centuries old tradition. By the late 1970s Italy's Red Brigades had won worldwide notoriety by gunning down judges, journalists, prison guards, ex-premier

Above: German police change the tire of their armored vehicle which had been punctured by a bullet in a siege of members of the Baader-Meinhof gang of terrorists.

Left: the burned-out remains of an Israeli bus taken over by 11 Palestinian terrorists. There were 41 deaths, including 9 of the terrorists, and 72 injured. It was the most tragic raid by Palestinians since Israel became a nation.

Aldo Moro, and other representatives of the establishment. Police blamed this left-wing group for most political terrorism in Italy, which, in 1978 reached a record average of six outrages a day.

But central and northern Europe had its share of killings, too. This time the major group responsible was a largely middle-class but left-wing band of Germans, known as the Baader-Meinhof gang from the names of two gang leaders. In 1977 the West German public prosecutor and a leading businessman, Hans Martin Schleier, were among the Baader-Meinhof's victims. Both in Italy and Germany assassination was designed to force government to take repressive measures, in turn provoking revolutions that would smash capitalism and reconstruct society.

Combating assassination in a modern urban setting poses huge problems for police. Killers can quickly vanish in a city as vast as Rome, New York, or London; and fast transport provided by cars, buses, trains, and aircraft means they can be far away in hours. In Italy, rivalry between three separate bodies of police has added to the problem.

Where leading personalities go in daily fear of death or kidnap many of the prominent and wealthy are forced to live in a security cocoon. Highly paid and trained bodyguards attend their homes, which are defended like some medieval baron's fortress. Chauffeurs versed in evasive driving bear their employers to appointments by unpredictable routes, at varying times and in cars built with special safety wheels, their floors reinforced against grenades, and surrounded by an armored shell, pierced by windows of bullet-proof laminated glass. But no protection can assure survival: five police guards died when the Red Brigades snatched Aldo Moro in the heart of Rome.

Assassins, it seems, are still today slaughtering their intended victims. Yet does assassination really work? It was shown that Caesar's killing brought about the opposite result of what his murderers intended. William the Silent's death did not win back the Dutch to Spanish rule. Lincoln's killing to avenge the South removed perhaps the South's best friend.

Right: the driver of Aldo Moro's car lies dead after the former Italian prime minister had been kidnaped. Five police guards also died in the attack by Red Brigade terrorists in the heart of Rome. The terrorists demanded the release of jailed members of their gang in return for Aldo Moro. When the government refused to interfere with the processes of law, the terrorists killed the former premier.

Below: members of the Turkish Popular Front manufacturing Molotov Cocktails. Chaos, murder, terrorism, are the methods used at the political extremes to have their grievances dealt with, or to force their minority political views onto those they cannot persuade by other methods.

Kennedy's assassination achieved no major change in US policy. True, Franz Ferdinand's assassination did indirectly, and with the massive bloodshed of a world war, free the South Slavs to unite into what is now Yugoslavia. Yamamoto's ambush was at least a propaganda victory.

But four in six of these assassinations did not accomplish what their perpetrators hoped for. Today there seems no sign that things have changed. Killing one leader does not destroy the ideas that he stood for. Rather it turns him into something of a hero and hardens the resolve of his successors to carry out his policies. Only if assassination triggers war or broad-based revolution is it likely to achieve its object.

This may well happen increasingly in future. Pessimists predict rising discontent as national prosperity everywhere is hit by dwindling supplies of fossil fuel. In such an atmosphere, assassination of leading politicians could intensify. But if – as dooms-day prophets hold – fuel shortage leads irreversibly to global poverty and famine, assassination as a means of overthrowing governments would solve – and set – no problems. Everyone would be too busy dying of disease and hunger to care who kills which powerless premier or president.

Whether or not this dismal prophesy comes true, the assassins' sects of yesterday and today will no doubt be forgotten and others' names will feature in the news.

Whoever the individual killer and his victim are, it may be argued that both represent a timeless pattern of antagonists. All leaders in any age are auto-matically candidates for an assassin's knife or bullet –

some as scapegoats, some as human sacrifices, some as father figures, or as combinations of all three.

One theory has it that as human sacrifice, assassi-nated leaders die in an old, almost universal tradition. Many peoples once chose a priest king for a year. The year up, the people killed their king, and put another in his place. Thus by imitative magic they thought that they assured the rebirth of the dying sun and of the seasons on which their crops and therefore food depended. Viewed in this light assassins of great men like Lincoln may be seen as "self-appointed priests of the people," killing off last year's priest king to make way for the next. But killing an individual invested with authority also carries Freudian overtones. For, in a sense, leaders are father figures whose authority we subconsciously wish to overthrow in order to assume their own positions for ourselves.

Because our criminal laws forbid the taking of another's life it follows that assassination can never really be justified. Many people are prepared to make an exception in the case of tyrannicide, however. Even respected philosphers have argued for it. The great 13th-century Italian theologian Saint Thomas Aquinas believed that natural law gave individuals the right to kill a tyrant for the good of the community. The 17th-century English philosopher John Locke saw the tyrant as a man at war with those he ruled, and his killing could be looked upon as an honorable military act. But in many cases, one man's tyrant is another's hero. Then, too, his death may have un-wanted repercussions. Lastly, once men start voting leaders out of office with the gun how shall we know who shoots for the majority?

Chapter 13

Scientific Disasters

Since the Industrial Revolution man has used his ingenuity and his technology to improve enormously his standard of life. He has also succeeded in overcoming to a greater or lesser extent some of the perils that have dogged him in the past. Disease, starvation, flood, drought; all these have to some extent been overcome. Prediction of earthquake and storm, cities less vulnerable to disastrous fire – these too he has achieved. But colossal strides in science and industrial technology have brought with them a whole new range of catastrophe and crisis. Pollution of land, sea, and air; frightful long-term effects of insufficiently tested medicines; ecological crises caused by the indiscriminate use of certain pesticides; poisonous industrial discharge on a massive scale; horrifying chemical explosions; alarming levels of radiation – these are a few of the new problems that technology poses.

Opposite: the Rio Tinto in south-western Spain has always been stained with salts of copper, which is widely deposited in the area. Since large-scale extraction and processing of the ores, however, the river has become appallingly contaminated and now supports no life at all. Must pollution always be the inevitable price man must pay for industrial growth and a high standard of living?

The Meaning of Pollution
A Worldwide Crisis

What exactly do we mean by pollution? In the United States alone road traffic emits a staggering 66,000,000 tons of poisonous carbon monoxide into the atmosphere every year. Experts estimate that as much as 10,000,000 tons of oil annually is spilt into the world's oceans through accident, carelessness, or sheer irresponsibility. Powerful pesticides frequently threaten to upset the entire balance of life on our planet. Chemical and other effluent has killed off much of the wildlife in North America's Great Lakes and the Mediterranean Sea. Seamen report that not a single stretch of the world's oceans, however remote, is free from garbage.

Until the Industrial Revolution, man was not equipped to do much in the way of conquering his natural environment. At most he did no more than scratch the surface of the earth. Technology and a soaring world population together have changed that vital balance between man's demands and the earth's resources. But not only does man take more from the earth than he replaces. Much of what is taken is misused and the wastes allowed to contaminate the air, the waters, and the soil. Pollution has created one of the most serious long-term crises of modern times. It is a problem that is only just being recognized, let alone solved. This artist's impression illustrates 13 major ways in which industrial and other pollution is wrecking our natural environment, from mountain top to ocean bed. Listed opposite, they represent the full range of what pollution really means.

1 The use by farmers and foresters of persistent pesticides, defoliants, and herbicides, which have damaging long-term effects upon wildlife.

2 Agricultural methods that reduce genetic variety, destroy wilderness, deplete soil structure, pollute with inorganic fertilizers, pesticides, and herbicides, all of which makes for an unstable ecosystem.

3 The construction of vast highway systems that encourage the wasteful and polluting use of the automobile, consume resources, increase water runoff and so deplete groundwater.

4 The construction of sprawling suburban communities that consume land, deplete city revenues, and add to air pollution with small, inefficient heating systems.

5 Vast city garbage tips that sterilize land, pollute whole neighborhoods, and often conceal illegally dumped toxic wastes.

6 Sewage effluent, treated or untreated, that over-enriches waterways, upsets the plant-animal balance, and squanders a valuable resource.

7 Industrial effluents that load the environment with persistent poisons and industrial waste heat that threatens many river ecosystems.

8 Cities that combine the kind of damage done by suburbs and highways.

9 Inefficient and incomplete burning of fossil fuels that raises the concentration of atmospheric pollution to dangerous levels.

10 Spillage from tankers, refueling ships, and offshore drilling operations accounting for some 10,000,000 tons of oil pollution every year.

11, 12 The building and use of aircraft that fill the upper atmosphere with particles from inefficiently burned fuels and also impoverish the lives of millions with their noise.

13 The dumping of chemical and other wastes at sea, which pollute the water and threaten to destroy the plankton on which all the earth's life depends.

The Indiscriminate Killer

A traveler making his way about the beautiful Mediterranean island of Sardinia will frequently see cryptic inscriptions scrawled on the walls of older houses: "DDT 1944." These are reminders of a massive United States Army program at the end of World War II to clear the island of malarial mosquitoes. DDT stands for dichloro-diphenyl-trichlorethane, a chemical compound that was first used as a pesticide in 1939. It works by penetrating the insect's skin and slowly bringing about paralysis and death. The US Army program was a great success. Today Sardinia is at long last free of the malaria-carrying mosquito and has a flourishing tourist industry and a new prosperity.

Sardinia was not the only part of the world to benefit from the new wonder pesticide. Similar US Army programs were carried out in the islands of the South Pacific. Since that time DDT had been used to wipe out disease-carrying insects throughout the world. As recently as 1955 the World Health Organization (WHO) tackled the problem in several South American states. Experts calculate that DDT may well have saved as many as 10,000,000 lives. Later the same compound was used in dust or powder form to control agricultural pests. Cheap to make and easy to apply, it was used on a massive scale. Something like 500,000 tons had been distributed on the earth's surface by 1969. It seemed that man had found a magnificent new weapon in his fight against disease and famine.

But the new weapon turned out to be two-edged.

Left: rats killed in the kitchen of an Indian house are sprayed with insecticide to destroy possible plague-carrying fleas on their bodies.

Above right: spraying DDT onto a makeshift building in northwest Argentina. It was part of the World Health Organization's program to eradicate malaria from South America.

Below right: analysts in a British Nature Conservancy Experimental Station carry out a postmortem examination on a barn owl. Tests showed that there were large amounts of DDT and other poisons, probably from treated grain, which was eaten by mice – later themselves to be eaten by the owl.

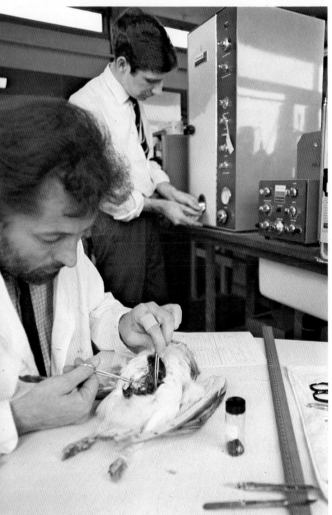

The problem is that DDT is a *persistent* poison – that is, it retains its poisonous character over a long period, in some cases several years. In addition, it is *cumulative* in its effect. This means that if a bird, say, eats insects containing small amounts of the chemical, those small amounts will not pass through the bird's system, but will build up in its fatty tissue until it reaches a fatal level. In 1954 Michigan State University sprayed elms with DDT to kill the elm bark beetles that bring Dutch elm disease. The spray certainly killed the beetles, but it also succeeded in wiping out the robins. The robins had eaten earthworms that had eaten leaves covered in DDT and the cumulative effect of the poison had killed the robins. This is a classic case of what experts call "biological magnification," meaning that the poison has an increasingly deadly effect as it works its way up the food chain. This cumulative effect of powerful organic chlorine pesticides such as DDT makes them hazardous not only to pests but to all animals that are part of the food chain, including man.

As far as man is concerned, the most frightening fact to emerge in the late 1960s was the discovery by scientists at the Miami School of Medicine that there was a correlation between high levels of DDT and deaths due to cancer, leukemia, and high blood pressure. According to the British author Lynette Hamblin, it was also noticed in several countries that breast-fed babies were receiving heavy doses of DDT. In parts of the United States human milk was found to contain as much as six times the permitted maximum dosage, while in Australia human milk often contained 30 times as much. But it was the discovery that herrings caught in the Baltic Sea contained high amounts of various chemicals that led to the Swedish government ordering a two-year ban on DDT in March 1969. The same year a number of other governments took heed of the scientists' warnings and imposed complete or partial bans. By 1970 such bans or restrictions were announced by the United States, Canada, Britain, Sweden, Denmark, Norway, Australia, New Zealand, and Japan.

Since World War II DDT has saved millions of lives, particularly in the underdeveloped countries. It has also eliminated numerous pests from the fields and orchards of the world. Malaria has never threatened people in the developed countries, and experts have already found safer pesticides to replace DDT. The threat to animal and human life was real enough. But thanks to Rachel Carson and her book *Silent Spring*, published in 1962, which drew public attention to the serious side effects of DDT, and thanks to the prompt action by governments, a long-term ecological disaster was averted. All the same, it is not really surprising if the undernourished peasant in Africa or Asia is indifferent to the fact that a miracle of modern science wipes out a few species of wildlife and poses a long-term threat to human health. After all, to him it simply means saving himself and his family from death by disease or malnutrition.

Pollution at Sea

Above: the supertanker *Amoco Cadiz* aground on rocks off the coast of Brittany, France in March 1978.
Opposite: attempting to clean up the mess along the shores of Brittany. The livelihood of thousands of people with a huge investment in tourism, agriculture, and fisheries, was put in jeopardy by the pollution.

At about 9.45 am on March 16, 1978 the 230,000-ton supertanker *Amoco Cadiz*, bound for Rotterdam from the Persian Gulf with a full cargo of crude oil, ran into trouble. The weather, already rough, was rapidly deteriorating, with strong southwest winds and heavy seas. The coast of France was about seven miles off the starboard bow. It was then that his crew informed Captain Pasquale Bardari that the giant ship's rudder was not responding – that he was in charge of a ship that was out of control. He immediately put out a warning by radio to all shipping in the area that the *Amoco Cadiz* was out of control and also telephoned the ship's owners in Chicago to obtain instructions as to how to handle the crisis. Their instructions were to call a tug or tugs at whatever the cost and make for a port on the southwest coast of England to dispose of part of his cargo.

The captain continued to send out warning signals to other shipping. At about midday the German tug *Pacific* came alongside the now helpless *Amoco Cadiz*.

By 4 pm the Amoco headquarters in Chicago had accepted a salvage contract with the tug's owners, Bugsier, and attempts began to put a line on board. All attempts failed however, and the *Pacific* finally withdrew from the rescue operation with night fast approaching. According to French reports, at 11.18 pm that evening the captain called on the French coastal authorities at Brest for assistance. But by then it was too late. The vast ship, with its lethal cargo, was already firmly aground off the French coast. The world's worst oil tanker disaster had hit the coast of Brittany.

The majority of the 220,000 tons of crude oil was washed up on the French coast, wrecking the livelihood of hundreds of Breton fishermen and the prosperity of an area that depends largely upon the tourist trade for its income. A month later thousands of volunteer workers were still clearing up the sticky black mess. The French premier, Raymond Barre, described the disaster as a national catastrophe. And indeed it is the scale of the catastrophe that is so frightening. The world's worst single man-made environmental disaster resulted from the wreck of just one great vessel. And the irony is that over 10 years earlier another supertanker went aground off the southwest coast of England, contaminating hundreds of miles of beach in Britain and France, destroying untold quantities of marine life, but teaching governments, oil companies, and other parties involved little apparently about how such crises should be handled.

The *Torrey Canyon* ran aground on rocks off the coast of Cornwall in southwest England on March 18, 1967. During the next few days approximately 100,000 tons of its 120,000-ton cargo of crude oil poured out into the sea. A huge slick 35 miles long and 15 miles wide threatened to destroy marine and wildlife on a then unprecedented scale. In fact 8000 oil-covered birds were thrown up on the Cornish coast alone and estimates suggest that as many as 50,000 sea birds died in all. It took at least three years for the fish population of this important fishing region to recover from the disaster. The affair was treated as a national emergency. Frantic efforts were made to find ways of cleaning up the mess. One way used in Britain was to treat the oil slick with detergent, but a report on the disaster published in 1968 showed that it was not after all the oil that caused the greatest destruction to marine life but the detergents! The wider use of bulldozer and shovel to clear away the mess from the Brittany beaches served to minimize the damage to fish and birds. Finally, after considerable delay due partly to bad weather, the British government ordered the Royal Air Force to bomb the wreck to set on fire the oil still in its hold. While this provided a dramatic conclusion to the disaster, in fact it succeeded only in releasing pollution into the air instead of the sea.

The English Channel is one of the world's busiest waterways, so it is hardly surprising that the two greatest supertanker accidents have occurred at its

western approaches. But massive oil pollution is not solely the result of dramatic events in crowded sea lanes. In her book *Pollution: The World Crisis* British author Lynette Hamblin describes what happened in January 1969 when one of the off-shore oil rigs at Santa Barbara "blew out." The Union Oil Company had drilled a well 3500 feet below the ocean floor of the Pacific. The well opened up a number of oil reservoirs separated by porous rock strata. Deeper levels contained oil at greater pressure than the higher levels, and it was this crude oil that burst into the sea through faults in the seabed. Every day for 12 days experts estimated that 21,000 gallons of the thick oil escaped. Finally, the well was plugged with huge amounts of chemical "mud" mixed with cement. But by then more than 250,000 gallons of sticky black oil had formed a huge slick. For some days it was kept from the Californian beaches by easterly winds, but then the wind changed. The slick eventually stretched for 200 miles and the coast was affected as far south as the Mexican border.

It cost a great deal of money to clean up after the Santa Barbara blowout. The United States Secretary of the Interior made the oil companies responsible for the clean-up operation in February 1969. It is believed to have cost them at least $5,000,000 quite apart from numerous private lawsuits. But it took almost a year before the beaches were reasonably clean and it was estimated at the time that the local tourist trade lost well over $10,000,000 during 1969.

The Santa Barbara disaster was unusual among oil pollution incidents because it was relatively easy to identify those who were responsible and to force them to pay up. With the more dramatic collisions and shipwrecks that occur with depressing regularity this is hardly ever possible. The British and French governments had to foot the bill for the *Torrey Canyon* operation, bombs and all, and that is the usual pattern. The advent of supertankers of 200,000 tons and over in the late 1960s brought new problems that have yet to find new solutions. Many of the oil slicks that wash up on the shores of the Mediterranean, the

Left: the remains of the supertanker *Torrey Canyon*, wrecked off the southwest coast of Britain in 1967. After polluting hundreds of miles of British and French coastline, the ship was bombed to destroy the oil remaining in it – thus polluting the air.

Right: a giant "vacuum-cleaner" barge one of the newest aids to clearing pollution at sea.

Atlantic, and the North Sea are the result of accidental spillage or – more frequently – of ships washing out their oil tanks at sea. In both cases it is practically impossible to identify the culprits. International legislation does exist. Since 1969 it has been illegal for any tanker to jettison oil inside territorial waters (that is, between 12.5 and 200 miles from any country's coastline) and within the entire English Channel, the North Sea, the Western Approaches, the Baltic, and the Irish Sea. If this legislation were observed, the only pollution in these areas would be from accidents like the *Torrey Canyon* or the *Amoco Cadiz*. But this is obviously not the case.

When the Norwegian explorer Thor Heyerdahl sailed his papyrus raft across the Atlantic in 1970 he

Above: part of the Brittany coast that had been affected by oil pollution. Even when the top levels of beach had been cleaned the lower levels remained sodden with oil for months afterward.

Above: erecting a temporary barrier against the spread of oil along the Brittany coast after the wreck of the *Amoco Cadiz*.

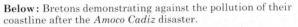

Below: Bretons demonstrating against the pollution of their coastline after the *Amoco Cadiz* disaster.

observed that the ocean was covered in tarlike clots that at times "stretched from horizon to horizon." Since Heyerdahl's frightening description of oil pollution in the Atlantic, experts have learned more about the subject. They now estimate that around 10,000,000 tons of oil are spilt into the world's oceans directly and indirectly every year. What more can be done? Stricter control of traffic lanes in the busy seaways like the English Channel would so something. Stricter enforcement of present legislation about discharging oil or oil-and-water might help. But ultimately, like so many industrial catastrophes, oil pollution on a sudden and enormous scale seems to be part of the price we pay for our industrial dependence on petroleum as a basic fuel.

Noise Pollution

An American journalist recently wrote an article about a mythical New Yorker who wandered into Central Park by mistake and almost died of the silence. He was apparently saved just in time by a blaring transistor radio. There is a grain of truth in the story. Some urban dwellers have become so accustomed to the din around them that they feel uncomfortable without it. For most people living in

Above and opposite: the high level of noise produced by jet air liners, trucks, cars, motorcycles and other vehicles and the rise in illnesses associated with high-level noise – stress, deafness, and some mental disorders – is seemingly the price industrialized nations have to pay for rapid modern transportation.

industrialized nations, however, the reverse is true. Noise, especially loud, jarring, unexpected noise, has become an increasing annoyance causing nervousness, headaches, inefficiency, sleeplessness, and even temporary deafness. For some, it has led to a permanent impairment of their hearing.

Scientists and engineers measure sound in decibels (dB) on a scale ranging from 0 for a sound barely audible to the human ear, upward to well over 100. The scale is logarithmic so an increase of 10 decibels represents a 10-fold increase in the intensity of sound emitted. To the human ear, however, a 10-decibel increase doubles the sound. This means that a business office with a decibel count of 58 sounds twice as noisy as a library reading room with 48 decibels of sound, but the office is actually ten times noisier in terms of sound emitted. Sound becomes annoying to most people at about 50 decibels and uncomfortable at about 80; it can affect hearing at 90

and becomes painful at 120. Short periods of intense sound can cause temporary deafness while loud noise over a long period of time can damage hearing permanently.

In recent years, the overall level of environmental noise has been rising about one decibel a year and is doubling the assault on the human ear every 10 years. Aircraft, trucks, trains, buses, and automobiles, jackhammers, and amplified music are all contributors to the growing cacophony. So, too, are household appliances such as vacuum cleaners, blenders, television and stereo sets, burglar alarms, and lawn mowers. There are also motor bikes and boats and transistor radios to intrude on what used to be the peace and quiet of woods, fields, lakes, beaches, and other open spaces. Together, all of these and other so-called modern conveniences produce enough noise to annoy a large percentage of the people living in technologically advanced countries, and there is plenty of evidence to show that the noise is causing a growing amount of psychological damage. Actual physical

damage, however, is most likely to occur in industry where workers are subjected to both loud and constant noise day after day, year after year.

Noise was for so long taken for granted in such industries as printing, shipbuilding, and textile manufacture and hearing loss was considered an occupational hazard. In past years, millions of workers had their hearing impaired by noise in these and other industries. Only recently has any serious thought been given to the possibility of preventing the damage by muffling the sound. A number of countries have now set noise standards for industrial plants, usually a maximum of 90 dB in areas where people work 40 hours a week. When noise levels exceed the standards, engineering changes to lessen or isolate the sound of safety equipment for the workers such as ear plugs or muffs are required. There are always companies that do not keep to the standards, because the cost of engineering changes would increase their prices – perhaps above those of their competitors. Where safety equipment has been supplied, workers frequently do not wear it because they find it uncomfortable or inconvenient.

What can be done to control industrial and environmental noise? Most experts agree that the best method would be to control it at the source; machines can be designed to make less noise. Design changes inevitably mean an increase in prices and no manufacturer is likely to make these changes until the consumer indicates a willingness to pay for them. Another solution which has been encouraged in industry is to muffle or isolate noise. Planners have begun to place housing and schools away from highways and airports and to build soundproofing into new buildings. A third method, and one now in wide use, is to outlaw noise through legislation. Many governments now ban horn-blowing for example, and

permit people to take to court those who exceed established noise standards. The laws are difficult to enforce, because offenders are not always identifiable and those affected by noise are not always willing to go to court.

The effects of noise pollution are less visible and dramatic than the more extreme effects of air and water pollution, and people seem less aware of the damage it can do. Yet noise probably has a greater and more immediate impact on more people than any other kind of pollution. Noise can be controlled but to do so requires public support and a willingness to foot the bill.

The Radiation Threat

On January 17, 1966 a United States Air Force B-52 bomber collided in mid-air with its refueling tanker near the coast of Palomares, Spain. The bomber dropped four nuclear missiles and in spite of the announcement that they were not explosive scientists and others long concerned with the dangers of a nuclear holocaust caused by accidents with nuclear weapons, expressed grave alarm.

One of the bombs fell without damage into a dry river bed. Another fell into deep sea water, not to be recovered until three months later. The remaining two bombs fell into farmland, and although they had no detonating device – and so did not explode – they broke up and released radioactive material. So great was the contamination that local crops had to be destroyed and 20,000 sealed drums of contaminated earth were taken to the United States for "disposal."

Hardly had the alarm and controversy over the question of nuclear weapons being ferried secretly around the world died down when, on May 11, 1969, a fire occurred at the Rocky Flats Atomic Plant near Denver, Colorado. The fire did $50,000,000 worth of damage to the nuclear weapons plant and damaged $20,000,000 worth of radioactive plutonium – one of

Above: a United States warship patrols off the coast of Palomares, Spain.
Left: thousands of barrels of contaminated soil from Palomares being transported to the United States. The soil became contaminated when two bombs fell and leaked radiation into the surrounding soil.
Opposite: the nuclear installations at Windscale in northern England. In 1957 large parts of the area surrounding the plant became contaminated and milk from local farms became unusable. Although the designs of nuclear power stations are improving they are still not perfect and can become dangerous under certain circumstances.

the most lethal materials ever produced by man – which posed a major threat to the whole region around the plant. Plutonium emits alpha radiation, which destroys the cells of the body, and when taken into the body – by breathing contaminated air, or through contaminated food or drink – causes death.

It seems, then, that not only must mankind live with the burden of "background" radiation – the cosmic rays from outer space, and radioactive substances in the earth's crust (plus further radiation from nuclear bomb testing) but also with the constant threat of a nuclear accident causing large-scale deaths, or even triggering a nuclear war. In the cases of Palomares and Rocky Flats, it was a "near miss." But the horrors of the nuclear explosions at Hiroshima and Nagasaki in 1945 cannot be easily erased. We know now that as a result of radiation, the survivors of a nuclear holocaust will face fever, nausea, loss of appetite anemia, vomiting, diarrhea, ulceration, and, depending on the dose, finally coma and death. The politicians meanwhile hope that the fear of widespread contamination by radiation may perhaps preserve nuclear peace.

To add to the possibility of increased danger from radioactivity there has been a growth in the use of nuclear power for peaceful purposes.

Nuclear power is a cheap, smokeless, and relatively inexhaustible source of energy. With the rapid depletion of the earth's stocks of oil, natural gas, and coal, it will assume more and more importance in the

radioactive material is stored in underground tanks. The tanks have to be constantly cooled to prevent the pressure from the hot liquid from bursting them. The material in them will remain dangerously active for *hundreds of thousands of years*. Some tanks have been dumped in the sea on the principle that even if the tanks eventually erode the material will be diluted sufficiently to offset any danger. This solution does not coincide with recent research, which indicates that the capacity of the seas to dilute the wastes has been overestimated.

To add to the hazards of pollution either through accidents to nuclear weapons, or storage of atomic wastes – there has been added a third use of nuclear power. Controlled nuclear explosions are now being used in civil engineering projects such as mining, clearing harbors, and excavating canals and reservoirs. Even though the devices are exploded underground, radioactive materials have been known to leak out through faults in the rock surface. Although the degree of fallout is only a fraction of that produced during atmospheric testing in the 1950s, it is nevertheless still a dangerous additional source of radiation.

It is the argument of the Atomic Energy Commission that the general public is not being exposed to more than a fraction of the maximum limit of permitted radiation dose due to strict control regulations. There is a growing body of scientists, politicians, conservationists and others who hope that these regulations

economic life of the nations of the world. The nuclear reactor at the center of the power station is cooled by circulating water which inevitably becomes contaminated and the radioactive material in it has to be removed. The problem that has dogged the question of nuclear-generated power is: What can be done with the radioactive waste? At the moment millions of gallons of the intensely hot, highly concentrated

will be maintained, and even tightened, in the future. As nuclear energy takes over from that provided by fossil fuels the possibility of an accident at a nuclear plant – which will release quantities of nuclear fallout comparable to that from hundreds of Hiroshima-sized bombs – will increase. Again, the AEC thinks that such a probability is nearly zero. But then somebody said the *Titanic* was unsinkable.

The Minamata Disaster
Japan: 1950

In the fishing village of Minamata on the southern island of Kyushu in Japan in the early 1950s cats began to fling themselves off wharves and drown. It was a signal of an approaching disaster that was to affect more than cats. They had eaten poisoned fish, and the poison had maddened them. Not long afterward, in 1953, the first sign of poisoning in human beings appeared, and the number of cases grew rapidly. Many of the victims died; others became ill

the brain and the central nervous system. As far back as the 19th century, hat workers poisoned by a mercury compound used in the manufacturing of felt hat-making gave rise to the expression "mad as a hatter."

In Minamata, analysts put forward the idea that the methyl mercury compound had been formed in the water of Minamata Bay when mercury discharged by the Chiso Chemical Plant along with its other wastes combined with methyl formed when microorganisms in the water broke down organic wastes there. The compound was eaten by fish and shellfish, which in turn were eaten by the fishermen and others of Minamata. The analysts could not check on their findings, however, because Chiso refused to permit them to study its production processes or test its wastes. It denied all responsibility for the poisonings and con-

Left: the Chiso plastics plant at Minamata, Japan. The company was forced to close down part of the plant in 1966 after it was found that mercury used at the plant had been discharged into Minamata Bay and had formed a highly toxic compound that was eaten by fish and shellfish.

Right: abandoned fishing boats at Minamata, the fishermen and their families were among the first to suffer from methyl-mercury poisoning. In the 1950s and 1960s the poisoning symptoms spread rapidly and became known as "Minamata Disease."

with convulsions, lack of muscular control, slurred speech, impaired sight, and other symptoms; babies were born blind, deformed, and mentally deficient.

Scientists identified the poison as a deadly combination of mercury and methyl. Even in its simple form, mercury has long been known to cause hemorrhaging, skin eruptions, kidney and liver damage, and intestinal disorders in human beings. When combined with some organic substances in a compound, however, it can be lethal causing damage to

tinued pouring mercury-laden wastes into Minamata Bay as it had been doing for years. The Japanese government also denied any knowledge of the cause of the "Minamata Disease" and refused to take action.

Stricken villagers, foregoing the traditional Japanese respect for authority, mounted protests against the company, won wide publicity, and gradually attracted the support of the Japanese people. In addition, 28 families went to court to sue Chiso for compensation. In 1966, Chiso finally closed down the processes that had spewed mercury into the bay and official tests soon afterward showed the company's wastes were mercury-free. Two years later, the government acknowledged that the company had been responsible for the mercury pollution.

By the mid-1970s, 150 people in and around Minamata had died of methyl mercury poisoning, and more than 1000 others had officially been declared victims. Chiso, which lost the long legal battle with the victims, had to pay nearly $100 million in compensation as well as contribute to the cost of cleaning up the bay – which brought the company to the brink of bankruptcy. Furthermore, the costs, both human and financial, seemed likely to grow. An additional 3700 people claimed compensation for damages and the list was still growing.

Other countries watching the Minamata tragedy

mercury in five cans of tuna fish and withdrew a million cans from sale. Britain and other nations also found excessive amounts in their studies. As late as 1972, not only fish, but humans, cattle and poultry were subject to large-scale poisoning in Iraq. The situation was so serious that the government ordered that anyone found dumping mercury treated grain into rivers should be summarily shot. In an effort to prevent further methyl mercury build-up in fish, 91 nations agreed in 1972 to a ban on dumping mercury and other pollutants into the sea.

For the people of Minamata, however, the tragedy continues. Few of those affected by the poison have recovered; most will live with the damage for the rest of their lives. In humans and other mammals, certain organic mercurials selectively and permanently destroy parts of the brain. The damage is not repair-

unfurl in Japan in the 1960s became concerned about the possibility of methyl mercury poisoning elsewhere. Mercury used in pesticides as well as mercury in industrial waste had found its way into waters all over the world, and they feared it would get into the food cycle by way of poisoned fish. In 1964, Sweden reported high levels of methyl mercury in fresh and salt water fish, and by 1970, many nations were checking the foods stocked in their own markets. The United States found excessive amounts of methyl

able. Because we are endowed at birth with a limited number of brain cells, which do not reproduce themselves, but decay with time to produce senility, additional damage should be avoided at any cost. At Minamata even those who escape poisoning suffer, for many of them must care for helpless husband, wives, or parents, or for crippled children. The saddest perhaps are the young women who fear to marry and have children lest the poison they may carry in their systems affect further generations.

Tomoko Uemura lies in her mother's arms, an incurable victim of the methyl mercury poisoning that damaged her brain before she was born.

The Thalidomide Affair
A Worldwide Disaster: 1960s

In September 1961 a 21-year-old British woman gave birth to her first child, a daughter. It was an extremely difficult birth, for the child's feet were attached to her buttocks and splayed out at an angle of 90 degrees. The mother had to have surgery to remove the child. On examination the baby was found to have neither arms nor legs. From one shoulder she had two jointless fingers, from the other, three. On one foot she had seven toes, on the other six toes and a thumb. She was one of 8000 children throughout the world

tion. The company had every confidence in the drug, which had undergone tests with laboratory animals and had passed through the clinical trials successfully.

In the late 1950s thalidomide was manufactured under license in several countries including Britain where it was put on the market under several brand names, mainly as Distaval, Tensival, and Asmaval, by a drug subsidiary of the giant liqor firm Distillers. But by 1960 there were disturbing reports of children being born in Western Germany with the deformation known as *phocomelia*. Phocomelia means resembling a seal's flippers. With this condition children are born with arms so short that their hands begin almost directly from their shoulders. To a lesser degree the legs show defects of growth. There are sometimes other deformities, such as malformations of the outer ear, eye defects, and the absence of normal openings

born deformed because their mothers had taken the new drug thalidomide, prescribed by their doctors as a tranquilizer or sleeping pill during the first few weeks of pregnancy.

The West German originators of the drug, Chemie Gruenenthal, had marketed thalidomide under the brand name Contergan. It was widely popular as a sleeping pill and could be bought without a prescrip-

in stomach or intestines. Phocomelia is a rare syndrome, most doctors going through a lifetime practice without ever seeing a case, but by 1961 there was something approaching an epidemic of phocomelia. Throughout the world, in fact, wherever thalidomide had been marketed under different trade names by different pharmaceutical companies, cases of limbless and deformed children were reported.

Above: a group of parents of thalidomide-damaged children in Britain meeting to discuss their special problems.
Below left: a young boy damaged by thalidomide taking part in normal school activities in spite of his handicap.
Below right: rehabilitating thalidomide victims. Compensation from companies that manufactured the drug that caused the defect has meant that at least some of the financial burden has been removed from parents wishing to provide the special facilities needed for the care of thalidomide children.

Distillers meanwhile had made an offer to the thalidomide children through their parents to set up a trust fund that would receive an income of £3,250,000 over 10 years. As a direct result of the press campaign, however, Distillers increased their offer and the eventual settlement to the children exceeded £30,000,000.

The question has been rightly asked whether the tragedy would have occured at all if the drug had been first tested on *pregnant* laboratory animals. In the wake of the disaster scientists did make these tests. Experiments with the New Zealand white rabbit in particular showed that specific doses of thalidomide, administered during a definite time in pregnancy, led to limb deformities in the offspring similar to those in human babies. It is an alarming fact that until the thalidomide tragedy there were no tests on pregnant animals for their possible effect on the human embryo.

Distillers withdrew thalidomide from the British market in November 1961. A year later the courts heard the first charges of negligence against the British manufacturers. The issue of compensation dragged on for 10 years. Then, in 1972 a British newspaper, *The Sunday Times*, began a forceful campaign of investigative articles that probed every aspect of the thalidomide tragedy.

The fact must always be borne in mind that, despite animal tests and human clinical trials, no new drug released for general consumption is absolutely safe. General release will often reveal new information about a drug. International drug companies have a duty to see that trials with new drugs are as comprehensive as the public has a right to expect. The thalidomide disaster must be the last medical disaster.

Chemical Catastrophe
Seveso:1976

Just after noon on Saturday July 10, 1976, a mixture of chemicals being used to make trichlorophenol, one of the ingredients in a powerful herbicide, in a reactor at the ICMESA plant near Milan, Italy, exploded forcing open a safety valve and releasing a cloud of chemicals into the atmosphere. The cloud contained dioxin, a by-product in the manufacture of trichlorophenol and one of the deadliest poisons known. Forming a cone shape, the cloud settled over a large part of the town of Seveso where it spread its deadly load on about 750 acres of market gardens, grain

area. By then 35 people had been hospitalized.

Local officials divided the affected area into Zone A, the most heavily poisoned section, and Zone B a less polluted area with "tolerable levels" of dioxin. Zone A, which eventually came to include about 250 acres of land and the homes of about 750 people, was completely evacuated, encircled with barbed wire, and put under the guard of troops to prevent residents from returning to retrieve contaminated possessions. In Zone B, an area of about 500 acres, the 5000 or more residents were permitted to remain in their homes, but children were taken out during the day to cut down on contamination, and non-residents were forbidden to enter.

Gradually, the early symptoms of poisoning, such as skin sores, cleared up for many of the Seveso victims, but a more serious and permanent skin disease, chloracne, took its place; children were especially hard hit. Some victims also showed marked person-

fields, grazing land, and on the houses and property of almost 6000 people before drifting away and eventually dispersing.

Within two days, many people in the fallout area were ill with sores on their faces, arms, and legs, and with diarrhea, vomiting, headaches, and dizziness. Thousands of birds had fallen to the ground dead, and small animals such as cats and rabbits were dying. Doctors, deluged with calls from frightened patients, contacted local public health officials to ask what the cloud had contained, but the local government could tell them little; ICMESA officials had said only that it might possibly have had "some material of a herbicidal nature" in it and gave no hint of real danger.

Not until the following Monday, nine days after the explosion, did ICMESA officials and those of its parent company in Switzerland, Givaudan, admit that dioxin had been present in the fallout, and five more days passed before a company doctor advised local officials to evacuate the most heavily contaminated

ality changes, and blood tests revealed that all the children from Zone A and many other victims, adults and children, had reduced numbers of white cells signifying less resistance to infection and a possibility of leukemia in the future.

Many feared the worst was still to come, however, for past victims of dioxin poisoning had developed symptoms over a period of years, and some had experienced liver and kidney damage and respiratory, heart, and eye problems as well as chloracne and nervous disorders. A few had died. Animals subjected to dioxin in laboratory tests had developed tumors and the number of their red as well as their white blood cells had been reduced.

Meanwhile, government officials and the scientific community struggled to find a way to remove the dioxin in Seveso so the people could return to their homes and their jobs. The poison had not only covered plants, grass, trees, and roads, but it had been tracked into houses on feet and had contaminated clothing

taminated area. Traces of dioxin have been found in the mud in Milan and in fruits and vegetables grown well outside the officially designated area of contamination, and many people in surrounding areas have developed chloracne and other symptoms of dioxin poisoning.

The end of the Seveso story will not be known for many years, if ever. Lessons already learned from it, however, could prevent a similar disaster in the future. First, early warning to potential victims could reduce contact with the poison; second, plants manufcturing toxic materials could be designed so that, in the event of an accident, the poison would be contained rather than released into the atmosphere; and third, the manufacture of trichlorophenol with dioxin as its deadly by-product could be eliminated as there are substitutes for the products in which it is used. Any of these measures could have reduced or prevented the disaster at Seveso.

Left: the ICMESA chemical plant at Seveso, Italy. It was from this plant that a cloud of deadly gas spread over the area when a safety valve on the reactor burst.
Above: one of the testers wearing special equipment removes a house cat poisoned by the fumes after the explosion.
Right: testers stacking contaminated objects for destruction after the area had been evacuated.
Below: this child, one of the many victims in Seveso has a skin heavily pockmarked with chlorachne due to dioxin poisoning from the ICMESA plant explosion.

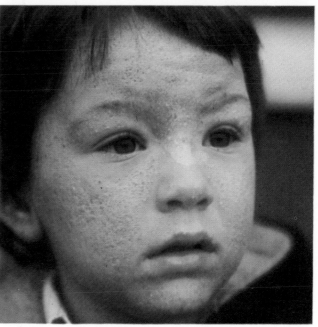

and household possessions. In past chemical explosions in which dioxin was released, the poison was confined to the factory. Even so, all efforts to remove it failed and the factories had finally had to be demolished. In Seveso, a year after the explosion, scientists and government officials still had been unable to find a satisfactory solution. One suggestion involved removing a foot of top soil from the entire area and burning it in a high-temperature incinerator. Another called for abandoning the area for many years, or forever.

To make matters worse, the area of contamination appeared to be growing. Some said the poison cloud moved haphazardly after the explosion releasing fallout on a far larger area than officials have admitted. Others said the poison was being spread by the waters of the Seveso River, which flooded in Milan several months after the explosion; by traffic on a major highway, which passes through the area; and by feet of people going in and out of the con-

Debris From Space
Canada: 1978

On January 29, 1978, six American and Canadian environmentalists studying wild life from a remote outpost in Northern Canada named Warden's Grove, came upon a crater nine feet wide and three feet deep gouged in the ice of a frozen river. Several pieces of twisted, perforated metal projected from the hole. After the find was reported scientists flew to the site, 150 miles east of the Great Slave Lake, and tested the metal debris for radioactivity. The reaction was positive. A five-day search costing upward of $1,000,000 had achieved its first object.

have been burned up as the satellite re-entered the lower atmosphere – but again, suppose it had not? And if instead of landing in a crowded street where safety precautions could at once be taken, suppose it had lain undetected on a rooftop or garden, saturating the surrounding district with its deadly rays. These were the questions people anxiously asked, and to a large extent they remained unanswered. The British writer Bryan Silcock contrasted the intense concern aroused by a fallen satellite that had killed nobody with the scant interest aroused by a flood in India that had killed thousands. He commented, "We understand what God sends us, but not what our scientists are up to in the heavens."

The situation is made more nightmarish on realizing that in January 1978 the earth's skies contained 4272 assorted metal objects sent up there by United States and Russian scientists. This number includes telecommunication satellites, satellites recording

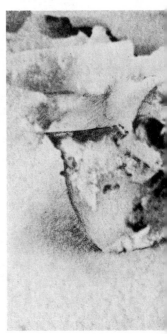

But the questions were only beginning. The debris were the fragments of a Soviet satellite, powered by nuclear fuel, that had spun out of control and crashed to earth. It had come down in one of the most thinly populated areas of the earth but that was only by chance. Circling the earth every 104 minutes, its two previous orbits had carried it over Spain, Tunisia, Central Africa, Madagascar, north over the Pacific, over California to central Canada, then southward, somewhat to the west of its previous path, over West Africa, northward between Australia and New Zealand and so to its final resting-place in the frozen wastes of the Northern Territories. No one was hurt, nothing appeared to be damaged. But suppose the radioactive debris had landed in a crowded street in Madrid or a Californian city, or in any other of the thousands of densely populated areas it had passed over? The nuclear fuel in its battery is presumed to

weather data, satellites spying on other countries and a considerable amount of debris from satellites that have come to the end of their useful life, as well as fragments jettisoned from them and from rockets at some stage. Since 1968 about 5000 man-made objects of this sort have re-entered the earth's atmosphere and burned up. In the 1960s at least two did not burn up but fell into the sea where they caused no harm.

The satellite that crashed in Canada was Cosmos 954, launched at the Tyuratam launching site in Central Asia on September 18, 1977. Western surveillance radar detected it as soon as it was in the air. One of a series of spy satellites, it was probably designed to observe movements of Western navies but it did not go as high as its predecessors, only about 150 miles above the earth. The flood of radio commands between Russia and the satellite indicated that it soon started to malfunction and by early

Below left: part of the Canadian search team of scientists looking for parts of a crashed Soviet space satellite.

Below: debris from a nine-foot-crater discovered by a government-sponsored wildlife mission and later proved to be part of the Soviet nuclear-powered spy satellite.

Right: a member of the Canadian Atomic Energy Board of Control packaging a radioactive piece of debris from a Soviet satellite in a military hangar at Yellowknife airport, Northwest Territories.

January American scientists were able to calculate that it would break up within the month. Requests to Russia for information concerning the satellite were at first countered with bland assurances. Increasing pressure was applied and on January 16 the Russians provided some definite information and a statement that there was "no danger of a critical mass occurring and therefore precipitating an explosion."

The radioactive battery of Cosmos 954 was about the size of a one-gallon vacuum flask containing about 100 pounds of Uranium 235. The heat generated during the decay of the uranium is converted into electricity and is a useful means of supplying energy for installations that are difficult to reach. American satellites also use nuclear batteries but prefer an isotope of Plutonium, which decays rapidly. Uranium 235 decays far more slowly and therefore remains potentially dangerous that much longer.

Cosmos 954 re-entered the earth's atmosphere shortly before 7 am on January 24. Mrs Marie Ruman of Yellowknife, north of the Great Slave Lake, said, "I thought, by golly, it's a jet on fire. I then realized it wasn't. . . . It was red flames, dozens and dozens of pieces following along with each other." A massive air-to-ground monitoring operation was mounted, United States aircraft flew over the area at different altitudes, and after the first debris was spotted more was located several hundred miles to the west.

Man will inevitably continue his scientific and technological researches. The discoveries he makes will contribute greatly to our knowledge and in many instances will significantly ease man's life on earth. But inevitably there will also be tragic setbacks, terrible accidents that kill or maim. Satellite Cosmos 954 was fortunately not one of these. That frightening event still waits in the future.

311

Chapter 14

Coping with Catastrophe

Man's power to halt the systematic cruelty of states and even of individuals is restricted. National laws and international agreements exist but cannot always be enforced in time. Man's powers are also limited when confronted with natural disasters, but if we can do little to prevent these we can do something to reduce the sufferings they cause.

The world's industrialized nations, whether in the West or in the East, have the resources to deal with their own disasters themselves. When hurricanes batter the coast of Florida or an earthquake destroys the center of Bucharest, the appropriate rescue operation is swiftly mounted and the work of reconstruction soon begins.

This is not the case in the so-called Third World – where unfortunately the majority of natural disasters occur. In times of crisis the underdeveloped nations need our help. However, in the past the right relief has often come too late. Is there a more efficient way of coping with their catastrophes?

Opposite: the aftermath of the earthquake that struck Peru in May 1970. Such natural disasters as earthquakes, famine, fire, and flood have always plagued man but as world population increases and cities become larger and more crowded a disaster in an urban area quickly assumes horrifying proportions. Help is almost always needed, help of the right kind – and swiftly. But is such help always forthcoming?

313

The Rescue Muddle

On May 31, 1970, a disastrous earthquake struck Peru. A 2500-foot cliff of rock and ice fell from the summit of Huascarán, the country's highest mountain, producing an avalanche of 80,000,000 tons of rock, ice, and mud. It swept down the valley at 180

miles an hour, overwhelming numerous villages and burying the flourishing town of Yungay in mud so thick that nothing remained visible but the tops of four palm trees in its central square. In the town of Huarás, chief town of the region, fully half the population died when their adobe houses fell on top of them. The earthquake killed 70,000 people, injured a further 50,000, and destroyed 200,000 houses.

In this mountainous area it was 24 hours before reports came through of the total destruction of the towns. A week after the earthquake two Mormon missionaries arrived in Chimbote on the coast to say that the town of Carás was still without relief supplies – and Huarás lay 50 miles farther inland, beyond the avalanche-struck valley. Two months passed before a proper aerial survey was undertaken by the United States National Aeronautics and Space Administration (NASA) to assess the extent of the disaster. After four and a half months there were still some villages that could be reached only by mule. Some relief supplies were not even getting to Chimbote, on the main road from Lima. More than 220,000 pounds of food, medicine, and clothes were held at Los Angeles Airport waiting for an aircraft to transport them to Peru.

The case of Peru is not exceptional. In November 1970 a tidal wave described by one of the few survivors as "a giant wall of water" hit East Pakistan, now Bangladesh. Around 1,000,000 people died. It was one of the worst disasters of the 20th century, and it

Above, above right, and **left:** scenes of destruction that resulted when in June 1970 80,000,000 tons of rock, ice, and mud, dislodged by an earthquake, rolled down the highest mountain in Peru and swept through the valley at its foot at 180 miles an hour. **Top left:** this aerial view shows the river of sludge produced by the avalanche. The magnitude of the disaster was made worse by the fact that aid was unable to get through to the survivors, both because of the inaccessibility of the area and the disorganization of relief.

was followed by one of the worst rescue operations. Local plans for dealing with flood emergencies were quite inadequate although floods are an ever-present threat in the Ganges Delta. The Pakistanis declined at first to declare the province a disaster area. Only a single Pakistani helicopter was available for flying in relief supplies.

International relief supplies were slow to begin and badly planned. The British scientific writer Dr Anthony Michaelis observed, "Tins of apple sauce, jars of honey, woollen socks, greatcoats and tents too difficult to erect filled the relief aircraft, while water distillation units, collapsible rubber dinghies and water purification tablets would have been more appropriate. Two tons of rice, blankets and drugs were flown in by the Luftwaffe, carried thousands of miles in a matter of hours, then finally dumped in an open field near the airport. Eventually they found their way on to the black market and never reached the refugees for whom they were intended." Six months after the disaster, half the financial aid raised in Britain was still in Britain because of the un-cooperative attitude of the Pakistanis.

Little can be done to prevent earthquakes, volcanic eruptions, hurricanes, or tidal waves, though some of these can now be forecast with varying degrees of precision. What can and must be done is to improve the measures taken afterward to relieve the suffering such natural disasters cause. Two issues are involved: firstly, relief must arrive as soon as is humanly possible, but, secondly, relief must be of the right sort. When the Agadir earthquake of 1960 reduced a city all set to become the "Miami of Morocco" to a mound of rubble, 15,000 people died. One relief organization sent washing machines although there was no running water.

Dr Michaelis studied the working methods of large international agencies like the Red Cross (and its Moslem counterpart, the Red Crescent) and private

charities such as Oxfam and War on Want. Without wishing to criticize the great efforts these agencies make, he proposed a new kind of organization, called by him International Rescue Organization (IRO). It would possess "the same prestige as the Red Cross and the universatility of the United Nations." The job of the IRO would be to set up large rescue warehouses packed with relief supplies to cope with any disaster. Warehouses would be strategically sited close to an international airport. Geneva, Panama, and Singapore were suggested as three suitable sites. The IRO would have a regional network in each continent staffed by small offices. These would be among the first to hear of any disaster in their area, which should mean that a smooth and rehearsed plan of operations could begin.

Clear and detailed information about the nature and extent of the catastrophe is a necessity in the initial stages. The regional office would request a photographic reconnaissance flight from the local air force to establish the data. The IRO would then fly its own men to the site of the disaster. "Their function," Michaelis writes, "would be to act as the eyes and ears of the regional office, which would by now begin to open its warehouse. Here again a planned procedure would be necessary to make sure that the right supplies go in the first planes."

A model on a national scale for this international force exists in the United States. It is the Office of

Emergency Preparedness and is an integral part of the President's Executive Office in Washington. When a disaster strikes in the United States help is first provided locally, then by the government of the State concerned. If their resources are insufficient the State Governor appeals to the President to declare the situation a "Major Disaster." It is then that the Office of Emergency Preparedness takes over. It can call

Left: a swarm of locusts often comprises as many as 10,000 million insects that can travel up to 2000 miles in a season and can cause almost complete defoliation of the arid regions they attack. By the early 1970s locust swarms had almost ceased to be a menace in East Africa, but political unrest in the areas most prone to attack has led to an alarming increase in sizes of swarms. There is already widespread famine in the Horn of Africa after years of drought and hundreds of thousands of people are in relief camps **(below)**.

Below left: two European nurses hold two of the many starving infants in their camp, both are too undernourished to be saved and will die.

upon the vast resources of the Federal Agencies and the Armed Forces. "There is no problem of resources here," said General G. A. Lincoln, one-time Director of the OEP, "we make a telephone call from the level of the White House. You know, you can't run fire brigades by committee."

But what works efficiently within the federated structure of the United States will inevitably hit political obstacles in the divided and constantly shifting world outside. The disastrous effect of political upheaval and continuous war can be seen in the harm done to the work of locust control in East Africa since the Ethiopian Civil Wars began. By the early 1970s damage from locusts had virtually ceased to be a problem in the region. Watch was kept on their breeding grounds and any gathering swarms sprayed at the earliest sign of danger. The overthrow of the Emperor Haille Selassie led to disturbances throughout the entire Horn of Africa. The local watch was neglected or actually forbidden as "an act of spying in an area of war." As a consequence, locusts, the ancient plague of the east, have been allowed to gather strength and are spreading rapidly, not only in Ethiopia, Somalia and Eritrea – the areas involved in the fighting – but into neighboring Kenya, Uganda, and Sudan.

The establishment of an IRO needs careful planning to prevent it turning into just another international charity, without power to act any more swiftly than

Above and below right: scenes after the earthquake of February 1976 in Guatemala. In spite of widespread damage and loss of life the Guatemalans soon managed to organize themselves and emergency relief supplies were being distributed by their own authorities by the fourth day. Foreign relief services, when they arrived later, were mainly either not needed, or were utterly useless.

its predecessors. Recent thinking has argued that a high proportion of Western aid to Third World countries is useless if not positively harmful.

The disastrous earthquake of February 4, 1976, in Guatemala killed 23,000 people and injured 75,000 more. But within three hours the airport was open. Most hospitals had escaped serious damage and by the second day were working again. They were running short of plaster for setting limbs – fractured limbs being the most frequent injury in earthquakes – and the needed plaster was later supplied by Oxfam. But four days after the earthquake the local authorities had dug slit trenches for latrines, organized emergency camps and blocked off roads in rural areas to serve as aircraft landing strips. All this was achieved before the foreign relief services became active. The immediate medical problem, with the exception of the plaster, was now over – but the armada of foreign aid brought many planeloads of American doctors, a complete packaged hospital, and 115 tons of drugs, including contraceptive pills, doctors' samples and a consignment of tablets manufactured in 1934. The doctors found little to do and a subsequent study of the work done by the packaged hospital showed that it had cost £30,000 for each patient treated! As for the drugs . . . the British writer Phillip Knightly of the *Sunday Times* reported what was done: "The Guatemalan authorities put three pharmacists to work to sort out anything that might be useful, but after three months they gave up, dug a trench near the warehouse where the drugs had been stored, and buried the lot."

Nor was medical aid the only relief fiasco in Guatemala. CARE (Cooperative for American Relief Everywhere) and CRS (Catholic Relief Service) imported 25,400 tons of food, although there was no evidence that Guatemala was short of food. The imports forced down the price of the local corn, preventing the

farmers from getting their usual price so that instead of helping them to rehabilitate themselves the aid actually hindered them. "We know we're poor," said the Guatemalans, "but please don't give us things. It causes a lot of dissension in our communities." Some agencies, however, the Red Cross among them, are obliged by their charters to give and are forbidden to sell. So some agencies gave materials away, others sold at less than cost with exactly the results the Guatemalans had predicted – envy and bitterness.

In the summer of 1978 a group of scientists, sociologists, doctors, and politicians met in London to consider plans for an international institute that could tackle disasters on a totally new basis. Research is to be carried out into the true needs of survivors. Shelter, for example, is considered a top priority by Western people but definitions of shelter differ widely and the housing sent out by Western countries is often never unpacked. Another recommendation is that an aid agency is most effective if it has estab-

Above: part of the consignment of 115 tons of useless drugs, and right and below, the packaged hospital that was not needed as Guatemalan hospitals were mainly undamaged.

lished links with the country before the disaster. It should also treat disaster-aid as part of a long-term development plan – and two good examples of such plans are the post-disaster schemes operated by the American agency World Neighbors, in Guatemala and by Oxfam, in Andhra Pradesh since the cyclones of 1977. It is worth noting that both Guatemala and Andhra Pradesh are cases where the local population made immediate and largely successful efforts to cope with the disaster themselves.

The best hope for helping mankind cope with the crises and catastrophes that will always affect him lies in encouraging among peoples in all countries this same determination to do as much as possible to help themselves. It is in our interest as much as it is in theirs to give them "a leg-up, not just a hand-out."

319

Above: "Eat, drink, and be merry, for tomorrow we die," was one way of looking upon death, especially when so much of mankind was overwhelmed by such catastrophes as the pestilences that periodically scoured the world until well into the present century. Modern medicines, sophisticated technology, and a greater awareness of the plight of others have all helped to reduce that feeling of powerlessness in the face of life's catastrophes and crises. But whenever man's arrogance, carelessness, or inhumanity comes to the surface, the grim reaper seizes his chance.

Index

C

industrial noise pollution, 299
Industrial Promotion Hall, Hiroshima, 209
infant mortality, 94
inflation
    16th century Spain, 162
    1923 Germany, *170*, 170-1
influenza
    effect on farming and industry, 134-5
    pandemic, 132-5
    preventive measures, *133, 138*
    spreading of, 119, 133
    symptoms, 134
    viruses, 119, 138-9
Innocent III (Pope), 221
Inquisition *see* Papal Inquisition
insecticides *see* pesticides
intercontinental ballistic missiles, *183*, 210, 279
International Bank for Reconstruction and Development, 179
International Monetary Fund, 178
International Rescue Organization, 316-18
Iraq, Mongol victory in, 185
Irish potato famine, 79, 81, *82*, 82-3
irrigation schemes, 92, *93*, 96
Irving, David, 202
Isabella I, 228
Israeli assassinations by Palestinian Arabs, *284-5*, 285
Issyk-kul, Lake, 122
Italy
    early assassinations, 248-9
    earthquake, 30-1, *30*
    Renaissance hospital in, *116*

J

Jaggar, Thomas A., 76
Japan
    attack on Pearl Harbor, 274-5, *276*
    earthquakes, 26-7, *26-7*
    Hiroshima and Nagasaki bombing, 206-9, 206-9 *passim*
    war with China, 274
Jarrow March, 176-7, *177*
Jauréguy, Juan, 259
Java, volcanic activity on, 76-7, *77*
Jekyll, Henry, 215
Jesuit church fire in Santiago, 108-9
Jesus Christ, 217, *219*, 220
Jews
    as Black Death scapegoats, 124, *125*
    conquest of Canaan, 182
    Nazi extermination of, *212*, 240-3
    segregation of, 240, *240*
Joelma Building fire, 100, *100*, 114
Joffre, Joseph, 198, *200*
Johnson, Andrew, 263, 266
Johnson, Lyndon Baines, 280, 282
José I, King of Portugal, 22
Journal of the Plague Year, A, 123
Julii, 251
Julius Caesar, *250*
    first invasion of Britain, 255, *255*
    military prowess, 251
    murder of, 12, 248, 250, *252*, 254-5, 286
    plot to kill, 253-4

reforms, 252
    rise to power, 250-2
jumpers, 239
Justin (Christian apologist), 218

K

Kambalda nickel mine, *163*
Kansas-Missouri floods, 40, 56
Kanto earthquake, 26-7, *26-7*, 34
Kapaho, eruption at, 75
Kapital, Das, 283
Kara-Khitai defeated by Genghis Khan, 184
Kasai, famine in, 88-9, *89*
Kashmir, famine in, 84
Kellog, Robert H., 192
Kelut, eruptions of, 76-7, *77*
Kennedy, Edward, *282*
Kennedy, Jacqueline, 278, 280, *280-1, 282*
Kennedy, John Fitzgerald
    as president, *278*, 278
    funeral, *282-3*
    murder of, 249, *280-1*, 281
    origins, 278
    presidential campaign, *278*
    threats to kill, 279
Kennedy, Joseph, 278
Kennedy, Robert, *282*, 284
Kenya
    Mount, 61
    woman at well, *80*
Khorasan, Genghis Khan at, 185
Khruschev, Nikita, 278
Khwarizm, Genghis Khan and, 184
Kiev, Mongol conquest of, 185
Kilauea, eruption at, 75
Kilimanjaro, Mount, 61, *61*
Kilrush, clothing distribution at, *83*
King, Martin Luther, 12, 284
Kircher, Athanasius, 118
KLM, 156
Kneller, Sir Godfrey, 168
Knightly, Phillip, 318
Knights Templar, *225*, 226
Koch, Robert, 131
Kodiak Island, tsunami on, *47*
Koga (Japanese admiral), 277
Köln-Lindenthal, 182
Komarov, Vladimir, 158, *159*
Königsberg bombing, 202
Korean War, 210
Krakatoa eruption, 40, *70*, 70-1
Krämer, Heinrich, 226
Kramer, Josef, 243
Kremlin, 106
Ku Klux Klan, *215*
Kufra Desert, *95*
Kurile Islands, 274
Kürten, Peter, 214
kwashiorkor, 87

L

La Befana, 50
La Compania church fire, 108-9, *108-9*
La Force, 235

La Guardia, Fiorello, 175
La Plata steamship, *46*
La Rochefoucauld, 235
La Roquette (Paris), 197
La Salle, René, 166
Labor Day Hurricane, 44, *45*
Lakehurst (N.J.), airship station at, 148
Laki fissure, 68, *69*
Lancaster bombers, 202-3
Landes (France), forest fires in, 113
Lane, Frank, 55, 74
Languedoc, 220, 222
Lanphier, Thomas, 276-7
lapilli, 62
Laporte, Pierre, 284
Larne, 262
Las Casas, Bartolomé de, 231
Lassa fever, 136-7, *138*
Lateran Council, Third, 220
Laurac, Guirade de, 222
lava, 62-3
    andesite, 61
    basaltic, 61, 68
    lapilli, 62
Lavaur, sieges of, 220, 222
Law, John, *166*, 166-7
    Madame, *167*
Leale, Charles, 266
Leclerc, Charles, 128, *128*
Lecomte (French general), 196
Lee, Robert E., 191, 265
Leeuwarden, burgomaster of, 260-1
Lefévre, Edwin, 173
"Legionnaires' disease," 137-8
Leibrecht, Joseph, 151
Leipzig as trading center during Thirty Years' War, 188
Leningrad, siege of, 181
Leroux, Georges, 200
Les Colonies, 72
Leukemia, 208
    DDT and, 293
Lieriksee floods, *49*
Lightning aircraft, 276-7
Lima, earthquake at, *28*
Lincoln, Abraham
    birthplace, 262, *262*
    Civil War role, 191, 262
    kidnap bids, 263
    murder of, 249, 262, 264, 266, *266*, 286
    opposition to slavery, 262
    physical appearance and condition, 262, *262, 267*
    rise of, 262-3, *263*
Lincoln, G. A., 317
Lincoln, Mary Todd, 264, 266
Lisbon Cathedral, 23
Lisbon earthquake, 22-3, *23*
Lister, Joseph, 118
Little Boy atomic bomb, 206, *206*
Lituya Bay, world's biggest wave at, 46, *47*
Liverpool Bay, submarine disaster in, *152*, 152-3
Livingstone, David, 237
llamas, 231
Locke, John, 287
locust control, *316-17*, 317
log cabin, Lincoln's birthplace, 262, *262*

Picture Credits

107(B)	The Bettmann Archive
108(L)	The Mansell Collection, London
109	*Radio Times* Hulton Picture Library
110(T)	The Bettmann Archive
110(B)	Scala
111	The Bettmann Archive
112(L)	Photri
112(R)	Keystone
113(R)	Australian News and Information Bureau
114	Compix
115(T)	Fox Photos
115(B)	Keystone
116	Photo Mauro Pucciarelli © Aldus Books
118(L)	Hildegarde MS Lucca/Photo Scala
118(R)	Reproduced by permission of the Trustees of the British Museum
119(T)	Glaxa Research Limited/Photo Behram Kapadia © Aldus Books
119(CB) (BR)	Gene Cox
120	The Mansell Collection, London
121	Roger-Viollet
122	British Museum/Photo John Freeman © Aldus Books
123(L)	*Radio Times* Hulton Picture Library
123(R)	The Mansell Collection, London
124	The Mansell Collection, London
125(TL)	The Mansell Collection, London
125(TR)	J.-L. Charmet
125(B)	Scala
126	The John Judkyn Memorial, Freshford Manor, Bath/Photo Mike Busselle © Aldus Books
127	Musée Carnavalet, Paris/Photo Bulloz
128	Roger-Viollet
129(TL)	*Radio Times* Hulton Picture Library
129(TR)	Aldus Archives
129(B)	J.-L. Charmet
130(T)	The Bettmann Archive
130(B)	J.-L. Charmet
131(T)	*Radio Times* Hulton Picture Library
131(BL)	Wellcome Historical Medical Museum
131(BR)	*Radio Times* Hulton Picture Library
132(L)	The Bettmann Archive
132(R)	*Radio Times* Hulton Picture Library
133(T)	The Bettmann Archive
134	Compix
135(L)	The Bettmann Archive
135(R)	Compix
136(L)	Keystone
136(R)	ZEFA
137(T)	World Health Organization
137(B)	Colorific!
138(TL)	Graham Harrison/*Daily Telegraph* Colour Library
138(TR)	Keystone
138(BL)	Paul Almasy/World Health Organization
138(BR)	Keystone
139(T)	Graham Finlayson/*Daily Telegraph* Colour Library
139(B)	Alan Hutchison Library
140	Sipa-Press/Rex Features
142(T)	Mary Evans Picture Library
142(B)	Ian Allan Ltd.
143	*Radio Times* Hulton Picture Library
144(TL)	The Bettmann Archive
144(BL)	The Bettmann Archive
145(L)	J.-L. Charmet
145(R)	*Radio Times* Hulton Picture Library
146(L)	*Radio Times* Hulton Picture Library
146(R)	The Mansell Collection, London
148	The Mansell Collection, London
149(L)	Ullstein Bilderdienst
149(R)	The Mansell Collection, London
150	Photri
151(T)	The Mansell Collection, London
151(B)	The Bettmann Archive
152(L)	*Liverpool Daily Post & Echo Ltd.*
152–153 (C)	United Press International
153(TR)	*Radio Times* Hulton Picture Library
153(BR)	*Liverpool Daily Post & Echo Ltd.*
154–155	London Fire Brigade
156	Frank Spooner Pictures
157(R)	Sipa-Press/Rex Features
158–9(T)	NASA
159(B)	Novosti
160	Victoria & Albert Museum, London/Photo Eileen Tweedy © Aldus Books
162	Keystone
163	Australian Information Service
164(TL)	Aldus Archives
164(TR)	British Museum/Photo Eileen Tweedy © Aldus Books
164(BL)	Fitzwilliam Museum, Cambridge
164(BR)	Aldus Archives
165(B)	Aldus Archives
166	National Portrait Gallery, London
167	British Museum/Photos Eileen Tweedy © Aldus Books
168	British Museum/Photo Eileen Tweedy © Aldus Books
169(T)	The Tate Gallery, London
169(B)	British Museum/Photo Eileen Tweedy © Aldus Books
170(TL)	Adrian Williams Collection
170(TR)	Archiv Für Kunst und Geschichte, West Berlin
170(B)	Bilderdienst Süddeutscher Verlag
171(T)	Ullstein Bilderdienst
171(B)	Bilderdienst Süddeutscher Verlag
172	The Bettmann Archive
173(L)	*The New Yorker*
173(R)	Compix
174	Compix
175(TR)	Compix
175(BR)	The Bettmann Archive
176	World Wide Photos
177(T)	*Radio Times* Hulton Picture Library
177(B)	Tennessee Valley Authority
178(T)	Society for Cultural Relations with the U.S.S.R.
178(B)	*China Pictorial*
179(B)	*Radio Times* Hulton Picture Library
182(T)	Reproduced by permission of the Trustees of the British Museum
182(B)	The Mansell Collection, London
183(TL)	Reproduced by permission of the Trustees of the British Museum
183(TR)	Imperial War Museum, London
183(B)	United States Information Service
184(T)	Aldus Archives
185(T)	Aldus Archives
184–185 (B)	The Metropolitan Museum of Art, New York. Gift of A. W. Bahf, 1947
186–188	British Museum/Photos Eileen Tweedy © Aldus Books
189(TL)	British Museum/Photo Eileen Tweedy © Aldus Books
189(TR)	David Paramor Collection, Newmarket
189(B)	National Gallery, London/Photo John Freeman © Aldus Books
190(L)	Photo Timothy H. O'Sullivan/Library of Congress
190(R)	*Radio Times* Hulton Picture Library
191	Courtesy of the Historical Society of Pennsylvania
192(L)	Library of Congress
192–193 (C)	Maryland Historical Society, Baltimore
193(TR)	The Mansell Collection, London
193(B)	Prints & Photographs Division, Library of Congress
194(L)	Musée Carnavalet, Paris/Photo J.-L. Charmet
195(T)	The Mansell Collection, London
195(B)	Musée Carnavalet, Paris/Photo J.-L. Charmet
196	Musée Carnavalet, Paris/Photos J.-L. Charmet
197(R)	Aldus Archives
198–199	Bilderdienst Süddeutscher Verlag
200(L)	Imperial War Museum, London/Photo Eileen Tweedy © Aldus Books
201	Imperial War Museum
202	Imperial War Museum, London/Photo Eileen Tweedy © Aldus Books
203(T)	Bilderdienst Süddeutscher Verlag
203(BL)	Victoria & Albert Museum, London. British Crown Copyright
203(BR)	Bilderdienst Süddeutscher Verlag
204	Keystone
205(R)	Hilmar/ZEFA

206(L)	U.S. Atomic Energy Commission/William H. Regan, Los Alamos Scientific Laboratory
206(R)	Los Alamos Scientific Laboratory
207	Keystone
208(L)	Rex Features
208(R)	Courtesy Office of the Assistant Secretary of Defense, Washington D.C.
209(TR)	Popperfoto
209(BR)	Rex Features
210–211 (L)	Rex Features
211(R)	Novosti
212	Imperial War Museum, London
214	Aldus Archives
215(T)	Metro-Goldwyn-Mayer Inc.
215(BL)	Black American News Service, Detroit
215(BR)	J.-L. Charmet
216	Vatican Library
217(T)	Queen's College MS 305 f.11 verso/Bodleian Library, Oxford
217(B)	Victoria & Albert Museum, London. British Crown Copyright
218	The Mansell Collection, London
219(L)	Staatliche Museen Press. Kulturbesitz, Frubchristliche-Byzantinische Sammlung, Berlin
219(TR)	The Mansell Collection, London
219(BR)	Mansell/Anderson
220	Archives de Toulouse/Yan
221(L)	Museo del Prado, Madrid/Photo Manso
221(R)	The Mansell Collection, London
222(T)	Photo Yan
222(BL)	The Mansell Collection, London
222(BR)	MS Bodley 270b f.123v Bodleian Library, Oxford
223(T)	Photo Yan
223(B)	Scala
224	Bildarchiv Preussischer Kulturbesitz, Berlin
225(TL)	Documentation Cauboue
225(BL)	Aldus Archives
225(R)	J.-L. Charmet
226	J.-L. Charmet
227(L)	The Mansell Collection, London
227(R)	Photo Friedrich Schult courtesy Nikolaus Barlach
228(T)	Werner Forman
228(B)	Aldus Archives
229(T)	Aldus Archives
229(BL)	Ferdinand Anton, München
229(BR)	The William L. Clements Library, University of Michigan
230	British Museum/Photo R. B. Fleming © Aldus Books
231(T)	The John Judkyn Memorial, Freshford Manor, Bath/Photo Mike Busselle © Aldus Books
231(BL)	Museo de America, Madrid/Photo Mas
231(BR)	The Royal Library, Copenhagen
232	The Mansell Collection, London
233(T)	The Mansell Collection, London
233(B)	André Held, Lausanne
234	Bibliothèque des Arts Décoratifs/Photo J.-L. Charmet
235(T)	The Mansell Collection
235(B)	Musée Carnavalet, Paris/Photo J.-L. Charmet
236	Aldus Archives
237(T)	Aldus Archives
237(BR)	The Mansell Collection, London
238(T)	Dwight Lowell Dumond, Antislavery, The University of Michigan Press, 1961
238(B)	Radio Times Hulton Picture Library
239(T)	Dwight Lowell Dumond, Antislavery, The University of Michigan Press, 1961
239(B)	Rex Features
240(L)	Keystone
240(R)	The Wiener Library
241	The Weiner Library
242	Imperial War Museum, London
243(TL)	Imperial War Museum, London
243(TR)	Artia/The Wiener Library
243(B)	The Wiener Library
244–245	Rex Features
246	Baptistery, Florence/Scala
248–249	Topkapi Saray Museum, Istanbul
250(L)	Mansell/Alinari
250(R)	Museo delle Terme, Rome/Photo Scala
251(R)	The Mansell Collection, London
252–254	The Mansell Collection, London
255(T)	MS Douce 208 f.154/Bodleian Library, Oxford
255(B)	Michael Holford Library photo
256(L)	Ferdinandeum Museum, Innsbruck
257(T)	Radio Times Hulton Picture Library
257(B)	Aldus Archives
259	British Museum/Photo Eileen Tweedy © Aldus Books
260(L)	British Museum/Photo Eileen Tweedy © Aldus Books
260(R)	The Mansell Collection, London
261	Rijksmuseum, Amsterdam
262–263	Library of Congress
264(L)	Library of Congress
265(T)	From the collection of The Union League of Philadelphia
265(B)	The Lane Studio, Gettysburg, Pennsylvania
266(T)	Library of Congress
266(B)	Meserve Collection, New York
267(T)	Alexander Gardner/Ostendorf Collection
267(B)	Library of Congress
268–269	Bilderdienst Süddeutscher Verlag
270(L)	Documentation Cauboue
271(TL)	Bilderdienst Süddeutscher Verlag
271(TR)	Ian Yeomans/Sunday Times Colour Library
271(B)	Bilderdienst Süddeutscher Verlag
272–273	Bilderdienst Süddeutscher Verlag
274	Popperfoto
275–276	Compix
277(T)	Courtesy Office of the Assistant Secretary of Defense, Washington, D.C.
278(T)	Camera Press
278(B)	United Stations Information Service
279	Radio Times Hulton Picture Library
280–281	Life © Time Inc. 1978
282(T)	John Loengard/Life © Time Inc. 1978
282(B)	Henri Dauman/Life © Time Inc. 1978
283(B)	Camera Press (Robert Jackson/Dallas Times Herald)
284	Israel Sun–Sipa Press/Rex Features
285(R)	Keystone
286(B)	G. Sipahioglu/Rex Features
287	Sipa Press/Rex Features
288	S. C. Bisserot/Bruce Coleman Inc.
290–291	Vernon Mills © Aldus Books
292	Paul Almasy/World Health Organization
293(T)	Photo by UNICEF
293(B)	Photo Geoffrey Drury © Aldus Books
294–295	Sipa Press/Rex Features
296(L)	Bill Eppridge/Life © Time Inc.
297(TL)	Rex Features
297(TR) (B)	Sipa Press/Rex Features
298(L)	Rex Features
298–299 (C)	Popperfoto
299(R)	Rex Features
300(T)	Keystone
300(B)	Popperfoto
301	Camera Press
302	Bob Davis/Aspect Picture Library
303	© Shisei Kuwabara represented by Orion Press, Tokyo
304–305	John Hillelson Agency
306–307	Rex Features
308–309	Sipa Press/Rex Features
310(L)	Brennan/Camera Press (Obs) London
310–311 (C)	Popperfoto
311(R)	Compix
312	Popperfoto
314–315	Popperfoto
316(T)	Gianni Tortoli/Photo Researchers Inc.
316(B)	Keystone
317(B)	Sipa Press/Rex Features
318–319	Sipa Press/Rex Features